W9-CPM-490

THE BIG FELLA

THE BIG FELLA

THE RISE AND RISE OF BHP BILLITON

PETER THOMPSON & ROBERT MACKLIN

WILLIAM HEINEMANN: AUSTRALIA

A William Heinemann book
Published by Random House Australia Pty Ltd
Level 3, 100 Pacific Highway, North Sydney NSW 2060
www.randomhouse.com.au

First published by William Heinemann in 2009

Addresses for companies within the Random House Group can be found at www.randomhouse.com.au/offices.

National Library of Australia
Cataloguing-in-Publication Entry

Thompson, Peter Alexander.

Big fella: the rise and rise of BHP Billiton / Peter Thompson, Robert Macklin.

ISBN 978 1 74166 710 3 (hbk)

BHP Billiton – History.
Mining corporations – Australia – History.

Other Authors/Contributors:
Macklin, Robert, 1941–

338.76220994

Jacket photographs: front © Dennis Jones/Lonely Planet Images; back © Reuters/Picture Media
Cover design by Natalie Winter
Internal design by Midland Typesetters, Australia
Typeset in Goudy Old Style by Midland Typesetters, Australia
Printed and bound by Griffin Press, South Australia

Random House Australia uses papers that are natural, renewable and recyclable products and made from wood grown in sustainable forests. The logging and manufacturing processes are expected to conform to the environmental regulations of the country of origin.

10 9 8 7 6 5 4 3 2 1

For Roderick Francis O'Loan, a friend indeed

CONTENTS

NOTE ON MEASUREMENTS AND CURRENCIES

Distances and altitudes in the narrative have been expressed, where practicable, in (rounded) metric units; but in quotations from other works, the original units have been retained.

Metric equivalents

1 inch = 25 millimetres
1 foot = 30 centimetres
1 yard = 0.914 metre
1 mile = 1.6 kilometres
1 pound = 0.45 kilograms
1 long (UK) ton = 1.016 tonnes
1 short (US) ton = 0.907 tonne
1 acre = 0.4 hectare

Whereas the mining industry deals in US dollars, all currencies here are given in Australian dollars unless otherwise stated.

INTRODUCTION

Global Australian

Miners are gamblers; it is the nature of the beast. And there have been no greater gamblers in Australia's history than the men of the Broken Hill Proprietary Company Limited and its latest incarnation, the dual-listed colossus BHP Billiton. From 'The Proprietary' to 'The Big Australian' to 'The Big Fella', the company has become the biggest diversified miner the world has ever seen.

A spirit of adventure and risk-taking (coupled with a ruthless edge) characterised the men who ran the separate companies until they collided and merged in one of the seminal mining events of the new century. And it was within this same spirit that the brash, young, South African-born chief executive officer, Marius Kloppers, ignoring the ancient lessons of Icarus, aimed at world domination in mineral resources with the launch of his hostile takeover bid for Rio Tinto in November 2007.

On a winter's day in 2008, just a few weeks before his 46th birthday, he sits tieless in the Copper Room on the 28th floor of the company's global headquarters in the QV building at 180 Lonsdale Street, Melbourne, in the middle of the contest he has codenamed Project de Bello – from the Latin 'to do battle and vanquish'. 'This would be a wonderful thing if we can get it done,' he says.[1]

Forces have been deployed on every front to identify the cost-cutting synergies and arrange the finance. BHP Billiton is set to press home its offensive with the announcement of a record annual profit for the seventh successive year: a phenomenal US$15.4 billion to the end of 30 June, a rise of 22 per cent, helped by a jump in commodity prices, higher production and an ability to pass on higher costs.

In terms of market capitalisation at that time, a combined BHP and Rio Tinto would have challenged Exxon, General Electric (GE), Microsoft and Citigroup at the top of the world league. 'The companies really do overlap in a way that is very, very significant and different from the overlaps between any two other mining companies in the industry,' Kloppers says. 'That applies in terms of operating jurisdictions, in terms of operating philosophies and also in terms of where we operate and share assets like Escondida, the Pilbara, the Hunter Valley and the Bowen Basin.'

Sir Robert Wilson, the former chairman of Rio Tinto who was involved in at least two earlier attempts to merge his company with BHP Billiton, was not so sure. Such a behemoth, he said, could well be too big to manage. And he added, 'What both companies would lose is actually the incentive to improve because it would be daft to deny that for decades BHP and Rio Tinto have been sharpened by rivalry. Take that away and what have you got? You've got, potentially, a big stodgy vegetable.'[2]

Wilson's theory remains to be tested. On 25 November 2008, the bid foundered against a backdrop of European Union opposition and a global credit collapse that saw capital and commodity markets plunge by up to 50 per cent. 'Marius's strategy was correct but he isn't clairvoyant so he couldn't factor in the worldwide crash,' says Ian Fraser, a former colleague who was closely associated with Kloppers' rise to the top.[3]

Kloppers himself was outwardly sanguine about his failure to pull off the deal. 'As you get to know me, I am the supreme realist in things,' he told the *Australian Financial Review*. 'We felt that, as a team, we did what we could in order to try and unlock those synergies. We couldn't do it. Admit defeat.'[4]

Within a matter of months, however, Rio Tinto's major assets were up for grabs after a plan to inject US$19.5 billion in Chinese capital into Rio faced collapse. Kloppers reactivated his team and in June 2009 BHP Billiton and Rio announced the biggest joint venture in the history of mining with a merger of their iron-ore operations in the Pilbara.

The 'supreme realist' knows that much of BHP Billiton's prosperity – and Australia's economic stability – depends on his company's increasing ability to satisfy the demands of the so-called Asian-commodity 'supercycle'[5] over the next two decades, a relationship that ensures BHP Billiton's pre-eminence in the national prospectus.

'The Big Fella', as chairman Don Argus christened the company in 2001, is one of the first great corporations to realise that, in the twenty-first century, globalisation is no longer a one-way street; that the developed world now depends on the rising stars of the so-called newly acquisitive nations (NAN) of China, India, Brazil, Mexico and Venezuela for its continued economic health.

Indeed, no less than two-thirds of global growth in 2007 came from emerging countries, whose economies expanded 6.7 per cent in that year compared with 3.9 per cent in Australia and 1.3 per cent for the United States, Japan and Europe. It seemed that within five years China – easily the biggest driver of global-resource demand – would account for 55 per cent of iron-ore consumption, 31.6 per cent of nickel and 42 per cent of aluminium. India was following a similarly powerful path of economic expansion, with the others close behind.

'The United States' GDP is US$13.5 trillion, China is about US$3.5 trillion, India, Russia and Brazil have got about the same sized economy at about US$1.4 trillion or so,' Marius Kloppers says. 'So India is 30 per cent the size of the Chinese economy at the moment, growing at a slightly lower rate but clearly a big step up over the past five years. It really is a question of how it develops over the next ten or 15 years, together with Brazil and Russia.'

Despite the economic downturn that began in the latter half of 2008, these irresistible forces are still reshaping the mining industry through a process of 'consolidation' – a polite euphemism for market dominance – into a handful of massive entities. And it is this dynamic that makes the saga of BHP Billiton so timely, so dramatic and so compelling.

The story behind the rise of BHP from the humblest beginnings in the Australian outback to starry heights on the great bourses of the world is as engrossing as it is unlikely. It has never been told before. Until now, readers and investors seeking the real story of BHP have had to content themselves with the daily spot news and views of journalists on the run, or a stream of officially authorised glossy publications designed with an eye to 'corporate image' and the share price of the day.

The Billiton story is even more elusive. We have had to chart new pathways through company archives and historical documents from the dark days of Dutch colonialism and South African apartheid to reveal Billiton's beginnings as a modest tin-mining company on the island of Belitung in Indonesia (at the time pronounced 'Billiton') and in the Netherlands East Indies. From there, it developed into an international miner via Royal Dutch Shell before being passed to the South African group Gencor, where it found itself leading the breakout from the collapsing apartheid barriers to stake its future in the world's financial markets.

The inside story of the courtship and marriage between BHP and Billiton comes direct from the courtiers with a frankness rarely revealed in the secretive world of corporate gamesmanship. However, *The Big Fella* owes nothing to company patronage: the access sought and received was without condition. Both strands of the story – the Australian and the South African – are told in the words of dozens of past and present BHP Billiton staffers, including three BHP chairmen and six chief executives, eyewitnesses to the drama, who were willing to speak without constraint, together with an extraordinary cast of academics, research scientists, politicians, lobbyists, miners, public servants and intelligence operatives with special insights into various aspects of the subject.

Indeed, our researches revealed BHP and its successor in the corporate world, BHP Billiton, to have such a network of linkages that it resembles a state within a nation. Few of Australia's 21 million people have remained untouched by its activities, whether through their employment in primary or secondary industry, their direct share ownership, or their superannuation-fund dividends.

Part I of this book describes the history of BHP as it forged its wildly unpredictable path to national corporate supremacy. Since that baking-hot day in 1883 when the mysterious Charles Rasp pegged his claim on the broken-backed hill near the New South Wales–South Australia border, the company has operated within an ambience of palpable excitement. Geology can provide a rough guide, but beneath its surface the earth twists and contorts and conceals its treasures in the most unexpected ways. More often than not, it confounds the prospector. Development costs are unpredictable. All that can be said with confidence is that they will be greater than the original estimate. And when the minerals have been garnered from their deep redoubts, the miner is at the mercy of the market – and markets, by their nature, are merciless. BHP learned that lesson many times, never more painfully than in the late 1990s when collapsing copper prices brought the company to its knees.

Even when the planets of good fortune are all aligned, the miner still cannot relax, since success on the share market brings its own perils. Here, too, BHP found itself more than once on the knife-edge of disaster, most dramatically in the 1980s when the buccaneers of the bourse led by Robert Holmes à Court made repeated raids on an undervalued flagship.

But it is this very sense of unremitting excitement that has attracted the big, bold personalities to the helm, almost from the beginning of BHP's unlikely journey – men such as George McCulloch, who organised the group of seven pioneers to sink the first shaft at Broken Hill that hit the line of lode that created BHP's famous 'Big Mine'; Guillaume Delprat, the Dutch polymath who transformed the rough miner into a steelmaker; Essington Lewis, who, through sheer force of personality and dedication, made it the foundation of the nation's secondary industry;[6] and Ian McLennan, a martinet who oversaw its discovery of massive oil, gas and iron-ore deposits. And along the way we reveal for the first time the crucial role played by the Australian geologist Professor Sam Carey in unlocking the great petroleum province in Bass Strait.

Part II of the book describes how BHP's new chief executive, Brian Loton, while under share-raider attack from Robert Holmes à Court, pursued an international expansion program unrivalled in his nation's corporate history. His acquisition of Utah International from GE in 1984 brought the coal mines of the Bowen Basin and the great Escondida copper deposits into the BHP portfolio – and seeded the corporate ranks, so long dominated by steel men, with a cadre of highly experienced coal and copper miners.

However, while the company has been driven by men (exclusively) from heady triumph to imminent collapse and back again, over time it developed an internal ethos that defied the idiosyncrasies of leadership. BHP saw itself as a bastion of quality and respectability, even if on several well-documented occasions BHP executives failed to measure up.

The US$2.5 billion purchase of the Magma copper mines in Arizona almost on the eve of the collapse of the world copper price and the failure of the hot-briquetted iron (HBI) plant at Port Hedland, Western Australia, after crippling cost overruns blasted the biggest hole ever seen in the company's balance sheet, while the environmental disaster at Ok Tedi in Papua New Guinea grew from a mindset that placed profit over the human rights of the powerless and the needy. The scandal of the $5 million shipment of wheat to Saddam Hussein – also examined here – plumbed the depths of corporate morality. And its architects compounded the situation when they sought its return – with interest – from that unconscionable regime. The 'gift' was patently a cold-blooded ploy to secure favoured treatment in the development of Iraqi oilfields.

Part III covers the history of Billiton, which began life as a purely Dutch company using immigrant Chinese miners to dig a huge open-cut tin mine on Belitung Island. At the same time, the antecedents of Billiton's one-time owner, Gencor, were exploiting cheap black labour to extract the mineral wealth of the gold, platinum and coal fields of South Africa.

Gencor thrived under the country's inhuman apartheid laws until Derek Keys, a newcomer to the mining industry, took over as chairman and chief executive and redefined the company's objectives for a world beyond apartheid. His successor, Brian Gilbertson, a gifted mathematician and former rocket scientist, then bought Billiton from Royal Dutch Shell in 1994 as a vehicle for transporting Gencor's principal mineral assets to the world's financial markets.

By the time Billiton merged with BHP in 2001, both companies had learned the hard way that commodity-price bonanzas are apt to end suddenly and dramatically. BHP's Magma copper mines in Arizona and Nevada cost it US$2.5 billion in write-offs when metal prices plummeted in the 1997–98 Asian financial crisis. Chief executive John Prescott and his chairman Jerry Ellis paid with their careers in BHP.

In desperation, Don Argus, the new chairman, turned to a tall, burly, motorbike-riding American with ideas to match his size and temperament. An engineer who had risen to president and chief executive officer of Duke Energy, Paul Anderson applied a nerveless resolve to BHP's problems. Indeed, according to Don Argus, 'That guy was the architect of the modern BHP Billiton. No doubt other people will lay claims to it, but this guy had a vision; he set the platform up beautifully.'[7] Anderson joined forces with Charles 'Chip' Goodyear, his chief financial officer, and within two years profits were soaring again.

Meanwhile, Billiton had suffered a similar, though less humiliating, deflation during the same period when its share price – and its reputation – plunged on the London Stock Exchange. The engrossing story of the way Brian Gilbertson and his chief financial officer, the bearded sage Mick Davis, revitalised Billiton for its marriage to BHP and how BHP's directors had to choose between merging with Billiton and acquiring another candidate, Western Mining, is told for the first time.

The Billiton merger, however, proved irresistible and the merged company took its place in the big league. In fact, two companies were created: BHP Billiton Limited (based in Melbourne) and BHP Billiton plc (based in London), both listed separately but operating as one business, with identical boards of directors and a single management structure. One casualty was Mick Davis, who discloses for the first time the real reason why he declined to join BHP Billiton and instead became a thorn in its side as the driving force behind the aggressive Anglo-Swiss miner Xstrata.

Part IV describes the working relationship between Paul Anderson and Brian Gilbertson to plot a new strategic framework for the merged conglomerate and then, with the course charted in 2002, how Anderson quietly returned to the United States, where he remains a director on the BHP Billiton board.

One of Gilbertson's first moves as chief executive was to approach Sir Robert Wilson at Rio Tinto about a possible merger between the two mining giants. Don Argus, however, became furious about being excluded from the talks and, after Gilbertson threw down the gauntlet for a test of strength, summoned a board meeting.

On 4 January 2003, Gilbertson was told to wait in his office while the board deliberated on his fate. In the event, he lost the power struggle – and his job – on a day of high drama that remains one of the most controversial incidents in Australia's corporate history. The behind-the-scenes story is revealed in full here.

Gilbertson's successor, Chip Goodyear, guided BHP Billiton through the shifting economic sands of the new century, in which sharp rises in the prices of energy, metals and minerals were accompanied by a revolution in world markets following the emergence of China and India as increasingly industrialised nations.

Goodyear and his successor in 2007, Marius Kloppers, have followed a strategy to develop only large, low-cost, long-life mines such as the Escondida copper deposit in Chile, where BHP Billiton owns a majority stake, its vast Australian iron-ore venture in the Pilbara and the world's biggest uranium mine at Roxby Downs.

'An awful lot of drivel is said about size not mattering,' says Mike Salamon, a Hungarian-born South African who followed the trail from Gencor to Billiton to the boardroom of BHP Billiton. 'BHPB is now up there with the oil supermajors in terms of scale. There is no mining company that has ever been anywhere near there before. And it's not an Australian company any more – it's a global business. Just look at the guys who run BHP Billiton and where they come from: CFO Alex Vaneslow – Brazilian; CEO Marius Kloppers – South African; Alberto Calderon, chief commercial officer – Colombian; Ian Ashby, the guy running the iron-ore business – Australian; Marcus Randolph, the guy running the steelmaking stuff – American. There's nothing like it.'[8]

The twenty-first century had produced a new-found and very public dedication to 'ethical behaviour', 'corporate integrity', 'a social licence to operate' and above all 'sustainability'. These objectives may have been partly initiated by rival miner Sir Robert Wilson[9] but were introduced to BHP by Paul Anderson in his March 1999 handwritten charter entitled 'Moving into the 21st Century', and then fulsomely embraced by his successors in the merged entity, most notably Chip Goodyear.

In a world of global warming and heightened environmental concern, 'sustainability' has since become a catchphrase within the organisation and is regarded by the company as a vital element of its public presentation. Whether it is practicable in an industry that is engaged in extracting a finite resource before folding its tent and moving on to new exploits is another matter. Some might well find it problematic, while others will, with some justification, label it little more than a public-relations facade.

Unquestionably, the company gives high priority to its image. Perception plays a role in the share price, in international relations, industrial harmony and, most importantly, in dealings with government. Political influence has always had its place on the company's boardroom agenda. Indeed, as will be seen, it is the historic association with conservative politics – both in Australia and South Africa – that draws BHP Billiton into the great issues of climate change and energy sustainability now confronting the planet. 'Our aim,' says Don Argus, in answer to the company's environmental critics, 'is to make a positive impact wherever we operate.'[10]

From the beginning, BHP aligned itself with the capitalist viewpoint. It led the campaigns against miners' rights. It crushed the industrial activists within its ranks. It flirted with right-wing radical causes. One of its chairmen helped to write the industrial policy of the nascent Liberal Party of Robert Menzies and supported it with generous funding thereafter. And the association between BHP and the Menzies family will no doubt provide one of the more engaging sidelights of this work.

But whichever side of politics has been in power, the company has been proactive in seeking to influence policy and to gain special concessions for its operations. According to the BHP Billiton code, all government subsidies are a wasteful, egregious interference with the marketplace . . . except all those that benefit the mining industry and BHP Billiton itself. And in this endeavour it has been extraordinarily successful. Federal- and state-government tax concessions, exploration subsidies, infrastructure developments and other contributions defy calculation. Former Labor prime minister Paul Keating says, 'The Commonwealth Government's considerations for BHP have been myriad.' And paradoxically this applied in particular to the Labor governments in which he was either treasurer or prime minister. 'Labor governments,' he says proudly, 'have always been kinder to BHP than conservative governments.'[11]

While BHP was 'The Big Australian' of the twentieth century, the effects of its influence were largely confined to the ancient continent that bred it. Many of these were benign. The company provided a vast treasure of export income that contributed to government programs of defence, development and social welfare. It created jobs. Its steelmaking added a new dimension to the Australian economy. Its mining ventures helped to develop regional and remote areas.

For Aboriginal people, this latter was a decidedly mixed blessing. In the early decades, they were ignored. Then they were exploited, their lives disrupted and debilitated by cashed-up miners and unlimited alcohol. BHP operated within the prevailing ethos of the day. When the wider community embraced notions of Aboriginal land rights, compensation and partnership, BHP responded – grudgingly, perhaps, but with an increasing sense of commitment.

In the twenty-first century, a new paradigm applies. The company has the power to exert its influence for good or ill in the world economy. Its top executives have ready access to presidents and prime ministers from more than a score of the countries in which it operates. And they take full advantage of the opportunities to influence the decision-makers. Whether they use that power for a greater good than the company's short-term profitability is a moot point.

'We are in long-life assets because only then can we build a really meaningful influence on the community that we're operating in; we contribute positively and get them to be on the side of further development,' Marius Kloppers says.[12]

By highlighting both the personal and historic aspects of the universal mining drama, this book will provide investors, bankers, financial analysts, journalists, environmentalists and the wider public – as well as many thousands of BHP Billiton employees – with a challenging view of The Big Fella's pursuit of its corporate goals and its 'licence to operate'. But even more enthralling to the authors has been the journey through the centuries, the twists and turns of serendipity, the brilliant insights of the executive officers on the bridge, the dedication of the miners themselves, the appalling errors, the battles won and lost – and through it all the gambler's spirit that forever rides the waves of fortune.

PROLOGUE

The Black Stump

In the eons following the Big Bang 13.5 billion years ago, gas and stardust throughout the universe repeatedly swirled together in massive balls of incredible heat that collapsed and exploded in supernovas. Such was the power of these atomic collisions that the light elements of hydrogen and helium were almost magically transformed; from the giant celestial furnaces poured the heavier elements such as iron and nickel. By around 4.6 billion years ago, they had become 1.4 per cent of a vast molecular cloud in the galaxy we now know as the Milky Way.

Slowly, the cloud reacted to the galactic forces surrounding it and formed into a nebula disc that rotated and began to concentrate much of its mass at the centre. The rotation speeded up, the disc flattened out and at the core the temperature climbed. After a million years, the pressure and density of hydrogen in the centre of the nebula reached a critical point; the star 'turned on' in a huge thermonuclear fusion.[1]

But while the star – our Sun – had captured most of the gas and dust in the collapsing nebula, at distant intervals the remaining debris gathered into clumps and then, through accretion, formed larger and larger bodies. Over the next hundred million years, these planetesimals grew to planets and settled into their orbits around the Sun. The Earth, third from the centre after Mercury and Venus, was a boiling magma ocean containing 28 per cent silicon, eight per cent aluminium, six per cent iron and four per cent magnesium. Down towards the end of the scale – below one per cent – were silver, lead and zinc, and almost at the tip was uranium.

There was no oxygen in the Earth's atmosphere, and as the planetoid bombardment continued, the iron and nickel sank to the centre. Then, as the planet grew towards its present size, gravitational attraction permitted an atmosphere to form from the gases released by mighty volcanic eruptions. And as the collisions tapered off, the Earth began to cool, forming a thin crust on its surface, mostly of the lighter silicate minerals.

By two billion years ago, the crust had developed tectonic plates, and through the process of continental drift the land masses gradually formed the geological and geographical features of today's world. Australia was contained in the supercontinent Pangaea, and as it broke up the Australian land mass would become part of the southern segment, Gondwanaland.

About 1.7 billion years ago, a huge rift valley developed within its boundaries, and as it filled with water and silt, volcanic eruptions began the process of precipitating the metallic elements such as iron and zinc from the rocks. For millions of years, the geothermal forces separated and collected the metals while other massive forces folded the rocks double then lifted them to form a mountain range. Ore bodies developed within the rocks; deeply formed minerals were changed to micas, and quartz was precipitated from fluids moving along fractures beneath the surface. The contortions of the Earth, folding and precipitating the metallic elements, continued for a billion years, but by 500 million years ago the region had gradually settled into part of a stable continental land mass.

One ore body was now about 2.5 kilometres long and from six to 23 metres wide, shaped like a boomerang plunged into the earth with its peak – a 'broken hill' – just above the surface. About 40 million years ago, as Australia began to separate itself from Gondwanaland, fierce winds, ice ages, mighty floods and other weathering ripped away the surface covering and further exposed the ore body.

The Australian continent drifted north, passing over some volcanic hot spots to produce Mount Warning on what would become the New South Wales–Queensland border, and then to create the last active volcano on the continent, Mount Gambier, in South Australia, whose final eruption took place 4000 years ago.

By then, the Australian land mass had been host to evolving life forms for perhaps 3.8 billion years and to human habitation for more than 50,000. The Aboriginal people had no knowledge of – nor need for – the mineral resources beneath their feet. However, in far off Mesopotamia, the settled peoples of the Tigris Valley had learned the art of extracting copper and tin from surface rocks and fashioning the resulting bronze into tools, weapons and religious objects. Soon, they would graduate to iron implements as communities in many parts of the world slowly mastered the rude technology of smelting ore to extract the precious metal.

While the nomadic Wilyakali people of the sandy red soil region around the 'broken hill' followed their traditional songlines through the desert seasons, on the other side of the planet empires rose and fell. And as metal technology provided them with the means to chart the courses of their sailing ships, the most venturesome went in search of a fabled Great South Land.

When the British navigator James Cook 'discovered' Australia in 1770, his political masters were unimpressed; his New South Wales was earmarked as a dumping ground for the nation's criminal class. But then, when white men discovered gold in astonishing quantities in the 1850s, visions of a southern bonanza returned and prospectors from around the world flocked to the ancient land. They followed the seams north from Victoria, and the vast penal colony took on a new identity as a thriving settlement, a lucky country of limitless potential . . . until the gold ran out.

They turned to grazing, and all across the grassy plains herders built up their flocks of sheep and mobs of cattle as the Aboriginal people retreated and fell victim to unaccustomed diseases caught in the wind.

Out in that part of Wilyakali country with the 'broken hill' they called Willyama – 'the place of the young people' – little changed. The emus, lizards and kangaroos provided a living for the Wilyakali along the creek beds and around the waterholes.

The wind swept in from the north and west; the rains fell from time to time; but the low mountain ranges stood as firm and unmoving as they had for untold millennia. The 'broken hill' made a jagged silhouette in the afternoon light.

PART I

The Prop

CHAPTER 1

King Charles

There is an elemental rawness to the town. The light is so harsh that shadows seem etched on the footpaths. The flies persist as of right. The locals measure their greetings; they know only two locations – Broken Hill and 'away' – and puzzled visitors often think they hear 'Hawaii'.

Though some mining continues at its extremities, the main ore body is long gone, consumed in the insatiable maw of industry. Yet its doppelganger remains, a dark presence slightly taller and much smoother than the original, dividing the town and looming over it. Made from a massive pile of tailings and fill that has been shaped to follow the old line of lode, it supports a lookout, a restaurant and a memorial to the 820 miners who have lost their lives – often in the most gruesome ways – in the quest to extract the riches from the ore body's ancient veins. 'Lead poisoning' dominates the early tragedies, but 'rockfall' also rates highly, as does 'crushed by machinery', 'fell down shaft', 'left cage prematurely', 'cut lip (septicaemia)', and the memorably Gothic 'entombed'.

Down on the flat, the centre of the commercial area is Argent Street and comprises strips of standardised American fast-food outlets, Australian country cafes, real-estate agencies and hotels, interspersed with anachronistic furniture and clothing shops. But the real character of the place is best observed in the houses that jostle up to its edges. Most are made from galvanised iron, as temporary and insubstantial as the Wilyakali's *gunyas*.

The houses have an unexpected and utterly incongruous twist. Some time in the 1950s during a wave of prosperity, a householder – no one remembers who – added a new feature to his iron box to give it a sense of bourgeois respectability and permanence: a stand-alone concrete facade boasting two Corinthian columns. The neighbours were instantly envious. Suddenly, it was a 'must have' for everyone on the block; and within six months the contagion had spread to every corner of the town. Some columns were fluted, others twisted like a pair of snakes mating; some were smooth, others patterned; some bulged in the middle, others rose straight and true to an Ionic or Doric capital just beneath the galvanised iron eaves. The newly house-proud miners and their wives painted them white or primrose or garish green. They planted flower beds at their base and watered them at dawn or in the dusty evenings as the Sun slipped beneath the horizon.

Sadly, the effect 50 years later is precisely the opposite from that intended. The growing gaps between the concrete facades and the iron boxes give the impression of ill-fitting wigs on old bald pates. Most of the flower gardens have long since shrivelled in the baking heat and the houses squat around the line of lode like small, resentful strangers, shimmering in the haze. They are a poignant illustration of the fleeting relationship between the human species and the great elemental forces: when one of our number discovers a prize, we gather in frenzy to harvest the riches; and when the most desirable bits are consumed, our interest fades . . . until the next time.

After a long decline, Broken Hill has been partially resuscitated by the mining boom that coincided with the industrialisation of China and India. But the day is fast coming when the mineral veins are all consumed and the last remaining evidence of human habitation has weathered away, the detritus buried – entombed – beneath the red sand blowing in from the west.

Standing atop the doppelganger, it takes no effort of the imagination to sweep away the hastily assembled impedimenta of the town and recreate the place in the mind's eye as a party of European explorers passes by the base of a jagged hill set in the endless flatlands of the outback. It is April 1844, and Charles Sturt, repatriated from command of the hellhole of Norfolk Island, leads his 15 men, 200 sheep, 30 bullocks, six dogs, six drays and a boat in his obsessive quest for the fabled inland sea. Just beyond the hog-backed hill, they are forced to camp by a sluggish stream for months before the rains arrive to replenish the inland watercourses and permit further venture into the unknown.

Among the party are John McDouall Stuart, who will later become the first European to prevail over the parched interior and reach the northern coastline; James Poole, the second in command whose namesake will help set the BHP saga in motion; and, even more remarkably, James Lewis, whose grandson will almost single-handedly turn the company into the biggest in the land. But it is Poole who deals Sturt's expedition the fatal blow when he returns from a scouting expedition in October to report the great discovery: the mighty inland sea glittering in the middle distance.

A joyous, triumphant Sturt sends the news back to Adelaide that soon they will broach 'these strange waters on which boat never swam, over which flag never floated. But both shall ere long.'

Alas, the mirage shimmers in tantalising retreat. An anguished Sturt will soon be blind and Poole dead of exhaustion, scurvy and misery. And for the next 16 years, only the Aboriginal people pass by on their seasonal safari.

In 1860 come Burke and Wills, a massive expedition even more elaborately equipped than Sturt's, yet still no match for the unrelenting wilderness. Then, from our perch 40 metres above the plain, new arrivals with sheep and horses may be seen making their way towards uncertain bends in watercourses, where they settle and build their rough shelters and solid homesteads on holdings half the size of Wales. Their ambitions too have the quality of mirages, and many depart defeated.

Mount Gipps station, which incorporates the broken hill at the southern extremity of the Barrier Ranges, passes from one owner to another until in 1875 George McCulloch, a broad, tough Scot, is appointed by his uncle and part-owner, the then Victorian premier, Sir James McCulloch, to run the 3626-square-kilometre property.

He is a good man for the job, well educated in Edinburgh and with practical farming experience in South America. He runs a tight ship, and the huge run with its 71,000 sheep begins to make a profit.

McCulloch has been granted a one-eighth share in the property and employs mostly single men, although his gardener, James 'Frans' Maygar, is married to Mary, née Smith, the daughter of English immigrants, who acts as the housekeeper. She not only cooks for the men, she salts the mutton, washes the clothes and fights an unending battle against the red dust that billows in from the north and west. Aside from the Aboriginal women who camp nearby, her only female companion is Meg, wife of the bookkeeper, George Lind. In the vastness of the outback, the small Mount Gipps community forms a tight bond.

McCulloch cares little for the rumours that gold has been discovered in other parts of the Barrier Ranges, and when the first strikes of silver are made at nearby Umberumberka (soon to be renamed Silverton), he refuses to permit prospectors on Mount Gipps, as they kill his sheep for tucker. And he threatens his men with the sack if they waste their time in prospecting instead of tending the stock and the boundary fences.

Silverton thrives. In the early 1880s, tents spring up among the bluebush. Ramshackle pubs open for business and never shut their doors. Bullock teams bring lumber and hard liquor. McGowan's Royal Coaches vie with their scarlet Cobb & Co rivals to ferry in the hopefuls. Solitary prospectors half-mad from the flies stagger across the baking plains, their boots collapsing, baring their feet to the fiery red sand. Nearby settlements such as Thackaringa have also struck paydirt. Barroom tales of the Victorian gold rush of the 1850s find new currency. Excitement shimmers in the harsh sunlight; hope turns to greed, dreams to wild obsession.

On 3 September 1883, a lone rider approaches the broken hill. Lean and sunburned, with a yellow beard, his hair worn thin beneath a battered felt hat, blue shirt open at the neck, muscular arms, moleskins belted around the waist and stuck into his riding boots, he dismounts at an outcrop of black rock. He is watchful, purposeful. He pulls out his *Goyder's Mining Guide* picked up in Adelaide on his last visit there and checks the rock against the pictures. He takes the hammer from his belt, breaks off some samples and weighs them in his roughened hands. Just as he thought, they are much heavier than the mullock that others have taken them for. He allows himself a moment of satisfaction, then packs them into a bag he has brought for the purpose. He remounts and turns his horse towards his two mates, the dam-sinker David James and his offsider, James Poole, who are working across the paddock.

As he guides his stock horse through that vast, silent landscape, it is certain that he shares that hum of excitement that has swept across the land, certain too that he carries a vision of what might flow from the discovery of the tin oxide that he believes is safely tucked away in his hessian sack. But whatever the outlines of that vision, whatever its depth or dimension, he could not know. No one could . . .

For more than a century, the rider's identity has been accepted as Charles Rasp, an edible-oil technologist from Germany who had arrived in Australia in 1869 aged 23. The principal source has been Archie Watson, who met him on arrival. Then a knockabout 20-year-old on his grandfather's property on the Upper Murray, Archie later became the first Elder professor of anatomy at Adelaide University. Celebrated as a genius by many – and derided as a crackpot by others – he would flee a piracy charge from his time on a Queensland kanaka boat[1] and haul up in Europe, where he studied medicine in Göttingen, Paris and London, including surgery under the great Joseph Lister. He and Rasp became instant mates and in later life were close companions until Rasp's death. Watson believed that Rasp was born on 7 October 1846 in north Germany. His parents were both dead by the time he was 12 and he lived for a time in Paris with an aunt. He was well educated and later trained in a big chemical company headquartered in Hamburg. Because he was fluent in English and French, he made his mark in the company's international marketing arm. But because of a persistent lung complaint, he set out for southern climes and after his arrival in Australia worked for the next 13 years on properties around the Murray-Darling.

He is said to have passed through Mount Gipps while droving sheep and to have been attracted by the broken hill, the black outcropping reminding him of tin mines in his native Saxony. And when he approached the manager, George McCulloch, for a job on the place, the rough-hewn 34-year-old Scotsman offered him £1 a week and his tucker. Rasp accepted.

More recently, however, Maja Sainisch-Plimer, whose geologist husband, Ian Plimer, is a leading authority on the Broken Hill deposit, has mined the past and uncovered a new vein. According to her research, 'Charles Rasp' was in fact the *nom de guerre* of a German Army deserter.

Indeed, the Sainisch-Plimer scenario is worthy of Charles Dickens, whose son, E. B. L. Dickens, was running a stock and station agency at Silverton at the time. Rasp, she says, was in fact Jerome Salvator Lopez von Pereira, the grandson of a Portuguese diplomat and his Saxon wife. After his return from France, Jerome enlisted in the Royal Saxon Army in 1865 aged 18. Then, in the siege of Paris during the Franco-Prussian War of 1870, he was overwhelmed by the desperate conditions in the German lines and when his close friend, Dr Emanuel Raspe, was killed in action on 2 December young Jerome deserted his army post, made his way to Holland and bought passage to Australia under the name of van Hengel. Once ashore in Melbourne, according to Sainisch-Plimer, he adopted the surname of his dead friend, grew a beard and passed himself off as 'Charles Rasp'.

If true, he would not have been the only European arrival to have started his life in the antipodes with a brand new identity. The gold discoveries had thrown Australian colonial administration into chaos. In the 1850s in Victoria alone, the population jumped from 77,000 to 540,000 in just two years. Indeed, the number of new arrivals exceeded the number of convicts who had been transported from the United Kingdom in the previous 70 years. When Charles Rasp stepped ashore in 1869 (in accordance with Archie Watson's account, but not Sainisch-Plimer's), the country's population had trebled from 430,000 in 1851 to 1.7 million; there was no time, no manpower and no inclination to check the bona fides of each member of the human tide sweeping ashore.

It is common ground among researchers that Rasp spent his first few years in Australia picking grapes at Lilydale, gold-mining in northern Victoria, working as a station hand on the Victoria–New South Wales border and tin-mining at Jingellic, a small settlement on the upper Murray River. In the early 1880s, he continued further north into New South Wales, working on various sheep stations and loading river boats on the Darling. He eventually pitched up at Mount Gipps sheep station in the Barrier Ranges and had his historic meeting with both George McCulloch and that blackened stump of a hill, shunned by silver prospectors as a heap of mullock.

By then, there was another factor at play in Rasp's quest, beyond the usual ambition among prospectors for untold riches. If, as he fervently hoped, he had discovered a lode of tin oxide, it would provide the shining key to unlock the heart of

25-year-old Agnes Klevesahl, the twinkling, buxom waitress in Café Kindermann, his favourite Adelaide coffee house.

Café Kindermann, with its marble-topped tables, newspapers and dominoes, was something of an institution in Rundle Street. Agnes and her shy little sister had been specially sponsored by Frau Kindermann from her home village in Germany to help in the business. A regular group of professional men gathered there, and though Rasp camped on the banks of the Torrens in the early days he was welcomed into their company. He reciprocated warmly, but in truth it was Agnes who drew him back to that sensual snuggery with its delicious aromas, sparkling surfaces and genial conversation. And while she was welcoming, even encouraging, she left him in no doubt: she would never give her hand to a penniless boundary rider of the wasteland.

So when he arrived at the dam-sinkers' camp with his 'tin' samples, he was not just arguing for a mining partnership but for his heart and soul. Nothing would divert him from his course. Fortunately, both men came from mining communities. David James was born in Wales in 1854 and had worked in the coal mines as a youth, arriving in South Australia with his mother and other members of the family in February 1877. They settled at Kapunda, and David became a contractor, building fences, sinking wells and excavating dams all over the state. James Poole had been born in a Cornish tin-mining region in 1848; he was a follower and would fall in behind his cobber.

Rasp later admitted, 'I had no idea of minerals. I was as green as could be.'[2] But such was the certainty in his demeanour that by lunchtime that day he had persuaded them to join him in pegging the hill so they could register their claim (which would be known as Block 10). That done, he set off for the little stone cottage on a distant Silverton hillside where he lodged the application with Constable Richard Connell, who doubled as deputy mining registrar.

But that was only half the battle. Now he had to confront George McCulloch. And that probably meant he'd be out of a job. Well, so be it.

On 5 September, after a billy of tea at the tumbledown shack of galvanised iron and wattle sticks that he called home, Rasp made his way to the manager's residence. He found McCulloch on the verandah of the big, stone, eight-roomed homestead known as Government House enjoying an evening smoke. The Scot had a soft spot for the quietly spoken German, whom he called 'the walking encyclopedia'. But when Rasp announced he was giving up his job and wanted to draw his pay, McCulloch rounded on him. 'Ye've been pegging the hill!'

Rasp admitted it and gave his reasons. In the telling, that sense of certainty that had gripped him in his talk with the dam-sinkers returned, and in the hour that followed, brought about a conversion in McCulloch worthy of St Paul himself. By the end of the evening, it was the Scot who was making plans to develop the claim. He roused the other members of the Mount Gipps team from their billets, and by midnight they had shaken hands on a deal. They were the syndicate of seven.

It was an unlikely combination. Philip Charley, the station's 20-year-old jackaroo, had been born at Ballarat on 2 September 1863. Orphaned at 12, he became a clerk in the Melbourne law office of Malleson, England and Stewart, but indoor work and the Melbourne climate undermined his constitution and his doctor advised him to depart for the dry interior. His employer and patron, J. C. Stewart, arranged with Sir James McCulloch for young Charley to work as a station hand at Mount Gipps, and within a couple of years the scorching winds of the West Darling district had cleared up his respiratory complaint; he had grown into a slim, sturdy, energetic young man, full of cheer and pleasantries.

George Urquhart, the sheep overseer, born in Inverness, Scotland, in 1845, arrived in Australia as an infant and grew up in Melbourne. As a young man, he was employed by his uncle, also named George Urquhart, who then owned, or managed, Kinchega station in northern Victoria.

They joined with Charles Rasp, George McCulloch, George Lind, David James and James Poole on that fateful night, each promising to contribute £70 from his pay or savings to meet the working expenses of their 'tin mine'. Over the next two weeks, they pegged out blocks 11 to 16, stretching across six kilometres of the area surrounding the hill. Each owned an equal share but, because of his position on the property, George McCulloch took a leading role. However, the driving force behind the enterprise in the early months was undoubtedly Charles Rasp. It was Rasp who took the rock samples to Adelaide to have them assayed. He told his partners he didn't trust the assayers at Silverton, but the real reason was his desire to see Agnes.

His plans – both mining and marital – suffered a serious blow when the initial assays revealed no tin but small amounts of lead and silver. Rasp said later, 'For 12 months it was really doubtful whether we could make anything of it.'[3] On the property, all hands were fighting the ravages of drought and, as if that were not enough, rabbits had reached plague proportions in the lush Victorian countryside and surged north and west into the Darling and the Barrier Ranges. As the dams turned to baked mud and the scant vegetation dried to a crisp, the rotting sheep carcasses and poisoned rabbits attracted clouds of flies, which tormented man and beast alike.

To finance more work on the claim, the seven partners agreed to split their shares in half and to sell one of their resulting fourteenth shares, provided they offered it to other syndicate members first. The result was a lottery of transactions in which 'cattle king' Sidney Kidman passed up a fortune when he bought half of James Poole's holding for six bullocks but then cashed it in for a few pounds; Poole later sold his other fourteenth share for £4500 and counted himself a winner.

David James disposed of a one-fourteenth share to a government surveyor, William Jamieson, for £110. Jamieson, who had come west to survey mining leases and settlements, would become a very active member of the syndicate. Later, the Welsh dam-sinker sold a further one-twenty-eighth share for £1800 to Harvey Patterson, owner of nearby Corona station.

Urquhart sold his whole one-seventh interest in the syndicate for £910 to Sam Hawkins, the Mount Gipps carpenter, and departed for Melbourne.

George McCulloch offered the new assistant bookkeeper, a young Englishman named Alfred Cox, a fourteenth share for £200, and when Cox haggled, he agreed to play three games of euchre against the 21-year-old to decide the price. Cox won, paid only £120 and left soon afterwards. That one share would make him a millionaire.

McCulloch then leaned on Lind to sell him one of his one-fourteenth shares for £90 to make up his 'loss'. In the event, Lind sold a fourteenth to McCulloch and a fourteenth to Rasp early in 1884 and left for Melbourne to join the staff of a bank. Charles Rasp and George McCulloch would end up holding three-fourteenths each.

The Linds' departure was a blow to Mary Smith Maygar the housekeeper, as it left her the only white woman on the property. And it is notable that her husband, Frans, was not included in the syndicate of seven. Indeed, a sense of mystery still surrounds Frans's fate. According to Broken Hill historian Jenny Camilleri, Maygar became 'discontented' with his life on the property and 'one day [in 1884] he rode away on his horse never to return'.[4] George McCulloch and Philip Charley discovered his remains the following year. His death was attributed to 'falling from his horse' and he was buried at Silverton on 3 May 1885. By then, George and Mary were living as man and wife.

Meanwhile, David James had begun to dig the initial 'Rasp's shaft', and the shares were attracting interest at brokers' offices in Silverton and among the bigger pastoralists in the region. Most of the buyers were steady men in their late thirties and, as new assays brought more encouraging results, they provided a sense of stability and direction to the enterprise. Station manager Bowes Kelly had arrived from his native Galway aged eight, had grown up in country New South Wales where his father was a policeman but followed his own adventurous spirit into the pastoral industry. He took up a small parcel and quickly involved himself in the management of the mine.

Another Irishman, William R. Wilson, recently appointed manager of the Barrier Ranges Silver Mining Association, bought a one-fourteenth share for £2000 – reflecting how sharply interest in the mine's potential was rising – and brought much-needed mining experience to the consortium. In September 1884, they had engaged geologist Norman Taylor, who declared that the ridge beneath the ironstone cap might well contain the biggest and most extraordinary lode of silver–lead ore in his experience. But it was the jackaroo Philip Charley who chanced upon a chunk of silver chloride in a pile of lead carbonate dumped outside the shaft. When he cracked it open, the chlorides sparkled in the sunlight. He had seen just such a phenomenon in Silverton a few days before.

William Jamieson, the surveyor shareholder, reacted immediately and had a boatswain's chair rigged up inside the shaft to examine the side more closely. It glittered in the lamplight, and samples assayed at 600 ounces of silver to the ton – encouraging but still not decisive. Shortly afterwards, an old miner, Thomas Low, approached Jamieson with 'confidential information'. At a certain hollow by the hill, he told him, he had discovered a pile of silver chlorides. He would reveal the location, he said, provided Jamieson kept it secret for a month so Low could obtain a share before the news broke.

Jamieson agreed. According to journalist and historian Alan Trengove, 'When he was shown the spot, Jamieson realised that the chlorides had fallen from a deceptively burnished outcrop high above, and that the discovery might be richly promising. He asked an Aboriginal boy named Harry Campbell to smash open the rock with a sledgehammer – and it cascaded silver.'[5]

Low bought his share but failed to hold it until the coming bonanza.

Each syndicate member was now called upon to contribute £100 as working capital, and they appointed Jamieson as general manager at an annual salary of £500. More miners were engaged and new shafts sunk.

A cross-cut at 40 metres revealed a silver lode some seven

metres across. Suddenly, it seemed that true riches were within their grasp. Little did they realise that further along the lode measured no less than 170 metres, making it the most valuable ore body of its kind in the planet's crust.

However, the syndicate partners knew it was time to float a public company to exploit the discovery. They elected McCulloch, Jamieson, Kelly and Wilson to draw up a prospectus for the new business entity: The Broken Hill Proprietary Company Limited. They capped the number of shares at 16,000, with a nominal value of £20 each – 14,000 to be retained by the syndicate as paid up to £19 and the remainder offered to the public at £9 each. From the £18,000 realised, £3000 would go to the proprietors to defray their expenses to date and the remainder to develop the mine.

Hopes were high as Jamieson – in a suit borrowed from fellow 'provisional director' Bill Wilson – set out for Adelaide, Melbourne and Sydney to promote the share issue. But the rough-and-ready prospectus did not engender quite the enthusiasm they had hoped for. While Adelaide and Sydney took up the combined 1000 shares on offer, Melbourne investors turned up their noses and Jamieson was able to unload only 162 shares of the 500 allocated to the influential southern bourse. The remaining 338 were reallocated to Silverton, which had already taken up its allotted 500.

As Jamieson made the long journey back to the small settlement they planned to call Willyama, Harry Campbell made another find. In the soft surface at the boundary between blocks 11 and 12, he uncovered specimens of ore within a mass of kaolin and quartz. He put them in a bucket and carried them into the manager's hut at the base of the broken hill. They would assay an astonishing 18,000 ounces of silver to the ton.

Harry had lifted the lid to the treasure chest.

Charles Rasp had never deviated from the pursuit of his German coquette. In his increasingly frequent journeys to Adelaide as word of the discovery spread, he moved up from the camp bed on the banks of the Torrens to the Exchange Hotel, and on his visits to Kindermann's coffee shop he pressed his suit with gifts and outings. As the gifts sparkled, so too did Agnes's eyes. But he was not without competition, and according to Archie Watson he used one-eighth of a one-seventh share to 'buy off' an ostler who duly 'faded from the scene'.[6]

Some months later – in late 1885 – he returned to Adelaide 'vastly excited'. 'Archie, I'm now a wealthy man,' he told Watson. 'I'm worth £20,000; I'm going for a trip to Germany and I'm going to marry Agnes.'[7]

Agnes accepted his proposal and they married in Adelaide on 22 July 1886. Rasp took his bride to Broken Hill to gaze upon the source of his wealth. Agnes became the only woman to go underground in Rasp's Shaft but could not leave quickly enough. Back in Adelaide, the newlyweds moved into a mansion called Willyama and soon afterwards they travelled to Germany. 'By the time he reached Hamburg,' Archie Watson told his friends, 'his shares were worth £200,000. Not long after his return their value was over two million.'[8]

Charles and Agnes Rasp travelled widely; the years 1900–1902 found them in Europe visiting the Niederwald National Monument near Frankfurt, built in 1871 to honour the dead of the Franco-Prussian War. The names included that of Emanuel Raspe. It was, perhaps, an unnerving experience for Charles Rasp. Had he been recognised as the deserter Jerome von Pereira, he would have faced a firing squad.

Agnes had social aspirations. The Rasps met Baron Field Marshal Richard von und zu Eisenstein in the fashionable resort town of Carlsbad, Bohemia, and invited him to visit them in Adelaide, which he did the following year. According to Watson, Agnes was cloyingly attentive to her guest.[9] While the social whirl spun endlessly at Willyama, Charles preferred to spend his time reading in his extensive library or smoking and talking with Archie and a few intimate friends. On 21 May 1907, he suffered a heart attack and fell dead behind a large sofa. His body was not discovered until the following day.

The other members of the original syndicate of seven

also had their lives transformed – for good and ill – by the great discovery. Mary Smith Maygar gave birth to George McCulloch's child, Alexander, in Melbourne in 1887, but since they were not married she gave the baby's father's name as Maygar despite his death two years previously. In 1892, George and Mary travelled to the UK, and the following year they married quietly at the London Registry Office before settling in a magnificent new home at 184 Queen's Gate, South Kensington. There, George lived the life of a gentleman of leisure and patron of the arts. He represented BHP in the British capital but rarely allowed his duties to interfere with his private indulgences. He died of cirrhosis of the liver in 1907, just over six months after Charles Rasp, the man who changed his life. He was 59.

Mary remarried in 1909 to the artist James Coutts Michie, and her work for the Red Cross in the Great War earned her an OBE. Her son Alexander Maygar McCulloch won the Diamond Sculls at the Henley Regatta and became an Olympic silver medallist in the London Games of 1908. Alexander married Jane Tennant and produced four children. He died of cancer while still a relatively young man. Jane remarried the brother of Egypt's obese, spendthrift monarch, King Farouk.

Mary returned to Broken Hill for a visit in 1925. By then, the Government House homestead was a ruin; she returned to her gracious Surrey home, which she had named Broken Hill. She died there after an eventful and truly remarkable life in 1945.

Philip Charley had been nearing his 22nd birthday when BHP was floated in 1885. His eight years of service in the outback had not only restored his health but also made him immensely wealthy. In 1886, he married 18-year-old Clara Evans of Adelaide and took his bride on a world tour. He then bought the historic property of Belmont Park at North Richmond on the Hawkesbury River, where he built a 25-roomed mansion and established a horse and cattle stud. He also imported the first Rolls-Royce into Australia – a 1907 Silver Ghost. Philip and Clara had five sons and three daughters; one son, also named Philip, was knighted in 1968 for services to the Royal Agricultural Society. Philip senior died in Sydney in 1937.

Following the launch of BHP, David James returned to Kapunda, where he bought a farm a few kilometres outside the township. He became mayor of Kapunda, chairman of the *Kapunda Herald* and president of both the Agricultural Society and the Racing Club. He established a racing stud on his property, Coalbrook Vale, and his filly, Auraria, won the Melbourne Cup in 1895. He was elected to the South Australian House of Assembly in 1902 and remained an unobtrusive backbencher for 16 years. He died in Adelaide on 21 July 1926, aged 72.

James Poole took up farming at Cunderdin, in Western Australia, but was compelled to abandon his property because of drought. He returned to Kapunda, where, in the closing years of his life, he was employed by Sir Sidney Kidman. He died in Kapunda on 29 September 1924, aged 76.

George Urquhart married in Melbourne and returned with his wife to the outback. He was manager of Tickalara station in southern Queensland for the Kidman interests and later settled with his wife and two sons at Black Hill station, near Silverton, which he managed for Kidman. On 14 May 1915, his horse returned riderless to the hut of shepherd Albert George Sutton, who found Urquhart's body where he had fallen, after suffering a fatal heart attack, aged 70.

After a suitable period of grieving the death of Charles Rasp, Agnes broached the outer defences of European high society and became engaged to the aged Baron Eisenstein, whose debts she repaid. But he died in a London hotel on the eve of their wedding. Indeed, according to Archie Watson, 'He took one more look at Agnes; drew his pistol; and shot his brains out all over her.'[10] Undaunted, Agnes switched her affections to another penniless German aristocrat, Count von Zedtwitz, whom she married in London in April 1914.

When the First World War broke out, the Count and Countess von Zedtwitz were in Berlin, where they remained until the war was over. The Count died soon afterwards, and Agnes returned to Adelaide in 1920 to discover that her assets had been confiscated by the Australian Government, which classified her as an enemy alien. In 1921, a special act of parliament, sponsored by Prime Minister Billy Hughes, reinstated most of her possessions, including her BHP shares, but by now she had become mentally unstable. At Willyama, tended by her faithful maid Anna, she converted the major part of her fortune to hard cash and hid it around the mansion. She barred the doors and windows and became a recluse until her death, childless, in 1936, aged 79.

CHAPTER 2

Silver and Scabs

In the early days, mining the BHP lode was at best haphazard and at worst dangerously amateurish. When the dam-sinker David James opened Rasp's Shaft, mineralogy didn't enter the equation; he chose a spot that was level enough to handle his rig. The first directors of The Proprietary knew only that they had three big tasks confronting them: securing miners to work the diggings, smelting the ore and transporting it to market. In all three, their approach was like the topography that surrounded their prize: raw and uncompromising.

At first, they benefited from the established settlement at Silverton, as miners, publicans and parsons alike shifted their operations the 25 kilometres to the new treasure trove. The miners were mostly prospectors down on their luck and in need of a few quid to survive while waiting for their own lucky strike. They would soon become too exhausted for extra-curricular prospecting and ever more dependent on the company's shilling. Then, as word of Broken Hill's riches spread, a small army made the long dusty trek to the fount, 1160 kilometres west of Sydney and just 48 kilometres east of the South Australian border.

The BHP bosses set tough terms. On their properties, they had ruled like autocrats; they saw no reason to change their stripes in the mining business. They even charged their miners four shillings from their first pay for the use of a shovel. It was an approach that would cause untold and unnecessary hardship to both worker and employer in the years ahead.

Working, housing and living conditions were appalling as the population soared. The miners and their families were surrounded by lead. It wasn't only in the mine or the tailings but in the air they breathed and in the dust that swirled around the streets and invaded their homes. Water was often so scarce that miners didn't waste it on washing themselves or their eating utensils – two essentials in the prevention of lead poisoning. Men were found writhing on the floor with unbearable stomach pains. Others were struck down with loss of appetite, premature ageing and impotence, broken constitutions and muscular tremors.

Standard mining techniques were ignored as miners worked out comparatively narrow sections in a two-metre stope. The 'roof' was supported by timbers until the cavities were supposedly filled by rock brought down from the surface. But since it took almost as much manpower to fill the cavities as to mine them, sections were often left open, and rockfalls were commonplace.

The first shipment of BHP ore – 48 tons – was carted on bullock wagons 280 kilometres to the South Australian railhead at Terowie, where it was loaded on to the freight train for Adelaide and thence to the Intercolonial Smelting and Refining Company's works at Spottiswood, outside Melbourne. The bullock wagons returned with mine timber, limestone, coking coal, foodstuffs, hard liquor and sundry other supplies for the isolated mining township. The only other route in was by paddle steamer up the Darling to a landing 150 kilometres from The Hill. But for much of the time the river was too shallow to be navigable.

The crude smelting process used at Spottiswood wasted a third of the silver, and in 1886 BHP imported two new 30-ton Nevada smelting furnaces that could treat 100 tons of ore a day at the mine head. And they snapped up much of the Silverton smelting equipment when those mines closed. Altogether, it was a rough-and-ready operation; and it succeeded only because the ore was so rich. In fact, they paid for the new plants from profits – the original £15,000 raised in the company float for development would never be needed.

Each BHP share retained its £19 nominal paid-up value, but by the end of the 1887 trading year they were selling for £174/10/–. When the Melbourne exchange opened in 1888, there was a frantic rush for scrip in any mine at Broken Hill, with BHP leading the field. In three weeks, prices had almost doubled, and by the end of February they reached the dizzy price of £409 per share.

In 1883, BHP had consolidated all seven leases within its direct control, but now three subsidiary companies (owning, respectively, blocks 10, 14 and, jointly, 15 and 16) were floated on the booming stock market, leaving BHP with three central and apparently richer leases (blocks 11, 12 and 13) along the crest of the outcropping lode. The new mines were Block 10, Block 14 and British BHP (blocks 15 and 16). At the edges of the BHP leases, beyond where the miner believed the limits of the lode to be, other companies – including Broken Hill South and Broken Hill North – raised funds from eager investors to develop their holdings.

In less than five years since Charles Rasp and his mates pegged the first claim, the mine was producing a third of the world's silver and was valued at £6.5 million. Yet no one knew that the hill contained an astonishing 280 million tonnes of ore, much of it intensely rich in silver, lead and zinc. That realisation would come only as new shafts were sunk and exploration techniques refined.

Soon after mining commenced, the township had been surveyed and the main streets named after the minerals that provided its *raison d'être*. In 1888, the *Broken Hill Argus* reporter Randolph Bedford described Argent Street as 'a huge dust heap, filled with hotels and flimsy offices and saloons; a two-chain-wide road knee-deep in dust and crowded with men from all the earth, selling at tremendous prices shares in alleged mines'.[1]

The local smelters now spread the lead poison to the wives and the children, whose mental and physical growth were stunted. Dust storms blanketed the area for days on end. Dysentery and typhoid raged through the tent and shanty town. The contrast between the miners' living and working conditions and the sudden, spectacular wealth of the proprietors was not lost on them and their families. Resentment festered, although the bosses seemed blithely unaware of it. In nearby Silverton, the assistant school teacher, gentle Mary Cameron from Sydney's North Shore, found common cause with the workers' plight. She converted to socialism, raged against injustice and published her first poem, 'Unjust', in *The Silver Age*. Later, she joined the utopian quest of William Lane to Paraguay and, as Dame Mary Gilmore, made her indelible mark in the nation's literary history.

However, 'human-resources management' aside, the BHP directors did know their limitations and were determined to hire the best brains to run the specialised areas of extraction and exploitation. That, too, was a characteristic that would distinguish BHP throughout its first 50 years.

Chairman Bill Wilson's brother Sam, superintendent of Silverton's Day Dream Mine, succeeded William Jamieson as general manager in 1885. But as the extraordinary size of the lode became clear, both he and the board realised that he was not really equipped for the task. Bill Wilson set out for America to hire the best.

In Colorado, site of the great silver rush of the 1870s, he found a top metallurgist, Herman Schlapp, to take control of smelting operations, and in Nevada he hired William Patton as general manager. Patton was a former manager of the famous Comstock Lode and signed on at £4000 a year – a breathtaking salary in Australia at the time. Both served the company well. Schlapp brought in new smelters to treat 10,000 tons of ore a week at the mine, and on his advice they chose to send their concentrate to Port Pirie, where they established a refining works before selling the silver to Australian banks and the lead to England and China.

Freighting the output to the coast remained a problem. The South Australian Government extended its rail line to the border, but the New South Wales Government refused to join it to the two nearby towns. So, at BHP's initiative, the locals formed the Silverton Tramway Company and in 1888 built a line to the South Australian border. The visiting Duke of Manchester found himself dragooned into an improbable journey to Broken Hill, where he opened the line by cracking a bottle of hot champagne over the steel buffers at the front of the carriage. Apparently offended by the waste, he repaired to Delamore's Hotel, shouted the bar and, with the help of the locals, quaffed the publican's entire stock to the encouraging strains of 'For He's a Jolly Good Fellow'. The Silverton Tramway soon became the most prosperous private railway in Australia.

Patton brought order and forward planning to the mining process and introduced square-set timbering to support the roof and walls of the underground mining stopes. He had pioneered the system in America and found no need for subsequent rockfill. His methods brought substantially increased efficiencies, although he would soon learn that the Big Mine (as it became known) was a different proposition from the hard-packed American mines he'd been used to. The Broken Hill ground tended to move or 'creep' when disturbed, and his Oregon-pine supports dried brittle and flammable. The miners lived in terror of the 'creep'. The author Ion Idriess, who worked in the mine as a youngster, wrote later:

> It is difficult to imagine anything more frightening away down below than the whispering, wheezing, shivering, grinding, straining, cracking, splitting, then shrieking of heavy timbers as they strain against the slowly increasing, implacable pressures of mother rock that finally explodes the great timber caulks into masses of splinters.[2]

When that happened, the miners would run for their lives. All too often, the rockfall beat them to the punch.

A way around the problem employed at Broken Hill was to abandon the underground mining in favour of the open-cut method. But that brought its own problems, with men (and horses) frequently falling to their deaths from the sides of the giant quarry. In fact, the miners – who began calling themselves 'slaves' – reckoned the bosses were more concerned about losing a horse than a man. A horse cost £40; a man could be replaced for pennies.

The response was as fierce as it was inevitable. In 1888, the men organised themselves into the Amalgamated Miners' Association (AMA) and demanded a better deal. The shocking disparity between the millionaire mine owners and those who dug their wealth from the bowels of the earth had touched a raw nerve. It struck at the heart of the newly forged Australian values based on the 'fair go'. It bred a savage militancy among the leaders, who would soon match their employers for arrant bullheadedness. By 1889, the AMA had by various means – not all of them gentlemanly – signed up all but 300 of the 5000 mine workers in the town. Then, satisfied with their bargaining power, they told the companies that they would not work with non-unionists and backed their demands with a strike. After only eight days, management capitulated. Henceforth, they would only employ unionists; they would even collect dues from members' pay packets and pass them on to the union.

But the initial victory was only the beginning of a slugfest that continued with rising resentment and bitterness on both sides for the better part of a century. Next year, the AMA supported their 'brothers' in the great maritime strike, and when the proprietors – led by BHP – appeared to back the shipowners, they threatened a lightning stoppage. The Broken Hill companies caved in almost immediately, reduced working hours from 48 to 46 a week and, according to the agreement, accepted judicial arbitration 'in the event of any future trouble'.

Within a year, the economic tide turned. Metal prices fell and depression loomed. By 1892, the directors of BHP were ready to fight back. They suspended any dividend for shareholders that year. They wanted cash reserves for a protracted struggle. Union leader Dick Sleath readied his men for the fight. Sleath was young and well made, a former mining-company promoter attracted to the union as an administrator and organiser. He resisted the radicals in his own ranks. He even sought to calm the wives and daughters who had literally tarred and feathered those recalcitrant workers deaf to the siren call of union solidarity. But once the lines were drawn, he proved himself an able organiser and an inspiring leader.

On 30 June, the companies declared that they would terminate the earlier agreement by 30 July. Thereafter, they would employ non-union miners by 'contract' and daily-award rates would remain unchanged for the unionists. Arbitration was out. And no discussion would be entered into. The battle had commenced, and for 18 weeks it took on many of the accoutrements of a civil war. The unionists opened with rousing speeches in Broken Hill's Central Reserve and repeated renditions of 'Rule, Britannia!' with special emphasis on the line that 'Britons never, never, never shall be slaves'. Declarations of solidarity from community and religious leaders also raised hopes and passions. According to the unionists' traditional chant, 'The workers, united, will never be defeated' . . .

The proprietors, led by BHP secretary William Knox, quelled a brief rebellion from small shareholders – partly triggered by Sleath, who bought a single share and tried to disrupt the annual meeting – then directed their forces from Melbourne's Scott's Hotel. Knox, an accountant with all the dewy-eyed compassion that distinguishes his profession, had been engaged by the BHP board at £75 a year in 1886. His clients typically came from his alma mater, The Scotch College, but as the mine unveiled its riches Knox concentrated on the main chance. Now, he had the opportunity to make his mark.

Once the unionists struck, Knox launched his battle plan: thousands of unemployed workers from the cities answered his advertisements and were signed up as strike-breakers. Arriving at Broken Hill, they ran a savage gauntlet from unionists and their supporters, but the New South Wales Government responded to Knox's call for troopers to maintain 'law and order'. The 'scabs' and 'blacklegs' made it through. Food and other supplies were assembled, together with flying squads to penetrate the picketing blockades at the mines.

Knox's ruthless regime succeeded. Within weeks, despite donations from other unions, the Broken Hill strikers and their families were in desperate straits. George Dale, a union historian, later wrote:

> Oh, the privations and sufferings of the latter portion of that struggle! What agonies were experienced; what degrading, humiliating, damnable straits were these downtrodden men and women of the Barrier driven to . . . 18 weeks watching the shrinking frames of underfed, ill-clad, ill-shod children of the working class . . . And all for what? – to appease the depraved minds and to fill the huge pockets and guts of a few bigoted, soulless, grasping capitalists who never have, and probably never will, do one single act likely to be of benefit to humanity, country, or God.[3]

On 4 August, Dick Sleath came to blows with a bank manager who refused to cash a draft from Newcastle miners.[4] The strikers took out their grievances on the blacklegs; street fights became commonplace; and when some strikers drifted back to work their houses were set on fire.

In the Central Reserve, calls for open rebellion increased until, on 15 September, Knox gave the signal and a massive contingent of NSW troopers descended on the town. They arrested Dick Sleath and all six of the union's leadership, the so-called Defence Committee, who were charged with conspiracy and sedition and placed in leg irons. It was the decisive blow. Now virtually leaderless, the strikers surrendered unconditionally on 6 November 1892.

In victory, BHP was unforgiving. It blacklisted 'union agitators', reduced the workforce and earned the undying hatred of the AMA. It rewarded Knox with promotion to the board of directors, taking the place of George McCulloch, who departed for the United Kingdom and his fatal rendezvous with the high life.

With the threat of the unions temporarily at bay, the board turned its attention to its other big challenges. First was the 'sulphide problem'. Beneath the oxidised surface ores was a fine-grained mix of silver, lead, sulphur and a zinc component that defied all attempts at separation. Small mountains of it accumulated, and for years it flummoxed the best brains of the industry. Some progress was made with mechanical water jigs and oscillating tables, set up in sheds beside the line of lode. The instruments were designed to agitate the mix and so separate its components. In 1896, BHP built a big plant on site to separate the silver and lead. Further refinements improved the process and a second unit in 1899 treated more than 600,000 tons annually. The remaining sulphurous material contained the zinc, which at the time was worth almost as much as the silver and lead together. But it was worthless until it could be separated out. More than ten million tons of these potentially precious tailings ranged tantalisingly around the line of lode.

It was not until the arrival of one of the most remarkable of BHP's overseas imports, Guillaume Daniel Delprat, that a solution (in both senses of the term) was found. Born in Delft in south-east Holland, home of an exquisite blue pottery and the magically talented painter Johannes Vermeer, Delprat was the son of the Dutch minister for war. He quickly established a reputation as a polymath and served his engineering apprenticeship on the infamous Tay Bridge in Scotland, which collapsed beneath a train that plunged into the river taking

75 of its passengers to their death. But the experience appears only to have reinforced his determination to bring all possible knowledge to bear on engineering problems. He took courses in physics at the local Newport polytechnic and explored the arcane mathematical world of differential and integral calculus in correspondence with his father.

He added Spanish to his command of English, French, German and Italian when he took several positions in Spanish copper and silver mines, and in 1892 he published a breakthrough article on 'the extraction of ore from wide veins or masses' in an American scientific journal. When BHP's general manager Alexander Stewart read it some years later, he alerted the board. In June 1898, Delprat accepted an offer to become assistant general manager of BHP, and on 3 September he arrived in Adelaide, where he was met by Stewart.

By now 42, Delprat was a dedicated self-improver addicted to the latest vogue, Pelmanism, better known today as Pairs, a memory game for children in which players seek to match pairs of cards. He was a man of great physical strength. He could crack walnuts between finger and thumb and on one occasion when his wife complained that a colleague was deliberately hurting women with an overly forceful handshake, he crushed the man's hand in his own.

His tastes were quintessentially European and included a passion for chess, French literature, fencing and lawn tennis. But he also possessed an appetite for adventure, and BHP certainly offered that.

Delprat's wife and five of their seven children arrived in Australia in January 1899 and, after a period in Broken Hill, settled in Adelaide from 1904. Delprat was soon promoted to replace the departing Alexander Stewart and began a peripatetic existence between Broken Hill, Port Pirie, Melbourne and, in time, Europe and the United States. However, his immediate concern was the sulphide problem, and it was all the more urgent because of the continuing fall in silver and lead prices on the international exchanges.

The mountains of 'waste' loomed over the town and spread their grit into every exposed orifice, whether human or artificial. It clogged machinery. It sent housewives into despair. It sickened and irritated the young and the elderly. And, most frustratingly, it mocked all attempts to release the untold riches contained within.

Delprat was in his element. First, he abandoned the oscillating process of extracting the silver and lead in favour of a technique he devised to make bricks of the slime, which he burned to eliminate the sulphur. The resulting lumps could then be smelted in the traditional manner. But that still left the zinc to be recovered, and in this he recalled a system used in Spain to extract copper from pyrites by dissolving the metal in water and then extracting it from the solution.

At the mine head, he worked with his chief metallurgist, A. D. Carmichael, and his associate, the brilliant Leslie Bradford. 'Boil the stuff and see if it will go into solution,' Delprat told Carmichael.[5] The chief was sceptical, but Bradford responded immediately. The result was not encouraging. For some unknown reason, the zinc, with a much greater specific gravity than water, would not sink. Carmichael was triumphant: 'It's no good. I told you so. It won't go into solution and I can't keep it down.'[6] Delprat studied the beaker. Then he poured it into another glass vessel held by Bradford. Again, the zinc-impregnated scum defied gravity and rose to the surface. Suddenly, the significance struck Delprat like a physical blow. 'Why, we've got the two separated,' he said. 'That will do just as well as getting into solution.'

The science behind the phenomenon – the action of carbonic acid to produce gas bubbles that held the mineral on the surface – would not be understood for some years, but for the moment it was enough that it worked. And, when combined with the work of a Melbourne brewer, Charles Potter, together with Leslie Bradford's and later E. J. Horwood's refinements, the flotation process unlocked a new bonanza. By 1911, BHP had produced 500,000 tons of valuable zinc concentrates.

Other miners at the deeper ends of the line of lode also cashed in on the new technology. One of the beneficiaries was the Zinc Corporation, which was incorporated in 1905 by a group of Australian mining entrepreneurs together with an up-and-coming American engineer, Herbert Hoover (who later became President Hoover, from 1929 to 1933). They used Horwood's method on a grand scale, providing the foundation of a business that through international expansion and merger would become the Rio Tinto group, with a $US25 billion annual turnover in 2006, second only to BHP Billiton itself among the great miners of the world.

Meanwhile, Delprat urged the company to transfer its smelting operations to Port Pirie on the eastern shore of Spencer Gulf, where they had access to greater supplies of water, limestone and ironstone flux. The board agreed, and while perhaps they didn't realise it at the time, this was not just the first step in BHP's departure from the source of its initial wealth but a radical new direction in the company's activities.

The ironstone would come from two intensely rich and rough-hewn eminences about 70 kilometres west of the shoreline on the other side of the gulf, Iron Monarch and Iron Knob. These had been owned since 1891 by the Mount Minden Mining Company. By 1896, Mount Minden's owner, Ernst Siekmann, was falling behind in his obligations to the South Australian Government and was faced with the possibility of losing his leases. BHP applied for them through one of its most active directors, John Darling, a wealthy Adelaide grain merchant with powerful political ambitions and a wide circle of support, not least through his brother Joe Darling, captain of the Australian cricket team.

Siekmann resisted, and Darling's ruthless determination over the next three years to overwhelm his opponent offended the sensibilities of some among the Adelaide Establishment and revived community resentment of BHP's winner-takes-all credo. A select committee of the Legislative Council was established to report on BHP's actions. Darling was accused of being a 'sharker'. According to one witness, 'In a mining camp, he would be lucky if he escaped lynching.'[7]

However, the committee was chaired by a shareholder, John Lewis MLC, whose son Essington had just begun work at BHP as a trainee engineer. His report gave the company a clean bill of health and confirmed BHP's ownership of the leases. In short order, the South Australian Parliament passed a Bill allowing BHP to build a railway from the mines to a jetty on the western shore at Hummock Hill, a tiny settlement that would be transformed in the coming decades into an industrial powerhouse and renamed Whyalla.

In the wake of the acquisition, Delprat and Darling would forge a close relationship, and as Darling rose to become chairman of the board they would operate as one of the most dynamic partnerships in Australian business history. Indeed, almost as soon as they acquired the iron leases they saw great new opportunities opening up. In 1901, the company spokesman Harvey Patterson told shareholders, 'The property is so gigantic . . . that I see no reason why it should not supply a portion of the requirements of the world for the manufacture of iron as well as flux for our smelters.' It was only one short step from that concept to the realisation that BHP itself could supply not just iron but its far more valuable and sought-after alloy: steel.

CHAPTER 3

Blood and Iron

So immense was BHP's original lode of silver, lead and zinc that the company would continue to extract its bounty until 1938. But as early as 1909 Delprat believed – and told anyone who would listen – that his was a 'dying mine'. In the previous year, he had produced a massive 600,000 tons of ore and the BHP board had paid generous dividends to shareholders. But now silver and lead prices were falling. The Americans and the Europeans were breaking contracts as they abandoned metallic currencies in favour of banknotes, which became legal tender in France and Germany in 1909; only the Chinese remained true to their word. As the situation deteriorated, the new chairman, John Darling, demanded a cut in labour costs.

That meant trouble at mine.

In 1906, BHP had reached a two-year agreement with the AMA for a twelve and a half per cent increase so that men on 7/6 a day now took home 8/7 and those above 8/4 received an extra 1/- a shift. No one among the miners was making a fortune, especially since basic foodstuffs were 30 per cent more expensive than in the coastal cities, but everyone was getting by. Now, management threatened the status quo.

The owners declared that they were faced with two options: close the mine until metal prices recovered or seek a better deal from the miners to avoid crippling losses. Closing the mines would cause immense hardship to the men and their families; so they opted to do 'the right thing' by the workers. Now that the agreement had expired, it was time to drop the twelve and a half per cent 'bonus'.

The unionists were outraged. BHP was wealthy almost beyond measure. It had distributed more than £11 million in bonuses and dividends to its shareholders. Productivity was up. Metal prices would bounce back as they always did. Once again, the worker was being made the scapegoat.

Delprat tried hard to reach a compromise. On one occasion, in 1909, he appeared at a union meeting in the very centre of unionist activity, the Trades Hall, where he used his muscular frame to part the boisterous crowd and reach the stage. 'Well, boys,' he began, 'here is Daniel in the lion's den.' But while they admired his pluck – and heard him in relative silence – when he offered a lower wage scale combined with a profit-sharing formula that would put money in their pockets when metal prices recovered, there were few takers.

The AMA leaders had imported the hard man of British unionism, Tom Mann, whose class hatred knew no bounds and whose rabble-rousing speeches were tough to resist. And there were plenty among the Australians who remembered the company outrages of 1892. The despised William Knox was now vice chairman of the board. So when Delprat announced officially on 7 December that the mine would close for Christmas and the bonus would cease on 1 January 1909, the combined unions responded with a unanimous resolution that they would resist the proposed lockout by BHP by refusing to work until the company agreed to pay the existing rate of wages.

The die was cast. By midnight of 1 January, the unionists had picketed the mine from one end of the lease to the other. And when word spread on 3 January that the New South Wales Government was sending a contingent of 50 police, the old hands could see the pattern of '92 returning. In a show of strength, all BHP employees marched on the mine eight abreast to demand back pay.

Delprat paid up, then asked for protection for 13 'scabs' who were going off shift. The union allowed them out unharmed, but when they reached the main streets they were set upon and, according to newspapers, 'roughly handled'.

In Adelaide, Darling raised the ante. 'If the police cannot maintain order, then the military should be called out,' he told *The Advertiser*. 'Either that or the government should give the mine owners power to protect their own property.'

Despite the best efforts of Mann and others to shame and goad the miners into 'solidarity' against the ruling class, enough men broke with the union to keep the mine in working order. Delprat arranged for them to march to work behind a brass band holding aloft a banner proclaiming, 'Behold, the Workers Think'. However, on Saturday, 9 January as they approached the mine, Mann and others stood in their way. As the two forces met, fights broke out and the police dashed into the fray wielding billy clubs. They frogmarched Mann and 27 others off to jail and on the way dealt out their own version of rough handling.

That night, a crowd gathered to protest. According to George Dale:

> What a procession it was – not one less than 15,000 men and women participating . . . and whenever a cop was observed he either received a 'back-hander' from a woman on passing or was spat upon. This happened not once but hundreds of times during that memorable tramp through the city's street.[1]

Dale may well have exaggerated the numbers but not the rage and resentment that swept the town. The court proceedings against Mann and his confederates – transferred to distant Albury to avoid trouble – lasted three weeks, and while the British agitator was found not guilty he was ordered to stop making speeches in New South Wales 'or in any way assist the strike'.

BHP agreed to attend a conference with the chief justice of the Arbitration Court, H. B. Higgins, but warned that it would not accept an adverse decision. Nonetheless, Higgins took evidence at Broken Hill and Port Pirie, where the union militancy was not as intense, before delivering his judgment on 12 March.

It was a resounding victory for the unions. The bonus was incorporated into the pay scale, for at least the next four and a half years. The miner, Justice Higgins said in his judgment, 'must dispute until he secures enough wherewith to renew his strength and maintain his home from day to day. He will dispute, he must dispute, until he gets this minimum; even as a man immersed can never rest until he gets his head above water.'

BHP appealed unsuccessfully to the High Court and the unions then sought to ensure that the strike leaders and activists would not be victimised if they returned to work. Delprat equivocated, promising only that the company would be reasonable in its approach. Mann and others tried to revive resistance but the Port Pirie workers would have none of it. So, in the face of a split, the union retreated. After 20 weeks, the strike officially ended on 22 May.

As in 1892, BHP reduced its workforce and blacklisted the trouble makers. Then, within weeks of the settlement, the lead price recovered, soaring up to £18 a ton, where it remained until the outbreak of the Great War. Had the miners accepted Delprat's compromise – and provided BHP had stuck to the bargain – they would have been substantially better off. Tom Mann went back to England, where, in 1920, he became a founding member of the Communist Party of Great Britain.

However, the strike only confirmed Delprat's view that the industrial convulsions were a symptom of his dying mine. Now was the time, he believed, for a major reappraisal of the company's future, and he found a staunch ally in John Darling. In late 1911, the board authorised its general manager to undertake an intensive six-month survey of the world's iron and steel industries and report his findings. Delprat farewelled his beloved brood in Adelaide and in the New Year left for Britain, Europe and the United States.

It was not his first overseas mission for the company. In 1907, he had travelled to Europe then returned via America, where he was impressed with new developments in steel technology. Now, he renewed his acquaintance with technical innovators, who reinforced his enthusiasm for the development of an Australian steel industry. One steelmaker in particular, David Baker of Philadelphia, seemed to bring the kind of clear-sighted approach to the issue that mirrored his own. He recommended that the board engage Baker to conduct an urgent feasibility study into the development of an Australian steel industry led by BHP. Darling secured board approval and Baker sailed for Australia with his daughter.

When Delprat returned, he submitted his report in a seven-page letter addressed to the chairman:

> The fact of the company holding an immense Iron Ore deposit in South Australia made it incumbent on us to find out if this Iron Ore could be turned into more profitable use than by merely using it as a flux in the smelters at Port Pirie.
>
> The demand for steel [in Australia] has grown steadily and today the requirements are such that the urgent necessity of having steel works in the Commonwealth is a well recognised fact . . . Very careful examination and boring [of Iron Knob] has convinced me that here we have a solid basis for an iron and steel industry, which will be sufficient for more than a generation, and I have further convinced myself that the quality of the ore is the very best that can be had for making steel.[2]

He then identified the Newcastle and Wollongong areas as sources for 'excellent coking coal' and after ranging over relative production costs, the availability of skilled labour, the best site (Hummock Hill), the type of blast furnaces and his consultations with state and federal ministers, Delprat concluded:

> I am of opinion [*sic*] that it is of great importance that the works should be started without loss of time. The great need for Iron and Steel Works in Australia is being realised by other men, and in a matter of this kind, it is a very great advantage to be first in the field . . . should the Board decide to proceed, I would suggest all possible despatch.[3]

His report was followed almost immediately by a more detailed analysis from David Baker in which he backed the move with figures showing big potential profits. However, he disagreed with Delprat's choice of Hummock Hill as the site of the steelworks:

> Nearly three-quarters of a ton of Coal is required above the weight of Ore necessary to make a ton of steel rails. And as the freight on a ton of Coal delivered to a point near the Ore – say Hummocky [*sic*] Hill – is 6/-, the extra cost for Coal in making Steel at that point is 4/1d, or $1.02.
>
> In addition, there is great scarcity of fresh water at Hummocky Hill, and as the Harbour at Port Kembla [near Wollongong] is too small and poorly protected to consider, my recommendation is to build the Blast Furnace and Steel Works on property having a water front in the Harbour at Newcastle, NSW.[4]

A week later, Delprat responded in a remarkable letter to Darling, 'I thoroughly discussed this point with Mr Baker and find that he is right and that I was wrong . . . Newcastle is certainly the best site we can take.'[5]

He then recommended that the company engage Baker to build the works as superintendent on a five-year contract at an annual $25,000 salary. 'It will take two and a half to three years to properly construct the plant,' he said, 'and two years more is not too much to enable Mr Baker to prove that the plant will fulfil his promises.' Darling agreed, and Baker set up his construction headquarters in Newcastle.

Again, BHP had chosen well. Baker was a tall, quietly spoken

Quaker who had spent 12 years with the Philadelphia Steel Company, three as manager of Illinois Steel, then a further three resuscitating Dominion Steel in Canada before establishing himself as a consulting engineer. He was immediately infatuated with Australia and enthused by the opportunity to establish a national steel industry virtually from scratch.

Australia's appetite for steel had reached a million tons annually, most of which was being imported. The only local competitor was the Lithgow works of Charles Hoskins, who had taken over a company with a troubled history, beginning with an attempt by the British industrialist John Lysaght to start a wire-netting works in 1883. Its location so far from the coast meant it could never compete on equal terms with BHP. However, Hoskins did have plans to move some of his operations to Port Kembla.

Baker didn't give a fig for the competition. His only concern was to bring his steelworks in on time and on budget – in three years at £1.5 million. Delprat gave him a free hand to import American experts and methods. He quickly assembled an enthusiastic team and pressed ahead on all fronts.

On 27 March 1914, John Darling died suddenly in Melbourne, leaving an estate of more than £1.5 million. By then, his powerful backing for the move into steel had the unequivocal support of the board and by June 1914 Delprat was able to report excellent progress:

> The blast furnace [at Newcastle] is nearly erected and ready for lining. The foundations of the Open Hearth Plant have been laid and the building will be finished on time. The foundations of the Rolling Mill are not quite completed but sufficiently advanced to allow the erection of the heavy machinery which had already been received on the ground.[6]

Other advances reported by Delprat included the electric power plant up and running; three of the 15 boilers completed, with the others well in hand; coke ovens on schedule; coal bin completed; a 200-metre wharf half-finished; railway lines laid; and workshops, offices and stores erected.

> At the Ironstone Quarries [in SA], two more working faces have been opened up showing excellent Iron Ore and a nest of five Jaw-breaker crushers are being erected at Hummock Hill at the end of the Iron Knob Tramway.
>
> The Jetty at Hummock Hill is being lengthened so as to end in deeper water, half of this work being already completed and conveyor belts are being installed on it to load the steamers promptly and give quick despatch.

Not even the outbreak of war on 3 August 1914 was allowed to interfere with the building schedule. On the contrary, it provided a new sense of urgency to establish an industry that could produce the vital munitions and war machines for the patriotic battle for king and country. In Delprat's words:

> Should any outside nation have the temerity to threaten the independence of this, our own country, they will find us quite prepared [with] swords and guns which, in the hands of the bravest among the brave – our Australian soldiers – will enable the Commonwealth to cry aloud, 'Hands off!'[7]

Patriotic enthusiasm for the Great War, however, was not so clear-cut at BHP's major operation at Broken Hill. Yet, ironically, it was – and remains – the site of the only outbreak of hand-to-hand warfare on the Australian mainland. On 1 January 1915, as 1200 men, women and children headed out of The Hill in open carriages for the traditional Manchester Unity Lodge picnic at Stephens Creek, two men under a Turkish flag opened fire from behind an earthen mound near the water pipeline about 50 metres from the tracks. Pandemonium overwhelmed the travellers as 18-year-old Alma Cowie fell dead from a bullet in the head. William Shaw also received a fatal shot and his 15-year-old daughter Lucy was struck in the arm. Alf Millard, who was riding his bike beside the train on a routine inspection of the pipeline, also took a fatal head wound.

In the confusion, the driver stopped the train as the fusillade continued. But at least it allowed two men – Shaw Hendry and Paddy Lowe – to leap out and run for a nearby house where, luckily, a phone line connected them to the Broken Hill police station. Inspector Henry Miller and all the constables he could round up were soon on their way to the scene.

Meanwhile, the two 'Turks' – Gool Badsha Mahomed, a young man in his early twenties, and 60-year-old Mullah Abdullah – broke off and made for Tom Campbell's stone hut on the western outskirts of the town. When he saw their rifles, Campbell slammed his door. The raiders opened fire and Campbell took a bullet in the side. However, the door held and the men ran towards an outcrop of white quartz with the police now in hot pursuit.

In the shoot-out that followed, Constable Robert Mills was struck on the thigh and seriously wounded. But the unluckiest victim was Jim Craig, 69, who, despite the pleas of his family, refused to take cover and went on chopping wood at the back of the nearby Cable Hotel. A stray bullet felled him stone dead.

When the Turkish guns fell silent, the police approached the outcrop and discovered Mullah Abdullah dead and the young Afghan, Gool Mahomed, dying. Documents discovered under rocks revealed the twisted motivations of the two men: Gool Mahomed 'because your people are fighting my country'; and the old man – whose Turkish antecedents were never proven – was revealed as distressed and culturally alienated. The final casualty list was six dead and seven seriously wounded.

However, despite the outrage at the very doorstep of Broken Hill itself, there were some in the town who saw the conflict in Europe as a war of the capitalists with little or no relevance to Australia. On at least one occasion, they 'bombed' the office of the pro-imperial *Barrier Miner*. In 1916, they elected a rabid anti-conscriptionist, Percy Brookfield, to state parliament, and when local Victoria Cross winner Roy Inman returned from the war he recalled that he had been 'stoned by mongrels at the train' when he enlisted. 'I would like to be at one end of the street with a machine gun and have them at the other end,' he said.[8]

On the Western Front, BHP miners found their skills in demand in one of the great victories engineered by General John Monash. The First Australian Tunnelling Company undermined a German position – Hill 60 – and packed it with explosives. At 3.10 am on 7 June 1917, Broken Hill's Captain Oliver Holmes Woodward pulled the switch that ripped the hill apart in an explosion that was heard 100 kilometres away and utterly demoralised the German defenders. On his return, Woodward became general manager of North Broken Hill Limited.

Industrial unrest continued at the BHP mine throughout the war, and in 1919, when the so-called Higgins Award was due to expire, the unions began agitating for shorter working hours and higher pay. In 1917, BHP had formed a 'company union' at Newcastle – the Iron and Steel Industry Employees' Protective Association – and pressured workers to join with an extra two shillings a day and an underlying threat to get in or get out. The concept was never accepted by the wider workforce and it would not survive beyond 1921. Now, at Broken Hill, carpenters in the mines struck for higher wages and the miners took the opportunity to demand better health-and-safety conditions. One miner said later:

> Our men were walking the streets of Broken Hill with death written all over their faces. They had dusted lungs which went from pneumonia on to tuberculosis; and then they just died. It was commonly said that miners did not live beyond [their] early forties in Broken Hill.[9]

The 1919–20 campaign for better conditions, which would be reprised in most of its essentials in the 2006 outcry against James Hardie Limited for compensation for asbestosis, galvanised community sentiment against BHP. Opportunists such as the shady Melbourne businessman John Wren donated £9000 to the cause to boost his reputation and the Melbourne *Herald* paraded the plight of sick and dying miners across its news pages. But the company refused to budge.

In Broken Hill, a new union leader, William 'Shorty' O'Neil, had followed his father on to the line of lode in 1917, aged only 14. Working initially on the surface at the Big Mine, the diminutive Shorty carried kerosene tins full of coal to fire a steam engine. Unionism was in his blood and he rose quickly through the ranks to leadership of the second largest of the Barrier unions, the moderate Federated Engine Drivers and Firemen's Association. He knew from his father and uncle the legends of 1892 and the battles of 1909, but nothing prepared him for the soul-destroying degradation of 18 months without pay. It was at this time, he said in a later newspaper interview, that he learned the lesson that became his catch cry: 'If you don't kick, you get kicked.'

At one stage, his father, Mick, dusted off his cobbler's kit and returned to his first trade repairing boots and shoes outside the Trades Hall building. Shorty was his shoeshine boy. The humiliation burned into his soul, even though the unions went on to win a famous victory. When the company finally surrendered, they had secured all their demands: an unprecedented 35-hour week; an end to night-shift work; a cessation of the deadly practice of firing explosives while men were working; and the introduction of a company-funded scheme of medical inspection and workers' compensation. But there was little time to celebrate. The world metal price slump of 1921 saw the workers laid off in droves and the O'Neils thrown back once again on union sustenance payments.

Nevertheless, the recession sparked the beginning of one of the most remarkable developments in Australian – and international – unionism. In 1924, the mining unions joined with others in the town to form a new and instantly powerful body, the Barrier Industrial Council (BIC). Disregarding the national arbitration system, the BIC dealt directly with the mine owners and, backed by compulsory union membership, came to exercise almost dictatorial powers over the running of Broken Hill.

Under the presidency of Paddy O'Neill and then Shorty, it silenced public dissent by taking over *The Barrier Miner* and then established a regime that some called a worker's paradise and others a reactionary dictatorship. It not only set wages and conditions but also prohibited married women from taking paid employment, regulated shopping hours, banned door-to-door canvassing by visiting salesmen to protect local jobs and declared Broken Hill 'dry' on Sundays so men would be sober for the lunchtime family roast.

Successive New South Wales premiers adopted a 'hands off' policy, and Shorty ruled as the unpaid president of the BIC until 1965, when he finally abdicated. In all his years at the head of the council, he suffered only one major defeat. And it could hardly have been more delightfully symbolic of the Australian outback. In 1960, he tried to ban the import of meat pies from Adelaide to protect the (inferior) local product. Broken Hill rebelled, and Shorty bowed to the inevitable. He knew his limits: you don't mess with an Australian's taste in pies.[10]

In his eighties, he had the undoubted pleasure of seeing his son Bill take over the presidency, but by then the industrial-relations movement had moved on; the closed shop and centralised wage-fixing were giving way to enterprise bargaining, and union membership was on a downward spiral.

At BHP, the transformation was even greater. And the man most responsible had, like Shorty O'Neil, begun his working life with the company on the line of lode. Indeed, both men gave their lives in different ways to BHP. They shared one characteristic – an authoritarian streak that brooked no dissent – but otherwise they occupied different polarities. Shorty O'Neil fought the ancient battles of injustice in the division of a nation's wealth; but first the wealth had to be created through industry and enterprise, and at BHP that role fell to Essington Lewis.

CHAPTER 4

Man of Steel

There was something in the Lewis DNA that compelled its men to push themselves and their endeavours to the limit. And, over three generations, BHP played an ever-increasing part in those endeavours.

Essington's grandfather, James Lewis, was a Welshman who arrived in South Australia on the brigantine *Rapid* in 1836 and eight years later joined Charles Sturt's quixotic expedition in quest of the inland sea. Some members of Sturt's party climbed the broken-backed hill to spy out the land ahead. While there, they collected mineral specimens to be sent back to Adelaide, where, amazingly, they were ignored, lost or both. Whether James Lewis was among them is not known, but on his return from Sturt's tragic ordeal in the wilderness he took up farming and worked from dawn to dusk to clear the land and grow a crop to feed his family.

His eldest son, John, strong and wilful, struck out on his own at 14. He headed first to Victoria and then north and west, working on cattle stations and in mining camps as he made his way through the red heart of the country and into the Northern Territory. In the 1870s, he reached Vashon Head, which forms an arm of Port Essington, north of Darwin, having crossed the continent by stages from Melbourne – a feat that had ended in disaster for Burke and Wills a decade earlier. It remained a source of great pride throughout his life, and the naming of his third son would serve as a living reminder.

John Lewis pioneered the rough cattle country in the far north and gained a reputation for the kind of endurance and enterprise that the country demanded. He retained his pastoral interests when he returned south and settled at Burra, only 150 kilometres north of Adelaide. Copper had been discovered in the area in 1845 in two lodes, one of which returned massive fortunes to its owners – a group of Adelaide merchants known colloquially as The Snobs. A population of 5000 crowded into the area and stripped the trees from the surroundings to support the mining stopes. By the time the lode was exhausted, the whole area had been cleared for farming, and when John Lewis established a stock and station business in 1876 with local partners Liston and Shakes the community was thriving.

The same year, he married Martha Brook, the daughter of a respected Burra family, and soon fathered three sons. The eldest, James, was named for his grandfather and would become a doctor; the second, Gilbert, would be a soldier. Essington made his appearance on 13 January 1881 at Burra district hospital.

Like his father, he exhibited a wilful independence early in life, and their relationship would be never less than turbulent. Young Essington was sent to St Peter's School in Adelaide, but at 13, shortly after his mother died, his father withdrew him and sent him for nine months to work on his cattle property, Dalhousie Springs, almost at the territory border. The youngster thrived in the outback, and his schooling would be interrupted several times by sojourns to the Springs. In Essington's sixteenth year, an eccentric bush character, James J. Murif, provided the first public glimpse of the personality that would come to play an extraordinary part in his nation's history.

In 1897, Murif set himself the task of riding his bicycle from Adelaide to Darwin dressed only in his pyjamas. In a concession to safety, he secured the flapping pants with bicycle clips and headed north. Some weeks later, he found himself beetling along the track between Dalhousie and Oodnadatta when a stationary horse team and dray hove into view. As he came closer, he saw that they had stopped for dinner. A fire was heating three quart pots for tea and a slim youth had arranged a rough tablecloth on the ground nearby. On it were a newly baked damper, corned beef, jam, a knife and fork and a pannikin. Two Aboriginal people sat in the shade of a nearby tree staring wide-eyed at the newcomer and his mode of transportation. Murif dismounted.

Recalling the event in his memoir, Murif says he and Essington swapped 'g'days' and the young man invited the traveller to share the tucker. Murif asked, 'Where's the boss?'

The youth smiled and replied, 'I am the boss.'[1] Essington reached out an arm towards a small linen tea bag, then stood up to throw a handful into each pot. Cutting off a few slices from the damper and sorting out the blacks' favourite pieces of meat, he gave a short, low whistle and up came the Aboriginal people. To these, he handed each his share of tucker, which they received in silence. 'You wantem more, you sing out,' he added as, taking with them two of the quart pots, they returned to their tree.

'I admired this manly child's way exceedingly,' Murif wrote. 'In "bossing" them, he spoke very civilly . . . in a quiet, cool, masterful manner. He offered to load me up with bread and meat but as I had resolved to break myself in to going on short commons, I would accept nothing more than a couple of apples. "It's rough to Blood's Creek. I don't think you'll get there tonight," were Essington's parting words. And he was right.'

Essington finally graduated from St Peter's in 1900 aged 19 and with a reputation as a fine sportsman. He wanted to study law but his father had other ideas. 'As you haven't got the brain and I'm damned if I'll give you the money, you'd better think again,' he said.[2]

His second choice – mining engineer – met paternal acceptance and he enrolled at the South Australian School of Mines and Industries. Part of the course involved practical work in a mine, and he chose BHP.

In the days following the federation of the Commonwealth of Australia on 1 January 1901, Essington Lewis reported for duty. He began quite literally at the bottom. Deep in the line of lode, the jut-jawed 19-year-old swung his pick with the hard men of Broken Hill. It was an invaluable experience, but he wouldn't be there for long.

While Essington Lewis fed the maw of BHP's never-ending appetite for ore and profits underground, his father made his own contribution in the genteel corridors of Adelaide's power elite, the South Australian Parliament. By now a formidable member of the Legislative Council, John Lewis not only chaired the select committee investigating BHP's acquisition of Iron Knob and Iron Monarch – and gave it the green light – but also sponsored a private member's Bill to build a railway from the deposits to Hummock Hill. The Bill passed and Lewis became a substantial BHP shareholder at precisely that time.[3]

By then, the interaction between politicians and The Proprietary already had a history. In 1888, BHP had engaged a lobbyist, T. F. DeCourcy Browne, to secure state-government funding of a dam on Stephens Creek. As negotiations dragged on, he targeted a former minister for mines, Joe Abbott, to press the case and met with him in the New South Wales Parliament's smoking room. Abbott didn't beat about the bush. According to the lobbyist, 'He wanted to know how many paid-up shares he was to get. I explained that . . . the few there were [would] not be distributed until the Bill passed into law.'[4]

BHP's general manager, John Howell, applied public pressure with a warning that unless the Bill were passed, the mine might have to cease production in six weeks. In fact, it would not become law for almost two years, passing through all stages on 11 November 1890. Its sponsor was none other than the new Speaker, Joe Abbott. The following day, the parliament erupted with cries of scandal from the member for West Macquarie,

William Crick. Bursting into the house, he confronted the Speaker: 'You got £2000 for putting the Broken Hill Water Supply Bill through . . . and the chairman of committees got £1000 . . . you are both a pair of thieves and robbers!'

Crick later withdrew his accusations and was welcomed back into the parliamentary fold. He was appointed postmaster-general in 1899 and served as secretary of lands from 1901 to 1904. Joe Abbott was knighted in 1892 and, still Speaker, took part in the framing of the Commonwealth constitution.

At the same time, BHP director William Knox had secured election to the Victorian Legislative Council in 1898, where he championed the cause of free enterprise as the member for South-Eastern Province. After Federation, he was elected to the House of Representatives where, on his motion, it was decided that each day's sitting would begin with prayers – a practice that continues to this day. Knox was the first member for the seat of Kooyong, whose most famous occupant, Robert Menzies, also had strong connections with the company.

Menzies' father, James, is invariably portrayed as a mere country storekeeper from Jeparit in northern Victoria. In his memoir *Afternoon Light*, the long-serving prime minister provides only the briefest mention of his father's subsequent career in Melbourne following James Menzies' election to state parliament in 1911 as the member for Lowan (which incorporated Jeparit). His son wrote, 'The nerves took charge when he made his maiden speech. After a few sentences, he paused, and collapsed. He made a good recovery, but it was an inauspicious beginning. He did not become a minister.'[5]

Nonetheless, he was re-elected twice, and though he lost his seat in 1920 he was sufficiently well regarded to attract the attention of BHP and worked as a consultant for them after he left the parliament. Then, in 1926, he joined the company full-time as 'statistical officer and tariff adviser' – BHP jargon for political lobbyist. In this role, he was part of the team seeking special protection of government against cheaper steel imports. According to a Tariff Board report of the time, without such protection 'the whole undertaking at Newcastle would not be a commercial proposition'.

The Bruce/Page government granted a tariff increase and in 1931 James Menzies spent much of his time in Canberra, where he enlisted Labor Party members to support further protection to 'save jobs'. According to historian Geoffrey Blainey, 'Some of the Labor Ministers unquestioningly accepted his advice and the speeches he helped them to compose.'[6]

As the younger Menzies rose to power and influence in conservative politics, becoming deputy premier of Victoria in 1932, the association between the family and the company became very close. Robert Menzies transferred to the House of Representatives in 1934 and was immediately appointed attorney-general and – happily for BHP – minister for industry. James Menzies was an active member behind the scenes in the Australian Industries Protection League from 1935 and remained a lobbyist for BHP until his death in 1945. The obvious conflict of ministerial interest has never been previously revealed.

Essington Lewis, who would become the enduring link between BHP and the Menzies family, rose steadily and inexorably through the ranks. From Broken Hill miner, he transferred in 1905 to the smelters at Port Pirie, and by 1909 he had charge of the wharf and stables there in addition to his duties as a shift superintendent.

The following year, he married Gladys Cowan, the daughter of a wealthy mining entrepreneur, but after the birth of their first child in 1911 she developed tuberculosis and lived in Adelaide. He would join her there two years later when Delprat, who sponsored his rise through the ranks, gave him key roles in preparing for the company's transformation from miner to steelmaker.

Lewis expanded the output of ironstone from Iron Knob and opened a limestone quarry at Melrose, Tasmania. When the Newcastle steelworks opened in 1915, he spent much of his time there learning all there was to know about steelmaking and copying endless details into the notebooks he habitually carried in his coat pocket.

But while Lewis worked closely with Delprat – and would become assistant general manager under him in 1919 – he was already forging a close relationship with the youngest director on the board, Harold Gordon Darling, son of the man with whom Delprat had worked so closely until the elder Darling's death in 1914. Remarkably, this new partnership would become even more significant to Australia's industrial development than the earlier alliance. Lewis and Darling – the tireless engineer and the patrician director – complemented each other perfectly as they worked together to construct a massive steel business and lay the foundation for secondary industry throughout the young nation.

Their friendship was cemented during a world trip in 1920 after the board had decided on a big expansion program at the Newcastle steelworks. Delprat had favoured the introduction of an American system known as Duplex, in which the pig iron was melted and cleansed of some of its impurities before being refined in open-hearth furnaces without the usual addition of scrap steel. It was expensive but had proven effective during the war in the great American steelworks. The board endorsed Delprat's recommendation.

However, when Lewis and Darling reached the US, Lewis quickly realised that the high cost of the process would be disastrous for Australia's relatively small industry. From Ohio, he cabled Delprat setting out the issue in great detail and strongly recommending that the decision be suspended at least until his return. Delprat, by then 64 and increasingly unbending in his opinions, refused to accept Lewis's view.

By nature a loyalist, Lewis was reluctant to oppose his mentor and patron. But when forced to choose between the man and the company, Lewis himself was unbending. Darling concurred and on 13 July he cabled the board:

> Referring to telegrams exchanged between E. Lewis and G. D. Delprat. Trust Board of Directors will reconsider whole

> question of Duplex. From information received consider first cost prohibitory. Adoption likely to prove fatal to Broken Hill Pty Co. Advise strongly against incurring any expense.

In Melbourne, Delprat – backed by David Baker – mounted a rearguard action with the board and they responded that installation of the new system would proceed as planned. Lewis was incensed. When he and Darling reached Britain, steel executives there confirmed his view that Delprat's bullheadedness was endangering the very existence of the company. He sent a series of urgent telegrams, endorsed by Darling, warning of a potential disaster unfolding. Finally, the board listened and suspended all further work until the travellers' return.

On the journey home, Lewis composed a report that not only damned the Duplex decision but also Delprat's choice of new coke ovens for the plant. Darling had it copied and circulated to all directors.

For some years, though not a director, Delprat had habitually attended board meetings. It was a mark of the esteem in which he was held, but it also reflected the ethos of the company, which relied heavily on the expertise of its top management. On this occasion, however, he was pointedly not invited, and with Darling leading the debate the board resolved to abandon the Duplex process. They would also have reversed the coke ovens decision but installation was too far advanced.

It was a humiliating blow for Delprat, who had given so much of his life to BHP, transforming it from the rough-and-ready miner to Australia's leading company in metallurgy, mineral exploration and now steelmaking. He offered his immediate resignation to the chairman, Bowes Kelly.

His next meeting with Lewis must have been excruciating for both men, since each held the other in high regard and affection. But both understood that the interests of the company came first. Delprat addressed the board and recommended Lewis as his successor, and on 18 February 1921 they made the announcement: Lewis would take over immediately as general manager on a salary of £4000, while Delprat would continue as 'consulting engineer' at his old salary of £5500 for the next 18 months. It was a wise gesture. Until his death at 80 in 1937, the remarkable Dutch expatriate would continue to speak publicly in support of his protégé, and of BHP.

Lewis confronted an immediate crisis. British steelmakers were claiming British Preference under the trade agreement between the two countries for their exports to Australia, even though they were merely processing cheap steel bars from Germany. The Americans had the advantage of economies of scale; and both benefited from sharply reduced shipping costs. At the same time, the Australian economy was slowing. BHP was fast losing money and market share.

Lewis attacked on three fronts. He began a regular round of visits to every element of his far-flung organisation seeking cost-cutting efficiencies. He had a particular affinity for the men and yarned easily with them while keeping his association with his white-collar executives strictly formal. He filled his bulging notebooks with facts and figures that would lead to new and better work practices.

He also confronted the unions demanding a deal that would staunch the flow of red ink. And to drive home his point, he closed the steelworks and threw 5000 workers on to the breadline. The lockout would last for nine months, and while he secured some reductions in the award, the benefit to the company's bottom line was in no way commensurate with the terrible pain and hardship caused to the working men and their families.

Thirdly, he opened talks with political parties and right-wing movements such as the Save Australia League, which wanted to destroy the Australian arbitration system. Indeed, BHP became one of the League's main financial supporters. And while Essington Lewis's venture into the political realm was not new to BHP, he expanded the process of government lobbying substantially. Subsequent top BHP executives would follow his lead. In the years ahead, their efforts would pay huge dividends to company shareholders.

It was Lewis himself who engaged James Menzies as in-house lobbyist in 1926, shortly after he was promoted to managing director. They would establish such a close relationship that on his death Lewis would write to Menzies' widow, 'Your husband was the finest and grandest man I have known.'[7]

Meanwhile, Lewis's efficiency, drive and his willingness to acquire new businesses that used BHP steel saw a massive expansion of company activity – and profits – in the late 1920s. So when the Depression struck in 1930, BHP was well placed to turn the crisis to its advantage. Indeed, Lewis would call the Depression a 'fiery furnace' that would 'purify' the economy from the 'false values' that had applied since the Great War. In words that would find an echo 60 years later when Paul Keating welcomed 'the recession we had to have', Lewis declared in the company's annual report, 'This period of adversity, although very unwelcome and unpleasant, is necessary to put us on a proper economic basis.'

With Harold Darling, who had risen quickly to the chairmanship, he planned a series of takeovers. Collieries, wire-makers, engineering companies and fabricators such as Lysaght Brothers all fell into the BHP cauldron. The only other steelmaker in the country, the Hoskins family's Australian Iron & Steel Limited at Lithgow and Port Kembla, gave up the fight and 'merged' with BHP in 1935.

The merger sparked cries of 'monopoly' from some politicians – notably Jack Beasley, who sat in federal parliament as the member for West Sydney alongside the former New South Wales premier Jack Lang. Together, they were known as Lang Labor and voted independently of the party then led by John Curtin. In parliament, Beasley accused BHP – with some justification – of creating 'a steel trust embracing the whole of the Commonwealth' and called for the company to be nationalised.

Beasley trumpeted the names of its major Australian

shareholders, which included the Fairfax and Syme families, and claimed that this compromised their treatment of BHP in the pages of *The Sydney Morning Herald* and *The Age*, respectively. However, the share register did not reveal the kind of political involvement he clearly craved.[8] The Menzies family, for example, was not represented, though Robert Menzies – now attorney-general and industry minister in Joseph Lyons' United Australia Party/Country Party coalition government – heaped his special brand of withering scorn upon the member for West Sydney in the debate. The motion for nationalisation was easily defeated.

At the time, Lewis had returned from one of his regular international fact-finding missions to stay abreast of industry and political developments. In Japan, he had been shocked to discover a nation in ferment. He wrote immediately to Darling: 'Japan may be described as a big gun-powder magazine and the people as fanatics; and any day the two might connect and there will be an explosion.'[9] Indeed, from his subsequent actions it is clear that Lewis, well ahead of his contemporaries, saw Japan as a rising military threat to Australia.

As soon as he left the country, he sketched out plans to fight back against possible invasion. BHP should immediately retool for the manufacture of munitions; and it should begin to build up massive stocks of raw materials. It should plan to build warships – minelayers, torpedo boats and small destroyers – at Newcastle and Whyalla, and make a start on an aircraft industry. '[The Japanese] are armed to the teeth,' he said, 'and I was informed that in emergency they could build 100 [fighter planes] a day.'[10]

In a meeting with Darling and W. S. Robinson, the early pioneer of Broken Hill mining companies now heading an international mining conglomerate, he secured agreement for a syndicate that would soon become the Commonwealth Aircraft Corporation. Its plant at Victoria's Fishermen's Bend would in time produce the Australian-designed Wirraway aircraft.

But when he took his concerns to the political arena, he was initially regarded as an alarmist. Whatever Japan's intentions, he was told, Australia was safe behind the impregnable fortress of Singapore. So he visited Singapore in 1937. He was not convinced: for one thing, Singapore had no battle fleet of its own. Behind the scenes, he continued to urge preparations for war.

Nevertheless, he authorised the sale of BHP iron ore and pig iron (the raw product of Newcastle's blast furnaces) to both Germany and Japan, reasoning that he was funding an Australian steel industry that provided the bulwark against military aggression. It was a self-serving argument, and it became untenable in 1938 when the Japanese secured the West Australian Government's approval to ship one million tons of iron ore a year from Yampi Sound in the north of the state to fuel Japan's furnaces.[11] Protests erupted and the federal government quickly responded. Prime Minister Lyons himself met with Lewis to warn him that his government was about to ban all iron-ore exports. They would give a 'diplomatic' reason – that Australia had barely enough for its own needs. Lewis accepted the decision without public demur. In return, Lyons agreed that BHP would continue to export pig iron to Japan from the Newcastle plant. The result was a political time-bomb.

The Port Kembla wharfies lit the fuse when they refused to load the freighter *Dalfram* with a shipment of pig iron in November 1938 on grounds that it would be used in the undeclared Japanese war against China. And when Menzies as attorney-general stepped in with the so-called 'dog-collar act' that allowed strike-breakers on the wharves, it exploded in wild controversy across the nation. By January 1939, 7000 wharfies and BHP workers were either on strike or locked out.

To his credit, Menzies confronted a mass demonstration at Port Kembla and put his case to union officials face to face. In the event, the unionists gave ground and loaded the ship. But Menzies' reputation would be forever tarnished with the soubriquet 'Pig Iron Bob'.

Coincidentally, as the BHP employees returned to work on 28 January, their colleagues at Broken Hill left the Big Mine for the last time. When they finally downed tools on that last shift, the company had extracted 12.3 million tons of ore, produced £54 million worth of metals and paid £14.8 million in wages. In the 56 years since Charles Rasp had pegged his claim on the ancient line of lode, BHP had become the largest corporation in the nation.

Meanwhile, the political scene was becoming increasingly chaotic, as Menzies broke with Lyons over a proposed national medical-insurance scheme and resigned from the ministry. Then, in April, the prime minister suffered a sudden, fatal heart attack. The Country Party leader, Earle Page, became caretaker prime minister until the senior partner in the coalition chose its new leader. But when Menzies was elected on 26 April, Page, a highly strung individual from a family with a distinguished military background, accused him of cowardice in not volunteering for service in the First World War and refused to serve under him. It was an outrageous charge, and Menzies was deeply offended. However, he did not allow it to divert him from the main game and accepted Governor-General Sir Isaac Isaacs' commission to head a minority government. He re-formed the coalition later that year when Page was replaced.

Back in 1938, as industry minister, Menzies had selected Essington Lewis to be chairman of the Commonwealth's advisory panel on industrial organisation. Now, one of his first acts as head of the new coalition government was to appoint him 'business consultant to the Department of Defence'. His task was to advise on the development of the industrial arrangements needed to fight a defensive war.

Lewis was happy to serve but frustrated by the indecisiveness within the upper echelons of government. When the 'Phoney War' finally ended in May 1940 with the German invasion of the Low Countries, Menzies at last grasped the nettle. On 21 May, Lewis flew secretly to Canberra in response to his summons. After brief amenities, Menzies said, 'Will you come and help the country by becoming director-general of munitions with a charter as wide as the seas and as high as the sky?'

Lewis: 'Yes, I will.'

Menzies: 'Can you gather about you all the best men in the industrial world in Australia?'

Lewis: 'Yes, I can. If I am to have a clear and wide authority, then I can get other men to share it.'[12]

The appointment was made public by Menzies the following day. Lewis's charter was indeed as far-reaching as the prime minister had promised. He controlled the production of all ordnance, explosives, ammunition, small arms, aircraft and vehicles, and all machinery and tools used in their production. He could acquire any building, issue contracts without calling tenders, delegate and revoke responsibilities at will, and spend up to £250,000 on any project without political approval. He would sit on the National Defence Committee and have the same access to the War Cabinet as the military chiefs of staff. And, though it was not mentioned formally, he would have unimpeded access to the prime minister.

Lewis, who abhorred publicity of all kinds, was not on hand to hear the announcement. He had returned to work in Melbourne. By now, he was 59 and had built a large home in Toorak, where he and Gladys – cured of her tuberculosis – raised their five children. He had also acquired a 3500-acre property, 'Landscape', in Tallarook, two hours' drive north of the Victorian capital. But for the next four years – aside from Wednesday-afternoon tennis in his Toorak grounds – he would have little time to spend in either of his personal redoubts. He established headquarters at Western House in Melbourne's CBD but spent most of his waking hours travelling to inspect munitions facilities or meeting with his board of fellow industrialists.

By common consent, he did a remarkable job. At its height, Lewis's directorate employed 150,000 men and women. They built ships, aircraft, landing craft and artillery. They established 213 armament factories and produced millions of rounds of ammunition. They channelled more than £300 million into armament production without a single accusation of corruption or double-dealing.

However, by retaining his role as chief general manager of BHP, declining a government salary and employing BHP personnel as his principal assistants, Lewis attracted powerful critics. Chief among them in the early months was Labor's H. V. 'Doc' Evatt, a former High Court judge, who accused him of a 'conflict of duty', thereby earning Lewis's implacable and undying hatred. Labor leader John Curtin and his deputy Frank Forde also spoke in favour of nationalising BHP. But when the Menzies government fell in 1941 and Labor took the Treasury benches, their attitude changed almost overnight. One reason was the return to parliament of Ben Chifley, who had lost his seat in 1935 and had been a key figure in Lewis's directorate of munitions as director of labour. He was unstinting in his praise of the BHP chief.

Indeed, by mid-1942 Prime Minister Curtin was so impressed with Lewis's work that he offered him a knighthood, despite the fact that such imperial honours were against Labor policy. Lewis declined, but when Curtin persisted he accepted the Order of Companion of Honour, an award usually reserved for Dominion prime ministers.

By then, with Japan threatening Australia's borders, unionists and industrialists had put aside their grievances and a new spirit of common purpose was sweeping the nation. Unfortunately, it didn't last beyond the immediate crisis and, embarrassingly for Lewis, one of the most troubled areas was the BHP Newcastle plant. In December 1943, a demarcation dispute between workers and executives over who would run various elements of the process led to a company lockout and at Port Kembla there was a series of stoppages until Curtin himself stepped in and oversaw a conciliation agreement.

By mid-1944, most of Lewis's war work was done. He had greatly expanded BHP's coastal shipping fleet hauling ore to Newcastle and Port Kembla to feed the engine of war, and used

BHP engineers to develop the nascent aircraft industry. His systems were running smoothly and the American industrial powerhouse was supplying materiel in an endless stream. He was able to turn more of his attention to BHP. Shortages of raw materials had cut into the company's profits during the war, but at the same time it enjoyed a massive expansion, particularly of steelmaking in New South Wales. Now, he undertook a world tour to discover the great technological advances made in steelmaking and secondary manufacturing of a range of steel-based products under wartime pressures. His notebooks bulged.

In May 1945, at 64, Lewis officially relinquished his government post and Curtin, in his final illness, wrote of his extraordinary efforts in Australia's time of peril, 'at the expense of your own personal convenience and whatever leisure you might have expected to enjoy'.[13] In truth, leisure was never a priority for Lewis, and he returned to the BHP headquarters in Collins Street, Melbourne, the day after his release.

While he had retained overall control of the company during the war, he had stepped aside from the boardroom, where Harold Darling and deputy chairman Colin Syme had taken up the slack. Now, he resumed his role as managing director, hopeful that with its increased capacity BHP would roar ahead. It was not to be. The Chifley government moved slowly to lift wartime restrictions and red tape; manpower shortages encouraged industrial unrest inflamed by communist union leaders; striking coal miners cut supplies of an essential component; and a resurgent Japanese steel industry cut into overseas markets.

Remarkably, in view of later developments, BHP suffered the misapprehension that Australia had very limited iron-ore reserves. Indeed, Lewis negotiated options over deposits in New Caledonia before investigating the distant Yampi Sound, where he took control of the leases in a deal with the West Australian Government.

In 1949, Lewis's longtime friend and ally Harold Darling began to suffer the debilitating effects of cancer. Gradually,

Lewis took over his duties, and when Darling died on Australia Day, 1950, Lewis was formally elected chairman of the BHP board. His elevation coincided with the installation of a new government in Canberra, elected in the previous December. At the head of the coalition, and leading the Liberal Party of his own creation, was Robert Gordon Menzies, in power in Australia for the second time. Lewis cannot have been displeased with the result. In 1944, when Menzies was laying the foundation for his new party, Harold Darling worked closely with him to develop its industrial platform. And while this has remained beneath the public radar until now, the association between the company and the new prime minister was sufficiently well known for the university students of the 1950s to raise their voices in tuneful satire: 'There'll always be a Menzies/while there's a BHP.'

CHAPTER 5

Supermac

Essington Lewis remained chairman for only two years and at 71 stepped aside for the astute and genial Colin Syme, whom he had recruited from Goldsbrough Mort in 1937 after they met on a trout-fishing trip in Victoria's Howqua Valley. Born in Western Australia in 1903 of Scottish and Northern Irish ancestry, Syme trained as a lawyer but found his true métier around the boardroom table, where he clouded the air with his ever-present pipe. He made a half-hearted attempt to understand the steelmaking processes but confessed he found it 'baffling'. His great strengths were in conciliating and coordinating the competing demands of the personalities within the organisation.

Lewis stayed on as deputy chairman, assisting Syme and the new managing director, Norman Jones, who had risen through the BHP ranks establishing a solid reputation along the way. He had joined the company in Newcastle at 17 and, encouraged by BHP management, qualified as a chemist after five years of night study while working as a labourer on the furnace floor. In 1938, he went to Melbourne as technical assistant to the general manager and impressed Essington Lewis as a solid performer.

However, the company's rising star was undoubtedly Ian McLennan, who for the next two decades would take over from Lewis as the guiding hand in the company's expansion. More than any other, he would be responsible for the development of the soubriquet that would prove more valuable than even he could have imagined: The Big Australian. For decades, it would be used to prise special deals from federal and state governments, and, despite the total transformation of the entity to BHP Billiton, it is still employed by the company's special pleaders today.

This was not Ian McLennan's intention, though he may well have approved. Born in Stawell and raised in Mooroopna in the Goulburn Valley of northern Victoria on 30 November 1909, he attended local schools before boarding at Scotch College, where his intelligence and natural athleticism won him high honours. He completed an engineering degree at Melbourne University and joined BHP in 1933 through the system of trainee cadetships – initiated by Delprat but formalised by Lewis – that sought out bright young prospects and developed and guided them through the company hierarchy to the limits of their ability.

In many ways, the system mirrored the Commonwealth Public Service, and much of the formality of the bureaucracy was retained. Executives always used titles when referring to each other and, in a long series of confidential interviews dated 1978–79 obtained by the authors and never previously revealed, Chairman McLennan said of his former colleagues, 'I still call them Mister, you know. I could never call them Frank Hockey [superintendent of mines and quarries] or Len Grant [Newcastle steelworks manager]. They were always Mister to me.'[1]

He spent his first two years at Whyalla and the nearby Iron Knob mine. '[This] oriented me towards raw materials, which had a great fascination for me all the time I worked with BHP,' he said. 'It is the heart and soul of BHP.'[2]

After a further year at other company mines in Western Australia and Tasmania, McLennan was posted to head office in Melbourne as assistant to Frank Hockey. He was already on a fast track to high office when he met and married a BHP secretary, Dora Robertson, in 1937. They would have four children, though McLennan, like Lewis and other top BHP executives, would spend an inordinate amount of time away from home. Family life suffered.

His first major executive posting was to Newcastle steelworks in 1940, but when Lewis became director-general of munitions, gaps were created in the organisational structure that assisted McLennan's rapid rise. By 1944, though nominally assistant manager of the steelworks, he had taken Lewis's place accompanying chairman Harold Darling in his travels around the country to inspect BHP plants.

After the war, like top company men before him, he made one of many world trips to stay abreast of steel technology and on his return pressed hard and successfully for the expansion of the Port Kembla plant to include a hot-strip mill and tinplate facility. Narrow-gauge steel strip coated with tin was essential for a huge range of white goods and other products, and McLennan convinced Lewis it was the way of the future. When Lewis secured board agreement, he called McLennan into his Collins Street office. 'Well, what do you think we should do about it, Mac?' Lewis said.

'Well, I think either Norman Jones or I had better go up there and spend a bit of time,' he replied.

'That's exactly what I think, and it had better be you.'[3]

There was a second string to the bow. McLennan also took over as general manager of BHP's recently acquired Australian Iron & Steel, partially located at Port Kembla. 'I still had my job as assistant general manager in Melbourne,' he said, 'but I was general manager of Port Kembla as well, and the intention was that I might do that for a couple of years.

'But in January 1950, Mr Harold Darling died, so that upset the applecart. Mr Essington Lewis became chairman of the company, Norman Jones became managing director and I became general manager of the whole company. This meant I couldn't spend the amount of time I had been spending at Port Kembla.'

However, during his period in Wollongong he forged yet another link between BHP and the government when nominated by Prime Minister Chifley to the Immigration Planning Council. The massive immigration scheme initiated at the time would help to solve the major impediment to the company's – and the nation's – growth. The first year's immigration target was 200,000. By the end of 1950, 'New Australians' made up 30 per cent of the BHP workforce. Perhaps unsurprisingly, the new Menzies government established three big migrant hostels around Port Kembla to accommodate them. The New South Wales state government followed up with large numbers of housing-commission homes. McLennan would remain the guiding light of the council for the next 17 years.

As the cold war deepened and the government judged international communism a major threat to national security, McLennan crossed another barrier between industry and government. In late 1950, he joined the National Security Resources Board, chaired by Prime Minister Menzies himself. The board had access to top-secret intelligence from home and abroad, and its deliberations were themselves highly secret. Once crossed, the barrier would never be fully re-established, and in the years ahead BHP operatives would boast of their access to intelligence sources within government. The benefits to their international negotiations would be incalculable.

The 1950s was a decade of uninterrupted growth, and in 1955 Prime Minister Menzies officially opened the hot-strip mill, declaring it 'a great historic event' that 'makes possible the success of hundreds of additional industries further down the line'. It was no exaggeration. The new plant increased steel-processing capacity by nearly a million tonnes a year and eventually provided product to roofing, white-goods and automotive industries throughout the country.

Moreover, in 1958 Menzies was joined at the apex of the Liberal/Country Party coalition by John McEwen, leader of the junior partner but minister for the highly influential combined Departments of Trade and Industry.[4] McEwen came from Chiltern, a neighbouring town to McLennan's home town of Mooroopna, and represented the area from 1934 until his retirement in 1971. A lean, autocratic figure who privately suffered an agonising dermatitis all his adult life, McEwen not only continued Menzies' close association with BHP, but as deputy prime minister he became the champion of protection for secondary industry.

As BHP expanded its steel output each year, McLennan became increasingly aware of the need to secure new sources of raw materials, particularly iron ore. 'I had a major amount to do with getting the exploration program going,' McLennan said. 'We could see Iron Monarch and [nearby] Iron Baron being worked out. So I put a lot of personal effort into trying to find new deposits.'[5]

The company recruited no fewer than 58 geologists and set them searching across the continent for the most economic ore bodies. After a false start in Queensland's Constance Range, they turned their attention to the Pilbara in Western Australia. 'For some strange reason, we in BHP didn't know as much about the Pilbara deposits as we should have,' McLennan said. 'They were known back in the 1880s. It's a bit of an indictment for most of us and particularly our geologists that they hadn't read up about these. We had one geologist who walked right past Mt Newman. Walked past it! So that was bad management and bad luck.'[6]

There was also a measure of selective memory in McLennan's recollections. According to a McLennan protégé, Stan Salamy, BHP's geological prospectors were ordered to confine their explorations to the coast as transport costs were thought to make inland iron-ore mining uneconomic. 'They didn't want to know about the inland,' he says.[7]

However, their luck would soon change in a big way. In 1957, an old prospector, Stan Hilditch, who had been grubstaked by a Kalgoorlie pump-maker, Charles Warman, discovered a massive iron-ore eminence in the eastern Pilbara about five kilometres from Mt Newman – and about 400 kilometres from the coast – which he named Mt Whaleback. He had been roaming the north for about six years in an old Thames truck with his wife Ella on a budget of $32 a week. And when he told Warman of his discovery, his partner was unimpressed.

'Look, Stan,' he said, 'iron ore is a cheap commodity. It's too far from the coast. I suggest you forget it.'[8]

At the time, Joe Lyons' 1938 decision to ban all iron exports remained in force, so the discovery was of little value. But in 1960, John McEwen took a submission to Cabinet – backed by BHP – arguing for the ban to be lifted to encourage exploration. Menzies agreed and, unbeknown to anyone in the industry (including BHP), Hilditch and Warman pegged their leases.

According to McLennan, shortly afterwards two executives from the giant American miner AMAX were heading back to the US when their plane was delayed in Sydney. While they were waiting, 'someone mentioned that there was a fellow called Warman [nearby] who reckons that he's got an iron-ore deposit. Would you like to meet him?'[9]

The Americans jumped at the chance and, after doing a deal that would turn Warman and Hilditch into multimillionaires, sought out an Australian company for a joint venture. They chose CSR, the big sugar and building-products company, then run by Sir James Vernon. According to McLennan, 'Jim Vernon knew a good thing when he saw one. He latched on to this. But then between them they couldn't do it, so Vernon came and saw us. I thought, "Oh gosh, here's the opportunity."'

What followed were 'tremendous negotiations', from which BHP ended up as the mine manager with 30 per cent, CSR with 30 per cent, AMAX 25 per cent, ten per cent to Mitsui C. Itoh and five per cent to Selection Trust of London.

The Americans then offloaded ten per cent to Mitsui C. Itoh and five per cent to Selection Trust in England. They were concerned that the Vietnam War, which was then raging, would cut the supply chain from Australia to its Japanese market by closing the sea lanes. It was a serious misjudgment. 'It's been probably the most successful iron-ore operation in the world,' McLennan said, 25 years before the China boom.[10] Subsequently, BHP acquired 85 per cent of the total shareholding and today exports 100 million tonnes annually from seven mine sites including Mt Whaleback, which is the biggest single-pit open-cut ore mine in the world.

On 18 April 2008, as the early Qantas flight carrying one of the authors touched down at Newman's long runway, the pilot slammed on the brakes and the passengers were thrown forward in their seats. As the aircraft taxied towards the neat airport terminal, the pilot came on the intercom. 'Sorry about that,' he said. 'There were a couple of eagles on the tarmac. To save hitting them, we applied some brakes.'

Welcome to the outback of the twenty-first century.

Mt Whaleback is now a vast crater five kilometres long, 1.5 kilometres wide and 430 metres deep. Six other massive BHP Billiton mines are also located in the East Pilbara, an area almost the size of New South Wales. All are connected by rail to Port Hedland, 400 kilometres from Newman. More than 70 locomotives and 4000 open cars carry the ore to the port, which can load 16,000 tons an hour into a steady procession of bulk carriers for the journey to China, Japan, Europe or Australian foundries.

BHP Billiton has reserves of 300 billion tonnes in the area. The company will still be carving out the ore in 50 years' time. Newman, a neat, nondescript town of 8000, is booming. It is so overcrowded with miners that tourists are waved away. There has been no room at the inn for the last four years. Shire president Lyn Craigie, bluff, blonde and hearty, says, 'We even tell the grey nomads to park out of town.'

It is a company town. 'The government does bugger all,' she says, 'and we're the powerhouse of the nation. BHP even built the airport and sold it to the shire for a dollar.' She loves the place. 'It's a great community, a terrific place to live if you can stand the pace.'

It was not always so. Mick Carroll and Fred Stojich have

worked at the Mt Whaleback mine since the late 1960s. 'Used to be a bloody Wild West town,' Mick says, sipping a drink in the covered verandah of Newman's Seasons hotel. 'None of us had mufflers on our cars,' he grins. 'Bloody rough place.'

Fred nods. He remembers driving one of the first two mechanical shovels loading ore into the trucks. 'No air conditioning in the shovels. So you'd open the front window and red dust would pour in on you. You couldn't see where you were going half the time.'

'The average worker would last about two weeks,' Mick says. 'We were getting 99 cents an hour. We were all at the single men's quarters – better known as the Sperm Bank – and the place was patrolled by security guards. For fun, we'd roar our cars and motorbikes around the town. More blokes got killed or injured driving home from work than at the mine. Made our own entertainment – drinking beer mostly. They put up a sort of open-air theatre.'

That was 1968, and the movies – beginning with *Dr Zhivago* – were projected on a bed sheet on a bare spot of ground between the pre-fab houses. Later, it became a drive-in. 'But you couldn't close your windows to hear the sound because of the heat,' Mick says. 'And when you opened them, the bloody mosquitoes were big as bats!'

As the population rose following the opening of the rail link to Port Hedland in 1969, the company built sporting facilities. In a famous early soccer match between Newman and Watson-Jaxon, the home side was soon plunging towards defeat. The spectators became so aroused at the refereeing decisions that the man in white fled from the field only 30 minutes into the game. According to the local rag, 'One of the spectators took over.' Newman lost anyway.

Soon, there were four Australian Rules teams in the town: the Tigers, Centrals, Pioneers and Saints. 'After the game, we'd all have a barbecue together, have a beer, settle a few scores maybe.' Mick laughed at the memory. 'There was a great community feeling. You didn't have to be invited. Everyone was in it.'

Not quite everyone. According to the official line, 'BHP Billiton Iron Ore has a long and positive history of working with the Indigenous people in the Pilbara.' This is untrue. Until recently, the Aboriginal people of the Pilbara were ignored, and even today an afternoon tour of Newman's dusty outskirts reveals a scatter of them staggering around stashes of booze. However, there are also signs that the company is serious in its 'aggressive targets' designed to achieve 14 per cent Indigenous indirect employment – and 40 apprenticeship positions – by 2012. Don Argus says, 'We have a commitment to the rights of Indigenous people wherever we go.'[11]

There are about 2500 Aboriginal people – including some 30 different language groups – in the East Pilbara, with the biggest group, of around 200, in the 'dry' community of Jigalong, 160 kilometres from Newman. Aboriginal contractors are working as drill-hole cappers – seeking out the hundreds of thousands of test drills (a few centimetres across) in the region, capping them with concrete to prevent animals and humans from injuring themselves and mapping them by the satellite-based Global Positioning System (GPS). The man in charge of the program, Craig Hoyer, says, 'They're doing up to 50 holes a day. It's working well.'

And when Prime Minister Kevin Rudd apologised to the stolen generations in parliament on 13 February 2008, the BHP executive team made the three-hour drive to Jigalong to share the event with the community when it was telecast at 6.30 am. As the sun rose on the vast purple plains of the outback, the Aboriginal community and the executives gathered in silence beneath an open-sided tent as the prime minister spoke to the nation: 'For the pain, suffering and hurt of these stolen generations, their descendants and for their families left behind, we say sorry. To the mothers and the fathers, the brothers and the sisters, for the breaking up of families and communities, we say sorry. And for the indignity and degradation thus inflicted on a proud people and a proud culture, we say sorry.'

Aaron Minchin, the sustainability principal at the mine, said, 'It was quite moving. We kept it pretty low-key. When it was over, we all shook hands and had a cup of tea. It was good.'

Serious social problems remain, and they are not confined to the Indigenous people. From the beginning of the Newman project, distance and isolation have had a profound effect on the miners and their dependants. According to journalist and author John McIlwraith, writing in 1979, 'Young women became so shattered by the isolation that they would walk out of their homes and on to a plane to the south, leaving the children in the house and a note on the kitchen table waiting for their husband's return.'[12]

Gavin Sinclair, a psychologist employed by BHP in the 1970s, criticised the company's 'paternalism', a them-and-us attitude reminiscent of the early days at Broken Hill. 'Many staff do treat the men "like animals",' he wrote, 'and then feel that an occasional freebie will fix things up. Such attitudes are anachronistic.'[13]

The result was a series of wildcat strikes followed by major disputes that shut down the mine for weeks on end. By 1976, one middle-level manager wrote, 'This company has lost only five days' production in the past seven years due to mechanical problems yet over the past 12 months we have had 60 days, at $1 million a day, lost due to strikes – that is, people-problems.'[14] In some years, the company lost a sixth of its production through strikes in the Pilbara.

The paternalism reflected Ian McLennan's attitude to personnel management. Stan Salamy, a short, quietly spoken man who joined the company after completing his PhD in 1955 and was regarded as being under McLennan's personal patronage, found himself the unwilling witness to the chief executive officer's modus operandi during his regular visits to Whyalla at the time. 'He was a difficult character,' he says. 'Whenever he would come to Whyalla, he would invite all the executives to dinner. You had to be suited and all the rest of it. They were held at the Directors' Cottage and the dinner was quite formal too.

'They were so embarrassing. After a while, he would select a topic – shipping, iron ore or steel – and he would hop into the person responsible. On and on he would go with this one poor bloke in the gun. It was very embarrassing.

'I tried one night to change the subject. He rounded on me. "Stan, keep out of this," he said. "It's nothing to do with you." So we just had to sit there . . . on and on he went.'[15]

Jerry Ellis, the future BHP chairman, saw a totally different side of McLennan. 'He was a wonderful man, a bit misunderstood. He was seen as being hugely authoritarian and a bit frightening to junior people,' he says. 'I carried his bag around the world in the mid-'70s and got to know him very well. He taught me a huge amount about self-discipline and how to organise your thoughts and behave in the upper echelons of business.'[16]

One of the reasons for Stan Salamy's favoured status was his scientific background. McLennan developed a powerful research unit within the company and in 1969 opened the Melbourne Research Laboratories, headed by an outstanding British scientist, Dr Bob Ward. By 1984, research-and-development staff within the group numbered more than 600 and new methods were discovered for galvanising iron, continuous coke-making and rolling head-hardened steel rails at Whyalla for the iron-ore railways.

In 1973, Dr Ward happened to see a young Perth inventor, Ralph Sarich, on the ABC program *The Inventors* demonstrating a revolutionary 'orbital' engine. Ward flew to Perth the next day and formed a new company with Sarich to develop the concept with BHP as a major shareholder. The results were outstanding, and today Sarich's fortune is estimated at $800 million.

At 85, Dr Ward is gently disillusioned by the company's approach to research. 'They have reverted to the "dig it up and sell it" approach,' he says. The Newcastle laboratories that housed 200 scientists and technicians when he retired in 1988 were now a shadow of their former strength. The Melbourne Research Laboratories had been sold. 'They went cold on research,' he continues. One result had been that they were 'left behind' in the development of geo-sequestration of CO_2 in coal-fired power plants. 'They could have been ten years ahead if they had started at the right time.'[17] (See Chapter 25.)

But it was BHP's exploration for oil and gas that triggered the big headlines of the McLennan era. When he joined the board in 1955 and became senior general manager, he learned that British interests were considering acquiring oil-exploration titles over a big area of the New South Wales coast – known geologically as the Sydney Basin – including BHP's southern coalfield. He immediately used the company's inside track to government to secure the leases ahead of the opposition. He then formed a new subsidiary, Haematite Exploration Proprietary Limited (named after the rusty red iron ore, hematite, to conceal the company's true quarry),[18] to undertake oil exploration within the exploration division. At the same time, he ordered a review of all geological surveys of the Sydney Basin.

The demand for oil and its derivatives – the 'blood of the earth', in Clemenceau's evocative phrase – had exploded in the 1950s, making crude the most prized natural resource on the planet. Its absence was the Achilles heel of the Australian economy. As the oldest continent, this was perhaps to be expected. Oil tends to be found in younger rocks. Nevertheless, minor finds had been made along the southern coastline since 1869. The first oilfield was established at Lake Bunga, near Lakes Entrance in the Gippsland Basin, in 1924, after Lake Bunga-1 was spudded in to drill for water and encountered small amounts of viscous, heavy crude at a depth of 370 metres. This led to the discovery of the Lakes Entrance oil pool.

The 64 wells drilled there between 1930 and 1941 produced a mere 3063 barrels of oil. During the Second World War, the Lakes Entrance Oil Shaft was excavated by the federal government and produced a further 4935 barrels. After the war, Lakes Oil took over the operation and a 1949 geophysical survey around Lakes Entrance indicated the presence of a number of structures with oil-bearing potential within the company's leases. Dr Nicholas Boutakoff of the Victorian Mines Department strongly suggested that exploration should be undertaken offshore in Bass Strait, where thick tertiary-age sediments included a number of large, relatively simple structures capable of holding oil.[19]

But neither Lakes Oil nor anyone else had happened upon the real treasure trove of black gold in the Lakes Entrance area. For the Gippsland Basin was in fact a major offshore petroleum province containing recoverable reserves of the order of four billion barrels of oil and ten trillion cubic feet of gas.

Elsewhere in Australia, small quantities of oil had been discovered at Roma on the Darling Downs (1927) and Rough Range in Exmouth Gulf (1953), but oil companies such as AMPOL were still importing all of their oil and petroleum products, and draining most of the country's foreign-exchange reserves in the process.[20] And big trouble was looming internationally, which made oil self-sufficiency, if possible, the nation's top priority.

As early as 1953, Shell analysts, operating with the proficiency of a secret-service organisation, forecast that the Anglo-French Suez Canal might be nationalised by Egypt. The Canal was Britain's lifeline to her rapidly vanishing Asian empire – and Australia's highway to Europe for her wool and wheat – but it was also a major tanker route for transporting two-thirds of the oil from the Persian Gulf to Europe's refineries.

Following the military *coup d'état* that deposed King Farouk of Egypt in 1952, Shell's rising star (and later chairman) John Loudon suggested to the French president of the Suez Canal Company that in order to avoid nationalisation of the Canal he turn over its ownership to the Egyptian Government and then lease it back, so that Egypt got substantial revenue while the company retained control of the waterway.

The suggestion fell on deaf ears. Loudon was told that if Egypt seized the Canal illegally, the company would expect France and Britain to reclaim it by military action. In 1956,

President Gamal Abdul Nasser nationalised the Canal, as Shell had foreseen, precipitating the Suez Crisis, in which Britain, France and Israel failed in their efforts to seize it through military intervention, forcing British prime minister Anthony Eden to tender his resignation.[21] Indeed, Menzies was himself humiliated when he led a delegation to Egypt only to be snubbed by Nasser.

Australia, of course, was east of Suez and although she imported most of her petroleum products from the United States much of the American crude came from the vast oilfields of the Middle East, which were beginning to look dangerously vulnerable to Arab nationalism. The 1956 crisis made the Menzies government even more anxious that BHP should drill for oil in the Sydney Basin.

Beginning in 1957, BHP's oil explorers sank a number of wells in the most likely looking prospects, but all came up dry. McLennan was disappointed but not discouraged. By now, he bestrode the organisation, his position unchallengeable, his faith in the company's future unshakeable. He did what BHP executives had done since the founding of the company: he looked overseas for the best brains available. He gave his general manager of operations, John D. Norgard, the task of discovering 'the best oilman in America', and after scouring the universities, oil companies and lists of private consultants, Norgard found just the man for the job.

CHAPTER 6

Bass Strait Bonanza

Wearing a snazzy bow tie and with his second wife Anne on his arm, petroleum geologist Lewis George Weeks touched down at Sydney's Mascot airport on Sunday, 6 March 1960. He had come out of retirement to make Australia, which he called 'the Cinderella continent' in terms of oil reserves, self-sufficient in petroleum products – and to get rich in the process. Weeks's life had been one long adventure, yet its most dramatic and rewarding passage had only just begun.

'Lewis Weeks was a thorough gentleman – a true, conservative East Coast American and one of the great oil finders,' says Russell 'Russ' Fynmore, who became head of BHP's oil-and-gas division (later BHP Petroleum).[1]

Born on a farm near Chilton, Wisconsin, on 22 May 1893 and brought up in a Christian family of 'frugal means', Weeks attended a one-room country school and worked his way through the University of Wisconsin to graduate in geology in 1917. In the years ahead, he searched for oil – usually successfully – in South America, Burma, France, Turkey, Saudi Arabia and Canada, played polo with British officers and shot wild boar in India, climbed the Himalayas, sailed up the

Amazon and became a legend at John D. Rockefeller's Standard Oil of New Jersey before his retirement in 1958.

In his memoir, Weeks says he received a phone call in late 1959 from John Norgard, who was visiting the United States, asking him to come to Australia to advise the company on where to drill for oil in the Sydney Basin. Weeks replied he wouldn't think of wasting the company's money on such a venture and suggested that Norgard consult other geologists. A few days later, Norgard rang back and asked whether he could visit Weeks to discuss the matter further. Weeks agreed and when Norgard arrived at his house on Bluewater Hill, Westport, Connecticut,[2] Weeks led him to a large map and told him the Sydney Basin would never produce 'more than a dab of natural gas'.

'You're in the wrong area,' Weeks said. 'You've got to go down to the water and get your feet wet. The oil-bearing rocks in Australia are the younger rocks, down to the south and out in the water.'[3]

When Norgard returned to Australia, he recommended that Weeks be hired as a consultant geologist. Keith A. Rowell, BHP's general manager for raw materials and exploration, agreed to a two-week contract at the rate of US$250 per day, plus travel expenses.[4] Following his arrival in Sydney, Weeks was taken on a tour of the Sydney Basin, where he was introduced to Dave McGarry, future managing director of Australian Oil & Gas. 'We had held the northern blocks of the Sydney Basin under licence for two years,' McGarry says, 'and had drilled several wells using percussion drills. We'd found a little gas but no oil. I was looking after our wells as a young geologist when Lewis Weeks turned up. BHP's licence covered the coal areas to the south of us, and Weeks wanted to drill a well in our block to see what was there. But he gave the Sydney Basin away before the hole was drilled, and I eventually got Shell to drill it.'[5]

Weeks returned to Sydney, where he had afternoon tea at the Australia Hotel with Murray Lonie, BHP's assistant general manager for raw materials and exploration, and chief geologist

Frank Canavan. His view was unchanged. The company's Petroleum Exploration Licence 25 was worthless. 'Weeks said there was no oil in the Sydney Basin and he was dead right,' Dave McGarry says.

The geologists were downcast, but only until Weeks replaced his teacup and asked, 'Is your company really interested in finding oil?'

Lonie brightened. 'You have some prospect in mind?'

Weeks allowed himself an enigmatic smile. For all his Christian humility, money was paramount. He had a new wife – the widow of his best friend Fred Sutton – and he had never earned more than $30,000 a year in his life. 'One thing oil geologists learn from sad experience is that even in the best of company you can pour out your ideas and be greeted with disinterest approaching disdain,' Weeks later philosophised in his memoir. 'Then later you find that somebody else has taken them and run with them, often scoring a touchdown. After this happens a time or two, you learn to reserve your ideas for some top decision-maker who trusts you and whom you trust to treat you fairly. In a consulting situation, it is even more necessary to be careful not to divulge too much too soon.'[6]

Lonie and Canavan took Weeks back to his hotel, and Lonie telephoned his boss, Keith Rowell. 'I think Weeks is on to something,' he said. They knew from John Norgard's report that the American had indicated southern Australia as the most promising oil-bearing region, but he had given no clue as to where BHP should start looking. The two men agreed he should be invited to Melbourne the following day instead of returning to the United States. On Friday, 18 March 1960, Weeks met Rowell in Melbourne and told him he knew where oil would be found but that he would speak with nobody but Ian McLennan.

Ushered into the chief executive's office at Essington Lewis House, the new company headquarters at 500 Bourke Street, Weeks began cagily. Nothing was a hundred per cent certain in the oil-exploration business, but McLennan would be wise to abandon all hope of a strike in the current BHP leases. 'That's good,' McLennan replied. 'It will save us some money.'

Weeks then said he knew of a more promising area that was accessible to 90 per cent of world markets. 'I've been aware of it since 1931,' he said, 'and have twice mentioned it in publications in the 1940s.'

So . . . the unasked question hung between them: if not the Sydney Basin, then where? Weeks prepared the ground. First, he'd need to do a proper magnetometer survey at a cost of £350,000. McLennan nodded. That would not be a problem. Then a further £1 million would be required for seismic surveys. BHP's net profit for 1959–60 was just £9.4 million, and these were enormous amounts, but McLennan kept his nerve. He accepted that figure, too.

Then there was the matter of Weeks's fee. How much would he require in the way of commission? Weeks had rehearsed his answer. His work had made billions for Standard Oil and other petroleum leviathans; now was his chance for a big pay day. Calmly, he said, 'There is a standard royalty payment throughout the world for introducing new oil-and-gas areas.'

He had thought of asking for five per cent but decided to settle for half that amount. He told McLennan he wanted a royalty of 2.5 per cent. McLennan looked him in the eye. 'Will you rely on me to do the fair thing?' he asked.

Weeks took a moment to size up the man. At 51, McLennan had maintained his athletic build, and the years of command had added depth and gravitas to his natural warmth of personality. 'Yes,' the American said. 'I will rely on you.'

So, the location . . .

'Come to your window,' Weeks beckoned. 'It lies out there in Bass Strait, and most particularly off the Gippsland coast.'[7] For a moment, McLennan was speechless. Bass Strait was notorious for wild weather and roaring winds. Its depth was greater than any offshore mining so far attempted. The costs could be horrendous. They would be operating at the very limits of technological advance. Yet, if they could pull it off, the benefits to the company – and to Australia – would be massive.

McLennan offered his hand. Weeks took it. McLennan would be as good as his word: when the massive Bass Strait field was discovered, Weeks would make many millions from his 2.5 per cent royalty.

The episode is a powerful legend within BHP. Weeks is romanticised almost as much as Charles Rasp. However, the behind-the-scenes reality is even more engaging and is revealed here for the first time. It involves an eminent Australian professor of geology, Samuel Warren Carey, who until now has been overlooked in the history of BHP. Yet without Carey's input, it is at best highly unlikely that the American would have been able to lead BHP to the vast oil reservoirs beneath Bass Strait.

There is no doubt whatever about the importance that Weeks attached to Professor Carey's work. Even before he had set foot in Australia, Weeks travelled the short distance between his Westport home and New Haven, Connecticut, to visit the Australian, who was then resident at Yale University, to sound him out on oil exploration in Bass Strait.

At 66, Weeks was Carey's senior by some 18 years and balding rapidly, while Carey's mane of curly silver hair remained firmly intact. But both were extroverts who enjoyed the limelight – indeed, Carey's lectures at Yale were so controversial that he was labelled 'a completely wild man', and his theories on continental drift and the expanding Earth caused some orthodox academics to shake their heads in disbelief and walk out of the lecture hall. 'Every lecture was a performance,' says Professor Pat Quilty, who worked with Professor Carey at the University of Tasmania and researched his life for a memorial for the Academy of Science. 'He believed the imparting of knowledge should be done in a memorable way.'[8]

Both Weeks and Carey had had a tough, rural upbringing. S. Warren Carey, as he preferred to be known, was born on a small farm on the Georges River near Campbelltown, 45 kilometres south-west of Sydney, on 1 November 1911, one of the six children of Tasman George Carey and his wife

Hannah Elspeth. 'When I started school,' he said, 'I had to walk three and a half miles to get there and then walk back again – right from the age of five.'[9]

After attending Canterbury High School, Carey won a scholarship in 1929 to the University of Sydney, where he studied science, taking geology as a fourth subject to chemistry, physics and mathematics. He came under the influence of the Welsh-born geologist, Emeritus Professor Sir Edgeworth David, one of the team who had located the magnetic South Pole as a member of Shackleton's expedition to Antarctica in 1908–09. David had retired as professor of geology in 1924 but he so inspired Carey that by the end of his first year the young man had no doubts he was going to be a geologist, 'a rock-hopper' in geology parlance.

Money was tight and he had to work his way through college: he literally conjured up cash by giving magic shows at children's parties as 'the Great Mystic S. Warren Carey'. When he graduated in geology with first-class honours in 1933, his plan was to study for his master's and then go to Cambridge, but first he signed on with Oil Search Limited, one of Australia's original exploration companies, to do fieldwork in Papua New Guinea. As an undergraduate, Carey had become aware of Wegener's ideas on continental drift,[10] a concept he pursued and developed for the rest of his life. It provided the basis of his doctoral thesis in 1938–39 on the tectonic evolution of New Guinea and Melanesia.

Then came the Second World War, and Carey was recruited to the Anglo-Australian special-forces outfit, Z Special Unit, and devised commando raids behind the Japanese lines in Papua New Guinea and South East Asia. His approach was suitably unconventional. On one occasion, he severely embarrassed the Australian and American navies in a practice exercise by planting limpet mines surreptitiously on the hulls of most of the warships in Townsville Harbour, an escapade that earned him official censure but huge kudos among the rank and file.

In 1944, Carey returned to Melbourne, where his wife

Austral and young family had been living after being evacuated from New Guinea. 'I resigned from the army to become chief government geologist in Tasmania,' he says.[11] He retained his government position until 1946, when he was appointed foundation professor of geology at the University of Tasmania.

One of the delegates at a continental-drift symposium organised by Carey in Hobart in 1956 was Chester Longwell of Yale University, who suggested that Carey should come to Yale as a visiting professor during his sabbatical year of 1959–60. Sam and Austral packed their bags and took their four children – Tegwen, Harley, Robin and David – to the USA. In that same year, Lewis Weeks had been elected president of the prestigious American Association of Petroleum Geologists (AAPG).

One of the AAPG members was another Australian geologist, Eric Rudd, whom Weeks had first met in the 1930s after Rudd had been awarded his master's at Harvard, then the leading geoscience school in the world. After graduating from the University of Adelaide, Rudd had used his savings from working for Oil Search in the Pilbara and Kimberley regions of Western Australia, Gippsland in Victoria and the Roma district of Queensland to pay for his tuition in America.[12] Returning to Adelaide in 1936, he had joined BHP as a geologist. He remembers walking up to the Top Cottage, the company headquarters in Whyalla, and handing his boss a pamphlet he had written on why BHP ought to get into the oil-search business.[13]

BHP paid little attention: instead of commissioning Rudd to explore for oil, it put him to work estimating its iron-ore and coal reserves. Even after he had become chief geologist in 1948, replacing Lockhart Jack, he had little success in persuading BHP to join the oil explorers.[14] But after he had resigned from BHP to become professor of economic geology at Adelaide University, Rudd had given a lecture attended by Ian McLennan in 1951. At question time, McLennan asked him, 'If you were to seek oil in Australia, where would you search?' Rudd replied, 'The north-west of Western Australia, Gippsland and the Roma district.' Two years later, AMPOL Exploration struck oil at Rough Range in the north-west; Australia's first commercial oilfield, at Moonie in the Surat Basin near Roma, was announced in 1960; and in 1966 BHP began its successful exploitation of the oil-and-gas deposits in Bass Strait off Gippsland.[15]

So Ian McLennan was nothing like the novice in oil matters that Lewis Weeks makes out in his memoir. Weeks had never visited Australia but he claims to have studied the geology of southern Australia as early as 1931 after what he describes as 'a chance conversation' in downtown Manhattan with an old-time prospector, who had advised him that Bass Strait was the place to look for oil. Dr Max Banks, Professor Sam Carey's associate at the University of Tasmania – 'lieutenant to Carey's captain', as he puts it – was dismissive about such an eventuality. 'I haven't got a suitable salt cellar here to take a pinch of salt,' he said. 'I know Carey did talk to Lewis Weeks about Bass Strait, but what they discussed I don't know, nor do I remember precisely when it was – but he did: there's no two ways about that.'[16]

In a 1996 letter in the authors' possession, Carey told his son, Dr Harley Carey, 'When I was at Yale, [Weeks] visited me many times to discuss the structure of Bass Strait.'[17] The issue clearly disturbed him. Before his death on 20 March 2002 at the age of 90, Carey left the following account of his meetings with Lewis Weeks, not just at Yale but in no fewer than four other locations: Copenhagen, New York, Westport and Hobart:

> At the International Geological Congress in Copenhagen in August 1960, I was in the mid-morning coffee queue when I felt a tap on my shoulder. It was Lewis Weeks. He said, 'I have been looking for you. May we have coffee together? I believe you have given a lecture about Bass Strait – please tell me about it. Broken Hill Proprietary has asked me to report on the petroleum prospects.'
>
> Sketching on the back of an envelope, I explained the tectonic structure, briefly summarizing my ANZAAS

[Australian and New Zealand Association for the Advancement of Science] address. Lewis paid close attention and asked several critical questions. Next day he again sought me out. With typical Weeks thoroughness he had carefully considered what I had said and came back with several relevant questions from it. A couple of months later in Hobart, I had a telephone call from him. He had come to Melbourne at the request of Haematite Proprietary, the petroleum exploration subsidiary of BHP, and immediately told them he was going to Hobart 'to see Carey'. He brought with him [Brian] Hopkins, Haematite Chief Geologist, and another from BHP. We met at Wrest Point and spent a couple of hours discussing the structure of Bass Strait.

In 1963, I went to Israel as a UN technical adviser and in April 1964 reported to the UN headquarters in New York. On 9 April, I attended a lecture at the New York Academy of Science and found Lewis Weeks was the chairman. He asked me to visit him next day at his home in Connecticut. I had rented an Avis car, so I drove up there arriving mid-morning.

By this time the airborne magnetic reconnaissance had covered the whole of Bass Strait and the more promising structures so indicated had been covered by ship-borne seismic reflection traverses. Weeks and I spent the rest of the morning sprawled on the carpet poring over the maps and gloating over the prospects so revealed. With his wife, we went out to lunch at the village and came back for another session on Bass Strait. We agreed that the structures off Gippsland looked excellent. There appeared to be several closed structures, with thousands of feet of sediment under them, and these sediments thinned out progressively towards the shore, pinching out at the Lakes Entrance unconformity, where the basal sandstone was saturated with oil. These structures just *had* to trap oil or gas or both.

I asked him how he intended to proceed because BHP, who held the licences through their subsidiary, Haematite, had no expertise in petroleum drilling or production even on land and

> still less at sea, and marine exploration was still in its infancy, especially in notoriously rough seaways like Bass Strait. He told me he had offered it to Shell but they had turned it down. But he had some old Standard Oil contacts who he thought he could interest in it. They had already had rough-sea drilling experience in Cook Inlet, which was every bit as stormy as Bass Strait.[18]

One of Professor Carey's postgraduate students, Dr Andy Kugler of Austin, Texas, recalls a lecture in which Carey discussed oil potential in Australia, particularly in Bass Strait. 'Just prior to that, he had been contacted by Lewis Weeks with respect to where they should be looking for oil in Australia; that was what Sam Carey actually told us in the lecture,' Kugler says.

'"Prof" had suggested there was a big fault zone between Australia and Tasmania and there were maybe up to a hundred miles of horizontal offset between the structure of Tasmania and the structure of Australia. In the zone between, which is Bass Strait, there had developed a basin which as far as could be told from onshore was getting into the Cretaceous period of the Mesozoic age, which is responsible for a lot of the world's oil, so on that basis he directed Lewis Weeks to Bass Strait as a place that BHP should be looking for oil.

'As far as I know, that's the only reason Lewis Weeks suggested they look there. It was a fairly straightforward lecture that "Prof" gave and there was no reason to believe he was embellishing anything. He was saying, "Okay, Lewis, if you want to find oil in Australia this is the place you want to go." "Prof" did not get any payment for his input but I never heard him bitch about it.'[19]

The Geological Society of Australia states unequivocally, 'Lewis Weeks, based on his knowledge of the Lakes Entrance Oil Shaft and Carey's sketch map of anticlines extending into the offshore Gippsland Basin, led BHP to take up exploration acreage.'[20] Professor Quilty adds, 'Sam's ideas on the evolution of the Gippsland Basin were critical, absolutely critical to the exploration of Bass Strait.'[21]

Ian McLennan was unaware of Sam Carey's input when confronted with the decision whether or not to proceed with the oil project in Bass Strait. Once again, the government became BHP's ace in the hole. The Menzies–McEwen Cabinet agreed to put up half the cost of the exploratory work. Chairman Syme said later, 'It was like putting your money on a rank outsider. Had the government incentives not been there, we would not have taken it on.'[22]

Serendipity also helped in establishing the organisational framework for the project. Once the early surveys showed that an oil find was possible, BHP needed a partner with expertise in the field. That could only come from one of the major companies, and when the Australians distributed tender documents to them there was a deafening silence.

'The managing director of Shell Australia visited me in my office,' McLennan said. 'He told me he thought we'd be left lamenting and no one would tender. Well, he was wrong.'[23] The Weeks connection proved valuable. By then, his professional alma mater, Standard Oil, was trading in Australia as Esso Standard Oil (Australia) Limited.[24] McLennan said, 'I think they had enough faith in Lewis Weeks to say to themselves, "Well, if Lewis thinks this is good, it's got a fair chance of being good."' After extensive surveys in 1962 and further work two years later, negotiations were finally concluded for a 50–50 partnership with Esso in May 1964.

Lewis Weeks had brokered the farm-out deal under which Esso would drill for oil and operate the productive wells, while BHP would pay its share of the operational costs and split the profits. Weeks's former employer offered him 'quite a few million dollars' for his royalty interest but he turned them down.

When state governments threatened to challenge federal jurisdiction over the oilfields – and the consequent distribution of royalties between governments – Prime Minister Menzies once again came to the rescue. According to McLennan, 'Sir Robert Menzies did a very large number of great things for Australia. This is one of the things he did. There could have been an interminable wrangle but Sir Robert Menzies, as soon as he heard about it, said, "Oh well, this might be a good development – let's not stand in the light." He virtually gave the states the rights and we had areas in each of those offshore waters of Tasmania, Victoria and South Australia. It was very largely due to the foresight of Sir Robert Menzies. BHP had zero to do with that. It was his own idea.'[25]

So Esso sailed the *Glomar III* exploration vessel from the Gulf of Mexico to Bass Strait. While it was in transit, Sam Carey had dinner with Dr W. A. Visser, who had been in charge of Shell's West Pacific exploration, at the International Geological Congress in Delhi on 15 December 1964. 'I asked him why he had turned down the Bass Strait invitation, as the aeromagnetic coverage followed by detailed ship-borne seismic-reflection surveys had produced exciting results, with every prospect of major production,' Carey says. 'He told me that they had been unsuccessful in a similar-looking prospect, and exploration and production in stormy sea regions was still in development stages. I assured him that he would regret that decision.'[26]

Glomar III spudded in Australia's first significant offshore well, East Gippsland Shelf-1 (later known as Barracouta-1) on 27 December 1964. The drilling site was 24 kilometres off the Gippsland coast in a water depth of 45 metres. Two months later, it hit gas – a spectacular hole-in-one that almost blew the drill-ship out of the water.[27]

The following year, BHP–Esso made a second major gas discovery at the Marlin field, and then the partnership hit the jackpot with the discovery of a colossal oilfield at Kingfish-1 in 1966 (1.2 billion barrels recoverable). John Norgard's daughter Susan Quail recalls, 'I was at home one night when Lewis called for Dad to say they'd found oil. It was celebrations all round.' Other fields were found in quick succession, including Halibut, Dolphin, Perch, Flounder, Tuna, Snapper, Mackerel and Bream, as well as more oil at Barracouta and West Kingfish.[28]

Royalties for Bass Strait were split seven per cent to Victoria and four per cent to the federal government. Then, John McEwen as trade-and-industry minister set the industry-wide price at $3.47 a barrel. At the time, the price for Middle East crude was less than $2. Altogether, it represented an exceptional deal for BHP.

BHP–Esso anticipated a flow of 350,000 barrels a day, and in one bound Australia had discovered enough crude to make it 70 per cent self-sufficient in oil.[29] The share price reflected Ian McLennan's faith in Lewis Weeks, topping $25 by the end of November 1968. BHP's former finance director Geoff Heeley says, 'Bass Strait was a very fortuitous development – a project which showed some foresight and, yes, it created a change in the whole structure of BHP.'[30]

Weeks's three-page royalty agreement with BHP–Esso had been drawn up by Paul Temple, an American attorney friend who worked with him at Standard Oil. Weeks agreed to give him 20 per cent of any deal. 'Paul grumbled,' Russ Fynmore says, 'because at the time it was before they had discovered anything, but afterwards that became a fortune.'[31]

Weeks himself was soon earning millions a year from the Bass Strait bonanza. His agreement stipulated that the royalty be paid at the 'gross wellhead value' of the oil and gas, without the deduction of any costs or taxes – an incredibly generous arrangement. His new financial status was reflected in the house that he and Anne bought at the very top of Bluewater Hill, overlooking Long Island Sound.

One of his advisers (and a close personal friend) was Sir Howard Beale, former Australian ambassador to the United States. 'Most of what Lewis Weeks knew about Australia – apart from the geological side of it – he learned from Howard Beale,' Russ Fynmore says. 'He really was a very good adviser to Lewis Weeks, including taxation arrangements with the Australian Government.'[32]

For tax purposes in the United States, he invested 1.378 per cent of the royalty in a company called Weeks Natural Resources (later Weeks Petroleum) to engage in oil exploration with the larger oil companies. He also employed James Daniel, a retired *Reader's Digest* editor, to compile his memoir from taped interviews. Weeks died on 4 March 1977 before the job had been completed, but his widow, Anne, published it the following year. There is no mention of Professor Carey anywhere in the work, and although many millions were paid in royalties from the Bass Strait oil-and-gas discoveries, he never received a cent.

In the last years of his remarkable life, Weeks was a generous benefactor. He built a new earth-sciences hall at the University of Wisconsin, a new YMCA pavilion at Westport and a new headquarters for the AAPG at Tulsa, Oklahoma. In Australia, he endowed the Lewis G. Weeks Gold Medal, presented each year by the Australian Petroleum Production and Exploration Association to commemorate 'the contribution to the Australian petroleum industry of Dr Lewis Weeks, who epitomised the purpose of the medal by his pioneering work in Bass Strait'. Its recipients include Professor Eric Rudd (1984), Dave McGarry (1986) – and, ironically, Professor S. Warren Carey (1996).

The early operational work in Bass Strait was difficult and dangerous. Divers laying the pipelines spent seven hours in a decompression chamber for every two on the ocean bed. The huge offshore drilling platforms were built in sections, assembled and hauled into position, where they were supported by 20,000-ton 'legs' driven 60 metres into the ocean floor.

The miners lived on the great platforms for weeks at a stretch and were helicoptered back to the mainland on leave. Accidents were commonplace, but in 1968 the country was shocked by a tragedy that took the lives of three visiting journalists. They were swept by a hail of flying metal when a helicopter suddenly dropped on to the platform and its broken rotor blade slashed into them. Hugh Curnow of the Sydney *Telegraph* was killed instantly; Peter Bourke of the Melbourne *Sun News-Pictorial* fell 40 metres into the sea after being knocked to the edge of the platform; Noel Buckley, a company PR officer, died later of injuries. Nevertheless, the pioneering work of the BHP–Esso consortium enjoyed wide public and political support.

The Menzies era had ended in 1966, and though McEwen could be relied upon to fly the BHP flag in Cabinet, he too resigned in January 1971. The prime minister of the day, John Gorton, brought a new and somewhat unnerving unpredictability to his dealings with the company. Tradition gave way to personal wilfulness and, at times, caprice. When teamed with Lenox Hewitt as his top adviser, Gorton became a knotty problem for McLennan and his team. Hewitt, a mordant character with the habitual expression of an angry parrot, had begun his career working in BHP's commercial department many years previously. The experience, it seems, was not recalled with unalloyed pleasure by either party.

McLennan, who had become BHP chairman in 1971, approached Gorton with one of the more remarkable proposals in Australia's industrial history: to reduce the oil price by a dollar from the McEwen figure to $2.47, thus cutting directly into BHP's profits. McLennan's reasoning was that the McEwen price was designed to make the relatively small Australian producers – such as Moonie and Roma in Queensland – viable entities. It was not designed for the massive flows from Bass Strait. At the time, imported oil was $2.10 a barrel.

According to McLennan, '[Gorton] was most enthusiastic. "That's the most statesman-like thing I've ever heard of," he said.'[33] At the end of the discussion, McLennan went to America, only to receive an emergency telephone call from Chairman Colin Syme to say the issue had 'blown up' and he'd better return immediately.

'I found that Mr Gorton had repudiated this arrangement and he wished to have further negotiations. We saw him – and Hewitt – at The Lodge,[34] because Mr Gorton had some fear of leakage taking place. This was a most difficult period indeed. We obviously adopted the attitude that we thought we'd done jolly well in reducing the price by a dollar. Well, it finished up we got virtually import parity for the oil.'

McLennan and Esso's Norton Belnap did secure an agreement that all the Australian refineries had to use Australian crude; only the finished product could be imported. But it proved to be of little advantage. 'After the OPEC countries started to put up the price of oil [in 1973], everybody wanted [the lower-priced] Australian crude.'[35]

By then, BHP was having to deal with an entirely new phenomenon at the national level: the Labor Government of Gough Whitlam, which still carried within its ranks hard men wielding the barely concealed baton of nationalisation. Most prominent among them was the long-time member for the Wollongong area, R. F. X. 'Rex' Connor, who not only secured the ministry of minerals and energy but Lenox Hewitt as his department's permanent head.

McLennan was aghast. He had dealt congenially and profitably with state Labor governments over the decades. But Connor quickly became BHP's bête noire. 'He never once achieved ministerial status in the state parliament where he was a member for many years,' McLennan said. In Canberra, however, his formidable bulk, conspiratorial reasoning and uncompromising delivery disarmed Whitlam, who promoted him to high Cabinet office. Indeed, on one occasion when both Whitlam and Deputy Prime Minister Jim Cairns were out of the country, he briefly became acting prime minister.

'He was, so he said, a great one for Australia developing its own resources,' McLennan said. 'I think the real fact of the matter was he was a great one for socialising resources.'[36]

Happily for BHP, Connor's career crashed in flames when, in pursuit of his 'socialising' agenda, he attempted to borrow $400 million in petro-dollars using a shady Pakistani go-between, Tirath Khemlani, after Whitlam had revoked his authority to do so. Hewitt's public-service career effectively flamed out at the same time.

Moreover, the changing of the guard in the Labor Party would usher in a somewhat surprising champion of the company's cause in Paul John Keating, who succeeded Connor in opposition as the party's spokesman for minerals and energy. 'Primarily the business I'm in, and have always been in, is the nation-building business,' Keating says.

He is sitting at a beautifully polished antique table in his Potts Point, Sydney, office in 2008. He is dressed in olive corduroys, an open-necked shirt and casual jacket with patched leather elbows. 'I was always sympathetic to BHP,' he says, 'if only because anyone who can build something that large – any group – its interests require consideration. And they always had consideration from me.'

He recalls his first interaction with the company: 'I had a call one Saturday morning from Ian McLennan – it must have been about 1977 or '78 – saying that BHP had had an approach from the Burma Oil company [for BHP] to take over their concessions on the North-West Shelf . . . it used to be called Woodside Burma or Burma Woodside . . . and what attitude would I take, because he said to get the project up it would take the life of a number of governments; so, representing the Australian Labor Party, what attitude would I take to BHP acquiring an interest?

'I said, "Well, I would encourage you to acquire it."

'He said, "I didn't expect that answer."

'I said, "I would encourage you to acquire it because I think this is the last of the Mohicans." He asked me what I meant by that, and I said, "Well, the increases in oil prices to $60–$70 a barrel in '73–'74, the OPEC-induced increases, lifted the price of all hydrocarbons. Therefore, if we could get the Japanese interested to take contracts, then we should take it. Because if it's a cartel holding up the prices, then inevitably the price will fall and then the chances of us being able to pick up a contract that large – six million tonnes, three trains of gas at two million tonnes each – would be slim."

'So I said, "You can say that this project would have the support of the opposition." So then, that gave him a fair degree of comfort and I think the kind of encouragement to go ahead and take the Burma interest.'

When they met shortly afterwards, Keating offered to take the matter further. 'I said, "If you like – because this is a really long project – I will put support for it in the Labor Party platform."' Keating says. 'So at the next meeting of the national conference of the Labor Party, either 1977 or 1979, I put an express provision in that we would support the development of the North-West Shelf gas field. So that meant we had a policy rather than a wink from some shadow spokesman's eye.'[37]

From the perspective of 1979, McLennan said, 'There are three major dates in the history of the company. The first was when Broken Hill was found; the second was when the decision was made to start in steel; and the third was when it decided to go into the oil business. The entry into oil and gas had a most major effect on the company. It's made it possible to develop in all sorts of other ways. It's kept it as the largest company in Australia.'[38]

It was indeed The Big Australian.

CHAPTER 7

The Image Makers

The Gorton and Connor imbroglios brought home to BHP's senior executives the need to resurrect the in-house lobbying operation once driven by James Menzies but which had seemed superfluous through the long years of Menzies–McEwen rule. During the 1950s and '60s, according to McLennan, 'Relations with the government were substantially handled by the chairman and the managing director. We never did want to go rushing to the government for every little thing that happened. But we did want them to understand our points of view on various things and that was done by personal interview.'[1]

Now, they developed their public-relations facility within the administrative division. They had taken the first tentative step in the mid-1960s by hiring Derek Sawer, a former Melbourne *Argus* journalist, to advise on relations with the press. Sawer came from a distinguished intellectual family. His brother Geoffrey was foundation professor of law at the Australian National University. Derek was born in Adelaide in 1918 and educated at Melbourne's Scotch College (by now BHP's educational alma mater). The Second World War interrupted his studies when he enlisted in the Australian Imperial Force and served in North Africa as one of the famous Rats of Tobruk. He was commissioned in the field and ended the war as a captain.

After demobilisation, he joined ABC Radio Australia in Melbourne before transferring to *The Argus* as a subeditor. When the paper closed its doors in 1957, he returned to the ABC; then, in 1967, he joined BHP. He had begun a commerce degree at Melbourne University and completed it during his initial months with the company. He quickly became a well-respected figure within the top echelon. McLennan and Syme consulted him frequently.

'I got on very well with McLennan,' he says. 'It was partly the Scotch College connection. He was dux in the same year as my brother Geoff. He was a very decent man. He saw himself as a sort of father figure to me.'[2]

Sawer says that, at the time, 'BHP was sort of a mystery all of itself'. His role was 'opening up the company' and allowing the public to see more of the way it operated. One of his first recruits was Juliana Hooper, a young Brisbane woman who had completed an Arts degree at the University of Queensland before working in McEwen's department of trade in London and Melbourne.

Sawer gave her the task of advertising manager. 'But they didn't call me the advertising manager,' she said, 'they called me a public-relations officer.' Her early experience said much about the company's ethos. 'The personnel manager said to me – and he didn't say it unkindly, he was preparing me – he said, "Women in this company have the status of fluff on the floor . . . you had better prepare yourself."' She laughed. 'I had the medical and failed miserably because I didn't have two testes, which was one of the requirements.'[3]

However, working with Derek Sawer helped Juliana over the early rough spots. 'I actually found they were a very fair company with a very fair ethos. After two years, they faced up to the fact that I was doing the job without the title and put me on the executive staff. Once I blended in, I was fine. There was a special dining room in the new building and I must say it was a fascinating phenomenon. You'd go to lunch and sit at a big table [where] there'd be people from the shipyards and from the iron-ore mines and the oil-and-gas fields all feeding in bits of information. There was this fabulous cohesive sense of being part of something.'

Her principal task was to help develop the all-important 'image'. 'Because the company was so big, it was always worried about being seen as being too powerful and too influential. This was when there was all that anti-cartel legislation in America. It was always a worry that they were earning big profits and that the profits were in proportion to the capital being invested. It was my job to put it all in perspective.'

Another priority was to secure recruits for the trainee scheme, which was now intrinsic to the company's modus operandi. 'Corporate image in the 1970s was about trying to attract the best young graduates,' she says, 'and you didn't do that if the literature you were putting out to universities was old-fashioned and fuddy-duddy. I was doing very up-to-the-moment stuff to try to make it attractive – just trying to present the company as a good employer and a good Australian.'

Her own experience with the men at the top reinforced her commitment to the job. Colin Syme, now knighted, personified much that was good about the company. 'He was the epitome of the old class of director: total probity; not about money; another world altogether. Corporate greed just hadn't happened,' she said. '[He] drove a very well-polished, well-loved old Holden. I thought it was wonderful that instead of having a very smart car he had a nice old car. He could have had all sorts of things but that wasn't the way they did it at BHP. Everything was done well, but not flashily. McLennan was the same. They were very solid citizens.'

Another indicator of the 'BHP way' was the preference of top executives for the Australian Club in William Street rather than the higher profile (and more snobbish) Melbourne

Club in Collins Street. Founded in 1878, the Australian Club became something of a BHP institution. Harvey Patterson, who was elected to membership in 1880, was one of the first BHP directors; he was joined by the first chairman, Arthur Blackwood, and after William Knox signed up in 1888 they established a 'BHP table' in the dining room.

At the Australian Club, they could promote the company's interests with fellow industrialists in relaxed surroundings, and by the 1970s Colin Syme and a later chairman, Sir James Balderstone, became presidents of the club. It was a measure of the esteem in which Derek Sawer was held that he too was invited to join.

The club was a significant element in the continuing development of the company's image. So too was the fact that many of the top executives had started their working lives as BHP trainees. Both Brian Loton, who followed McLennan, and James McNeill, the chairman after Sir Colin Syme, had begun as trainees. According to Juliana Hooper, 'At the time I was there, a lot of very senior management were people who had started with the company virtually when they were 14, so it wasn't patrician – a lot of the management was actually meritocracy. Sir Colin was a lawyer, whereas the next two chairmen [McNeill and McLennan] were company officers who had come up through the ranks.'[4]

Throughout the 1970s, the whole public-relations strategy would become one of the most potent forces in the company's armoury. And by the end of the decade, when once more they had the friendly ear of a coalition government, under Malcolm Fraser and McEwen's successor, Doug Anthony, they had built the image of the company to commanding heights.

Derek Sawer left in 1982. 'When McLennan retired,' he said, 'it was expected that Fred Rich would follow him as CEO. He was general manager administration and we all wanted him to take over. But he went home one night, sat on his sofa and died. The board insisted on bringing in one of those British headhunting firms to find the successor. I wasn't inclined to wait around.'[5] He bought a sailing boat and a home at the coastal town of Portsea. 'He became a ship's chandler,' Juliana Hooper said. 'He loved his boats.'

While the company sought Sawer's replacement, his role was filled temporarily by Ian Crawford, who began with the company in the 1960s as the public-relations officer for the oil-and-gas division. 'He was in a very different mould,' Juliana Hooper said. While he had reported to Sawer, Crawford's American connection through Esso meant he enjoyed a measure of independence. He also had a more aggressive approach to the task. However, he was passed over for the permanent role in favour of Sydney-born journalist Peter Maund, who had arrived in Melbourne in 1954 to work on the *Herald*. He transferred to the infant Channel Nine in 1956 as director of news and current affairs before crossing the fence to public relations with the State Electricity Commission in 1972.

When he applied for the BHP job, he had a lengthy interview with chairman Jim McNeill. It revealed the comparative naivety of the company in presenting itself to the world. 'We talked about this and that for some time, which amused me because it didn't revolve around what the real business was,' he says. 'So finally I said, "Should I take up this position – or you appoint me – what would you expect me to do?" And he said, "Well, we expect you to tell us what to do!" That was the sort of relationship that was expected at the beginning.'[6]

In fact, senior executives and the board would soon be swept up in a sharp learning curve as the company became embroiled in a takeover battle. But in April 1982, Maund looked forward to a relatively peaceful life as director of public affairs and government relations. The chief public-relations concern was with the steel factories, which were shedding workers in an attempt to stay competitive with their international rivals; but with a change of government in 1983, Prime Minister Bob Hawke and Treasurer Paul Keating created a new paradigm . . . or so the PR team believed.

'It became pretty apparent that we had to step up our dealing with government,' Maund says. Despite Keating's present-day protestations that he gave the company 'special consideration', Maund says that publicly at least, 'There was no love lost between Keating and BHP. He always used to have a go at BHP whenever he could. Paul Keating thought BHP was the epitome of evil and the people who ran it were evil people who were rapacious. So we appointed Jock McGregor full-time in Canberra. He later became company secretary of BHP.'[7]

In fact, Keating says, 'I did BHP an inordinate number of favours in Bass Strait as treasurer over the years. Bass Strait was characterised by these small hydrocarbon pinchouts outside the main reservoirs. And what the Commonwealth used to do was second-guess the production costs and put on differential excises per field. That meant that some gas reserves would be left. They wouldn't do them because it wasn't worth their while to do them. So I did them a big favour, I thought, in terms of efficiency in that I changed the tax treatment of Bass Strait so that the fields were taxed as one so they could make their own choices about whether they developed this field or that field. And this brought far more rationality into the development.'[8]

Nevertheless, the perception was that Keating was hostile to the company, and McGregor was joined in Canberra by Peter Laver, who had been with BHP since 1959 as a trainee. Laver would spend several years associated with the public-affairs unit in its various guises. He attended Melbourne University on a BHP fellowship and took a degree in metallurgical engineering. Soon afterwards, he was awarded a special cadetship that allowed him to visit all of the company's operations around Australia, including spending six months at the Port Kembla steelworks. Back at headquarters, he worked for two legendary general managers, Mark Pitt and Jack Richards. This brought him to the notice of Ian McLennan, whom he assisted for the next two years.

'Over the years, I found myself doing a lot of work with the public-affairs people,' Laver says. 'I was seconded to the area as a "steel man" in 1983 and with Jock McGregor I developed the "roadshow" for bureaucrats and legislators at a time when the steel business was under cost pressures. Malcolm Fraser wanted us to wear a hair shirt. And when Hawke came in, he and [New South Wales premier] Neville Wran wanted to fix the steel industry in a hundred days. They had inquiries going in Sydney and Canberra; I practically lived between the two."[9]

When Robert Holmes à Court made his raid on the company in 1984 (covered in detail in Chapter 8), the pace and intensity of Laver's work multiplied overnight, while Maund's annual budget leapt to $9 million in an all-out public campaign against the raider. And in 1985, Derek Sawer returned part-time to oversee the publication of the massive book *Australians in Company* to mark BHP's centenary. 'They wanted to make it a great and glorious thing,' Sawer says. 'So we spared no expense.' The result was a coffee-table-sized tome. 'When I read it recently, I thought it was corny,' he says.[10]

By the mid-1980s, BHP was able to point to a trebling of group sales over the previous decade to $5.4 billion annually. At the same time, shareholders' funds also trebled and by the end of 1984 stood at $5.3 billion. Group profit had passed the magic $100 million mark in 1972. Now, it had leapt to an astonishing $639 million. The company employed more than 59,000 Australians and, with an average of three dependants per wage earner, that meant BHP alone supported almost 250,000 people at a time when the population of the Australian Capital Territory and the Northern Territory together numbered fewer than 300,000.

Meanwhile, 'The Big Australian' tag had entered the language. 'It was one of Derek Sawer's coups actually,' Maund says. 'The *Herald* newspaper and others were a bit sour about BHP – particularly its size – and there was a great hubbub, for example, when the first profit of $100 million was announced. It was sneered at, and this phrase, "The big Australian", was used by the *Herald* in a derogatory sense. However, Derek thought, "Let's make the best of it," and he turned it into something to make people feel good about BHP.'[11]

Maund entrenched the concept with a change of company logo. At the time, it featured a ladle pouring molten steel. 'A lot of the senior executives had their grounding at Newcastle or Wollongong,' he says, 'so it was not only the outward symbol of BHP but it was indicative of the general culture.' His new logo – a stylised map of Australia incorporating the BHP initials – signalled a radical change. 'It was a different colour for each of the divisions – red for steel, blue for petroleum and so on – but it was also an attempt to change the thinking.' It had the great advantage of reflecting a new reality. With the acquisition of several highly profitable global assets in coal and copper (explained in detail in Chapter 9), BHP was becoming a significant international player.

Peter Maund was succeeded by the first woman to hold a high executive position in the company, Carol Austin. Melbourne born and with science and economics degrees from Monash and the Australian National University, she was chief economist at the Australian Industry Development Corporation when recruited in late 1989. She found her gender much less a problem than it had been for Juliana Hooper. 'My biggest problem was that public affairs didn't have a lot of credibility on my arrival because it wasn't given a high status and didn't have a lot of influence,' she says. 'It hadn't been central to policy making. In changing the focus, I had the support of the board, Brian Loton and the senior-executive team. I got on very well with them. I restructured the staffing to give it much more of a public-policy perspective.'[12]

She was also determined to recast the company's image, which at the time was driven by a massive advertising campaign featuring the character actor Bill Hunter in macho mode. 'I canned all that Bill Hunter stuff,' she recalls. 'Harry Miller rang me up and said that I was destroying the reputation of the company and damaging the image of BHP. But we weren't a consumer brand; you don't do mass advertising for an organisation like BHP. My focus was on building images in the communities where we operated.

'The money that I saved on that I put into upgrading the science awards, into exciting children about science and encouraging them to be scientists and engineers.'[13]

She says her science training alerted her to the greater environmental issues: 'I could see that the environment was going to be a major area of concern, so I set up an environmental task force to do an audit of the status of environmental management within the company.' The problems varied between the divisions. 'Carbon taxes were on the table even back then,' Carol Austin says, 'as was energy efficiency, pollution, remediation of mine sites – that was important, not walking away and leaving it for some other group to clean up the mess.'

The initiative led to the development of an environmental department in the company. When the company's Ok Tedi gold and copper mine in Papua New Guinea began to attract critical publicity, 'I was greatly in favour of defusing it . . . of managing these things by making them understandable,' she says. 'It's always better for journalists to write from knowledge than scant information.'

Her unit, with a staff of 12, did not have a major government-relations focus. 'When we would go to government to lobby a minister,' she says, 'I would accompany the head of the relevant division and would work with him on a strategy to handle that. Where there were group issues, or where the issues were very high level, I got involved; where they were considered operational divisional issues, the division handled it. Steel had its own government-relations unit. Steel had a lot more issues with state government.'[14] The power of the New South Wales unions ensured that steelmaking, which dominated the economies of Newcastle and Port Kembla, would always be high on the state government's agenda.

She says that, during her five years with the company, 'Every year, there was a senior-management meeting and the flavour became much more international; it became a more globally focused organisation.'

Peter Laver returned from an operational role in the Pilbara iron-ore development in 1992 to take over the role of general manager external affairs, which then incorporated government-relations and public-relations functions. Carol Austin reported to him, he said, until she left in 1994. Carol recalls that, aside from an annual performance review conducted by Laver, she dealt directly with chief executive officer Brian Loton and the then chairman Sir Arvi Parbo.

The operations of BHP's corporate image makers and in-house lobbyists were becoming progressively more sophisticated. Peter Laver says he also developed an economic team that worked on developing forecasts for exchange rates and commodity prices in conjunction with the chief executive officer. But a hard core of trained journalists would be tempted away from their vocation to burnish the company's image by releasing stories favourable to BHP and deflecting those that put it in a poor light.

The process gained a new dimension when Laver and chief executive officer John Prescott recruited Graham Evans in 1995. Evans was born in Melbourne, raised in Colac and Ballarat, and graduated from the University of Melbourne before embarking on a bureaucratic career in the Commonwealth Public Service. He was seconded to be principal private secretary to Prime Minister Bob Hawke for three years from 1983 before serving in a number of senior positions, including secretary of the departments of primary industries, resources and energy, and transport.

Laver had met him during his time with Bob Hawke. 'That was when I spent all that time in Canberra,' he says. 'When Graham joined BHP, his operations would come increasingly under the office of the chief executive.'[15]

Evans says, 'I didn't have any background in the media, and in communications, for that matter. And I certainly didn't see my role as a lobbyist. What I was concerned to do was get a much closer identification of the external-affairs function with the business direction of the company.'[16] Working with John Prescott, he developed the economics group to forecast global and domestic economic activity. 'We started doing country risk analysis, and this had both economic and political dimensions,' he says.

In doing so, he revived the company's association with Australia's intelligence organisations. 'We talked to people in government, we talked to academics but we relied mainly on foreign affairs, [which] gets an input from the intelligence agencies.'

However, despite his underplaying the role, Evans's group was vitally concerned with lobbying both state and federal governments. And invariably the ministerial door was wide open. Paul Keating says, 'I think the question about what is in the interests of BHP and its shareholders vis-à-vis the interests of Australia often coincides.

'And often the political system would do them a favour but the favour would more often than not scrub up as good policy. In other words, they were not given a favour out of bad policy, they were given a favour out of good policy.

'And whenever they pushed the limit too much – and they do this occasionally – then sometimes they'd stub their toes and get a "no". But they always took the opportunity of discussing their circumstances before they moved on things. Often, a "no" for BHP would not be a bald, public no, it would be a soft, private no, way ahead of anything they might otherwise have done. But it's probably true to say that both political parties have had an upbeat view of them. Certainly, the Labor Party has. And for those in the Labor Party interested in building businesses – and I was one – the background thinking which we would do with them would be friendly and conducive to their benefit.'[17]

In the Howard years, BHP Billiton operatives such as Bernie Delaney, whom Evans recruited from the steel division, would develop networks within government and among like-minded lobbyists that would have a profound effect on government policy, not always to the ultimate long-term benefit of Australia. Indeed, as detailed in Chapter 22, BHP Billiton would take a leading role in the behind-the-scenes struggle to reverse government policy and abandon the agreement to ratify the Kyoto Protocol. In so doing, Australia became a major impediment to the international effort in the battle against climate change, the quintessential political and environmental challenge of the twenty-first century.

PART II

The Predator

CHAPTER 8

The Buccaneers

When the Labor Party took power in Canberra in 1983, Bob Hawke and Paul Keating immediately began the deregulation of the economy, removing tariff protection and opening up the financial and banking sector to free-market competition.

During the 1970s, Keating had visited many of Australia's mining assets when he was Labor's shadow minister for national resources. 'I liked the mining industry because it was a successful, internationally competitive export industry,' he says. 'It wasn't laying down in a sort of rut of tariffs and protection; it was out there doing something.'[1] But, he added, the industry was being held back because the Australian dollar was overvalued, making its resources uncompetitive in world markets. One of his first acts in 1983, therefore, was to float the Australian dollar and allow market forces to decide its true worth.[2]

Brian Loton, who worked his way to the top after joining the company as a metallurgical engineer at the Newcastle steelworks in 1954, says, 'We got on very well with the Hawke and Keating government opening up the economy, floating the dollar and reducing the rigidities. The company certainly benefited from it.'[3]

Indeed, Loton would use the Hawke–Keating financial revolution against a succession of punishing takeover battles by consolidating the steel industry at home and expanding the company's interests abroad. It would be a life-and-death struggle.

BHP was now a $3 billion business employing 60,000 people, with three times that number of shareholders, many of them long-term loyalists. It was a tempting quarry for the buccaneers of the bourse. Asset-rich and underperforming on the share register, the company was made to order for a squadron of corporate raiders who were spearheading the greatest takeover frenzy Australia had ever seen. Leader of the pack, which included Alan Bond, 'Last Resort' Laurie Connell, John Spalvins of Adelaide Steamship, Ron Brierley of Industrial Equity and the gruff, burly, football-mad John Elliott of Elders IXL, was the tall, softly spoken Robert Holmes à Court.

'Enigmatic' was the adjective most commonly appended to the West Australian with the unusual surname; indeed, he was the *rara avis* of Australian business: not only an enigma but, in the words of his friend and one-time legal partner Nicholas Hasluck, 'ingenious, constantly inventive and always pragmatic'.[4]

Michael Robert Hamilton Holmes à Court had been born to British parents in the South African mining hub of Johannesburg on 27 July 1937 and raised in Rhodesia, where the family farmed. Young Rob, as he was known, was educated at Michaelhouse, an English-style, fee-paying school in Natal. He was soon in the business of making money. At the end of term, the fledgling entrepreneur drove his classmates home in exchange for their travel allowances; he also turned his hobby of photography into a business, taking photographs of students and selling the prints.[5]

The Holmes à Court family shifted to New Zealand, where Rob studied agricultural science in anticipation of life as a gentleman farmer. But in 1962, he suddenly changed tack when he moved to Australia and began studying law at the University of Western Australia. While at university, he met Janet Lee

Ranford, a young science teacher, whom he married in 1965. When he started his own legal practice two years later, Janet and his mother, Ethnee Holmes à Court, were on the staff.

From the beginning, the young solicitor-barrister specialised in finding pathways through the mire of Australian company law. 'Basically, I'm not a businessman or a banker, I'm a lawyer,' he said with one of his puckish grins to explain the unconventional methods that had made him Australia's first billionaire.[6] His private company, Heytesbury Securities, which owned a controlling interest in his flagship Bell Group, was named after a distant relative, Lord Heytesbury, the nineteenth-century British ambassador to Moscow. Holmes à Court used the Heytesbury insignia and wore a Heytesbury signet ring on his little finger in the blue-blood manner.[7]

For less than $100,000, he bought control of a threadbare woollen mill and made it profitable, then moved into natural resources after acquiring the Bell Group, an engineering and transportation concern. In his office high above St Georges Terrace in downtown Perth, he displayed a painting entitled 'Melbourne Burning', which, in the style of Hieronymus Bosch, depicted people writhing in an inferno.[8] The painting could be seen as a metaphor for his relationship with Melbourne-based BHP, which would range over a seven-year period from hostile to inflammatory.

By the time he went after BHP, Holmes à Court had developed a formidable track record, even giving Rupert Murdoch a run for his money in the 1979 battle for control of Sir Reg Ansett's road haulage, airline and television empire. He entered the 1980s with $100 million in cash and strategic stakes in a range of companies. What made the coming battle for BHP especially piquant was that Holmes à Court clashed with John Elliott in 1981 when he bid $120 million for the agricultural and pastoral company Elder Smith Goldsbrough Mort. The battle culminated in a reverse takeover in which Elders appeared to buy Elliott's jam-maker Henry Jones IXL but in fact Elliott and his directors ended up controlling the new company.

Sir Ian McLennan came out of retirement at 72 to become chairman of Elders IXL, with Elliott as chief executive.[9] Having passed the mandatory retiring age for directors, McLennan had been obliged to relinquish the chairmanship of BHP in 1977, but Elders' articles of association were specially altered to let him take the chair. Sir Norman Young, the displaced chairman, described McLennan's action as 'a strange combination of conceit and blind self-interest'.[10] But Elliott, then just 40, wasn't going into these uncharted waters without his tried and trusted friend McLennan at the helm. 'He was very tough, very straight, very smart and a very good negotiator,' Elliott says. 'He taught me a lot.'[11]

Holmes à Court pocketed a $16.5 million profit from this first skirmish with Elliott – by buying low and selling at the takeover premium – and turned his attention to Britain. There, he took over Lew Grade's Associated Communications Corporation (ACC) after it was almost sunk by Grade's disastrous venture into film production with *Raise the Titanic*. 'It would have been cheaper to lower the Atlantic,' the ageing showman grumbled to the press. Overnight, Holmes à Court demoted him, in the words of one commentator, 'from film mogul to third spear-carrier on the left'.[12]

Holmes à Court then turned his guns directly on Elliott's Elders IXL and his newly acquired Carlton & United Breweries, the makers of Foster's lager. Elliott fought him off but again Holmes à Court retired with a healthy addition to his war chest. 'Money is one of the tools of the trade I am in,' he told reporters in one of his pithy little homilies.

His first tilt at BHP was made on 15 August 1983 through one of Bell's newly acquired subsidiaries, Wigmores Limited, the West Australian distributor of Caterpillar tractors. Sir James McNeill, BHP's chairman, was puzzled. 'Who are Wigmores?' he inquired.[13] It was a good question. No one in Melbourne's financial community seemed to have heard of the audacious interloper. The bid had no chance of success. Wigmores was capitalised at just $39 million and its Part A takeover offer of two Wigmores shares for one BHP share amounted to a market value of $3.715 billion. The offer closed with acceptances for a mere 0.23 per cent of BHP's shares.

Undaunted, Holmes à Court changed Wigmores' name to Bell Resources, then on 20 February he announced an offer for BHP of seven Bell shares for four BHP shares aimed at increasing his holding in BHP to just under eight per cent. Casually puffing one of his cigars, he announced that BHP would be far more attractive to stockholders if it were split into three separate companies – petroleum, minerals and steel – confirming the suspicions of the company faithful that he intended to dispose of many assets in the biggest fire sale Australia had ever seen. John Clark, executive general manager in charge of corporate affairs at BHP House, the company's new customised headquarters in William Street, says, 'There was a lot of concern among us who were not right in the action but on the edge that we were going to be owned by someone we didn't know and then broken up for financial reasons.'[14]

Jerry Ellis, then manager of the Port Kembla steelworks, sought to reassure his workforce. 'Look, we have a set of owners now who are remote from us,' he told them. 'If Holmes à Court takes us over, we'll just have another set of owners. Life will be unchanged. Just get on with the job.'[15]

Holmes à Court might have been Western Australia's favourite adopted son, but his main adversary at BHP, 54-year-old Brian Thorley Loton, scion of a wealthy West Australian family, had actually been born in Perth and educated at the prestigious Hale School. He was also a lot tougher than some people gave him credit for. 'Brian was my boss – I reported directly to him, so I saw him quite often,' says John Clark, who marvelled at Loton's stoical capacity to withstand the multiple pressures of his office. 'I've known him all my life. I'd met him at university – we were in the same university college, although he was two years ahead of me. While he was fighting off Holmes à Court, he said, "It's business as usual." That was his approach:

that this thing should not interfere with the work of the management committees or our operations.'[16]

John Prescott, who had followed Loton into Newcastle in 1958 and was now general manager of BHP's transport subsidiary, says, 'Brian Loton had been Ian McLennan's right-hand man – he was much younger, of course, but was regarded as a brilliant metallurgist-cum-engineer. Brian was really the driving force behind the development of the company, certainly in the '80s and for a while before that.'[17]

Loton and his chairman acted swiftly to neutralise Holmes à Court's new offer. BHP announced a one-for-five bonus issue to its shareholders and splurged on a nationwide advertising campaign. There was plenty to shout about: the Bass Strait operations were making millions and the new Jabiru field in the Timor Sea off the north-west Australian coast was producing astonishing results, while the dramatic purchase of Utah International, described in the following chapter, had brought some of the rich coal mines of Central Queensland into the BHP fold.

Loton and McLennan also engaged Macquarie Bank's executive director Graeme Samuel[18] and Morgan Stanley's vice president Charles Tait to fend off the raid. Samuel says, 'I spent, oh gosh, 18 months, almost every day, up at BHP on the executive floor there in what was called The Bunker assisting in the various matters we had to deal with in terms of the takeover by Holmes à Court. The initial catalyst of the process was when Potters Partners, which traditionally had been the broking house of BHP, decided to act as the broker for Bell Resources in the acquisition of shares in BHP. And that caused a great deal of consternation at BHP because they felt that Potters had switched horses. We'd been brought in to advise and assisted in the whole series of processes that occurred over many, many months.'[19]

One problem, he says, was Derek Sawer's public-relations 'coup' over The Big Australian nickname: 'That was not good because it was focusing on the "big" rather than the

"Australian".' Big was not necessarily good. 'Secondly, we were in the midst of an entrepreneurial boom and the takeover merchants were seen as the great heroes of the share market. If you weren't one of them, you were seen as being staid, stodgy, conservative, ripe for takeover and appropriate to be taken over.'

However, he says, the biggest challenge was the corporate laws that permitted partial takeovers. In the wake of a bid, the big institutions would sell most of their shares to secure the takeover premium while small shareholders would hold on. But once the acquisition was completed and the takeover premium disappeared, the institutions would buy back into the company at the lower price. Indeed, Samuel recalls the 'outrageous threats' made by some institutions to Macquarie Bank demanding that they 'back off' and permit the takeover to succeed. 'There was one particular institution that behaved very, very badly,' he says, 'an investment-fund manager that behaved very badly indeed.'[20]

Samuel was also caught in a clash of cultures. While Holmes à Court operated almost alone, BHP had a system of 'institutional governance' that made tactical manoeuvring difficult. 'We spent weeks with the BHP executive analysing who would be best to approach Robert Holmes à Court to talk to him,' he says. 'I felt the best thing was to pick up the phone and ring him, but no, we had to work out who would be the best person.'

Finally, Samuel called Holmes à Court's lawyer, Peter Petrachus, whom he knew, and they arranged a meeting at Holmes à Court's Spring Street apartment in Melbourne's CBD. 'He was quite a strange individual,' he says. 'He was a combination of strange and charming – he would often let you sit there for half an hour without saying a word.'

Meanwhile, Peter Maund had been extremely industrious. 'We decided to make much more noise in the community,' he says. 'Until then, BHP preferred not to beat the drum too much in public. But because of the need to win hearts and minds, suddenly my budget went up in one year to $9 million to spread the word.'[21]

Almost overnight, he created the BHP Awards for the Institute of Excellence and invited New South Wales governor Sir Roden Cutler VC as the chief judge. 'It was nationally televised,' he says. 'That was part of the push to improve the image of BHP in the minds of the people and to try to impress upon them that it should not be broken up.'

Other initiatives followed in quick succession. An advertising campaign with the new company logo, featuring the stylised map of Australia, blanketed the airwaves. 'The other wing of it was the measuring of the effect of the campaign, particularly with shareholders,' Maund says. 'Previously, it was quite difficult to get the board to take opinion polls seriously. Now, they commissioned a wide range of private polls, not just the general public but socio-economic breakdowns, and most particularly the shareholders.

'We needed a huge majority of the mums-and-dads investors to believe that the invaders should be repelled. And as it turned out, the ordinary non-institutional shareholders were 85 per cent fiercely opposed to any break-up of BHP. This was important not only to have in the armoury in case of an extraordinary general meeting, where the shareholder votes would count, but also to use to show them there was a solid backing for the company.'

Jim McNeill was due to step down as chairman in mid-1984 and be replaced by Sir James Balderstone. While Holmes à Court's bid was still on the table, the outgoing and incoming chairmen flew to London in April 1984 to reassure the London investment community that they had no intention of allowing this interloper to interfere with BHP's operations. Indeed, the Bell offer succeeded in boosting Holmes à Court's stake in BHP to just 4.5 per cent.[22]

BHP's shareholders had no reason to regret their decision to stick with the management when Brian Loton reported a profit of $442 million for the previous fiscal year, a figure greatly enhanced by his achievement in retooling the steel division, which had suffered from a slump in world prices since 1982 and had desperately needed modernisation.

But these were no more than preliminary rounds to the main event, and they attracted little more than passing interest from John Elliott, who was busy expanding Elders' operations in South East Asia and elsewhere. Elliott had attended the University of Melbourne on a BHP scholarship and The Prop was his first employer. 'The problem with BHP in those days was it was a great bureaucracy, dominated by the steel business,' he says. 'I'd done an honours degree in economics and it didn't seem to be the opportunity to the road to which I aspired. I think they lost most of the scholarship holders, some pretty smart guys. After I did my MBA in 1965, I joined McKinsey [the New York-based management consultants]. Rod Carnegie, who ended up chairman of CRA [Conzinc Rio Tinto of Australia], was the senior partner in Australia. My first job there was to write up the profits of BHP because there was a study in the offing where BHP were going to use McKinsey or one of the other consulting firms, so I spent the first three months analysing BHP. We didn't get the job.'[23]

John Elliott started to take a closer interest in BHP through Balderstone, a pastoralist with strong ties to Elders, the Liberal Party and BHP's largest institutional holder, the Australian Mutual Provident Society. 'I was federal treasurer of the Liberal Party, so Jim Balderstone was a good friend of mine,' Elliott says. 'He'd put me up for the Australian Club a few years earlier.'

The two men went into the trenches together when Bob Hawke called a federal election for 1 December 1984 after less than two years in power. Hawke, however, demolished their candidate, Andrew Peacock, and returned in triumph to The Lodge, while Elliott retreated to his office in the executive suites opposite the old IXL Jam Factory in Garden Street, South Yarra.

Having achieved a 50 per cent share of the Australian brewing market with Carlton & United Breweries' amber nectar, he decided it was time to 'Fosterise the world', starting with the purchase of a British base that would also give him access to Continental Europe. In April 1985, Elders strategists

Peter Scanlon and Andrew Cummins flew to London to seek out the most suitable prospects.[24]

Elliott's craggy face broke into a huge grin when he read their reports, which revealed that the self-satisfied, asset-rich brewers of the United Kingdom were among the most undervalued companies in the world. According to Elliott, Allied-Lyons plc, which had been created by the 1978 merger of Allied Breweries, makers of Teachers whisky and Beefeater gin, and the food and catering group J. Lyons and Co., owners of the eponymous Lyons Corner Houses, purveyors of tea and cakes to the masses since 1909, was 'the most moribund of them all'. Employing more than 70,000 people, Allied-Lyons was four times the size of Elders and second only to Bass Charrington as the biggest brewer in Britain.

Elliott planned to gain control of Allied for £1.7 billion (about $3.4 billion at that time) and recoup up to £1.2 billion by selling off the non-beer divisions and another £400 million by selling 50 per cent of each of Allied's 7000 tied houses (hotels and pubs) to the publicans. If things worked out, he would get his British brewing base for virtually nothing; but first he had to find the necessary funds.

Elliott was as Australian as Foster's lager, yet there was a distinct Runyonesque quality about him. With his shock of curly hair, immense rubbery features, swaggering gait and booming laugh, he seemed made for New York City – the first stop on his fund-raising safari. Boldly informing investment bankers that Elders was about to launch the biggest takeover in the history of the United Kingdom, he fished a piece of paper out of his pocket revealing the details of his master plan and asked them to stump up £2 billion. He didn't quite succeed: when he returned to Garden Street, he had secured credit lines totalling £1.8 billion.[25]

As it happened, Brian Loton, an altogether more conservative figure, had also been trying his luck in the gilded salons of Wall Street. Having seen the effectiveness of BHP's advertising campaign, he had decided to drum up demand for BHP stock and thus make it as expensive as possible for a predator to mount a takeover bid. With the portfolios of Australia's major institutions already bursting with BHP shares, he looked to the United States for new investors. In May 1985, Loton and his chief financial officer Geoffrey Heeley pitched BHP's prospectus to analysts, fund managers and investors after merchant banker Morgan Stanley set up meetings in New York and four other American cities.

The Americans listened politely to the visitors and then asked some pointed questions: why should they invest in an Australian mining company such as BHP when Australian banks – for example the National Australia Bank, whose stars included the 46-year-old Don Argus – were a much more appealing proposition?[26]

While Brian Loton was still abroad, Sir James Balderstone and David Adam, BHP's general manager corporate affairs and chief legal officer, received a 'goodwill visit' from Elliott's chief strategist, Peter Scanlon, who floated the idea of forming an investment partnership between Elders and BHP. The objective would be to afford BHP some measure of protection against predators and, at the same time, improve Elders' financial credibility in the United Kingdom. Balderstone was well aware of BHP's long association with Elders through Sir Colin Syme (who had been a director of Elder Smith) and, now, Sir Ian McLennan. He stalled for time but did not dismiss the idea out of hand.

Elders, meanwhile, had started buying up Allied shares through IXL, an associate company in which Elders held a 49 per cent stake, with the remaining 51 per cent split between two merchant bankers in Monaco: Richard Wiesener, a former finance director of Henry Jones IXL, and Bob Cowper, a former Elders director who had played Test cricket for Australia. Elliott hoped to build a ten per cent holding in Allied before making a public takeover bid. However, news of his intentions leaked out through the banking system and in September 1985 he was forced to announce a premature bid after acquiring only six per cent of the company. The shares had cost an average of £2.05 each, and he offered Allied shareholders £2.55 for their stock.

The chairman of Allied-Lyons, Sir Derrick Holden-Brown, a former naval officer, described the bid in the British financial press as 'an act of sheer piracy'. The City of London pinstripes closed ranks around their endangered brethren and were generally antagonistic towards the Australian interloper. 'Our bid shook the Establishment,' Elliott says.[27]

Back in Melbourne, Elliott and Scanlon called on David Adam to propose that BHP become directly involved in Elders' bid for Allied-Lyons. They suggested BHP underwrite $500 million of the planned equity issue of the bid vehicle, named IXL, in exchange for a 9.9 per cent interest in Elders.[28] The timing was unfortunate. Balderstone was accompanying Brian Loton on a flag-waving tour of Europe and neither had any desire to become embroiled in a hostile takeover bid in Britain that might further antagonise the City of London towards Australian companies.

Nevertheless, discussions continued intermittently between Scanlon and Elliott for Elders and Loton, Adam and Heeley for BHP, but the sticking point was always the same: as Scanlon put it, '9.9 per cent of Elders was not a large enough investment for BHP to take seriously.'[29]

In the end, BHP referred the matter to a seminar of its executives at the Burnham Beeches hotel in the Dandenongs, where it was quietly kicked into touch.

Then, in November, Elliott pulled off a major publicity coup when the Prince and Princess of Wales accepted an invitation to attend the first Foster's Melbourne Cup at Flemington. Prince Charles told him at their first meeting, 'There's a lot of discussion over the dinner table at our place.'

'What's that about, sir?' Elliott inquired.

'Well, I'm strongly supporting your bid for Allied-Lyons and my father is totally against.'

Sitting in his new office in Charter House, a yellow-brick

building opposite the Mitre Tavern off Collins Street at the 'big end of town', John Elliott lights a cigarette and chuckles at the memory.

'Philip regarded Elders as upstarts from the colonies, whereas Charles had been educated here at Geelong Grammar, so he had a very different attitude,' he says. 'That was the memorable day he got up in presenting the Melbourne Cup and said, "This cup should be frothing over with Foster's." It was in every newspaper, on every TV in the UK – it was fantastic for us.'[30]

Allied-Lyons, however, had powerful friends in Westminster, and the Elders bid was referred to the Monopolies and Mergers Commission, which had the power to veto it. 'The whole question was, "Were we financially strong enough to mount the bid for Allied-Lyons?"' Elliott says. 'We had to figure out how we could get some additional strength into Elders. Then we realised BHP was in trouble and that Holmes à Court was going to own them.'

Indeed, 'The Hacca', as he was now known to financial writers, was back. Brian Loton declared on 20 December that there was an 'element of sham' in Holmes à Court's trading methods. 'BHP is prepared and will ensure that the control and direction of the company will not change,' he told a press conference to announce BHP's half-yearly results. 'In the end, someone or ones is going to get very badly burned. It won't be BHP.'

On 16 January 1986, he received a swift riposte when Bell Group outlaid $240 million to buy BHP shares from seven institutions, and 19 days later – at 10 am on 4 February – Holmes à Court called on Sir James Balderstone to tell him that he was making a 'partial bid' of $7.70 cash, or one Bell share and $2.50 cash, for each BHP share. Balderstone was stunned. The bid was worth $1.925 billion and would give Holmes à Court 39 per cent of BHP's stock and control of the company.

'I presume you will be welcoming this good news for your shareholders,' Holmes à Court told him. 'The price is high and I'm sure you'll be very happy.' Controlling himself with some difficulty, Balderstone replied, 'I don't think that's the situation.'

But Holmes à Court continued, 'You previously refused us a seat on the board when I hadn't asked for one, but the position has changed and I now want one.'

Balderstone replied, 'That will be very difficult. I don't believe my co-directors would agree under any circumstances.'

Holmes à Court's response was, 'Well, that is a condition of our offer.'[31]

David Adam then joined the discussion and, after a lot of verbal sparring, Holmes à Court departed an hour and a half later. When the BHP board convened at 3 pm that day, far from endorsing the new bid it unanimously rejected it. At a press conference in the basement of BHP House, Brian Loton told reporters, 'We are not treating this light-heartedly. This is a disruption, or a threatened disruption, to a very important part of Australia's industrial life.'

On 10 February, Balderstone raised the question of a strategic defence over lunch with John Elliott and suggested that Elliott speak to Brian Loton. 'We were chatting to BHP just socially,' Elliott says. 'We said, "We'll offer you a bit of free tactical advice. I'll send my best strategist in – Peter Scanlon – and see if we can work out a defence for you." Holmes à Court was playing the options market pretty well and he was forcing the price up. He was buying his options, then buying the stock against his options, making money on his options – it was a very clever ploy. He was gaining more and more shares. There's no doubt BHP would have been taken over if we hadn't intervened.'[32]

As Elliott saw it, BHP's problem was that its executives 'didn't have those sorts of skills – takeovers were not in their bag of tricks. They were a big organisation and they felt they couldn't be vulnerable because they were BHP, very much a head-in-the-sand attitude. Although they'd done very well in oil, iron ore and coal, the mentality of the company was still the steel business: most of the people like Brian Loton and the others had all come up through steel.'

In the BHP Bunker adjoining the boardroom, the eight-man defence team headed by David Adam and Graeme Samuel applied tight security rules. 'To prevent leaks, papers that were very sensitive were individually numbered, with the instruction that they were to be shredded once dealt with,' Peter Maund says. 'One evening, we gathered to wait for Loton to return from a meeting with Holmes-à (that's how the Bunker people identified him). Their meeting was held in a hotel suite at the top of Collins Street. Loton returned and reported that, upon meeting, he and Holmes-à sat and had a short exchange. Then Holmes-à sat silent. Loton was not going to blink, so they both sat without speaking. Eventually, Loton decided to end the game and strode out.'[33]

The chief executive officer then opened a new front where, he believed, BHP would have a natural advantage: a direct appeal to the federal government. Treasurer Paul Keating was sympathetic to BHP's cause but troubled by the request. 'Brian Loton, who's a substantial bloke, came to see me and Bob Hawke wanting us to stop Holmes à Court acquiring the company,' he says. 'I said to him, "Brian, I don't know how you can ask us to say that someone who wants to buy your shares on the market can't buy them." Even though I would have liked to have done Brian a favour, I didn't quite see how we could.'[34]

Nevertheless, he and Hawke arranged for the company to put their case to a full Cabinet meeting. 'The chairman and all the executive directors of the company came with a bevy of lawyers, including their spokesman Graeme Samuel,' Keating says. 'There would have been about 12 or 13 of them. They sat on one side of the Cabinet room around the old Cabinet table, the square one; they took up one side of the square. And they went on with their case and we heard them sympathetically.'

Samuel has a different memory. 'It was a very uncomfortable experience,' he says. 'I never wanted to do it, never thought it was the wise thing to do; and when you don't feel comfortable about the argument, it's very difficult indeed. So I was in rather an invidious position, and appropriately the government ministers – particularly Keating and [Gareth] Evans – tore us to shreds. They just said, you know, you've got no right to be here.'[35]

Keating says that Brian Loton spoke to him after the meeting. 'I said, "We'll have Holmes à Court there [in the Cabinet room] tomorrow," and he said, "I know, Paul, I've got to tell you, he's fantastic; you know he's his own financial adviser, his own lawyer, his own analyst and his own operator. He's phenomenal."

'And the next day, we had Holmes à Court. And he just came in by himself. He had answers to all the things we raised. If you had to score the events, he won the event: his logic was more compelling, the delivery of the story was more real, in the sense that he was doing it.'

The raider from the West had won the day. Keating voiced the will of the Cabinet: 'The market must decide.'

Back at the Jam Factory, BHP became known in Elders' war games as 'Elephant', not only because of its size but because the elephant was Elliott's lucky charm – elephant motifs adorned his ties, and dozens of elephant ornaments decorated his office. Elliott put a new proposal to BHP on 26 March 1986, two days before the Easter holiday, in which BHP would take up one thousand redeemable preference shares in Elders for a total amount of $1 billion.[36] With Holmes à Court beating at the door, the BHP board considered the proposal the next day, and Brian Loton telephoned Elliott to say the directors thought it was worth pursuing.

Meanwhile, the share price of Allied-Lyons had risen sharply and was now too high to make it an attractive takeover target. Without waiting for the Monopolies Commission to deliver its verdict, Elliott sold nearly all of his Allied shares, banking a profit of $83.5 million. He still had ambitions in the United Kingdom and still needed BHP's support, but Brian Loton and co. were moving too slowly for his liking. 'We decided the only way for us to get our extra equity,' he says, 'was to take a strong stake in BHP.'

Elders finance director Ken Jarrett arranged a meeting with merchant bankers Wardley Australia to discuss a new loan facility of $1.87 billion in conjunction with the National Australia Bank, the ANZ Banking Group and the Bank of Tokyo. At the same time, Andrew Cummins updated his research on BHP, which indicated four scenarios, all of them positive from Elders' point of view:

1. Elders would buy 20 per cent of BHP, which would persuade BHP to make a $1 billion investment in Elders.
2. If BHP did not agree to that investment, Elders would sell to Holmes à Court and give him control of BHP.
3. If neither BHP nor Holmes à Court played ball, Elders would hold the balance of power and be able to determine the future of BHP.
4. BHP was always a sound investment anyway, offering definite advantages to Elders shareholders.

Elliott had circled Thursday, 10 April in his diary as the day he planned to launch the share raid. On the eve of battle, everything in Garden Street appeared rosy, but behind closed doors frantic scenes were taking place. In one room, Elliott was authorising his brokers to pay up to $7.36 for each BHP share, a rise of 80 cents above that day's closing price; in a second room, he and Jarrett were negotiating the necessary finance with a coterie of the bankers led by National Australia Bank's Don Argus.

Argus had joined the National after leaving school in Brisbane and, as well as becoming a star hockey player, had worked his way from the post room in the suburban Redcliffe branch to the chief executive's office. He lifted his bank from third to top of the Big Four. It brought him into contact not only with John Elliott but with Alan Bond, Larry Adler and Robert Holmes à Court. 'Buccaneering days,' Argus later described those times. 'I ran the credit-risk area of the bank at the time and saw all the deals.'[37]

Indeed, as chairman of BHP Billiton, he told the authors,

'I knew exactly what was happening that night [in Garden Street]. I can remember walking out of the Elders meeting when everyone else was there and John was doing his usual thing. I said, "I'm out of here. You don't need me." He said, "Bloody get back here," and I said, "Not in this environment; you deal with me separately."'[38]

In a third room, Peter Scanlon was negotiating a $1 billion preference-share deal with two BHP executives who remained blissfully ignorant that their company was soon to be the target of a share raid by these very same people.

At 10 am on 10 April 1986, Elders went into the market in the biggest buying spree in Australian stock-exchange history. 'We bought 18 or 19 per cent of the company for $1.8 billion, much to the delight of our three Melbourne stockbrokers,'[39] Elliott says. 'As I recall, the going rate was about two per cent. I think I shaved a bit off it, but they made a lot of money.'

During the morning session, more than a hundred million BHP shares changed hands at $7.36, giving Elders ten per cent of the company. By the close of business that day, this had risen to 15 or 16 per cent, while overnight buying in London and further buying in Melbourne on 11 April took the number of shares purchased to 231,028,581, or 18.56 per cent of BHP's capital.[40] Says Elliott, 'One of the two men at the National Bank who lent me a billion dollars was Don Argus – a good man, an outstanding man.'[41]

Elliott's so-called white-knight defence of BHP was designed to give Elders extra leverage in its bid for a British brewery and, at the same time, prevent Holmes à Court taking over BHP. Holmes à Court – codenamed 'Warthog' by the Elliott team – was at home in Perth with a head cold when he learned that he had a rival bidder for BHP; he packed his bags and headed for Melbourne.

Brian Loton had been speculating with Sir James Balderstone about the identity of the mystery buyer of BHP shares when Elliott telephoned BHP House and confirmed their suspicions that Elders was the guilty party. 'We were in the driving seat,'

Elliott says. 'We could sell out to Holmes à Court, which we never had any intention of doing provided we got some cooperation from BHP. Within a week, we'd convinced BHP they'd better put a billion into Elders.'

First, BHP bought Elders convertible bearer bonds for $200 million, amounting to 12 per cent of the company's issued capital, and then began preparing an analysis of the $1 billion preference-share proposal. When Elliott, Peter Scanlon and stockbroker John Baillieu turned up at BHP House for a meeting, Loton assured them he would recommend the issue to a meeting of the BHP board the following morning.

John Elliott told the BHP representatives, 'Holmes à Court is going to fix you right up.' But BHP was still reluctant to embrace any scheme that involved investing in Elders and turned down every one of Elliott's proposals.

Graeme Samuel says that at one meeting Elliott fatally alienated the BHP executive. 'Although Elliott was part of the Establishment, in just one movement they pushed them too far and it got the board very much on the defensive,' he says. 'I think they demanded the chairmanship be handed over to Elliott or a nominee but suddenly it created a tension that blew the whole thing up. It was the squeeze of the orange that got the pip.'[42]

The showdown meeting between Elliott and Holmes à Court took place in Elliott's South Yarra flat at 10 am on Saturday, 12 April. For two long hours, devoid of chit-chat, let alone chivalrous gestures, each man offered to buy the other's holding in BHP, with Holmes à Court cheekily suggesting to Elliott at one point that a takeover of Elders might free him to pursue his interest in politics. 'We'd get control [of BHP],' he said, 'and you'd get to be prime minister.'

The BHP board had convened at the same time and when that meeting broke up Loton telephoned Elliott to report that the directors had approved the $1 billion proposal. Elliott, who was president of Carlton Football Club among his many other duties, went off to the football and watched Carlton beat St Kilda by 88 points. 'Holmes à Court was an exceptionally difficult person,' he says. 'One day, I was negotiating with him in his Spring Street apartment near the Windsor Hotel. We must have spent three hours seeing if we could work something through and he said, "Well, I've got to go out for dinner." I said, "I've got to do something too, so we'll resume at 9.30 in the morning." We resumed at 9.30 and it was as though the previous day's discussions hadn't taken place. That happened to me many times. He'd wipe the slate clean and start again. The other thing he did, which was a great artform on his part, was he used meetings to glean data. He and [Kerry] Packer were the best I've ever seen at it – Packer was good. You'd go and see Packer and he'd ask you question after question. Holmes à Court would ask you a question which you would answer and you'd ask him a question and he would sit there and say nothing. In fact, if you weren't careful you'd start talking again. I used to sit there: there were ten-minute silences when I met him, quarter of an hour silences.'[43]

Graeme Samuel says, 'The problem was the two of them could never reach agreement; they just didn't trust each other. And that worked to our advantage.' Holmes à Court had roughly 20 per cent of the company, Elliott also had around 20 per cent – together 48 per cent – and neither trusted the other, while BHP trusted neither. 'Suddenly, you've got a very nice triangle,' Samuel says. 'And playing that triangle off against each other and reaching an ultimate accommodation was what Morgan Stanley and Macquarie Bank had to do.'[44]

Elders' sweetheart deal with BHP had more than doubled shareholders' funds in the company from $688 million in 1985 to $1.86 billion in 1986. This information was reported to the Monopolies Commission, which gave Elders a clean bill of health in September 1986. By then, however, Elliott's attention had switched from Allied-Lyons to a new target: the giant Courage Brewery, ranked fifth in Britain with more than 5600 tied public houses and 386 bottle shops. Its owner was the Hanson Trust, run by Lord James Hanson in London and Sir Gordon White in New York.[45]

'Lord Hanson had just bought Imperial Tobacco,' Elliott says. 'He wanted the tobacco side – a great cash-flow business – but he didn't want the brewing side. So prior to the Monopolies Commission concluding in our favour, we had already negotiated a purchase price with Hanson. When the Monopolies Commission approval came through, we bought Courage for $3.5 billion. It wasn't all one-way traffic in our efforts to help save BHP. It was win–win, absolute win–win. By that time, the BHP share price was a good deal higher than our price – we had won there, we had got our money, we had taken over Courage and we had started to Fosterise the world.'[46]

While Elliott was abroad that September, a ceasefire, if not exactly a truce, had been brokered in Melbourne that gave Elliott and Holmes à Court seats on the BHP board in exchange for a commitment that neither would buy out the other without making a tender in cash for all outstanding shares – a multi-billion-dollar proposition that was beyond the reach of either man.

After eight months of vituperation, writs, court cases, TV appearances and hostile press conferences, BHP veterans had never witnessed scenes to match those that unfolded on Monday, 15 September, when Elliott and Holmes à Court arrived separately at BHP House. Secretly, they completed the documentation to become BHP directors and then lunched with the other board members. Shortly after 3 pm, Sir James Balderstone and Brian Loton appeared at a press conference flanked by Elliott and Holmes à Court, all four smiling broadly.

Holmes à Court described the deal as a 'triumph of common sense'. 'It brings to an end a very wasteful exercise in corporate warfare,' he said. 'It means that all the parties, the shareholder blocks, the company's board, its management, can all work together now with the object of improving the company. And I certainly pledge Bell's support to bringing that about.'[47]

Elliott concurred: 'As Robert Holmes à Court said, the aim will now be to improve the performance of the company rather than fighting peripheral issues.' Sir James Balderstone was at his most diplomatic: 'With the contribution of Mr Holmes à Court and Mr Elliott, BHP will continue to generate profits and growth guided by an independent board appointed by and answerable to shareholders as a whole.'[48]

There was no sign of John Elliott, however, when Holmes à Court attended his first board meeting at 9.30 am on Friday, 19 September. He had returned to London to complete a few matters concerning the Courage takeover. 'We wanted to get on with our brewing operations, so in the end there was a stand-off at BHP,' Elliott says. 'We were friendly with Balderstone and Loton, and they didn't like Holmes à Court at all. He came from the West, so he was the aggressor; we weren't.'

Geoff Heeley found the whole takeover episode distasteful. 'It was an interesting era and a very stressful era,' he says. 'When something goes on for three or four years, it becomes difficult, and as far as I'm concerned it's one of those issues which a lot of us were very happy to put behind us.'[49]

'A lot of credit goes to Brian Loton,' says John Clark. 'One of the protections against Holmes à Court was to have a viable and vibrant business. Brian was very good at stroking the public, the shareholders and the bankers. He was very focused. Few people could have done it, but he was an absolute professional.'[50]

Brian Loton, his steely-grey hair now white and his leonine profile still firm, smiles contentedly over a drink at the Dorchester Hotel in Park Lane. 'Well, others could probably describe it better than I could,' he says modestly, 'but I can only say that the people involved had unsustainable strategies.'[51]

In October 1987, John Elliott had been staying not far from the Dorchester at the Elders house at no. 1 St James's Street. 'I'd just got married again and we had our honeymoon in England,' he says. 'The Ritz was just around the corner and we'd eat there often. We also had a house up in Hertfordshire and a house in the South of France. I'd had a nice two weeks off, my football team had won the premiership and we were running along quite well.'[52]

On Sunday, 18 October, Elliott and his wife Amanda[53] were driven to Heathrow airport for the flight back to Melbourne. Before they landed at Tullamarine, the fair financial wind gave way to a fiscal tornado that would scatter all the Australian raiders in the confusion of a stock-market collapse.

CHAPTER 9

Utah Unbound

Through all the *Sturm und Drang* of the 1980s, Brian Loton quietly advanced his main objective of turning BHP into a multinational company that could reap a great harvest from overseas investments. 'We don't underestimate the difficulties of going multinational,' the 56-year-old chief executive told the *New York Times* during a flying visit to the United States in the company Gulfstream jet in 1985. 'But we aren't daunted by them. We have been involved in the international world for a long time.'[1]

BHP's quest for offshore assets had come after many years of operating with foreign companies in joint ventures at home. 'Every major international resource company interested in venturing into Australia has, sooner or later, to knock on BHP's door,' says Arthur Reef, a consultant to AMAX, the American mining company that partnered BHP in the Pilbara iron-ore operation. 'Those knocks have resulted in countless joint ventures. The experience has been invaluable to BHP.'[2]

The Prop had already infiltrated the American steel and oil markets, producing around 40 per cent of its revenues in American dollars, while 85 per cent of its costs were paid in the cheaper Australian currency. The margin was such that every one-cent swing in the exchange rate represented a US$13 million shift in BHP's profits.[3]

The man who provided Loton with a golden opportunity to boost the company's American assets was John Francis Welch Jr, the blue-eyed Irish-American boss of the massive General Electric Company. Welch was known to corporate America as 'Neutron Jack', because, it was said, whenever he took over a company the buildings remained intact but the people vanished. On becoming the youngest-ever chief executive of Thomas Edison's old firm in 1981, the 45-year-old had embarked on a five-year program of acquisition and divestment, closing 73 plants and facilities and slashing GE's staff from 411,000 at the end of 1980 to 299,000 at the end of 1985.[4]

When he applied his cast-iron rule of 'fix it, sell it or fold it' to one of GE's main subsidiaries, Utah International Inc., BHP was presented with the chance to acquire the American miner's valuable assets not only in the United States but also in South Africa, Peru, Chile – and Australia itself.

Jack Welch's predecessor, Reginald H. Jones, had purchased Utah in 1976 as a hedge against inflation for US$2.3 billion[5] in the largest acquisition ever seen in the United States. 'The chairman of Utah, Edmund Wattis "Ed" Littlefield, was on the board of General Electric,' says Tim Winterer, a mining engineer who had joined Utah in the iron country around Cedar City in south-western Utah in 1960. 'He convinced Reg Jones that GE ought to have a minerals division, but when Jack Welch became chairman he said, "What are we doing with this mining company? Get rid of it!"'[6]

Welch wanted consistent income growth from all of his sectors, and the cyclical nature of the minerals market in which prices fluctuated wildly according to the laws of supply and demand concerned him. 'I didn't like the natural-resource business, where I felt events were often beyond your control,' he explains.[7]

The Utah Construction Company, founded in 1900 by Littlefield's grandfather Edmund Wattis and his brothers

William and Warren Wattis, had built the massive Hoover Dam on the Colorado River and the bomb-proof silos that housed intercontinental ballistic missiles. In between, Utah diversified into mining with the purchase of the Marcona copper mine in Peru, the Pathfinder uranium mines in Wyoming and the Navajo coal mine and power plant in the Four Corners area of the south-west United States, where the borders of Arizona, Colorado, New Mexico and Utah all meet.

The company moved from Ogden, Utah, to new headquarters in San Francisco and changed its name to Utah Construction & Mining Company, which first came to Australia to work on Victoria's Eildon Dam and the Snowy Mountains Scheme. Its excavation expertise made it a natural contender for open-cut mining, with the result that one of its subsidiaries, the Utah Development Company, largely developed the Central Queensland coal deposits to supply metallurgical (or coking) coal to a thriving world steel industry.

The existence of coal in the Bowen Basin had been known for many years but, owing to lack of demand, the Queensland Mines Department had never conducted a detailed geological survey of the area. In the late 1950s, Utah geologist Richard Ellett searched the basin for minerals suitable for large-scale open-cut mining, especially iron ore and coking coal. As a result, Utah took out exploration permits covering 2400 square miles and hired local geologist Don King, who located the gently sloping sides of the coal seam through test drilling. The Blackwater open-cut mine was opened by the Queensland premier, Jack Pizzey, and Littlefield's predecessor as Utah's chairman, Marriner S. Eccles, at a ceremony at the mining site on 11 May 1968.

On the Utah side, the prime movers in the deal with the State of Queensland had been its president, Alexander M. 'Bud' Wilson, senior vice president Keith Wallace and Ralph Long, who became Blackwater's first manager. The most powerful advocate in the Queensland Government was Johannes Bjelke-Petersen, who became premier in August 1968 following Jack Pizzey's sudden death. The Kingaroy peanut-farmer-turned-politician was quick to take the initiative in promoting the state's minerals abroad, particularly to the Japanese. Dignitaries turning up at a reception in Tokyo found that the centrepiece was a large ice sculpture in the shape of Australia, with the state of Queensland highlighted in blue. 'During the evening, the ice melted and the southern states gradually disappeared until only Queensland was left,' says Gillespie Robertson, one of the Utah marketing men present. 'Then we found out that the blue was really made of plastic.'[8]

The Utah men soon became aware that Bjelke-Petersen was somewhat touchy on the question of interstate rivalry. Robertson, who had worked at Utah headquarters in San Francisco, was posted to Sydney when Utah opened its marketing department in Australia. 'We'd been advised that Sydney was the commercial hub of Australia,' he says. 'This was a big mistake. The Queensland Government didn't appreciate it at all, so the office was quickly moved to Brisbane.'[9]

Under the Central Queensland Coal Associates Agreement Act, Utah and its Japanese partner, the Mitsubishi Development Company, were given the right to develop export coal mines at Blackwater, Goonyella, Peak Downs, Saraji and Norwich Park. The Queensland Government agreed to pay for roads, water supplies, hospitals and other facilities in the area and claim only a low royalty rate of five cents per ton until 2010 in return for profitable rail-freight charges.[10]

'The mines were all open-cut and were located in cattle country in the Bowen Basin but not very good cattle country, probably ten acres per cow and 20 inches of rain a year,' says Tim Winterer, who became Utah's chief engineer in Queensland in 1969. 'I often met Bjelke-Petersen – he was quite a character, a down-to-earth guy, very religious. We were happy with the deal and I think he did a good deal for the state, too, although he was criticised because it was thought the royalties were too low. We ended up building a dam for the railroad and turning it over to the Queensland Railways Department, and we paid for the terminal at Hay Point.'[11]

Utah quickly became Australia's largest exporter of coal. The tough-guy Australian actor Rod Taylor was hired to front a series of 'good corporate citizen' TV advertisements extolling the company's virtues. 'Well, it's a long way from Hollywood to Hay Point, but that's where I am right now,' Rod declared. 'South of Mackay, Queensland. The Utah Development Company built Hay Point. Utah is Australia's largest exporter of coal. You know, they tell me, over the last decade, hundreds of millions of dollars have been spent up here. The important thing for Australia is that every time Utah spends a dollar it inspires other industries to spend $4. I learned there's enough coal up here to last for hundreds of years, so development can continue to grow, the towns are going to grow larger, and the jobs are going to be increased. Utah is going to spend a lot more money in Australia, as will other industries. Utah believes in backing Australia.'

Jack Welch, however, did not believe in backing Utah. 'It was clear in my mind the first day on the job that it had to go,' he says.[12] Matters came to a head in late 1981 when Bud Wilson, who had stayed on as Utah's chairman, was called to GE's corporate headquarters at Fairfield, Connecticut, to explain a $75 million shortfall in revenue after the Japanese had refused to accept contracted shipments of coal and a major labour dispute had broken out with the Australian mining unions. Within GE, it was holy writ that the company always made its numbers. If one business faltered, the others were obliged to make up the difference. But it was clear to Welch that Utah's variable performance would prove an unacceptable drag on GE's other divisions.[13]

In 1982, after just one year in the top job, he went looking for a buyer. His mission got off to a rocky start when American natural-resources companies turned him down. According to Brian Loton, it was Ed Littlefield, one of Welch's largest shareholders, who suggested that BHP seemed to be a natural fit for Utah, whose massive open-cut mines in the Bowen Basin complemented BHP's coal-mining activities in New South Wales.

Welch's deputy John Burlingame first raised the possibility of selling Utah to BHP in a private conversation with BHP's chairman Jim McNeill during a visit to BHP House on 23 August 1982. 'Utah wasn't offered to anybody else,' Brian Loton recalls. 'Jack Welch and his people had decided that BHP were the logical buyers and it would be worth more to us than to anybody else, which is quite true.'[14] As we shall see, there was in fact another prospective buyer – revealed here for the first time.

Burlingame valued all of Utah's assets at a colossal US$3.5 billion – which was actually half a billion dollars more than BHP's capital value at that time. Nevertheless, BHP's directors decided at a board meeting on 10 September to enter into negotiations with GE – a decision that marked the turning point in The Big Australian's modern history. The directors accepted that if they didn't buy Utah, BHP would revert to being a company with faltering steelworks and an ageing oilfield in Bass Strait, a company that was primarily dependent on one country – Japan – for most of its revenue. 'Brian Loton's vision of the Utah acquisition was that it should be used to expand the company overseas,' says John Prescott, then general manager of BHP Transport. 'Although the principal assets GE were offering were the coal mines in Queensland, Brian saw that Utah should be used to diversify BHP out of Australia because BHP was outgrowing its Australian market: steel was much more stagnant than it had previously been, the heydays had gone, there was a Labor Party in office in Canberra and after the early experience of a Labor Government in the early '70s nobody was quite sure just how socialist they'd be and how much control they'd try and exercise. It turned out they didn't, but we didn't know that when we were acquiring Utah. But Brian had this vision and he managed to implement it.'[15]

Utah's profits from its Queensland operation had soared from a modest $8 million in 1970 after all taxes, royalties and costs had been deducted to $137 million in 1976, the year it was snapped up by Reg Jones to diversify GE's portfolio following the

First Oil Shock. No other company operating in Australia had ever made so much money. At the same time, BHP recorded a profit of $63.5 million, less than half of Utah's. And while BHP employed more than 60,000 Australian workers, Utah made do with just 2700. Since then, Utah continued to produce enormous profits despite Jack Welch's innate abhorrence of the fluctuating nature of commodity prices.

Under Utah's deal with the Queensland Government, coal was transported from the mines to the Hay Point terminal in trains consisting of six locomotives and 148 wagons carrying 8500 tons of coal worth $400,000. Every week, more than 70 such trains hauled the rich coking coal down to the coast to bulk ore carriers queuing up to take their cargoes to Japan and Europe. And each week the Utah Development Company rang up another $3 million in clear profit.

This arrangement seemed so beneficial to the American miner that in 1977 investigators from the ABC's *Four Corners* program asked why the deal provided relatively few benefits to the Australian public but gave a huge return to Utah's American shareholders. On the program, Doug Anthony, then federal minister for national resources, defended Utah as 'a pathfinder of coal development in Queensland . . . they went in, they explored the area, they developed it when coal prices were very low and they made a success of it'.

Paul Keating, the shadow minister, sounded a more nationalistic note. 'While we certainly do need a proportion of foreign capital,' he said, 'the control and ownership of Australian resources ought to be the prime requirement of Australian resource-development policy.'

Much of Utah's success, it was revealed, emanated from the deals it had done with the Queensland Government. State taxes and royalties paid by Utah in 1976 accounted for less than four per cent of the company's total revenue, or $21 million, while rail freight to the Queensland Government amounted to ten per cent, or $56 million. At the same time, the company's profit was nearly 25 per cent of the revenue, or $137 million.[16]

The first meeting between representatives of BHP and GE to discuss Project Utah was scheduled to be held in Honolulu, roughly halfway between the head offices in Melbourne and New York, starting on 21 September 1982. Jack Welch told his vice chairman John Burlingame and senior vice president Frank Doyle to work out the best strategy, while Paolo Fresco, GE's Italian-born, London-based vice president, was summoned to the States to lead the GE negotiating team.[17]

On the BHP side, Brian Loton chose David Adam, an executive director for more than five years, as team leader and co-opted Bill Hunter, chief finance officer since 1979, to manage the intricate financing arrangements. In the ensuing reshuffle, Geoff Heeley, who had been treasurer, became acting finance director and Graeme McGregor replaced Heeley as treasurer. The two other members of the negotiating team were Russ Fynmore, head of the oil-and-gas division, whose brief was to examine Utah's American energy subsidiary, Ladd Petroleum, and Dick Carter, general manager resource planning and development.

Both teams checked into the Kahala Hilton Hotel. Two of GE's team, vice president Standley 'Stan' Hoch and tax counsel Walter Beaman, were alarmed when they arrived at the conference room at 8 am on Tuesday, 21 September 1982 to discover that hotel staff had placed a noticeboard outside the door with 'General Electric' boldly spelled out in white plastic letters.

The GE men were discussing this lapse in security when they were joined by David Adam and Bill Hunter. Someone had the bright idea of rearranging the letters to form an anagram that converted 'General Electric' into a mythical corporation called 'Carter Gellee Inc'. From then on, Project Utah was known as 'Carter Gellee'.[18]

Negotiations got off to a promising start, with the BHP team learning that GE were looking for a price based on the discounted present value of future estimated cash flows. GE agreed to supply additional financial estimates to enable BHP to evaluate Utah's various businesses. Its team also turned over a valuation of Utah prepared by Morgan Stanley the previous year.

The following month, Graeme McGregor was on his way to Mexico for a meeting of the International Federation of Accountants when he received instructions from Melbourne to go via New York and retain the mergers and acquisitions specialists Sullivan & Cromwell to advise BHP. Both BHP and GE had agreed to negotiate directly with each other, but BHP needed counsel's opinion on United States acquisition and tax laws.

'Utah would probably have preferred to stay with GE, where they were autonomous, as opposed to being merged into a bigger mining company,' McGregor says.[19] However, the wishes of the Utah staff – and their counterparts at BHP Minerals – took second place to the urgent business at hand, as the two negotiating teams shuttled between Melbourne and New York. 'There were some hiccups early in the piece,' McGregor says. 'Quite frankly, one of the things that worried our negotiators was a meeting where GE put a different team of negotiators in and tried to start afresh, which we didn't think was appropriate.'[20]

After haggling, GE reduced the value of Utah's assets, minus Ladd Petroleum, which it decided to retain, to US$2.85 billion, whereas BHP's figure for the same package was US$2.375 billion. 'We simply can't afford it,' David Adam pleaded on one occasion. 'I'll just have to put myself into your hands.'[21]

By agreement, Brian Loton and Jim McNeill kept their distance from the negotiations. 'I was helping in the background, as it were,' Loton says. 'I knew Jack Welch reasonably well and met him at functions in San Francisco a few times during the negotiations.'[22]

As 1982 drew to a close, a couple of other Utah assets had been taken off the table, and the asking price whittled down to US$2.6 billion, enabling a letter of intent to be signed in mid-December. 'There were handshakes all round,' says Carrol Houser, human-resources vice president at GE, Utah and subsequently BHP, who later wrote a history of the Utah acquisition at Brian Loton's request. All that remained was for BHP's directors to give their approval at BHP's regular December board meeting in Melbourne.

The manager of Utah Development's operations in Australia since 1982 was James T. Curry, a civil engineer and Stanford business graduate who had once been Ed Littlefield's assistant. He was based in Eagle Street, Brisbane, overlooking the broad sweep of the Brisbane River. The talks had been kept so secret that he was blissfully unaware of the drama unfolding around him. 'I'd been down in Melbourne to see if we could find somebody to go on our local Utah board and I'd approached one of the members of the BHP board,' he says. 'He later told me that he knew this was going on and he knew I didn't know. He was terribly concerned that he had to keep going along with this charade.'[23]

Jack Welch was in a celebratory mood when he arrived at the Park Lane Hotel in New York for the annual staff Christmas dinner-and-dance party. He was chatting and joking with senior executives and their wives when things started to go wrong. At 11 pm, John Burlingame was called off the dance floor and when he returned half an hour later he was visibly shaken. 'Jack,' he whispered, 'the deal's off. I got a call from Paolo. He said that BHP just called him to say its board couldn't go through with it. They can't swing it financially.'[24]

Welch was devastated: he had been counting on BHP to take this ill-fitting piece of the GE corporate jigsaw off his hands. After Christmas, he ordered Burlingame and his team to get into a huddle with BHP to resurrect Project Carter Gellee and work out a new deal. If BHP couldn't raise the full asking price, Welch said, then GE would simply have to remove some more of the assets from the inventory.

On 27 January 1983, GE announced it had reached a tentative agreement to sell Utah International Inc. and the

Utah-Marcona Corporation to BHP for US$2.4 billion in cash.[25] Under an agreement signed on 19 April, GE would retain the oil-and-gas producer Ladd Petroleum, as well as Utah's interest in the Pathfinder uranium mines in Wyoming, the Trapper steam coal mine in Colorado and some land-development properties in the United States.[26] 'Various things were done,' John Prescott says. 'We sold down the Queensland coal interests to Mitsubishi, Mitsui and a bunch of Australian banks, and we didn't take the oil interests that were in the original package. We got the price down and finally went ahead with it.'[27]

Meanwhile, Graeme McGregor, who was casting the BHP net ever wider in the United States, met a polite young analyst with the New York investment banker Kidder, Peabody. His name was Charles Waterhouse Goodyear IV but everybody called him 'Chip'. 'I've been familiar with BHP for many, many years, but my first direct experience working with them was in 1983,' Chip Goodyear says. 'BHP were looking for some oil-and-gas acquisitions in the United States and I worked with Graeme McGregor, who was the treasurer at the time.'[28]

The Utah acquisition was finally concluded on 2 April 1984 when David Adam handed over BHP cheque no. 0001, drawn on the Morgan Guaranty Trust Company of New York, for US$2,268,447,750 to GE's Stan Hoch at the Wall Street offices of Sullivan & Cromwell. In return, he received a brown satchel containing the Utah share certificates.

The following evening, BHP hosted a dinner at New York's Metropolitan Club. Murmuring broke out among the 80 guests when Robert Holmes à Court showed up unexpectedly as one of the new partners in the restructured Utah coking-coal joint ventures in Queensland. In a speech, David Adam welcomed his adversary as 'Australia's answer to T. Boone Pickins', a remark that failed to raise a smile from its target. 'David was irritated that this corporate raider had insinuated himself into the BHP celebration,' Carrol Houser writes. 'However, it was a minor irritation. In spite of it all, the evening was an extremely pleasant occasion.'[29]

In Brisbane, Brian Loton, accompanied by Bud Wilson and Jim Curry, announced that the Utah acquisition had been completed. As the TV cameras rolled, all of the expanded Central Queensland Coal Associates Joint Venture participants signed the agreement papers. There was one absentee: Premier Bjelke-Petersen, who was supposed to sign on behalf of the Queensland Government. Boarding Utah's Learjet, Utah's John Wruck pursued the premier to North Queensland, catching up with him at Townsville airport. The documents were signed on the wing of the aeroplane.

In a message to employees, Loton said that the Utah acquisition enabled BHP 'to further diversify our mining interests. It will reduce our dependence on the fortunes of the world steel industry and it also means with Utah's substantial mining interests we will gain greater access to more markets.'[30]

Early the following morning, a BHP–Utah team headed by Brian Loton boarded the BHP plane and headed for Tokyo. For ten days, the group visited business partners, customers, trading companies, bankers and government representatives in Japan, South Korea, China and Taiwan to show the flag and reassure everybody that BHP and Utah would continue to honour all existing commitments.

But not everybody was happy. Carrol Houser says BHP Minerals employees were openly critical of their new American colleagues. 'Their attitude was, "Who the hell do these Americans think they are? We acquired them, we did a lot of work on this, we know about coal and we know about mining. Now, all of a sudden we're frozen out."'[31] The BHP staff believed the acquisition should have opened up new overseas assignments for many Australians, so there was a lot of resentment in the ranks when Utah was given a huge amount of independence.

'I was very impressed when BHP took us over that they didn't try to press their culture on us at all,' Jim Curry says. 'I was put in charge of consolidating the Utah mines into the BHP mining operations. I was given a seat on the board, with the title of chief general manager of BHP Minerals. They wanted Jerry Ellis to get some experience on the mining side, so we put him into the slot as my deputy.

'I was spending half the time in Melbourne and half in San Francisco. We had a house in South Yarra next to the Botanic Gardens and a house in California. We'd move down there for a month and then go back to the States. I had an office in BHP House. I didn't have much staff at all, mostly people reporting to me who were in charge of big operations everywhere, so my job was to make sure everything was running as it should.'[32]

Incredibly, the Utah holdings contributed almost 20 per cent of Broken Hill's profits in the first full year under its new owner, mostly from the Queensland coal mines and those in New Mexico at the Navajo Indian Reservation, which supplied two non-BHP coal-fired power plants.

The acquisition had also brought some risks: Utah owned gold and coal deposits in politically explosive South Africa, as well as the Escondida copper holdings in strife-torn Chile. Says Geoff Heeley, who was closely involved in the Utah transaction, 'When I joined the company in 1956, we had steelworks at Newcastle, Port Kembla and Whyalla, we had some iron-ore mines in South Australia and we had the iron-ore deposit in Yampi Sound – I don't think we'd even opened Koolyanobbing at that stage[33] – and we had coal mines in Newcastle and Port Kembla. We had limestone quarries in South Australia and New South Wales and manganese ore in Groote Island,[34] but basically it was a steel company.

'When we acquired Utah, it was a very substantial organisation; it included coal mines in the Four Corners in the US, it included the Escondida deposit – at that stage it was only a known deposit, it wasn't being mined – coal mines in Queensland and a whole stack of other assets. It was a very major acquisition and it was a roaring success.'[35]

News of the Utah deal attracted the keen eye of Bob Wilson, a young Londoner working as a strategist for Rio Tinto Zinc (RTZ). He said to his chief executive, Sir Alistair Frame, 'BHP did really well to get themselves into a bilateral position on that transaction.'

'Oh,' Frame replied, 'I never mentioned it but actually GE asked me if we'd be interested and I said, "No, it's too big."'

'You can't have done that!'[36]

Wilson laughs heartily at the memory but still finds it incredible. 'I can see if he was just looking at "We've got to buy all of it or nothing" then he might have come to a snap decision,' he says. 'But you've got to be a little more creative than that: there are several ways of trying to do things – maybe a joint venture or agreeing with BHP or someone on a split of assets. I was probably a bit rude at the time.'[37]

Wilson was working on a copper project in Panama that was being touted as the best undeveloped copper prospect in the world when word reached him about Escondida. It seemed to him that the part of Utah that BHP had in mind – the real target for them – was the Queensland coal mines. As GE had placed no value on Escondida in the transaction because of the vast expense of opening it up, Wilson thought he might still be able to snaffle it from under BHP's nose.

He suggested to Alistair Frame, 'Why don't you send a note to Brian Loton and say that I happened to be passing through Melbourne and would like to talk about whether there might be one or two things in Utah that they're not really interested in?'

Frame complied, and, after a brief meeting with Brian Loton, Wilson was siphoned off to meet David Adam and Bill Hunter.

'I'll do you a favour,' the visitor told them. 'There's a bit of stuff you picked up down there in Chile – not a very nice place anyway. Would you like me to take it off your hands?'

'We don't know what we've got yet,' the BHP men countered. 'We don't know how we're going to manage it. Thanks for coming and talking – we'll call you back sometime.'

Wilson went away empty-handed then, but he would be back. He knew from his experience in the copper industry that Escondida contained a massive lode of copper, and he, and indeed BHP, would reap a rich harvest.

CHAPTER 10

The Hidden One

Minera Escondida is located in the Atacama Desert, an almost rainless plateau on the western side of the Andes. 'I dreamed up the Atacama Project after working in Chile for several years as a geological consultant for Codelco [Corporacion Nacional del Cobre de Chile – Chile's state copper company and the dominant force in world copper],' says J. David Lowell, the legendary American mining engineer-cum-geologist credited with finding more copper than any other explorer. 'I became familiar with all the large copper deposits in Chile and noticed on a one-to-a-million map that they line up absolutely in a straight line.'[1]

The alignment convinced him that there must be another big deposit up there in the baking Mars-like terrain among the high sierras. He designed an exploration program based on a belt 32 kilometres wide that ran for 500 kilometres between two known deposits at Chuquicamata in the north and El Salvador in the south. Utah International and Getty Oil Company were brought in as 50/50 joint venturers, while Lowell negotiated a contract that allowed him to plan and manage the project and receive a finder's fee or a percentage interest in any mineable discovery.

In January 1979, a convoy of four-wheel-drive vehicles set off from Antofagasta, a port in northern Chile, and headed for the first likely point along the 500-kilometre belt. Altitudes ranged from 2500 to 4000 metres, which in the Chilean view was not considered very high. It was so hot and dry that the prospectors hung their tents with pictures of forests and rivers to remind them what they looked like. Speaking from his mining office at Rio Rico near the Mexican border in Arizona, Lowell says, 'The air is terribly clear up there and the stars shine like little light bulbs – it's a place where many astronomical observatories are located. At night, you could walk out away from the tents and it was totally quiet. The only sound was the blood in your ears.'[2]

Over the next two years, Lowell did so much walking over rough ground to check out significant outcrops that might indicate the presence of copper that his boots wore out and he spent days at a time without any footwear. 'We were not looking for an underground mine,' he says. 'We were looking for an open-pit mine.' Whenever he found a likely prospect, the crew drilled a row of boreholes at 500-metre intervals – unusually wide spacing for exploration, but the type of ore body they were looking for would have been hard to miss. 'It would have dimensions of thousands of metres.'

One promising site 170 kilometres south-east of Antofagasta had been staked five times by Codelco and two or three other major companies. 'They had filed claims on the property, looked at it carefully, decided it wasn't worth drilling and dropped it,' Lowell says.

There were relatively small outcrops indicating a porphyry copper system and the rest of the area was covered with *chucha*, a powdery surface of bleached rock. One outcrop on top of a ridge had some leached capping. There was a difference of opinion about the significance of the leaching, not least because it was in the middle of the Atacama Desert, one of the driest places on earth – so where had the water come from?

'There's a water table under all parts of the desert, sometimes 300 metres deep,' Lowell explains. 'In an ordinary part of the world, the water would come from rainfall and would penetrate downwards. This water was rising from the water table to the surface and in the process picking up salts containing copper minerals. I think I was probably the first one to understand this process and that contributed to the discovery, although I would have to admit I didn't have a great deal of faith in my conclusions. But I felt it was well worth drilling at that spot.'

Dave Lowell, son of an Arizona rancher, had spent so much of his 53 years in the outdoors that his features seemed to have been chiselled out of sandstone. He and his team burned the midnight oil trying to pick a name for the claim that, to mislead the opposition, would give the impression it had been staked by a small miner. Lowell suggested calling it 'San Francisco', a commonplace name for such claims, but Donaldo Rojas, a Chilean who was staking claims for the project, disagreed. 'No, no, a small miner would be more romantic than that,' he said. 'We should call it La Escondida – the Hidden One.' The name reflected the explorers' intention of keeping the site secret from rival companies and, if they hit paydirt, it would also describe the hidden jewel they had found among the dross.

Lowell returned to his office at Antofagasta, leaving the drilling to his Chilean assistant, Francisco 'Pancho' Ortiz. 'After five holes, Pancho telexed me for permission to stop the drilling on the basis of negative results,' he says. 'I told him to keep drilling and the next hole was Pozo 6 [drill-hole 6].'

On 14 March 1981, Pozo 6 struck 1.51 per cent copper at a depth of 240 metres. The rotary drill bit had intersected the main Escondida ore body of high-grade copper. The deposit was three kilometres long and one kilometre wide, with ore grades averaging 2.5 per cent, rising to five per cent in isolated pockets.

The find created a sensation at Utah headquarters in San Francisco. 'We had drilled and drilled in that area and were about to give up when we sunk a drill-hole right into the middle of the Escondida deposit,' Jim Curry says. 'It was very exciting, although at that time Chile was a questionable place to do business.'[3]

Only a decade earlier, Chile's foreign-owned mines had been nationalised by the Marxist regime of President Salvador Allende. But in 1973, Allende was violently overthrown – and killed – in a right-wing military coup led by General Augusto Pinochet. With Chile's economy tottering, the new president denationalised foreign-owned mines and welcomed investment from abroad.

'Utah International were scared to death that Escondida would be expropriated by the government again,' Dave Lowell says. 'Most of us who were living in Chile at the time thought that was unlikely with Pinochet's government, but the company was afraid to invest their own money – they wanted 100 per cent project finance.'

But before anything else could happen, controversy erupted when three Utah employees and one Getty employee claimed to have discovered Escondida. 'None of these fellows had even been to the Escondida project but as soon as the discovery was made they claimed credit for it,' Lowell says. 'They also shut me out of the fun of participating in the definition drilling. I was technically separated from Escondida as soon as the discovery was made. There was a lot of bad feeling at that point, and to add insult to injury they put their names on a monument at the drill-hole that first intersected Escondida but left my name off. That sort of thing often happens when an important discovery is made; in fact, it's more the rule than the exception.'[4]

One year after the discovery, Robert N. Hickman was brought in as president of Minera Escondida. Hickman had started with Utah in 1960 at the Lucky Mac uranium mine and then, after a stint at head office in San Francisco as a development engineer, was appointed mine superintendent at Island Copper, Utah's iron and copper project in British Columbia.

'Both Utah and Getty recognised that Escondida was an extremely important property,' he says. 'As president of Minera Escondida, I did all the sales and then I arranged the financing to develop the mine. We went to the governments of the companies we were going to sell to – primarily the Japanese, the Germans and the Finns. In Japan, it was the Japan Import Export Bank. The Japanese had never lent before to any entity where they had a minority share. And Chile at the time was still under Pinochet.'[5]

Then, in 1984, Texaco bought Getty Oil and in August the following year put its 50 per cent stake in Escondida up for sale. At RTZ, Bob Wilson saw his chance. 'I knew that Utah had a pre-emptive right to acquiring that 50 per cent interest,' he says. 'This was also a pretty depressed time for the copper market, and Chile wasn't flavour of the day as far as most people were concerned because this was still almost the heyday of the Pinochet regime, even though that was foreseeably going to come to a close before this project was up and running. That made me focus on trying to get alongside Utah. I saw them with the then chief executive of RTZ, [Sir] Derek Birkin. We introduced ourselves along the lines that, "We don't want to go bidding against you – you've got a pre-emptive right, we know that – we don't imagine you want to go for 100 per cent of this yourself. Is there a way in which you and us can get together and think about doing a joint venture?"'[6]

Indeed there was; Utah's parent, BHP, was pleased to share the costs of development. 'We ended up arranging a consortium to buy Texaco's holding,' Bob Hickman says. 'We initially held 60 per cent, RTZ got 30 per cent and a Japanese consortium led by Mitsubishi held ten per cent.[7]

'To entice the World Bank into the thing, we gave the IDC [International Development Corporation, the private-investment arm of the World Bank] an option to buy up to five per cent of our 60 per cent share, and they ultimately bought 2.5 per cent. They also put up some funds. We made those arrangements on 17 October 1985 – my 60th birthday.'[8]

So BHP now found itself with a 57.5 per cent interest in Escondida. Just over a year later, the BHP Gulfstream headed across the Pacific with Brian Loton, Graeme McGregor and Robert Holmes à Court, who, as we have seen, had joined the BHP board on 15 September 1986. 'We went a roundabout way – refuelled in New Zealand, stayed overnight in Tahiti, refuelled on Easter Island and then went into Santiago,' Graeme McGregor recalls. 'We had a look at Escondida and held discussions in Santiago about the Chilean economy – Pinochet was still in power and it was a pretty closed economy; in many ways, it was a gutsy decision to invest there.'[9]

Jim Curry found Holmes à Court 'aloof and arrogant: he had all sorts of strange ideas – that we should sell off the Chilean copper operations because they weren't any good.' Bob Hickman, however, says that after a visit to the copper fields in northern Chile, Holmes à Court changed his mind. 'We did a job on Holmes à Court,' he says. 'He brought his wife and his daughter. His wife was a very able person. None of them had ever been to South America before. We took Holmes à Court to northern Chile, but before we took him to Escondida we took him to Chuquicamata, one of the biggest industrial enterprises in the world. He could see it was as big as any industrial enterprise in Australia and he could see Escondida might be important, but he never understood how good Escondida was until he first looked at Chuquicamata, which had been operating at that time for 50 years and was getting down to its basic ore body. They laid out these big cross sections so he could see where these tremendous ore bodies had been and how they'd mined them. Then we went to Escondida and we took out the cross sections we had for Escondida and they looked just like Chuquicamata when it was brand new. Holmes à Court, who was our biggest critic, became a fan of Escondida. When he went back to Australia, he dropped his opposition. He was a horse-racing fan and he named one of his horses Escondida.'[10]

In 1987, BHP and Utah formalised their alliance with the creation of BHP-Utah Mineral International Corporation, thus becoming one of the largest mining and minerals operations in the world, with major operations in Japan, Europe, the United States and South America. There remained the business of Robert Holmes à Court and John Elliott to tidy up. Graeme McGregor found Holmes à Court a particularly difficult proposition. 'He was a poker player but he was also a man of very fixed views,' McGregor says. 'Some of his ideas I didn't agree with and argued strongly with him at finance committee meetings because I didn't like the potential outcome of some of the things he was proposing. It's no secret he wanted to break the company up – not only that, but some of the other financial engineering of gearing up certain parts of the company would have had disastrous results.'[11]

Despite their differences, Brian Loton discovered that Holmes à Court could be 'a very charming person. I had a trip with him to London when he owned all those theatres,[12]' he says. 'I was there on company business and he was there on Standard Chartered Bank business, so we just happened to travel together. He invited me to go on his plane, a Boeing 737, and we flew from Perth, stopped for fuel somewhere and landed at Luton. In London, we saw Michael Crawford in *The Phantom of the Opera*.'[13]

In July 1987, the Hawke government was returned to a third term, giving Treasurer Keating the opportunity to complete his wide-ranging financial reforms. But for the empire builders and asset strippers, a particularly brutal nemesis was near at hand.

On Monday, 19 October, New York's Dow Jones index fell 22.62 per cent. 'Black Monday' on Wall Street produced 'Black Tuesday' in Australia when the All-Ordinaries index lost 24.3 per cent.[14]

'I was in the air on my way back to Australia when it happened,' John Elliott says. 'I got off the plane. I can remember there were press everywhere. I knew nothing about it. That Sunday night, there had been a huge storm in London – a cyclone that had brought all the trees down. We'd left that night – you lose a day – and arrived in Melbourne on Tuesday morning. I got off the plane, went home, had a shower and went to the office. I thought, "There's been a gross overreaction here." We had a big superannuation fund and we told the super boys, "Get into the market." They did and it paid off handsomely.'[15]

Holmes à Court made it clear to financial writer Terry McCrann, who called him that day, that he would liquidate all his assets, real property as well as shares. But the only buyer he could find was among his enemies. 'Holmes à Court had never been part of the [Brian] Burke–[Alan] Bond Catholic Labor mafia,' McCrann says. 'Yet Burke's government would buy all his Perth properties. And Bond his company Bell Group. Not of course to help him, but to plunder the billion dollars-plus of cash that was inside the Bell Resources offshoot.'[16]

However, what the media never discovered at the time – or subsequently – is that Burke had also reached an agreement with Holmes à Court to buy his entire BHP shareholding. The sale did not proceed because Treasurer Paul Keating vetoed it.

Both Holmes à Court and Burke approached Keating separately. '[Holmes à Court] wanted me to let the West Australian Government acquire his interest in BHP, which I refused,' Keating says. 'He'd talked Premier Burke into taking that interest up.'[17] When Burke contacted him, Keating says, he told him, 'The state's got no business buying this.' Burke protested in vain. Keating says he was most concerned that if the company ran into trouble, the relatively small West Australian community would have to bear the brunt of it. '[Those] problems would come to my doorstep,' he says. 'Anyway, I refused him. Holmes à Court was very cranky on me about that. He said, why would I turn him [Burke] off it? I said, "Well, I've got the national-interest considerations here, you know." So he held the stock.'

Holmes à Court was attending a BHP board meeting in the Directors' Cottage at the Port Kembla steelworks when he received a message that Merrill Lynch had withdrawn his billion-dollar line of credit. Jerry Ellis, who was managing the steelworks at the time, says, 'My wife was entertaining Janet Holmes à Court somewhere in the country near Wollongong, so they were summoned to hurry back. I think he had a helicopter on standby to whisk him away.'[18]

'Holmes à Court wasn't totally ruined but he was gone,' says John Elliott, who was also present at the board meeting. 'We concluded – erroneously, as history would say – not to proceed to buy BHP ourselves. Elders could have bought him out and that would have given us control of BHP. We looked at it very hard. We could have bought BHP for $1.2 billion: look at it now, it's worth over $100 billion. Staggering.

'One of the things that concerned us was that BHP weren't in control of any of their pricing. The steel business was controlled by government pricing, while oil, iron ore and coal were commodities, so we would have been at the behest of economic times. Then we spent a couple of years undoing things. The undoing of it in the end was that we formed a holding company, Harlin, which basically bought BHP's equity in us.'[19]

BHP had indeed sold its Elders shares to Harlin Holdings in exchange for redeemable preference shares in Harlin that, with accrued interest, would amount over time to a debt of more than $1 billion.

Brian Loton recalls, 'It was a difficult period, obviously, and you can see it pretty clearly in retrospect now. Every generation has its difficulties and challenges. As I said, [Holmes à Court and John Elliott] had unsustainable strategies and we managed the business until reality dawned.'[20]

Graeme Samuel believes BHP had a lucky escape. 'If I think about what would have happened had the whole of BHP been acquired by Robert Holmes à Court – in the context of what ultimately happened to John Elliott and Elders – the company could have just imploded.'

An increasingly desperate Holmes à Court offered his shareholding to Kerry Packer, who declined. Paul Keating says, 'I know a group of people said to him, "Why don't you take the steel business? You give BHP the stock and they give you the steel business?"

'I know the ACTU said this to him because [steel] needed a whole lot of workplace changes to make it work. The ACTU said, "You take it, we'll make it work." But no, he wouldn't do it. You see, in the end, Robert Holmes à Court wasn't a business builder; he was in the end a speculator, a great speculator, the cleverest one we ever had, but he was a speculator and so his refusal to do anything about the BHP steel division meant that he was locked in the BHP clockwork of events and they had to clear out that equity interest in some way, and he had all those debts to the banks.'[21]

The financial meltdown, however, had not stopped work on Minera Escondida. 'We had an approved budget of $1.143 billion and we did it for $863 million, so we saved a hell of a lot of money,' Bob Hickman says. 'The financing was all tied to the negotiation of acceptable sales contracts; that gave the buyers – the Germans, the Japanese and the Finns – the upper hand in negotiations. We had great difficulty making the sales contracts and we didn't complete that until mid-1988. We had a big signing ceremony at the World Trade Center in New York City.

'Then we started the construction. We did our own pre-mine stripping of some 180 million tonnes of waste in order to get to the ore body – that was the longest line in the development. We finished the job in 29 months. Originally, it had a 36-month schedule, and that's one of the reasons we under-ran the budget.'[22]

Dave Lowell's contract gave him a five per cent participating interest in any successful discovery, but at the last minute Utah demanded a $3 million cap on the value of the interest. 'I agreed to it, which was a mistake on my part,' Lowell says. 'I'm quite sure they would have agreed to three per cent instead of five per cent and no cap. The difference for me would have been several billion dollars.'[23]

The Los Colorados concentrator started processing ore

in November 1990, and the first shipment was logged as sailing from Antofagasta on 31 December 1990. 'Truth is,' Bob Hickman says, 'it pushed off 1 January 1991 but the company was so anxious to have it in calendar 1990 that we signed the documents 31 December 1990.'[24]

By this time, the geologic fraternity had given Lowell full credit for discovering Escondida. 'BHP commissioned an article about the Escondida discovery, giving me the credit, which was distributed to people who participated in the opening of the mine.'[25]

The adjacent Zaldivar ore body had been found at the same time as Escondida. Lowell staked a claim that covered half of that ore body, which became BHP Billiton's Escondida Norte in 2005. 'I was paid a finder's fee for one and a half discoveries,' Lowell says. 'It added up to $4.75 million.'[26]

Over time, Escondida would be developed into the world's largest copper mine, producing 1.483 million tons of copper in 2007 and providing BHP Billiton with one of its most valuable assets.

One of its strong supporters, Robert Holmes à Court, would not live to enjoy its bonanza. A heavy cigar smoker and diabetic, Holmes à Court died of a heart attack on 3 September 1990 at his stud farm near Perth. He was just 53 years old. His rival, John Elliott, the old Carey Grammarian, president of the Liberal Party, president of Carlton Football Club and self-made millionaire, attempted a management buyout of his Elders group through Harlin Holdings in 1989. He failed and took heavy losses. Following an investigation by the National Crime Authority, he was charged with fraudulent foreign-exchange manipulation. When acquitted, he sued the authorities – an action that resulted in his financial ruin. Elliott's wealth had once been estimated at well in excess of $50 million. He had owned a big house in Toorak, a villa in the south of France, a holiday home at Flinders and three big farms in the country.[27] He lost the lot.[28]

The battles for control of BHP through the 1980s had made its management more aggressive, more acquisitive, sharper, smarter, more worldly wise. The steel industry, however, had been defying gravity for so long that the Labor government had mounted a rescue operation in the shape of a five-year Steel Industry Plan under which the steel unions promised to refrain from industrial action in return for guarantees from BHP relating to security of employment. Productivity increased from 150 tons per worker per annum in 1982 to some 250 tons in 1984.

'We didn't do a bad job on the steel industry,' says John Prescott, who took over as head of BHP Steel in 1987. 'We gradually got political acceptance for an enormous downsizing in steel and we gradually got workforce acceptance for the need to do it. There was a huge restructuring, many redundancies – all handled voluntarily – and massive reinvestment in the industry to make what was left efficient. I inherited a loss and within a couple of years turned that around to a $650 million profit. We'd turned a very difficult industry into a profitable industry, but it was quite clear to me that even that amount wasn't something one should be too happy about. The conclusion one was left with was that this was not the best industry to be in.'[29]

As the 1980s closed, Brian Loton added the deputy chairman's role to his chief executive duties. 'Brian was very much the old-style business gentleman, a very determined guy,' says Lance Hockridge, who joined BHP in 1978 straight out of the University of New South Wales in a labour-relations role. 'He certainly knew his stuff. He could be on the one hand personable but on the other hand had that touch of ruthlessness about him. The bottom line was that most of my peers were very respectful of Brian.'[30]

The new chairman, replacing Jim Balderstone, was Estonian-born Sir Arvi Parbo, the driving force behind Western Mining, along with Hugh Morgan. The 1990s, however, began unpromisingly with a recession that followed the oil-price spike induced by the First Gulf War.[31] Then, in May 1991, while retaining the deputy chairmanship, Loton passed the chief executive officer's baton to John Prescott. 'My relationship with

Arvi Parbo was excellent – he's one of the great mining figures,' Prescott says, 'and my relationship with Brian Loton was also very good – I wouldn't have been appointed CEO without his support.'[32]

John Barry Prescott was born in Sydney on 22 October 1940 and educated at North Sydney Boys High School and the University of New South Wales. 'I studied industrial relations at university and joined BHP in 1958 at Newcastle Steelworks,' he says. 'There were distinctions in those days between commercial trainees and cadets, and I was a commercial trainee rather than a cadet, but I became a cadet – cadets were the higher-regarded group.'

Lance Hockridge says, 'I met John the first day I joined the company – at that time, John was assistant manager of Fleet Operations and I was in the shipping and stevedoring department. He happened to be in Sydney on business and I was introduced to him.

'The issues that were running in those days were all about industrial relations, and so I had a good deal to do with John. When he became general manager transport, I became his manager personnel; and then he dispatched me to Port Kembla into my first operational role. We were pretty close for about ten years, then he became executive general manager steel, and while I would see him from time to time I didn't have much to do with him. Then the wheel turned again and he became managing director, and while I didn't work directly for him, being part of the executive group one has that kind of interaction.'[33]

As though to emphasise the end of an era of extraordinary expansion, The Big Australian had outgrown BHP House, which was closed down, and company headquarters were moved from William Street to the monolithic BHP Tower at 600 Bourke Street. No one could have predicted then that by the end of the new decade Broken Hill Proprietary Limited would have been brought to its knees and, shortly afterwards, would have ceased to exist in its then current form – largely because it had gone tilting at windmills in the Arizona desert.

CHAPTER 11

Mother Magma

Jeremy Kitson Ellis, by now chief executive officer of BHP Minerals, knew he was approaching San Manuel when two huge smokestacks loomed like beacons out of the cactus-strewn Arizona scrub. It was the spring of 1996 and Jerry Ellis was making his first visit to the little copper-mining town since BHP had completed its US$2.4 billion takeover of the Magma Copper Company.

Described by one industry insider as 'affable, charming, pleasant, polished but not super-smooth, good-humoured',[1] Ellis travelled the 56 kilometres from Magma Copper's corporate headquarters on North Oracle Road, Tucson, with Magma's president and chief executive, the Irishman J. Burgess Winter. Everything looked fine as the little convoy of company cars threaded its way down Highway 77 from the mountain town of Oracle towards the Lower San Pedro Valley.

Indeed, the two men had every reason to celebrate the trans-Pacific deal that had made BHP the largest publicly traded producer of copper in the world. Winter had made a fortune from selling his Magma stock to BHP, and Ellis thought he had landed one of the great mining prizes of all time. Neither man had any inkling of the turbulent times that lay ahead for their companies.

'Jerry Ellis was instrumental in bringing in the Magma deal – it was the last thing he did as minerals chief executive,' says Graeme McGregor, who was executive general manager of BHP at that time. 'The full board was meeting in Melbourne and they had sent me to New York to sign the papers.'[2]

In Arizona, the little convoy approached a crossroads among the grey-and-white-speckled boulders, so different from Ellis's birthplace, Hardy Country in England's rural Dorset, but more akin to the country where he had been raised in rural Western Australia. 'I went to primary school in York in the West Australian wheat belt and secondary school in Northam, also in the wheat belt, so I grew up as a young Australian,' Ellis says. 'I've lived here pretty much all my life, although I went to Oxford for a few years. I didn't get an Australian degree. Oxford only give out BAs but my subject matter was engineering and then if you stay on the books long enough you can buy yourself an MA, which I did – it cost me £10 – and my official post nominal is MA Oxon.

'The first company I worked for was ICI in England and then I moved with ICI to their subsidiary ICI Australia, which has morphed into Orica. So the first five years of my working life were with that company as a process-control engineer.' He joined BHP in 1967 as an organisation planning officer and worked with a team of American consultants, Cresap, McCormick & Paget, who had been hired by the then administration manager, Fred Rich. 'I worked with them for a couple of years and it gave me a good insight into the company.'[3]

The left-hand road led to the San Manuel mine, the largest underground copper mine in the United States, visible on the escarpment as a collection of gaunt steel towers and winding gear that hovered over the shafts, in the words of one Australian mining executive, 'like Don Quixote windmills'.[4] The right-hand turning was South Reddington Road, which went to the town, the mill, the smelter and the electrolytic refinery. The desert sun – still low on the horizon – blazed over man's despoliation of the biblical wilderness.

San Manuel had been built at an elevation of 1000 metres on the north-eastern flank of the Santa Catalina Mountains. It rarely snowed at this altitude, but when it did the tailings seemed to have been draped with white blankets and the saltbush sprinkled with balls of cotton wool. The township was so close to the smelter that the prevailing winds sometimes enveloped it in clouds of sulphurous smoke that soiled washing and engulfed children in their playgrounds.

It was a huge day in the little town's history. Since early morning, cars had been pulling into the parking lot outside the conference centre on South McNab Parkway. The centre was packed with Magma employees, each of whom were given a little commemorative copper anode stamped with the words 'Magma Copper Company: 5 May 1910–18 January 1996. *Our history is the springboard to our future*.'

'Soon after the BHP purchase was announced, Jerry Ellis came to San Manuel and spoke to us,' says Matt Foraker, an electrical engineer with a master's degree in mathematics who worked at the smelter. 'He talked about how wonderful everything was and how it was going to be so great. He had to talk to a lot of concern because the people in that room could already smell that something nasty was coming.'[5]

Magma Copper had been founded in 1910 by William Boyce Thompson, a mining engineer and Wall Street financier.[6] It took its name from the district of Magma in Pinal County, 50 kilometres north of San Manuel, where Thompson also operated copper mines. Exploration of the San Manuel area began in the early 1940s during a steep increase in demand for copper. Test drilling started in 1943 in the Red Hill area of San Manuel and shortly afterwards Magma Copper paid a reputed $28 million for the claims. In 1952, Magma used a federal loan of $94 million to build the mine, the plant, the railroad and the company town. Production from the mine began in 1954.[7]

'For a miner like me, it was a wonderful place to work,' says Onofre 'Taffy' Tafoya, one of 4500 people who moved to San Manuel. 'If you were a good worker, you always got a job there, you got good financial credit anywhere in town. When I hired in there in 1956 at the entry level, which was as a chutetapper, the pay was $14.35 for eight hours. What made it so damn attractive to me was that I was working as a labourer in a brickyard before that for less than $1 an hour, so to me it was a promotion.

'The chutetapper was the man down at the copper face with a double-jack: a 16-pound sledgehammer with a shortened handle. You sit there and break rocks all day long. It was damp down there but the ventilation was pretty good. The mine was so damn big. When we were at our very best, we had over 600 miles of drifts and tunnels and raises down there. The working people used to call the mine Mother Magma, because it was like having a big old titty that you could go suck on all day long. It paid out money all the time – you get what I mean? "Hey – I see you bought a new car." "Yeah, Mother Magma."'[8]

In 1995, Magma Copper was producing high-quality copper cathode and copper rod from its operations in San Manuel, Miami and Superior – all mines in Arizona – the Robinson mine at Ely, Nevada, and the Tintaya mine in southern Peru. Magma Metals, a division of Magma Copper run by the stalwart John F. Champagne, operated the smelting and refining complex at San Manuel.

The company had come back from the brink of disaster a few years earlier and was now turning a healthy profit thanks to a revolutionary agreement between unions and management. The turn for the better started in November 1988 when the private-equity firm of Warburg Pincus Capital arranged funds for Magma to buy out its two largest shareholders, Newmont Mining Corporation and Consolidated Gold Fields. Burgess Winter, senior vice president of BP Minerals America, was brought in as chief executive.[9] Years of conflict between management and the United Steel Workers of America, largest of the ten unions at Magma, brought the company to the verge of bankruptcy. Winter embarked on a radical program to improve efficiency and reduce costs. A joint committee was set up to develop a sense of mutual purpose that would change things dramatically from confrontation to cooperation.

'Burgess was responsible for the turnaround in the company, with two key executives, Brad Mills and Marsh Campbell,'[10] says Matt Foraker. 'He hired consultants King, Chapman & Broussard (KCB), who created what was called "The Voice of Magma", a committee consisting of approximately 150 people throughout the company at all levels: it included forklift drivers, underground miners and members of the board of directors. People were selected because they stood out as influential in the business. Even though a guy was only a forklift driver or a welder, if he was seen as somebody people listened to, and counted on and trusted – one of the good guys, so to speak – he was selected.

'The Voice of Magma crafted the Magma Charter, a set of principles that was also a statement of accountability. It was a document about what the company was going to be and it introduced a sense of trust and alignment between the unions and management. It was unprecedented.'[11]

Bradford 'Brad' Mills was born in Washington DC just after the Korean War, the son of an investment banker who was working temporarily in naval intelligence at the Pentagon. He graduated in geology at Stanford University and took his master's degree at the Stanford School of Business in mineral economics. After spending ten years in exploration field geology, he became director of corporate development of the gold-and-copper miner Echo Bay, and three years later moved to Magma Copper at Tucson, Arizona.

'I joined Magma as the vice president business development and over the next five years completely transformed that business,' he says. 'We had a wonderful chief executive in Burgess Winter. Through the five years of the copper boom, we were able to grow the company very successfully.'[12]

From 1988 to 1994, productivity increased by 86 per cent, production costs were slashed from more than 80 cents per pound of copper to less than 60 cents per pound, and output was cranked up from 400 million pounds to 700 million pounds per year.

Under a 15-year labour contract with a seven-year no-strike clause, there were no layoffs in several years and the unions altered job rules so that workers could pitch in wherever they were needed. 'A welder who works in the mine will now come and work in the smelter on a busy day there,' says John Champagne.[13] Magma's average wage for a miner was $15 an hour, but $2.25 of this, or 15 per cent, was a 'gain-sharing' bonus paid for greater efficiency. To earn it, each miner had to dig roughly 570 pounds of ore a day, on average, rather than the 350 pounds that was typical in 1988.

On 2 February 1995, Magma announced record net income for 1994 of US$87.4 million, or $1.38 per share, compared with $21.9 million, or 40 cents per share, in 1993. '1994 was a monumental year for Magma Copper Company,' Burgess Winter commented in the company's annual report. 'Major accomplishments have dramatically transformed Magma into a competitive international copper producer. These include: the acquisition of the Tintaya mine, purchased from the Peruvian government in November 1994; the start of construction at our Robinson mine near Ely, Nevada; the completion of a major smelter expansion at our San Manuel smelter; net cash operating costs of 58 cents per pound for the year; and record Magma source production. The combination of our growth and cost-reduction programs has made 1994 the best year in Magma's history.'

A few months later, Winter was approached by Jerry Ellis, who had been told about the great promise of Magma Copper by two of his United States-based BHP executives, Bob Hickman and Glen Andrews, group general manager of the copper division. 'Probably right,' Jerry Ellis says in an interview. 'Most of my dealing was with Burgess Winter and John Vogelstein [of Warburg Pincus].'[14]

'Myself and Glen Andrews recommended the acquisition of Magma,' says Bob Hickman, who became group general manager for business development after returning to San Francisco following the successful opening up of Escondida in 1990. 'We went to San Manuel, we went to the smelter, we went in the mine, we talked to all the principal people and we had all of our engineers and metallurgists on the property. We knew the property very well. It wasn't bad for a block-cave operation, but they were running out of ore in the main [mine] – they needed a new development there.

'Jerry Ellis was my boss and he used to split his time between San Francisco and Melbourne: he had two offices. Between the phone and teleconferencing, we put together a package that we thought was doable and then it was recommended. When it became clear it was something that should have been favourable for the company, the responsibility for it transferred to Melbourne. It was basically done by Jerry himself, along with Melbourne staff. Then Jerry did all the direct negotiations with Magma. It didn't turn out to be a very successful acquisition; in fact, it was ultimately one of the things that brought down BHP.'[15]

On 12 July 1995, Jerry Ellis met with Burgess Winter, Donald J. Donahue, Magma's chairman, and Vogelstein, the Warburg Pincus vice chairman who was also a Magma director. There was already a history between the two companies. Magma Copper and BHP Minerals had formed a joint venture two years earlier to bid for the El Abra copper deposit in northern Chile.[16]

'El Abra was a copper-oxide deposit and we didn't feel confident that we could do it alone,' Ellis says, 'but nor did Magma, so we decided to make a joint bid. The Magma fellows and the BHP blokes in San Francisco worked together on putting a bid in for El Abra – that's how we started working together; that's when we got an appreciation of their skills in so-called SX/EW winning of copper.'[17]

The El Abra bid was unsuccessful but the companies remained on cordial terms.[18]

In October 1995, Brian Loton, John Prescott and Jerry Ellis met with Burgess Winter and John Vogelstein to discuss the price at which BHP would acquire Magma. Later that month,

Winter, Vogelstein and Brad Mills flew to Melbourne and on 30 October BHP and Magma entered into a confidentiality agreement to enable BHP to conduct due diligence of the American company's assets.[19]

The takeover deal was announced on 30 November. BHP's cash tender offer of US$28 a share did not require the approval of BHP's shareholders, and Magma's largest shareholder, Warburg Pincus Capital, agreed to tender its 26 per cent stake.[20]

The deal gave BHP a fully integrated copper operation that would use Magma's smelter, described as 'state of the art' by the *New York Times*, to transform mined copper ore into pure metal. The smelter could process more than a million tons of copper concentrate per year, enabling Magma to also process copper from outside sources. There was also a railroad to carry ore the 11 kilometres from the mine to the smelter and transport the finished product to Hayden, 48 kilometres away, for distribution on the wider rail network. It provided BHP with immediate access to the American copper market, essentially giving it global reach.

'The key focus of this acquisition is growth,' Graeme McGregor told the *New York Times*. '[It] will create great synergies.'[21] BHP financed the deal with internal cash resources and existing lines of credit. This would increase the company's debt initially, but the deal would save US$30 million to $40 million a year over time through redundancies.

Burgess Winter became executive general manager and chief executive officer of a new entity, BHP Copper Group, which would control all of The Big Australian's copper interests in the United States, plus Escondida in Chile and Ok Tedi in Papua New Guinea. Based in San Francisco with BHP's other major American acquisition, Utah Mining, BHP Copper would produce roughly ten per cent of the world's copper.

John Prescott and Burgess Winter declared, 'The creation of the new BHP Copper Group has the unanimous support of the BHP and Magma boards and is a very positive and exciting development for the industry and each company's shareholders.'

On the New York Stock Exchange, Magma Copper shares jumped US$6.25 to $27.65 – a rise of more than 29 per cent. 'I cannot think of two other companies that have as good a fit as these two,' Anthony P. Rizzuto Jr. of Bear Stearns told the *New York Times*. 'This was clearly driven by strategic factors and would not make sense for other companies.'[22] The London-based *Mining Journal* nodded approvingly that 'there appears to be very little risk associated with the takeover'.[23]

BHP Copper, however, soon found itself immersed in serious problems. Some of these difficulties should have been spotted by the BHP team on the ground. One Australian mining executive says, 'When I heard about the acquisition, I remember thinking, "Who on earth would buy that?" There was one per cent copper, which is okay – except it's not okay at a couple of kilometres down. I couldn't believe Jerry and the boys had forked out $3.2 billion for that.'[24]

Daniel L. Edelstein, copper-commodity specialist with the United States Geological Survey (USGS) in Washington, says, 'It was a good time, a positive period – copper prices were relatively high and the prognosis was for increasing demand. But the copper price suddenly took a downturn. They were looking at a mine that was at the end of its useful life and needed a significant investment to go deeper. They were exhausting the upper ore body in the San Manuel mine and they were having to put investment work into the lower ore body, known as Kalamazoo or the Lower K.'[25]

Specialists from the United States Environmental Protection Agency (EPA) had inspected the mine in 1992. 'Mining of the one-billion-ton San Manuel ore body will continue until 1995 when the ore is expected to be depleted,' says a copy of the EPA report in the authors' possession. It continues:

> Magma also owns the Kalamazoo ore body, a faulted segment offset from the San Manuel ore body. The Kalamazoo ore

> body is located approximately one mile to the west of the San Manuel ore body, between 2500 and 4000 feet below the surface. Magma Copper Company began to develop the Kalamazoo in 1990 and is currently mining at a rate of 6000 tons per day. A long-term [15-year] labour contract was agreed to in late October 1991 in anticipation of fully developing the Kalamazoo ore body.[26]

Expectations at BHP were nonetheless high. The bullish Daniel Roling, an analyst at Merrill Lynch, believed demand for copper was likely to remain strong in 1996, sustaining the current copper price of around $1.30 a pound because of rising copper use in the housing, transportation and machine-tools industries. Others were not so optimistic. New mines were due to come on stream in Indonesia and Chile in 1996 and 1997, adding ten per cent or more to the global copper supply. 'Bringing on that much supply should soften prices,' said Leanne Baker, a metals analyst at Salomon Brothers. 'I am negative on copper.' She added that the BHP share offer 'is a valuation Magma shareholders should be very happy with'.[27]

Indeed, Magma's shareholders were ecstatic with the price BHP had paid for the American company, which some analysts later calculated as five times higher than its true value. Nobody was talking in those terms yet.

'I wasn't actually part of the negotiating team but as soon as we bought Magma I had to visit there and gained a bit of an understanding of what it was all about,' Peter Laver says. 'We were taken on a fairly extensive tour of the place. The hosts were Burgess Winter, Brad Mills and the Magma people. John Prescott was there and all the senior minerals people: Jerry Ellis, Dick Carter and the crowd from San Francisco, Tim Winterer and Keith Wallace. We played golf and had dinner at the chief executive's house, which was an amazing spread sitting in the hills looking down over Tucson. We've been prey to a few sweet-talking people occasionally and he was one of them.'[28]

Had the price of copper remained buoyant, things might have turned out very well. But the deal was star-crossed. 'Well, there's no doubt it was a shitter,' Jerry Ellis says, allowing himself a rueful laugh. 'All these "what ifs" . . . it's a bit like playing golf: "If I'd played better golf yesterday, we'd be the club champions."'[29]

As the analysts were mulling over Magma's prospects, the 48-year-old trader Yasuo Hamanaka stayed late at his office on the third floor of the Sumitomo Corporation near the Imperial Palace in Tokyo to deal in copper through third parties on the New York Mercantile Exchange (Nymex). It is immaterial whether he won or lost that day. For ten years, he had crushed the competition with huge buy-and-sell orders that enabled him to dominate the market. He would often stay in his office until 3 am to conduct transactions in the New York and London markets.

While his company accounts showed that his division had created huge paper profits for Sumitomo, a secret ledger recorded losses running into many millions of pounds. Hamanaka's double-dealing began to unravel in December 1995 – just after BHP had bought Magma – when the United States Commodity Futures Trading Commission and Britain's Securities and Investments Board, which oversee commodity markets in New York City and London, asked Sumitomo to cooperate in an investigation of suspected price manipulation. Sumitomo then started its own inquiry and in June 1996, only two weeks after the birth of the BHP Copper Group, Sumitomo admitted at a news conference that Hamanaka had racked up more than US$2.6 billion in losses through unauthorised trades conducted off the company's books. (Hamanaka was sentenced to eight years in prison for fraud and forgery in 1998 and was released in July 2005.)

The revelation drove down copper prices by as much as ten per cent in London and New York, a fall that coincided with the serious downturn among the Tiger economies of Asia, one of the biggest markets for copper and copper-intensive products such as electrical wires, motor vehicles and pipes. 'The moment copper prices fell to the extent that they did – down to about

60 cents a pound when we'd effectively done the economics on a dollar a pound – it was always going to be a struggle,' says Graeme McGregor. 'There had been a fair bit of manipulation by the Sumitomo trader in Japan who had effectively created a false market. Then there was oversupply – the LME stocks were at record highs; most people for a while kept producing on the basis that they weren't going to be the one to shut down facilities. Escondida was producing but not nearly to the extent it is now. It was a very high-grade mine – they were talking 2.16 per cent copper for a 50-year mine life and the original grade was very high, so it was in a vastly different situation to Magma, which was .7 or .8.'[30]

Down in Melbourne, John Prescott was having difficulty accepting the sudden shift in BHP's fortunes. The operating profit after tax to the end of May 1996 was a colossal $1.293 billion. In BHP's annual report, the Magma acquisition had been presented as one of the highlights of the year. Suddenly, things looked very gloomy indeed.

'Magma was something I wasn't very happy about,' John Prescott says, speaking for the first time about the debacle that followed. 'The copper price really carked. It had been between 120 and 140 US cents a pound – probably 120 was a more continuing figure; we in those days regarded a dollar a pound as about the average price you could expect through the cycle but at one stage it dipped to 60 cents. The problem with the minerals business is that you dig the stuff up and you eventually run out of it.

'BHP had had the good fortune over the years to have a number of deposits that didn't run out as quickly as most did in that industry – Broken Hill lasted more than a hundred years and is still going. Escondida is a hundred-year asset. Cannington, the silver mine in Queensland, is a hundred-year asset. The iron-ore mines in Western Australia are probably thousand-year assets. The world wasn't growing its mineral consumption in the 1990s quite as rapidly as it is today; in fact, there had been stable iron-ore consumption for 20 or 30 years and not a lot in copper, so the challenge in the '90s was how the hell do you grow a minerals business when there's not a lot of growth in the consumption of the metals? The thrust was to diversify the minerals we were seeking to produce and to diversify some of the activities, and to some extent to go downstream to create a market for our own minerals. That was entered into with a degree of confidence because we had had seven or eight very successful years and we regarded ourselves as having some pretty good operators.

'But when the copper price fell out of bed we were pretty badly hurt. We had just made a couple of acquisitions that had looked okay at the time but looked like dogs by '97 or '98. We slowed down the development of Escondida because the cash flow wasn't quite as good as it had been. Then we had a couple of what would have to be regarded as strategic errors, not least of which was the direct iron plant in Western Australia, and then we had some problems in Rhodesia. We had two or three things bank up on us at the same time, so the minerals business went from being boomingly successful to struggling for a while.'[31]

Burgess Winter's team at BHP Copper included Brad Mills, Marsh Campbell and Craig Steinke, all of whom were well aware of the special relationship that had existed between the Magma management and its workforce. At the time of the acquisition, Mills, a large, athletic bear of a man with a big smile, was the chief operating officer for Magma. 'They moved me back on to the strategy side of the combined group,' he says in an interview in the chief executive's office of Lonmin, the former Lonrho mining empire, overlooking the gardens of Buckingham Palace. 'The Magma executives had two-year golden handcuffs – it was part of the way that Magma compensation was set up – and it was helpful from a merger perspective because BHP wanted to keep our people. I spent 18 months trying to sort out strategy issues inside BHP, but I became quite disenchanted.

'I really didn't like anything to do with BHP. I thought it was amateur hour. Magma was a company that had mediocre assets and was very well run, and BHP was a company that had extraordinary assets mediocrely run. BHP people in charge of the Magma assets were a complete disaster. They managed to destroy a lot of value and in the process destroy some careers – it was ugly.'[32]

Matt Foraker says, 'Magma had a rule you weren't allowed to dress too nice because it created an air of "I'm better than you". So at Magma you weren't even allowed to wear a tie – but BHP changed all that. We had the best union/management in the world, we had teamwork, we had a voice, and people were wondering, "Is BHP going to destroy this?" Burgess Winter was one of the first resignations: I don't think he lasted a year. John Champagne and the Magma Metals controller Craig Steinke – the great guy who hired me – all resigned. They saw the writing on the wall.'[33]

John J. O'Connor, an outspoken Dubliner appointed head of BHP Petroleum in 1994, took a particular interest in Burgess Winter's departure. 'He made it very clear he wanted out of the subsequent marriage,' O'Connor says. 'When John Prescott would have these thousand-man, offsite leadership meetings, Burgess would sit up on the stage with him, reading the newspaper. He was clearly trying to get bought out, which is, I'm sure, what happened.'[34]

'Burgess Winter created himself a heck of a good deal by selling Magma to BHP,' says Gary Dillard, editor of *Pay Dirt* magazine based in Bisbee, Arizona. 'He had a good chunk of the stock and he also got severance pay as chief executive. When you look at what Magma had as assets, BHP certainly overpaid.'[35]

One additional problem was that Bob Hickman, an American, and Glen Andrews, a Canadian, both competent ex-Utah operatives, were no longer there. 'Bob left almost immediately after the acquisition and Glen only stayed maybe another year,' Brad Mills says. 'When Burgess Winter left, they employed Jim Lewis as the head of the copper group. He brought Australian-steelmaker mentality to copper, which was challenging.'[36]

Lewis, who became executive general manager and chief executive officer of BHP Copper, joined BHP as a research officer in the 1970s and worked in the coal and steel divisions. His strengths were corporate strategy and development. To introduce a more hands-on management, Lewis appointed Bill J. Walls on 31 March 1997 as senior vice president and group general manager for business improvement. Walls was described in a BHP press release as 'a seasoned financial executive, certified public accountant and graduate of the Harvard Advanced Management Program (AMP), with 24 years of experience in commercial, operational and administrative areas'.

Matt Foraker says Bill Walls's arrival at San Manuel triggered dissension in the ranks. 'He came into the Magma operation like he knew everything,' he says. 'His work produced massive resignations of Magma managers and administrators. He represented everything Magma Copper had fought to overcome during '93 to '96. He was one of the most arrogant and self-important characters I have ever met. The Magma view: "Employees are good. Empower and develop them to become as productive as possible." The Bill Walls view: "Employees are bad. Eliminate as many as possible and still be able to operate."'[37]

All the promise and goodwill at the time of the takeover had evaporated in the hot, dry Arizona air. Concern about Magma's future reached new heights when in late April John Prescott had the dismal task of passing a virtual death sentence on Newcastle's steel industry with the announcement that BHP would cease making steel there from 1999. If that proud city, where life for generations revolved around the huge plant on the banks of the Hunter River and where most people referred to the company as 'The BHP', could be axed, the question had to be asked: was anything sacred?

Since the 1982 slump in steel prices, BHP had spent a colossal $5 billion (US$3.8 billion) upgrading its steel operations. Jobs were shed and productivity more than trebled, but it hadn't been enough. The Newcastle works still could not compete with cheaper producers abroad and was losing millions.

'More than anything else, the closure was technology-driven,' says Lance Hockridge, who was sent to Newcastle by John Prescott to manage the shutdown (and was later unfairly blamed for the closure). 'Port Kembla evolved into the flat-product steelworks and Newcastle produced the long products,' he says. 'There were many proposals in the '70s and '80s right through to the early '90s to reconfigure the Newcastle steelworks, none of which was taken up for various reasons.'[38] The Newcastle operation dated back to 1912, and steelworks required continuing investment to stay in business. In the 1980s, Smorgon established a long-products business. 'They competed directly with BHP in the same product range but using the much more efficient technology based on scrap recycling,' Lance Hockridge says. 'Labour relations were an issue but the reality is that no amount of tinkering with labour cost would have made any difference to the fundamental issues. That certainly wasn't the reason why the steelworks was closed.'

There was little consolation in the fact that BHP would continue turning out rod and bar steel products from Newcastle after 1999 – the steel would be shipped in from Whyalla. In Newcastle, 3000 people, many of them middle-aged European migrants who had worked for BHP since their arrival in Australia, would lose their livelihood. One disillusioned citizen scrawled a sign in chalk outside the Church of Christ in Mayfield, a suburb that provided a big percentage of the workforce: 'Jesus Fixes BHP, Broken Hearted People'.[39]

'Initially, there was an emotional reaction, but it settled down quite quickly as we were able to explain the reasons behind the closure,' Lance Hockridge says.[40]

The question for the BHP board in Melbourne was whether the company could now afford to wait for the copper cycle to take an upswing or whether it would have to cut and run in Arizona as well. Either way, there was going to be blood on the boardroom carpet, and Mother Magma was far from the only problem that the miner was having with its ventures into copper.

CHAPTER 12

One Little Tremor

The Ok Tedi in Papua New Guinea is a tributary of the 1000-kilometre Fly River system, which has a total catchment of 76,000 square kilometres. The Fly discharges between 3000 and 7000 cubic metres of water per second from the western high country into the Gulf of Papua. More than 50,000 people live along its banks and floodplains. It is now an environmental disaster area.

At a mine-closure workshop in 2006, the managing director of Ok Tedi Mining Limited (OTML), Keith Faulkner, said, 'This region should have seen greater and more sustainable benefits than it has in the 25 years OTML has been in existence. Insufficient thought was given 25 years ago and since then to the effects of its social and environmental impact. But Ok Tedi was a tough project to get started in the first place 30 years ago.'[1]

It was indeed.

Ok Tedi is a misnomer; the mine is actually on Mt Fubilan in the Star Mountains, first penetrated by a Westerner, the Australian kiap (patrol officer) Des Fitzer, in 1963. Five years later, geologists working for the American miner Kennecott discovered copper and gold deposits in the mountain and for the next six years negotiated with the PNG administration during the transition to independence from Australia in September 1975.

The following year, the talks broke down and Kennecott withdrew. According to Richard T. Jackson, mining consultant and historian with continuing links to the project, 'After a brief interregnum in which the government managed the project, BHP put together a consortium with Amoco and a mixture of [then West] German companies. BHP and Amoco each held 30 per cent of the shares in Ok Tedi Mining Limited, the Germans held 20 per cent and the PNG Government the remainder. From 1978, serious negotiations began over the future development of a mine on Mt Fubilan.'[2]

In 1977, Jackson, his associate Robert Welsh and economist Craig Emerson[3] were contracted by the PNG Government to report on the impact of the Ok Tedi project. 'Unfortunately,' Jackson says, 'what should have been its companion volume, an environmental impact assessment, was not commissioned until after this date; it was eventually commissioned by OTML and issued in seven volumes in June 1982.'[4]

Meanwhile, BHP as the operator was under pressure from the PNG Government to begin mining and thus provide much-needed foreign exchange, since the only other comparable revenue source was the Panguna copper mine in Bougainville. The then BHP treasurer, Russ Fynmore, who was in charge of financing Ok Tedi, visited the mine several times. 'The Papua New Guinea Government would have to share responsibility for what happened,' he says. 'Ok Tedi had a gold cap and the copper was underneath. The government was very concerned that we would just mine the gold cap and walk away, so they wrote the contract in such a way that we had to go on with the copper mine – which we always intended to do – but then when the environmental issues arose, they wouldn't let us walk away because the copper was valuable and they wanted their royalties.'[5]

BHP was itself keen to start extracting the gold cap to secure its own returns on the project. It engaged the big American construction company Bechtel in combination with Morris Knudsen International (BMKI) to build the first stage in 37 months. Work began in June 1981 on a 'fast track' schedule that almost immediately ran into trouble. According to Jackson, 'From April 1982 onwards, matters appear to have deteriorated.' The *Kyoten Maru* sank off Townsville with US$1.3 million worth of cargo for the project. Heavy rains hampered road construction. And when the rains stopped, there was an almost unprecedented drought, and the Fly and Ok Tedi became unnavigable. 'The low water flow was to last for six months,' he said. 'The project ran out of cement in July, and fuel and food supplies were low.'[6]

Cost overruns reached US$100 million. A proposed hydroelectricity plant was abandoned. By 1983, the project was eight months behind schedule. According to Jackson, the German shareholders pressed the OTML board to ask the PNG Government to allow them to dispense with a tailings dam. 'Whilst the case for no tailings dam had been strongly argued by BHP in 1978–79,' he said, 'this was the first time since the project agreement's signing that the issue had been raised.'

The PNG Government resisted. 'From the start of the project, the PNG Government tried to take as firm an attitude as possible on the matter of tailings disposal,' he said. 'In 1979, during negotiations held at a stage when world metal prices made the whole project appear sub-marginal, the consortium proposed to dump all tailings into the river system. This provoked a vigorous response from government, which rejected it out of hand and, in return, imposed a wide variety of environmental conditions on the project. Fortunately, gold prices rose very substantially and the consortium felt able to accept the costs these environmental safeguards imposed. These included the tailings dam at Ok Ma.'[7]

Now, in the face of further cost overruns, OTML submitted new plans on 12 December 1983 that eliminated the dam.

They demanded an immediate response. Three days later, the PNG Cabinet rejected it. Stalemate followed, but not for long. The dam was reinstated within two months but, when construction began, the operators were unaware that the mine was in a seismically unstable region. Minor tremors had caused some dislocation but work was able to proceed. On the night of 6 January 1984, however, something happened that would disfigure and deform the project for the rest of its life. Some say it was 'one little tremor', others that it was a 'land slip' caused by water drainage beneath the slope, and others that BMKI's work at the site precipitated it. But whatever the cause, the effect of the massive avalanche that obliterated the work on the tailings dam would be devastating.

OTML, now effectively controlled by BHP, returned to the PNG Government on 23 January with a request to 'defer' the tailings-dam construction for two years. Two days later, against the advice of some of its experts, the government acceded, thus saving up-front project costs of US$84 million. Gold mining started almost immediately. In May 1984, the first gold pours began at the mine site and the first tailings entered the river system. 'The plan was to build a dam but the area was too volcanic and they could never get the dam to stay in place,' Russ Fynmore says. 'That's why the decision was made to dump all the refuse in the river.'[8]

Soon after mining began, two environmental disasters occurred. On 14 June, a barge carrying 2700 drums of sodium cyanide, a key element in the gold-extraction process, capsized in the Fly River on the way to the mine. Only 117 were recovered. Five days later, there was a serious leak of cyanide solution from the mine into the Ok Tedi. The company said nothing about the accident for two weeks until piles of dead fish, snakes and crocodiles appeared on the riverbanks. A government report damned the mine's 'interim tailings scheme'. The government gave OTML one year to produce detailed plans for the copper-mining phase of the project to include construction of a permanent tailings dam.

Australian National University anthropologist Dr Colin Filer, who has worked in the region for two decades, said, 'One year later, the other members of the consortium [aside from the government] declared that they were not prepared to invest in the facilities required for copper production and simultaneously undertake to build the dam.'[9]

The government's response was to close down the mine for six weeks in February and March 1985 until the other partners changed their tune. Another year passed, the original tune was played again and this time the government's opposition was muted. In February 1986, parliament ratified the Sixth Supplemental Agreement between the state and the mining company, allowing the latter to proceed with copper production despite the absence of a tailings dam, provided only that it undertook to study the effects of discharging waste materials into the river system and report back to the government by the end of 1988.

However, just as the deadline expired on 1 December 1988, events elsewhere conspired to produce the worst possible result for the villagers of the Ok Tedi region. Rebellion broke out in Bougainville and would soon close the Panguna copper mine, PNG's only other major source of foreign exchange. And in the world's commodity markets, copper prices began to recover.

OTML immediately responded by raising its output to 80,000 tonnes a day to take advantage of the higher prices but with a corresponding increase in the noxious waste pouring into the river system. And the cash-strapped PNG Government sat on its environmental hands for a further ten months. When it did respond, it released the company from its obligations provided it would 'continue to study the feasibility of various waste-retention options, upgrade its own environmental monitoring program and take some steps to compensate the people living downstream of its operations'.[10]

The need for 'compensation' had entered the equation following growing complaints from villagers downstream of dead fish and polluted water. The tailings sediment contained a toxic mix of sulphur and other chemicals from the ore body itself, plus the acid used in the separation process. The company secured the use of a vessel, *Western Venturer*, to monitor fish populations in the Fly River.

In late 1987, Glen F. Andrews, who joined Utah in 1970 and gained experience in copper mining at the Island Copper mine on Vancouver Island, was brought in from BHP's San Francisco office as general manager. He ran Ok Tedi in 1988 and 1989. 'I flew in with King Air – at that time they had an airstrip – and lived with my wife in a house on stilts at Tabubil, a nice little town site but it needed a lot of improvements,' he says. 'The mine was 6000 feet up the mountain and had been operated rather loosely. You couldn't run that mine without impacting the river. The tailings dam had broken before I got there and we started a system of dredging to collect the sediment and keep it out of the Fly River.'[11]

Meanwhile, at BHP headquarters chief executive officer Brian Loton and his team fought off the Holmes à Court share raid, acquired the undeveloped Escondida copper mine in Chile and bought out its OTML partners, Amoco and two of the German investors, giving it a 60 per cent interest in Ok Tedi.[12] And by January 1988, the copper price hit a high of US$1.50 per pound, producing an end of year profit of K24.2 million,[13] 42 per cent of PNG's total exports. 'With the release of these figures,' Filer said, 'OTML was able to portray itself as the prodigal son who had saved the economy when the loss of [Panguna's] production had threatened devastation.'[14]

From that point on, the company's senior executives displayed a growing confidence – perhaps even a touch of arrogance – in their capacity to match each report of escalating physical damage to the Fly River system with an even more impressive list of economic benefits to Papua New Guinea as a whole.

An American anthropologist, Stuart Kirsch, who surveyed the area from August 1987 to May 1989, reported that the lower Ok Tedi had been turned into 'a 75-kilometre long sewage canal'; overflows of sediment in flood periods prevented crops from growing at all; and 'the entire Ok Tedi river system has been destroyed' to become 'an environmental horror'. 'What is at stake,' he said, 'is nothing less than the future of the entire Fly River and possibly parts of Papuan Gulf and Torres Straits as well.'[15]

He recommended that a compensation plan be devised for the people who lived and owned land along the Ok Tedi river system while scientists continued to investigate the effects of the discharge on the Fly River itself. Filer says, 'The sad irony in Kirsch's recommendation is that [they] should have been receiving fair and reasonable compensation according to the government's own rules from the moment the government itself allowed OTML to begin mining operations without the tailings dam.'[16]

But even in 1989 the only people receiving compensation from OTML were the traditional owners of those areas that the government had leased out to the mining company back in 1981, at a time when all parties still thought that a tailings dam would be built.

In fact, these groups had received only K3 million in that period. Now, in June 1989, Ok Tedi landowners sought K13.5 million in compensation in a petition to the district office. 'One may imagine,' Filer says, 'that the recipients of this petition did not regard it as the sort of document which deserved the attention of a mining warden in Port Moresby.'[17]

OTML responded with a proposal for a 'Development Trust' of K25 million via a levy paid to the government for each tonne of ore processed and waste mined.[18] The company's contribution would return each of the 30,000 beneficiaries a mere K83 a year. Village leaders of the local Yonggom people resolved to petition the national government. At the same time, the international environmental community bestirred itself. The Papua New Guinea Council of Churches passed a resolution condemning the dumping of waste in the Ok Tedi; the German Council of Churches paid two scientists from the Starnberg Institute to visit the area and report; the International Water Tribunal and the Australian Conservation Foundation also produced damning reports.

BHP's director of corporate affairs, Carol Austin, says she lobbied internally for a more active public strategy on Ok Tedi. 'But there were tensions between what Corporate wanted to do and what was done. Ok Tedi came under minerals division and when you have autonomous business units they ultimately have the say.

'I wanted to see regular flights taking half a dozen journalists up there to show them the mine, explain what was happening. The environmental people in the department that I dealt with expressed the view that this would cause disruption and that the long-term environmental damage was reversible. And that was the advice that was given to senior management.

'Certainly, there was the question of the mining bringing to the surface the heavy metals – but this was put in terms of "this is what happens when you get internal disturbances". The other side of it was the income that was being generated; but certainly the advice to the management at headquarters given by the environmental department was not that we are doing devastating damage to the environment and we need to cover it up. They maintained to me that they were comfortable about what BHP was doing at Ok Tedi.'[19]

However, in June 1992 the Yonggom community leaders travelled from the banks of the Ok Tedi to the Rio Earth Summit, where they attracted the interest of the world press. Their provincial leader Isidore Kaseng threatened to close the mine by any means available unless the government agreed to negotiate a better compensation package. Kaseng was briefly arrested. Protests threatened to disrupt the mine. The shadow of Bougainville – by now a shooting war – loomed ever larger. In May 1994, celebrating the tenth anniversary of the mine's operation, BHP's most senior Papua New Guinean representative, Kipling Uiari, called the environmental protests 'not true, wrong and nonsense' and regaled his audience with a list of the economic benefits the mine had delivered:

- More than K330 million to the national government from taxes, royalties and dividends.
- The creation of 5000 jobs.
- K12 million spent on education and training.
- Health services to more than 10,000 people in the area.
- Growth of local industries supplying the mine.

Clearly, there were two very different perspectives at play. Confrontation was inevitable; but when it occurred it took a totally unexpected form.

John Gordon, partner in the Australian law firm Slater & Gordon, later reflected on his company's decision to challenge the might of BHP in a Victorian court. 'If you asked a lawyer to devise a scenario for the case he or she would least want to embark upon,' he said, 'I suspect it would be something like this: your clients are impecunious; they live in another country whose government is opposed to their claim; they live in villages without phones, four hours by plane and many hours by boat from the capital; your opponent is the biggest company in Australia; they engage one of the country's biggest law firms to act for them; the litigation is vigorously contested; and you have to fund it yourself.'[20]

That, he said, was the situation his company found itself in when it agreed to represent 30,000 landowners of the Ok Tedi in a multimillion-dollar claim for damages against BHP in 1994. In May and June, four test cases were issued in the Supreme Court of Victoria seeking injunctions to restrain the dumping of tailings into the river system and compensation for the damage caused.

BHP responded that they were 'more than happy' to fight the case. But if so they totally misread the situation. The publicity surrounding the incendiary legal battle would engage and intrigue Australia for the next two years. Television programs such as *Four Corners* and *60 Minutes* would send crews up the Fly and over the mountains of Western Province to picture 'Stone Age communities' devastated by the greedy and unrepentant mining giant. Suddenly, 'The Big Australian' was a term of opprobrium. BHP had never known anything quite like it.

Inside the courtroom, Slater & Gordon had secured the services of Julian Burnside QC, whose involvement in the case would not only bring him high national regard but also affect his own attitude towards society's worthier causes. His advocacy on behalf of the 'subsistence lifestyle' of the Yonggom would become a textbook source in the field. BHP's team claimed that because the villagers were subsistence dwellers who did not use money as a means of exchange theirs was simply a loss of amenity; accordingly, 'there can have been no economic loss and hence no monetary damages could be awarded'.

Burnside responded, 'The reason economic-loss cases involve money is because money is what we use for our economy. The lifestyle of the Papua New Guinea natives in gathering food, fishing and [hunting] game and using it to eat and sell is no less an economic activity because it is not translated through the medium of money.'[21]

The judge agreed. BHP then challenged the jurisdiction of the Supreme Court of Victoria and attempted to settle the claims directly with the local landowners. This too was unsuccessful. The company worked with the PNG Government to develop legislation[22] that would prohibit legal proceedings, or giving evidence in legal proceedings. 'But it didn't end there,' John Gordon said. 'In the event that BHP and OTML were ordered to build a tailings dam, they would be entitled to reduce [any] compensation payable dollar for dollar. Given that the cost of a tailings dam would far exceed the total amount of compensation payable over the life of the mine, this would effectively end all payments of compensation.'[23]

But then, in an extraordinary provision, the agreement provided that, even if a tailings dam were ordered and BHP/OTML reduced their compensation commitments accordingly, they could elect, apparently in their absolute discretion, not to proceed with construction of the dam as ordered.

The Bill enshrining the agreement incorporated draconian

punishments for anyone seeking to take legal action against it, including a fine of K100,000 plus K10,000 a day for each day the offence continued. 'As if all that was not enough,' Gordon said, 'the agreement then provided that if someone was able to successfully obtain a judgment for damages against BHP or OTML, BHP could then sue to recover the amount, no doubt at the same time as criminal proceedings were brought against [the defendant] and their lawyers for having dared commit such a heinous offence.'

When the proposed legislation was revealed, Gordon & Slater applied to have BHP punished for contempt of court. And as word spread, 1800 shareholders inside BHP's September 1995 AGM in Melbourne and a crowd of placard-wielding protesters outside demanded answers. Chief executive John Prescott refused to accept responsibility for the PNG legislation. 'In the final analysis, it is the sovereign government of Papua New Guinea that has the accountability and responsibility for this matter,' he said.[24]

In the legal wrangle that followed, a new agreement was drafted removing the offending passages and in June 1996 the parties reached an out-of-court settlement. BHP agreed to implement a 'feasible tailings containment system', to pay K40 million to villagers in the worst affected areas on the Ok Tedi and a further K110 million to all affected persons.

For Gordon & Slater, it was a great victory. However, four years later BHP was back in the courts facing claims of breach of contract over the settlement. These proceedings would further despoil the company's environmental reputation.

The prevailing view at BHP headquarters seems to have alternated between confusion and outrage. Graham Evans, the head of public-relations damage control, says, 'You have on the one hand the company paying taxes and royalties and compensation for environmental damage in Ok Tedi – and having invested significantly in the social and economic infrastructure of the Western Province – and yet [we] were attracting very adverse newspaper headlines.

'The issue was coming up in a pretty ugly way at AGMs, and senior management was appearing in Federal Court. They and the board found it very hard to reconcile the two.'[25]

Evans sought to distance BHP from the issue by engaging an outside public-relations firm, Offor Sharp, in 1999. The contract, signed by Evans's employee, Michael Spencer, would keep Offor Sharp well rewarded until 2007. 'We delivered a tightly controlled and highly strategic public release to diverse and often aggressive stakeholders in PNG, Australia and the US,' Tim Offor said. 'Media coverage was limited because direct engagement over the complexity of the issues meant few critics were prepared to provide media comment. As a result of the release strategy, there was no civil unrest in PNG and [OTML's] two listed shareholders contained potentially damaging media coverage.'[26]

In fact, since the 1996 judgment, BHP's 'feasible tailings containment system' had become the dredging program in the Ok Tedi at an annual cost of $30 million. It was ineffective. The pollution was poisoning the river ever further downstream. After a thorough investigation, the World Bank had told the company on 20 January 2000, 'The Ok Tedi mine needs to be moving toward closure as soon as possible. Preparations for closure should be initiated without delay given the traditionally long lead time associated with social impact mitigation measures.'[27]

The major stakeholders would soon agree, some more enthusiastically than others. Unfortunately for BHP, there was still a series of shoals and reefs to be negotiated before clear water could be glimpsed; and nor were they the only lurking threat to the company's carefully nurtured reputation.

CHAPTER 13

Black Gold

John J. O'Connor was recruited in 1994 from the US giant Mobil Oil to take over from Peter Wilcox as head of BHP Petroleum. At the time, O'Connor was one of three executive vice presidents in Mobil's exploration and production division with responsibility for Europe, Africa and Russia. 'I had worked with P. J. Wilcox in the Middle East,' O'Connor says. 'He must have given my name to John Prescott.'[1]

Within weeks of his arrival in Melbourne, O'Connor proved to have a mind – and style – of his own. He worked not at BHP Tower but at the BHP Petroleum office in Collins Street, enjoyed partying and drove a Porsche around town. 'We executives were all given an allowance to buy company cars,' he says. 'They all bought BMWs – safe cars – while I bought a Porsche. I was in the newspapers all the time; that got up their nose, I'm sure. Melbourne is extremely parochial – I always get the sense that it's run by about 50 families.'[2]

The maverick image grew among O'Connor's colleagues on the BHP board when he expressed the view that his division should concentrate on big cash-producing assets, dispose of the remainder and invest its Bass Strait earnings in high-risk, high-return growth.[3] 'The petroleum piece of the business was pretty much coasting along,' he says, 'although they had done a number of innovative developments, not least of which were the floating production storage offshore vessels (FPSOs) that they had off Western Australia. But it was clear that both Bass Strait and North-West Shelf had to be augmented with new stuff, so we started looking outside Australia.'

In Pakistan, he secured a block that subsequently became the highly profitable Zamzama field[4] before turning his attention to the Gulf of Mexico, where the company controlled some smaller assets. 'BP had a large swathe of exploration blocks in deep-water Gulf of Mexico, which they owned 100 per cent,' he says. 'They wanted to reduce their exposure, and after lots of other companies had turned them down we accepted the commitment.

'We acquired 44 per cent of this swathe of blocks – might have been a hundred blocks – and that was really the key transformational event. We took a risk; we stepped out from hundreds of feet of water into thousands of feet of water in an area where data was very sparse. That's how BHP has ended up with this 44 per cent equity – it was through that deal with BP.'[5]

O'Connor then hired Norman Davidson Kelly, a London-based oil executive, to act as a roving diplomat for BHP Petroleum. 'He was the head of business development and he had a good track record,' O'Connor says. He had done deals in North America and knew his way round international mergers and acquisitions. 'I felt that BHP Petroleum needed to be shaken up, needed new blood, needed people with a more broad-based view. The whole point was trying to change the strategic direction of the business, trying to be a bit more worldly wise and trying to find some new things.'

O'Connor's strategy was applauded by Don Argus. 'John O'Connor actually broke the BHP cultural mould,' he says. 'John was one of these guys that actually challenged the strategic direction of the company.'[6] However, his challenge was not an unalloyed success. And his hiring of Davidson Kelly – known to his friends as NDK – was an unmitigated disaster.

Born in Scotland and educated at Exeter College, Oxford, NDK was a friend of Sir Malcolm Rifkind's, the former British foreign secretary and fellow Scot who joined BHP as a consultant after he had lost his parliamentary seat.[7] In Melbourne, NDK gravitated towards Tom Harley, a pipe-smoking, Oxford-educated great-grandson of Australia's second prime minister, Alfred Deakin.[8] 'Harley was a dilettante-ish sort of person who flitted in and flitted out,' O'Connor says. 'He had a number of different irons in the fire, I guess."[9]

Tom Harley had joined BHP on 3 April 1984 and by 1996 was group manager financial structuring in BHP Petroleum. He had very close links with the Liberal Party and introduced Davidson Kelly to Robert Hill, a Cabinet minister in the Howard government who later described NDK as 'outgoing and gregarious'.[10]

At BHP, the circle around the two Oxford graduates became known as the 'Harley Davidson boys'. The nickname was steeped in irony; both men could hardly have been more different from the ruffians of the road. The Old Oxonians dressed fashionably, spoke with plummy accents and revelled in the atmosphere of stately privilege in Harley's Melbourne Club.

In 1995 and early 1996, Davidson Kelly and Harley arranged for BHP to ship 20,000 tonnes of Australian wheat, valued at $5 million, to sanctions-hit Iraq, an initiative that would later embroil BHP in one of the more unpleasant controversies of its long history.[11] The wheat shipment was described as a humanitarian gesture, but internal documents, produced at the subsequent Cole Inquiry,[12] showed that some BHP executives were hoping to persuade the Iraqi regime to allow it to develop the country's lucrative Halfaya oilfield once the United Nations had lifted its sanctions. The oilfield, in southern Iraq, had the potential to produce 300,000 barrels of oil a day from a reservoir estimated at two billion barrels.[13]

Eight years later, the $5 million was returned with

$3.25 million interest, though the entire amount found its way to the pockets of Norman Davidson Kelly. BHP Billiton had earlier arranged to receive 25 per cent of the repayment; in the event, it got nothing but a humiliating dose of public opprobrium.

Harley met with Australian Wheat Board (AWB) executives on 23 June 1995 in Melbourne, where he learned that Charles Stott was a key figure as regional marketing manager for the Middle East. According to author and journalist Caroline Overington, who was among the first to expose the scandal and who covered the Cole Inquiry for her newspaper *The Australian*, Stott was very well connected in Iraq. 'Stott liked to boast that he had more contacts in Baghdad than any other Western businessman,'[14] she wrote.

Between September and November, Davidson Kelly discussed the means of financing the wheat shipment with other BHP executives, including O'Connor, Graham Evans, director of government relations and external affairs, and his associate Peter Laver. 'I was asked to deal with the political issues and the Corporate Centre approval process,' Harley said, 'and to assist with researching aspects of some of [the] options on Mr Davidson Kelly's behalf.'[15] He also spoke with Charles Stott at AWB.

On 19 September, Davidson Kelly and Harley sent a joint memo to O'Connor recommending that 'US$5 million be spent to purchase a Letter of Credit (LOC) to be issued or backed by the Central Bank of Iraq in favour of the Australian Wheat Board'. The LOC would be redeemable into either oil or cash no later than 2000 and bear an interest rate of ten per cent per annum, the memo said.[16]

> This transaction will cause the Australian Wheat Board to ship about 20,000 tonnes of wheat to Iraq.
>
> The purpose of the transaction is to establish favour with the Government of Iraq in anticipation that sometime prior to 2000 the LOC may be exchanged with the Government of Iraq as a down payment for entry to the HCF [Halfaya] concession. However, no certainty exists in this respect.

> The transaction complies with the terms of the UN embargo on Iraq because the AWB has an exemption for this wheat sale and our arrangement is a back to back financial agreement. The LOC will only be settled in oil if the embargo has been lifted.
>
> The most significant risk taken with this proposal is that a new regime takes control in Iraq that will not honour obligations. The value of the LOC will have to be assessed annually and any diminution will be written off against profit. The worst case is that the US$5 million will have to be written off completely, in which case it will be deductible against income.

John O'Connor made light of the cost, saying it represented 'about half the cost [of drilling] one dry hole' in the search for oil. However, according to Tom Harley's statement to the Cole Inquiry, BHP managing director John Prescott expressed 'reservations' about the deal. On 9 October, Harley penned an internal 'note' on the situation. It was unclear, he said, what Prescott's objection was, but two possible causes were, 'The payment of funds by the company for "goodwill" to the Iraqi Government being akin to some form of bribe,' or 'opening the company to the allegation that it is aiding an international pariah'.

However, a week later Prescott signed a memorandum containing the proposal from Davidson Kelly with the notation, 'I would agree provided we proceed via Dept of Foreign Affairs and gain UN Sanctions Cttee approval.'

Harley said in a statement to the inquiry, 'Mr O'Connor told me around this time that he wanted to proceed with a wheat shipment . . . at this point I believe there was a firm internal proposal to move forward with a wheat shipment based on a letter of credit.' However, he said, he later considered 'various gift based options' and spoke with John Freakes, a senior Department of Foreign Affairs and Trade official. Freakes later sent a fax to Stott at the AWB noting that AWB's 'recent application' to send the shipment to Iraq had received United

Nations approval on 28 November 'for the supply of wheat from a third party [i.e. BHP]'.[17]

Stott sent the fax on to Harley on 4 December with the handwritten notation, 'Tom, Looks like all systems go. Charles 4/12'.[18] The following day, Tom Harley said, he drafted 'at least part of' a memorandum that went to John Prescott. Headed 'IRAQ', it said:

> The Australian Department of Foreign Affairs and Trade (DFAT) through the Acting Director Middle East and Africa Branch, Mr John Freakes, has stated that the Company is free to pay the Australian Wheat Board (AWB) for the supply of wheat to Iraq.
>
> DFAT's approval has been obtained following the satisfaction of their requirement that the AWB gain approval from the UN Sanctions Committee for the supply of wheat by a third Party. The Sanctions Committee last week approved the AWB's application.
>
> It is now proposed that we proceed to arrange with the AWB for the shipment of up to US$5 million of wheat as soon as possible. It is proposed that this be done on a straight forward grant basis.

Prescott responded to the memorandum – 'Ok to proceed' – on 9 December. Charles Stott then organised for the MV *Ikan Sepat* (Sour Fish) to load the grain in South Australia and transport it to Umm Qasr for arrival in Iraq on Australia Day 1996. The Iraqi deputy minister for oil, Faiz A. Shaheen, wrote to O'Connor in April saying:

> We are delighted that your *first* shipment of grain arrived in Iraq. Many thanks for your efforts and that of BHP and we hope that additional shipments can be made successfully in the near future.
>
> We have been informed of the good presentation made by your staff on the development of the Halfaya field and the

> Ministry is awaiting the next round of discussions where more progress is expected to be made . . . [emphasis added][19]

Since the successful shipment in January, NDK had envisioned a series of subsequent wheat sponsorships to the increasingly desperate Iraqis under the sanctions regime. Indeed, Charles Stott left his position at the AWB in early 1996 to join BHP Petroleum as international business-development manager, reporting to Davidson Kelly.

However, the attitude of DFAT to further shipments soon became a complicating factor. In April, when Stott had joined BHP, he sent an email to NDK and Tom Harley that raised hopes for DFAT approval. However, they were dashed the following month when Harley received a fax from DFAT's assistant secretary Mark Pierce providing a 'substantive reply' to the issues. 'Ministers[20] have decided not to endorse the proposal that some wheat be shipped against payment by a five-year letter of credit,' Pierce wrote, 'and they therefore decided that no submission containing any such proposal should be put to the UN sanctions committee.'[21]

Pierce also noted that Harley's 'colleagues' had raised the possibility of 're-formulating' the US$5 million shipment to become a loan rather than a gift. 'The department takes the view that, if the gift arrangement were re-formulated into a credit arrangement, the requirement of notification and disclosure to the UNSC sanctions committee would not have been met,' he said. 'This would not be acceptable procedure. As far as the department is concerned, the sale in January is a closed matter and must remain closed.'

John O'Connor now says he kept the Iraq project at arm's length. 'I was on a green card when I worked for Mobil in the US but still had an Irish passport,' he says. 'I had started the process of applying for American citizenship. When the deal about looking at Iraq surfaced within BHP Petroleum, I took counsel from Skadden, Arps, a leading law firm in the US, and the advice was, "If you want to keep pursuing your US citizenship application, have nothing to do with anything to do with Iraq." In essence, that kept me totally separate from anything that was being done.'[22]

O'Connor's passport problems were remarkably fortuitous, and he departed BHP in August 1997. His successor was Philip Aiken, who had joined as the company's executive general manager corporate development in May. Tom Harley became global practice leader in May, reporting to Aiken when Aiken took over from O'Connor. At the same time, Norman Davidson Kelly became group general manager, new business opportunities. Charles Stott returned to AWB in 1998.

For the next two years, all was relatively quiet on the Middle Eastern front. Norman Davidson Kelly had become an internal consultant to BHP Petroleum in November 1998, then international consultant in September 2000. In May 1999, Harley was promoted to BHP vice president mergers and acquisitions and says he had 'very little' to do with Iraq.

Then, at 12.57 am on 2 May 2000, Charles Stott at AWB sent an email to Davidson Kelly: 'Norman, In January 2001, it is 5 years since BHP supplied the grain, and payment of US Dollars 8,052,550 becomes due. We need to start thinking about what we want to do, as the system will need to be appropriately warmed up, starting a least 6 months in advance if we want to recover the debt. Happy to discuss. Cheers, Charles.'

Davidson Kelly copied his response to Harley: 'Tks. Let's discuss. N.' and Harley replied, 'Yes, The Canteen Thursday? Thos.'[23]

Harley told the Cole Inquiry, 'I believe my reference to "The Canteen Thursday" is a reference to having lunch in London on the following Thursday, which was 11 May 2000.' However, he would not be able to keep the appointment.

On 9 May, Davidson Kelly sent an email to Philip Aiken with a copy to Harley:

> I don't know how familiar you are with the details, but there is the strong possibility that the Iraqi's [*sic*] will owe BHPP [BHP

> Petroleum] a total of around US$8 million under a debt which crystallises in 6 months['] time.
>
> I would prefer to fill you in in person, or Tom can easily do that. I think it would be a good idea for Tom and me to work through the issues with Jim Lyons and Charles Stott, who were involved in the original transaction. It is quite complex as there are DFAT and UN issues to address.
>
> We could then discuss with you a recommendation either to proceed to attempt recovery, with a draft plan of action, or a recommendation that we drop the whole thing. I would be reluctant to recommend the latter course of action without at least an internal review, as there is a lot of potential cash at stake. No hurry, and Jim is on leave until early June in any event. N.[24]

Aiken responded, 'I never cease to be amazed. Will be fascinated to hear this one.'

Harley said:

> I recall that Mr Aiken was with me in New York and Houston at the time Mr Davidson Kelly's email was sent and that I spoke with him several times a day in person while we were there. I recall him asking me what the 'debt' to Iraq was all about. I recall saying to him words to the effect that there was no debt. I do not recall his response or any other aspects of the discussion other than his incredulity at the notion that the Iraqis might owe BHPP money . . . I am not aware of what, if anything, followed from this email.[25]

In about mid-2000, Aiken began negotiating an arrangement with Davidson Kelly to 'exit' BHPP; part of the deal was that Davidson Kelly's company Tigris Petroleum would take over BHPP's role in seeking the development of the Halfaya oilfield. Tom Harley told the Inquiry:

> Mr Aiken informed me that Mr Lyons was assisting with drafting the arrangement that was being negotiated. I was

not involved in the negotiations with Mr Davidson Kelly. Mr Aiken said he did not want me to be involved. I do not believe he told me why.

When the negotiations were completed, Aiken wrote to the Iraqi oil minister, Amir Al-Rashid, on 13 September reminding him of the wheat shipment:

As you will recall, BHPP made a major contribution to the alleviation of suffering of the Iraqi people with the cargo of grain delivered on the MV *Ikan Sepat* in January 1996 prior to the institution of the United Nations 'Oil for Food' programme.

It has been a great frustration to BHPP that circumstances have prevented us from implementing the Production Sharing Agreement which we had negotiated in relation to the Halfaya field.

Following our recent Strategy Review, BHPP has come to the conclusion that it would be in the best interests of all parties to hand over to a new organisation, The Tigris Petroleum Corporation, the responsibility for continuing discussions with the Ministry for Oil in relation to oil-and-gas developments in Iraq. In the event that normal political relations are resumed, BHPP has the right, subject to your approval, to participate in those projects . . .[26]

On the same day, he signed a letter To Whom It May Concern transferring all BHPP's 'right title and interest relating to all Iraqi Assets and Liabilities' to Norman Davidson Kelly's company, Tigris Petroleum Corporation Limited, registered in Gibraltar:

In particular, BHP Petroleum has assigned to Tigris all its rights to receive value from the Grain Board of Iraq, or its assignee, in relation to the cargo of grain delivered by the Australian Wheat Board to the Iraqi Grain Board in January 1996 on the

> MV *Ikan Sepat*, which cargo was financed by BHP Petroleum at a cost of US$5 million which rights are hereinafter referred to as 'Grain Board Receivable'.
>
> Tigris is hereby authorised to discuss the Grain Board Receivable with the appropriate parties and to negotiate details and terms of payment as Tigris in its sole discretion shall deem appropriate, without further BHP Petroleum involvement. Payments made in relation to the Grain Board Receivable should be made as directed by Tigris.

In May 2001, Charles Stott, now general manager international marketing at the AWB, wrote to the chairman of the Iraqi Grain Board, Yousif M. Abdul-Rahman, 'regarding the repayment to Tigris Petroleum for the grain shipped on the MV *Ikan Sepat* January 1996'.[27] He enclosed a letter from Norman Davidson Kelly in which NDK said that, in consideration for prompt settlement, Tigris would be prepared to waive its right to compound interest on the 'loan'. He suggested two payments – $3.875 million on 1 June and $4.062 million on 1 December. Stott concluded his covering letter, 'Would be grateful if you would pass the letter on to the appropriate authorities for their consideration.'

At the same time, Davidson Kelly wrote to Philip Aiken to bring him 'up to date on the steps we have taken to recover the outstanding loan made by BHPP to Iraq in January 1996'. He said Tigris and AWB had made a direct approach to the Iraqi vice president, Taha Yassin Ramadan, who had referred the matter to Council. 'Even if we get the green light,' he said, 'I expect the actual repayment process to be complicated', and it 'will be linked to shipments of Australian wheat and therefore made over a period of time'.

In the event, the Iraqi authorities accepted their obligation and repaid the 'debt' – a total of US$8.35 million – through the AWB 'loading up' the cost of wheat shipments. By agreement with Norman Davidson Kelly, AWB paid themselves a US$500,000 collection fee.

The separation agreement between BHPP and Davidson Kelly contained a provision for BHPP to receive 25 per cent of anything collected from the Iraqis, but the arrangement was subsequently waived. The result was that BHP outlaid US$5 million for no return and Davidson Kelly recouped the entire US$8.35 million 'repayment'.

It was not, however, the end of the story. The episode would return to haunt the company in the years ahead. Indeed, it would bedevil a series of chief executive officers and weaken its international bargaining position as the industry entered its international consolidation phase. Meanwhile, its future partner in BHP Billiton had embarked on a journey that would excite the envy – and avarice – of the mining world.

PART III

The Partner

CHAPTER 14

Billiton

Billiton's remarkable history began on 27 June 1851, 32 years before Charles Rasp scoured the broken hill for black oxide of tin, when six Dutchmen stepped ashore on a white-pebbled beach on an island off the eastern coast of Sumatra in search of the same mineral. The island was Belitung, which they pronounced Billiton.

In the eighteenth century, copious quantities of tin had been found on neighbouring Banka Island and the explorers suspected that little Belitung, measuring just 79 kilometres by 77 kilometres, also contained rich deposits in its rugged terrain and low hills. Their expedition had been financed by Prince Henry of Orange, and one of the explorers was Vincent van Tuyll van Serooskerken, a Dutch aristocrat. With the motto *Virtus vim vincit* (Virtue defeats vice) on the escutcheon, a succession of knights, courtiers, generals, ambassadors and statesmen had borne the van Tuyll name for a thousand years. Following the French occupation of the Netherlands in 1795, Vincent's father Carel Lodewijk van Tuyll van Serooskerken fled to England, where he married Marie Louise Gildemeester, daughter of a former Dutch consul-general to

Portugal. Vincent was born in the English spa resort of Bath on 13 March 1812.

The previous year, a British army had defeated Franco-Dutch forces in the East Indies and occupied Dutch territories to deny their spices, merchandise and bullion to the rampaging Emperor Napoleon. The viceroy of India, Lord Minto, who had accompanied the military expedition, appointed his protégé, Stamford Raffles, as lieutenant-governor of Java and its dependencies. Raffles banned torture (including water-boarding, which had been pioneered by the Dutch in the Indies), introduced trial by jury and established British residencies in many of the main centres of population. To Banyuwangi on the eastern tip of Java he sent Alexander Loudon, a Scottish soldier whose family name would run through Billiton's history for more than a hundred years.

When Dutch settlers were slaughtered in 1812 by followers of the Sultan of Palembang, a state on the eastern coast of Sumatra, the Sultan was put to flight and Raffles seized Banka and Belitung islands as reparation for the massacre. He allowed Belitung's Malay ruler, the *depati*, a vassal of Palembang, to stay in power on condition he kowtowed to the British resident on Banka. Raffles had great plans for Belitung. 'Billiton lies in the direct track of the trade between Europe and China, passing through the Straits of Sunda,' he wrote, 'and would afford a convenient port of refreshment for our China Ships and might be expected to become a most extensive entrepôt between Europe and China.' He continued, 'Billiton is said to be rich in ores of various descriptions and would form a most valuable and important link in our series of stations, and would always ensure us to every advantage in the trade of the archipelago.'[1]

The powers-that-be in Westminster, however, did not share Raffles' vision and returned both islands to the Netherlands under the Anglo-Dutch Treaty of 1824, an act of folly that was savagely denounced by *The Times*. 'Of all the blunders of Lord Londonderry [the former British foreign secretary],' The Thunderer raged, 'this sacrifice of the Eastern Archipelago to the Dutch was in itself the most impolitic, and to the British merchant the most odious.'[2]

After the restoration of the House of Orange, the van Tuyll family had returned to the Netherlands. Carel Lodewijk became gentleman of the bedchamber to King William I and was rewarded with a title, Baron van Tuyll van Serooskerken. His twilight years were spent as a gentleman farmer on the family's estate at Hillegom, which he bequeathed to Vincent, along with his title and large tracts of the Canadian wilderness that he had unwisely bought on time payment.

Tall and handsome, with masses of curly hair and a full beard, the rakish young baron ignored the moral injunction of the family motto and used his charms to seduce an improbable number of young women during his travels in England, Germany and North America. He finally settled down at the age of 32 when he married Charlotte Mansfield in London on 8 August 1844 and took her home to Hillegom.[3]

By the late 1840s, the demands of Vincent van Tuyll's creditors in Canada had almost bankrupted him and he began speculating in mining enterprises in the Indonesian archipelago. Tin mining was concentrated on Banka Island, where large numbers of Chinese had been imported to work the state-owned mines. The authorities in Batavia (now Jakarta) largely ignored Belitung's scattered communities of humble Malay farmers and fishermen until the beginning of 1850, when van Tuyll and Prince Henry asked the Prince's brother, King William III, to grant them the mineral rights on Belitung. Their request was granted and a small syndicate was formed. Van Tuyll was so optimistic of its chances of success that he created the name 'Bilitonia' as a middle name for a daughter born that year.

One of the syndicate's members was John Francis Loudon,[4] 30-year-old son of the Scotsman Alexander Loudon and his Dutch wife Susanna, known as Santje. After serving as British resident at Banyuwangi, Alexander had assumed the much more lucrative post of collector of customs at Semarang. He had taken Dutch citizenship and made his fortune through extensive holdings in the Javanese sugar trade. Santje had presented him with six sons: the first – Hugh Hope Loudon – was born in 1816 when she was just 15, and the last – William Beylon Loudon – was born in 1827, only a year before her untimely death at the age of 28. Alexander imbued his sons with a spirit of adventure, while his wealth paid for a good education and a place among the Dutch bourgeoisie back in Holland for each of them. A lithograph of John Francis Loudon made in 1845 shows a dandified young blade in cravat, waistcoat, cutaway jacket and tight breeches.

The syndicate's first act was to commission Dutch mining engineer Dr J. H. Croockewit to prospect for tin on Belitung. Croockewit duly enlisted the help of the *depati*, who, fearing Belitung would be inundated with foreigners like Banka Island, told the Dutchman he was wasting his time: there was no tin on the island. After a three-month search, Croockewit concurred. 'The island of Belitung contains no tin ore in its soil,' he concluded, 'that is, not in such form as has been found and could be worked on Banka up to now'[5] – an astonishing finding considering parts of the island were pitted with old diggings from earlier tin-mining endeavours and the streams contained rich alluvial deposits of the mineral. In fact, Banka and Belitung were at the end of a narrow belt of tinstone extending from Lower Burma through the Malay Peninsula to the East Indies.[6]

In Batavia, Loudon discussed Croockewit's report with another engineer, Cornelius de Groot, and decided it was fallacious. He asked the governor-general if he could undertake a second expedition to Belitung. This would be a much grander affair – an alliance between the Dutch aristocracy, represented by Baron van Tuyll, and bourgeois entrepreneurs like himself.

On arrival on Belitung in June 1851, they were greeted by the same *depati*, who offered them refreshments in his pavilion. When the man refused to eat any of the food himself, Loudon feared it had been poisoned and warned his companions. Loudon then told the *depati* that the Dutch Government was determined to find ore on his island whether he liked it or not, and if his party failed in its mission an even larger party would be sent. The *depati* saw the wisdom of this argument. According to Loudon's diary, 'tin was discovered 24 hours after our arrival'.[7]

Baron van Tuyll sailed back to Batavia to report the success of the mission and to claim an interim mining concession on behalf of the syndicate, while Loudon, a large straw hat shielding his balding pate from the blistering sun and dressed in a red frock-coat and black breeches, supervised the excavation of four large pits at spots where oxide of tin had been discovered. The following year, van Tuyll and Prince Henry were given a government mandate to develop the Dutch tin industry abroad. At the same time, the syndicate's concession to all mineral rights on Belitung was extended for the next 40 years. Mining operations then began in earnest.

The authorities on Banka refused to allow Loudon to employ members of its workforce, so he hired 60 Chinese workers from Singapore to organise a *kongsi*, or cooperative, to employ coolies from Hong Kong, Canton (Guangzhou), Amoy (Xiamen) and Swatow (Shantou).[8] Their first job was to clear rainwater out of the flooded excavations using ancient treadmill pumps. The fledgling mining project encountered many difficulties: tropical diseases – cholera, typhoid and malaria – wiped out more than a third of the workforce every year for the first several years; money was in short supply; pirates were a constant menace; management techniques were poor; and accidents happened.

Billiton plunged deeply into debt.

Further misfortune followed when Baron van Tuyll, at just 48, died in The Hague on 17 March 1860. Nevertheless, six months later, on 29 September 1860, the tin-mining company NV Billiton Maatschappij (the Billiton Society) came into being when articles of association were approved at a meeting of shareholders in the Het Groot Keizerhof hotel in the Dutch capital. The company took over the mineral concession and issued 5000 shares, each worth 1000 gilders; one of the most enthusiastic investors was Prince Henry. With an injection of fresh capital, rich alluvial deposits were soon discovered on the east coast of the island.[9]

'The founding of Billiton is always deemed as 1860, but that was a convenient date to register the company in Holland when they knew they had a resource on Belitung Island that would produce tin,' says Paul Everard, a Shell marketing executive who became an executive director of Billiton in the 1980s. 'By the 1860s, Billiton had become one of the leading tin producers in the world.'[10]

From the outset, Billiton was a purely Dutch company and Belitung was a company island: Billiton Mij (an abbreviation of Maatschappij), or the Billiton Tin Company as it was known in England, owned the mines, the barracks, the commissariat and the hospitals. The company simply leased its mines to the *kongsi* and advanced sufficient money to finance each year's mining operations, including food and medical supplies for the miners.

The advance was repaid in the form of tons of tin ore delivered from the open-cut mines to the company at a fixed price. After paying off the labourers, the remaining profits were distributed among the *kongsi*'s shareholders. Billiton then made its money by smelting the ore and selling the tin ingots on the open market. The first public auction of Billiton tin was held in Batavia in April 1863; three years later, *The Times* of London reported that 'very large quantities of tin are steadily arriving in this country from Banca [*sic*] and Billiton'.

John Francis Loudon rapidly amassed a large fortune from tin mining and, like his father, from sugar refining. In 1869, he returned to the Netherlands, where he excited envy among the *haute bourgeoisie* by buying the fabulous 250-piece De la Villestreux collection of Delftware to decorate the large house he had bought in The Hague. The Loudon family's stocks rose substantially in 1871 when John Francis's younger brother James, a former colonial minister, was appointed governor-general of the Netherlands East Indies, an appointment that would enable him to keep an eye on the family's tin-mining investment.

Output from the Belitung mines increased dramatically over the next 20 years – so that when the Billiton concession was renewed in 1892, the Dutch Government insisted on a new arrangement under which it took five and a half per cent of the gross revenue, plus a large share of the profits.

James Loudon had wanted his eldest son Hugo to follow in his footsteps in the country's diplomatic service. The young man, however, had a mind of his own and, after graduating as a civil engineer, worked on land-reclamation projects in Hungary and built railways in South Africa. As the nineteenth century drew to a close, he forged a relationship with another rising star of the Amsterdam Bourse, Royal Dutch Petroleum, which would play a vital and unexpected part in Billiton's chequered history.

Royal Dutch had discovered oil in the sweltering jungles of north-eastern Sumatra in 1890. Regrettably, after a few years' production the wells started pumping nothing but salt water. The news of this commercial disaster reached Amsterdam in July 1898. To the grave embarrassment of one of its principal shareholders, the Dutch Royal Family, the value of Royal Dutch's shares plummeted. The company's boss, August Kessler, knew that if he failed to find productive new fields – and quickly – Royal Dutch would be at the mercy of his competitors, John D. Rockefeller of Standard Oil of New Jersey and Marcus Samuel of London-based Shell Transport and Trading.

Royal Dutch's experienced American crews drilled 110 wildcat wells on Sumatra without finding any new oil. In desperation, Kessler dispatched Hugo Loudon, who had been sent to the East Indies as technical manager and had quickly established himself as Kessler's right-hand man, to the little principality of Perlak on Sumatra, where oil seepages had been discovered among the pepper trees. The area had only recently been pacified following bloody clashes between the Dutch Army and Perlak's overlord, the Sultan of Aceh. Loudon discovered that a local prince, the Rajah of Perlak, favoured cooperation with the colonisers – an act that had provoked his Muslim subjects to declare *jihad* against him.

Hugo Loudon radiated natural charm and his name was known throughout the Indies; he realised Perlak's internecine conflict presented him with a unique opportunity. With a diplomatic elan that would have impressed his father, he explained the benefits that oil royalties might bestow on the warring factions and succeeded in brokering a truce between them, thus enabling exploration work to proceed.[11]

Geologists had so far been largely ignored by the oil industry, which saw them as scientific theorists possessing none of the technical virtues of engineers. But in a radical departure symptomatic of Royal Dutch's desperation, a couple of geologists had been included in a drilling team for the first time. Loudon told them to select the most promising drilling sites among the pools of seeping oil.

Drilling began just before Christmas 1899 and only six days later a huge gusher burst from the wellhead. Royal Dutch shares doubled in value in a single day – and Hugo Loudon had started his meteoric ascent to the very top of the oil industry. When Royal Dutch, now commanded by Kessler's formidable protégé Henri Deterding, merged its assets and operations with a faltering Shell in 1907, retaining the latter's famous pectin shell as its trademark, Loudon became managing director and later chairman of the Royal Dutch Shell Group.[12]

Meanwhile, Billiton had become well established in the mining and smelting of tin and lead, initially with a smelter on Belitung and then a much larger one in Singapore. It had also acquired a coat of arms: a fist clenching a geological hammer over an armorial shield bearing three ingots of tin. Billiton was so successful that on New Year's Day 1924 the Netherlands Indies Government, after casting a predatory eye over the company's balance sheet, insisted on increasing its stake to five-eighths of the stock, leaving private investors with a minority holding of just three-eighths. A joint public–private enterprise, the Billiton Joint Mining Company (GMB),[13] was set up with a 25-year concession to mine the tin deposits on Belitung.

Tin and lead production commenced in the Netherlands in 1928 when a smelter was opened at Arnhem. However, Billiton's fortunes plunged in 1929 when the price of tin tumbled even before the Great Depression of October that year had bitten deeply into world markets. Prices continued to fall during the 1930s, with disastrous consequences for Belitung, where thousands of Chinese miners were laid off and repatriated at the company's expense. Belitung's standard of living slumped, creating widespread hardship among the Malay population; it did not recover until tin prices revived at the end of the decade.[14]

By now, Vincent van Tuyll's grandson was president of Billiton, and he led the company into new ventures, exploring for nickel in Celebes (Sulawesi) and gold in Dutch New Guinea (Irian Jaya), and expanding into bauxite mining on Indonesia's Bintan Island and at Paranan in the Dutch colony of Suriname, South America. A zinc smelter was also built in the village of Budel in southern Holland in a 50/50 joint venture with North Broken Hill Limited to process ore from Broken Hill.[15]

Billiton's activities in Holland were abruptly halted when German panzers overran the Low Countries in May 1940. Queen Wilhelmina escaped to London and the Dutch financial empire went with her. Under a decree of 24 May 1940, the Royal Netherlands Government, 'temporarily residing in London', expropriated all Dutch assets outside of the Netherlands for the duration of the war.

In the Pacific, Japanese troops occupied Belitung on 10 April 1942 following the surrender of the Allied forces on Java and Sumatra. Billiton's European managers destroyed much of the mining equipment and flooded the underground mine at Kelapa Kampit and were punished with a harsh internment that many did not survive. The Japanese handed the Belitung mines over to an affiliate of Mitsubishi, which drove the remaining Chinese miners back to work. Small quantities of tin ore were exported to Japan before Japanese shipping was destroyed by the United States' submarine blockade of the East Indies.

Meanwhile, the Arnhem smelter had been destroyed in the fighting, but at least one Billiton subsidiary was still producing tin. With $8 million in United States Government funding, the Tin Processing Corporation designed and built the Longhorn Tin Smelter at Texas City and from 1942 churned out large quantities of metal for the Allied cause. Bauxite was also shipped to the States from Billiton's mine in Suriname to be turned into alumina and then aluminium, another vital war material, especially in aircraft production.

Following Japan's surrender in August 1945, 350 years of Dutch colonial rule came to an end with President Sukarno's declaration of Indonesian independence. Billiton resumed operations to meet industry's demand for vast amounts of tin and aluminium in the post-war boom in consumer products – but with a new partner when the Indonesian Government assumed the Dutch Government's majority five-eighths shareholding in the Billiton Joint Mining Company.

'The physical task of rehabilitating the mines – repairing and replacing equipment, removing water from the underground mine at Kelapa Kampit – was daunting,' historian Mary F. Somers Heidhues writes. 'The workforce had been decimated. European supervisors and technical personnel were brought in, some from internment camps, some from the Netherlands. Thousands of labourers were needed; yet many had died, fallen ill, or had fled the mines to squat in rural areas, planting cassava to survive.'[16]

Knowing its days in Indonesia were numbered, Billiton invested in new mining and smelting operations in Rhodesia, Thailand and Holland itself. As predicted, the Indonesian Government told Billiton at the end of February 1958 that it was no longer willing to continue the joint venture. The company was liquidated on 1 March, 98 years after Billiton Mij had been formed in The Hague.

'Billiton was quite well compensated for the loss of its Indonesian mines, and in the 1960s it diversified quite heavily into downstream enterprises, particularly in Holland,' Paul Everard says. 'It went into a whole variety of metal-derived manufacturing activities and also took some exploration blocks in the North Sea. But essentially it was a very difficult period because Billiton had lost its *raison d'être* as a mining company and at the end of the decade was running into cash-flow problems.'[17]

Billiton's fortunes might have foundered if Hugo Loudon's brilliant son, John Hugo, following the family's new dynastic imperative, hadn't followed him into Royal Dutch Shell. Taking over in 1959 as chairman of the group's committee of managing directors, composed of the most senior executives of the two parent companies, John Loudon made a series of decisions that would lead to a completely new phase in Billiton's corporate life.[18]

Loudon was then 54, a charismatic, six foot one inch, tanned, broad-shouldered oil man, possessing the diplomatic skills of his grandfather James and the technical knowledge of his father, Hugo. He was fluent in five languages – Dutch, English, Spanish, French and German – and the trusted associate of Middle Eastern potentates and European royalty. In London, he lived in a fashionable Grosvenor Square apartment with his wife, Marie van Tuyll van Serooskerken, a direct descendant of Baron Vincent van Tuyll.[19]

The world oil market had become more vulnerable than ever to the vicissitudes of Middle Eastern politics. The 'Seven Sisters'[20] lost their stranglehold on much of the world's oil supply after Monroe 'Jack' Rathbone, chairman of Lewis Weeks's old company, Standard Oil of New Jersey, slashed the posted price of Middle Eastern crude by 14 cents – seven per cent – a barrel in September 1960 without consulting the oil-producing countries. Shell and the other Sisters were forced to make similar cuts under the terms of their secret treaties, but feared the consequences. John Loudon, by now chairman of Shell, warned his associates, 'You can't just be guided by market forces in an industry so essential to various governments.'[21]

Rathbone, however, was from the refining end of the oil business – a downstream man – and had no experience of handling the explosive nationalistic forces at work in the oil-producing countries. Representatives from Venezuela, Saudi Arabia, Iraq, Iran and Kuwait gathered in Baghdad, which was in a state of turmoil over his unilateral action: tanks and armed soldiers patrolled the streets, expecting a CIA-engineered coup similar to the one that had ousted Mohammed Mosaddeq as prime minister of Iran in 1953 for nationalising the British-owned oil industry.

The five oil producers were the source of more than 80 per cent of the world's crude-oil exports. At the meeting, the representatives decided to set up the Organization of Petroleum Exporting Countries (OPEC) to defend themselves against the greed of the Western oil companies. OPEC would be an instrument of collective bargaining and a means of self-defence against incursions into their domestic politics. Rathbone had triggered a revolution that would profoundly impact on the oil companies and their billions of customers.

The harder John Loudon worked in these difficult times to ensure Shell's oil supply from the Middle East, the more he realised that his company could no longer rely solely on the production of oil and gas for its revenues.[22] In his dark, wood-panelled office at central office – never 'head office' in Shell parlance – in St Helen's Court in the City of London, he contemplated a new strategy of diversification. While remaining devoted to the oil market, he urged his associates to investigate new areas of business in chemicals, mining, metallurgy, nuclear energy and coal.

One of the companies on Loudon's wish list was Billiton, described by one of Shell's biographers as 'an important but obscure mining company, focused in a few far-distant islands'.[23] Loudon, of course, knew all about the company from family connections. By now, Shell's international operations had been moved from St Helen's Court to a vast seven-acre site, crowned by a 26-storey tower block, near Waterloo Station. It was here that Loudon received the news from Melbourne that the BHP–Esso partnership had struck huge reserves of oil and gas in Bass Strait. The Australian oil bonanza could so easily have been Royal Dutch Shell's, and the oil extracted from Bass Strait would have eased the group's critical supply problems during the ensuing decade.

Loudon stepped down as Shell chairman in 1965 but remained chairman of the board of supervisory directors, a position from which he fought a valiant but largely futile battle to safeguard Shell's Middle East interests following the disruption of oil supplies caused by the Arab–Israeli Six-Day War of 1967 and the sequestration of Western oil interests in Libya following Colonel Muammar al-Qaddafi's rise to power in 1969.[24]

It was against this background that the Dutch members of the committee of managing directors, the venerated CMD, proposed that the company buy Billiton and diversify into metals and minerals. Loudon's successor as chairman, Sir David Barran, later described the acquisition as 'very much a Dutch-run venture. They made a very good case for doing it and we said, "Yes, fine" and more or less told them to go ahead and get on with it.'[25]

In 1970, Royal Dutch Shell bought NV Billiton (renamed Billiton International) for US$123 million in preference to acquiring the much larger miner Rio Tinto. 'Rio executives were terrified that Shell was going to take them over,' Paul Everard says, 'but Billiton was seen as a good first step and it was partly that mindset that led them to Billiton rather than Rio. It fitted in quite well with Shell's risk-averse profile.'[26]

Dave Munro, a young Englishman who became a Billiton director in 1997, provided a slightly different slant. 'Billiton had got into trouble,' he says, 'and I understand Shell had been told to buy it by the Dutch Government in order to rescue it – otherwise it would have gone bust.'[27]

After sustaining early losses, Shell sold off all of Billiton's non-metal assets and reduced its workforce from 10,000 to fewer than 5000. The restructured company's revenues helped

Shell to weather the First Oil Shock, which followed the outbreak of the Yom Kippur War in 1973, and to survive further oil shortages as OPEC, flexing its muscles, raised the price of crude oil again and again.

'Billiton had to fit into the Shell structure but nobody in Shell knew anything about metals, so we tended to have a much higher degree of independence,' says Everard, who became president of aluminium. 'For example, I did a lot with Worsley in Western Australia, which was our major aluminium investment.' (The Worsley Alumina Project would open in April 1984 after more than two decades of planning and negotiations.)

Unlike other Shell acquisitions, Billiton retained its name and its famous logo: the three tin ingots stacked one on top of the other. Belitung Island itself had fallen on hard times. In 1971, Brian Loton, then a 41-year-old rising star at BHP, flew there after the Indonesian Government offered the company a contract to reopen the now-defunct tin workings. Loton drove the 60 kilometres north-east from the capital, Tanjung Pandan, to the Kelapa Kampit mining camp. 'Everything was exactly the way the Dutch had left it – the houses, the hospital, the sports fields,' he says.[28]

Loton and his colleagues undertook a comprehensive geophysical study, which located a larger and richer tin deposit at Nam Salu. As a result, BHP resumed mining on Belitung around 1975 and continued until 1983, when the introduction of tin-production quotas led to a decision to close down operations. 'We looked at Banka and other islands for another mine to make the operation profitable but we couldn't find one,' Loton says. 'It wasn't a success.'[29]

In May 1985, BHP sold its interests in Belitung Island to the German miner Preussag. Three years later, Loton commissioned a new zinc/lead mine at Cadjebut, Western Australia. BHP's partner in that joint venture was none other than Billiton International. Meanwhile, the man who would take Billiton to new heights was beginning his own ascent to the top of the pile.

LUCK'S A FORTUNE: Charles Rasp was the first prospector to peg the broken hill, in the belief it was a potential tin mine . . . and in the hope it would win him the hand of Agnes, the coffee-shop waitress.

RASP'S HUT: Rasp lived in this bizarre mix of iron, wattle and daub on Mount Gipps station. (© Charles Rasp Memorial Library, Broken Hill)

THE BROKEN-BACKED HILL, 1886: Note the family picnicking in the foreground. (© Charles Rasp Memorial Library, Broken Hill)

BROKEN HILL SMELTING WORKS, c.1887: Bullock teams hauled the coke, firewood and flux to the BHP smelters. (© Charles Rasp Memorial Library, Broken Hill)

BROKEN HILL OPEN-CUT MINE: The open-cut mine turned out to be even more dangerous than the early shafts, as men and horses often fell from its precipitous slopes. (© Charles Rasp Memorial Library, Broken Hill)

THE FIRST FIFTY TONS OF ZINC CONCENTRATE PRODUCED AT BROKEN HILL, 1903: (from left) E. T. Henderson, assistant metallurgist; Leslie Bradford, metallurgist; J. A. Lindsay, chief engineer; G. D. Delprat, general manager; R. Spier, university student; E. J. Horwood, works manager; G. Hylton, mill superintendent; (at rear) M. Petch, foreman tinsmith. (© J. G. Williams/BHP Billiton)

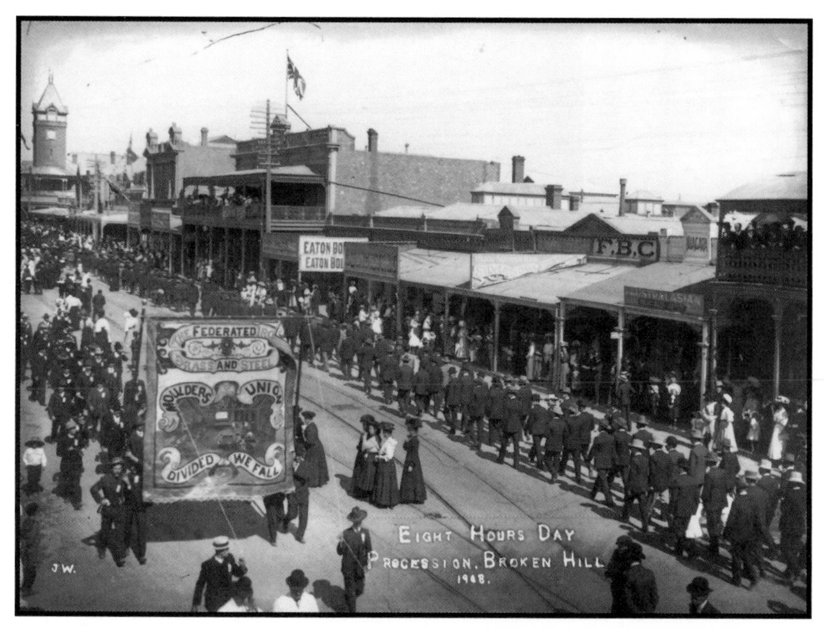

EIGHT-HOUR-DAY PROCESSION DOWN ARGENT STREET, 1908: BHP's proprietors and the miners fought bitter battles over wages and conditions. (© Charles Rasp Memorial Library, Broken Hill)

TOM MANN ROUSING THE WORKERS OUTSIDE THE BROKEN HILL TRADES HALL, 1909: After his return to England, the union leader became one of the founders of the British Communist Party. (© Charles Rasp Memorial Library, Broken Hill)

UNDERGROUND IN THE BIG MINE: BHP had early problems with cave-ins and sought the help of top American experts. (© Charles Rasp Memorial Library, Broken Hill)

BROKEN HILL LOOKING SOUTH-WEST: Flimsy miners' shacks jostled for position near the line of lode. (© Charles Rasp Memorial Library, Broken Hill)

DUST STORM COMING: When it reached Boken Hill, it would mix with the smoke and lead dust from the smelter to torture the lungs of the miners and their families. (© Charles Rasp Memorial Library, Broken Hill)

GUILLAME DELPRAT, 1915: As BHP's general manager, the Dutch-born polymath would transform the company from miner to steelmaker. (© BHP Billiton)

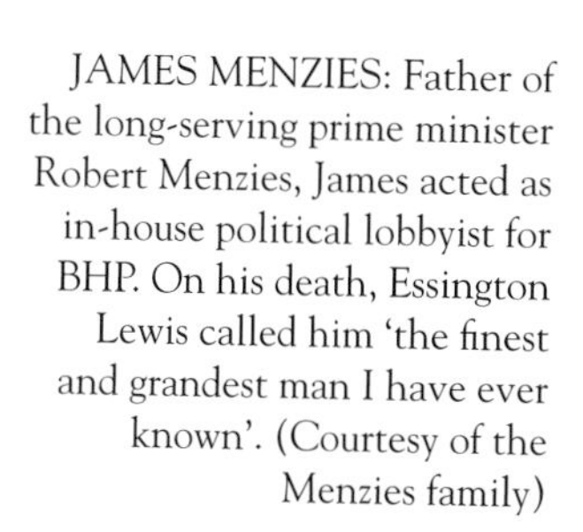

JAMES MENZIES: Father of the long-serving prime minister Robert Menzies, James acted as in-house political lobbyist for BHP. On his death, Essington Lewis called him 'the finest and grandest man I have ever known'. (Courtesy of the Menzies family)

3 OCTOBER 1941: On the occasion of the flight of Commonwealth Aircraft Corporation Pty Ltd's first fighter-bomber, the Woomera. Left to right: Sir Alexander Stewart; H. G. Darling (chairman of BHP); L. J. Wackett (manager and director of CAC); Senator Gordon Leckie; Essington Lewis (director general of aircraft production). (© BHP Billiton)

IAN MCLENNAN: Born in country Victoria in 1909, Ian McLennan, as BHP's chief executive officer, was a 'martinet' to some and a 'lovely man' to others. Under his benevolent dictatorship through the 1960s, BHP grew to become The Big Australian. (From *Seventy-Five Years of BHP Development in Industry*, BHP)

16 AUGUST 1950: At the unveiling of the Memorial Plaque to men who died in the Second World War when SS *Iron Chieftain* and SS *Iron Knight* were sunk by enemy action, relatives of the dead were presented to Essington Lewis, shown (above) greeting J. S. Swainson and (below) delivering a speech to mark the occasion. (© BHP Billiton)

ROCK HOPPER: Samuel Warren Carey in New Guinea, 1942. He targeted the Bass Strait oil find.

OIL SEARCHER: Lewis G. Weeks in 1960. He was called in by BHP and consulted Carey on where to drill in Bass Strait.

PIONEER: An early drilling rig searches for oil in Bass Strait in 1967. (© National Archives of Australia)

RAIDER: Big John Elliott in 1988 . . . he staged a huge share raid on BHP. (© Rod Fleming, licensed by www.scran.ac.uk)

LEGEND: Brian Loton fought off the corporate raiders in the 1980s as BHP's chief executive. (© Brian Loton)

COURTSHIP: The wooing of BHP's Brian Loton by John Elliott and Robert Holmes à Court during the takeover crisis of 1984–85, as seen through the eyes of cartoonist Geoff Pryor of the *Canberra Times*. (© Geoff Pryor/National Library of Australia)

'DON QUIXOTE WINDMILLS': The striking winding gear above the shafts of the San Manuel copper mine that tempted BHP into buying it. (Courtesy of Onofre Tafoya)

COPPER MAN: Jerry Ellis was chief executive of BHP Minerals when the purchase of Magma Copper was negotiated in 1995. He was later chairman of BHP. (© Monash University Archives, IN6721)

THE DON: Following the Magma disaster, Don Argus took over as chairman of BHP from Jerry Ellis in 1999 and championed BHP's merger with Billiton in 2001. He clashed with new chief executive Brian Gilbertson in 2003, resulting in Gilbertson's resignation, and then worked more harmoniously with chief executives Chip Goodyear and Marius Kloppers. (© Reuters/Picture Media)

PROJECT BARDOT: Brian Gilbertson in his BHP Billiton office with his inspirational photograph of Brigitte Bardot in 2002. As chief executive, his attempt to negotiate a merger with Rio Tinto chairman Sir Robert Wilson in 2002–03 led to his resignation after a controversial board meeting. (© Peter Braig/Fairfaxphotos)

MR FIXIT: Mike Salamon, 'the best operations guy in this business'. (Mike Salamon collection)

MR COOL: Chief executive Charles 'Chip' Goodyear signing an iron-ore deal in China in 2004 (© Reuters/ Picture Media)

THE BIG DIG: A small section of the enormous open-cut pit at the Escondida copper mine in northern Chile, one of the jewels in BHP Billiton's crown, which it shares in a joint venture with Rio Tinto. (© Reuters/Picture Media)

STRIKE: Chilean miners shout slogans during a meeting in Antofagasta in August 2006 in support of a strike at the Escondida copper mine. After a 25-day stoppage, the miners reached a deal that reputedly made them the highest-paid workers in South America. (© Reuters/Picture Media)

HEAVY METAL: BHP Billiton chief executive-elect Paul Anderson (left) and his chief development officer, Mick Davis, address analysts in London during the BHP Billiton roadshow in March 2001. Davis's resignation as soon as the merger was finalised shocked investors. (© Reuters/Picture Media)

THE CAKEHOLE: An aerial view of the hydrometalurgical circuit at BHP Billiton's controversial Olympic Dam uranium mine near Roxby Downs, South Australia. BHP Billiton trumped Mick Davis's Xstrata by buying the mine from Western Mining Corporation for $9.2 billion in 2005. (© Reuters/Picture Media)

PAYDIRT: A train loaded with iron ore departs from BHP Billiton's Yandi Mine in the Pilbara. (© Reuters/Picture Media)

ORESOME: A gigantic bucket-wheel reclaimer loads ore at the BHP terminal at Port Hedland. (© Reuters/Picture Media)

STRATEGIST: Marius Kloppers in his office at 180 Lonsdale Street, Melbourne, in 2009. The South African-born wunderkind made a hostile bid for Rio Tinto shortly after taking over as chief executive from Chip Goodyear in 2007. The bid failed, but in 2009 BHP Billiton negotiated the merger of its iron-ore assets with those of Rio Tinto in the Pilbara, subject to regulatory approval. (© BHP Billiton)

CHAPTER 15

The Big G

On a mountainside in the Brazilian state of Pará, Brian Gilbertson – the man who would be largely responsible for BHP's peripeteia – stood in the swirling red dust watching gigantic shovels scoop tons of high-grade hematite iron ore from the Carajás open-cut mine. 'See that mountain over there,' his guide from the world's biggest iron-ore miner Companhia Vale do Rio Doce (CVRD)[1] told him, pointing to the horizon. 'When we finish here, we're going over there – that one is full of iron ore too.'[2]

As one of Derek Keys' young lions at the South African precious metals specialist Gencor, Gilbertson knew all about gold, platinum and diamonds. But at that moment in Brazil – in 1990 – he saw that his company would have to diversify into base metals if it were to join the major league of miners: a resurgent BHP, the British-controlled titan Rio Tinto, Harry Oppenheimer's Anglo American (Gencor's main competitor in South Africa), and CVRD itself.

'The large South African groups had built their fortunes on gold mining and then on coal mining, platinum mining and so on, but the bulk commodities like iron ore weren't there on the scale of the international producers; there also wasn't much in the way of nickel and absolutely no bauxite,' Gilbertson says. 'I saw on that visit to Brazil that we had to find some way to operate internationally.' On his return, he reported his view to the Gencor directors and Derek Keys. 'If you had anything vaguely positive to offer, he would encourage you to get on with it,' he says. 'So we started looking around for opportunities. We always thought that BHP had among the finest assets in the industry.'[3]

Gilbertson is a charismatic figure with a rough-hewn face and a boyish grin, a nuclear physicist with a love of opera and an encyclopaedic knowledge of the Renaissance. He is known in mining circles as 'The Big G', a tag that could equally have been applied to Gencor in its heyday. Myths abound about both. According to *The Economist*, 'browbeaten staff would greet Gilbertson's arrival by helicopter by declaring that "the ego has landed"'.[4] But the helicopter pad had been on Gencor's roof in the heart of Johannesburg for the previous 40 years and Gilbertson was simply continuing a company tradition by using it. The difference was that the helicopter now had twin Messerschmitt engines, state-of-the-art avionics and a decor designed by his wife, Rensche.

The London offices of his new company, Pallinghurst Resources, named after the street of his former home in Johannesburg, is on the seventh floor of ultra-smart Wilton House at 54 Jermyn Street, next to Wiltons restaurant and surrounded by bespoke men's stores. Fortnum & Mason is the local corner shop; there is a view of Big Ben and the Westminster spires. Gilbertson is in his shirtsleeves behind his glass-topped desk; a thick grey thatch of hair frames his face like a helmet; the eyes are black and searching. Born in the township of George on the garden route in Western Cape on 15 August 1943 and raised near Bothaville in the heart of Afrikanerdom, Gilbertson says, 'My father went out to South Africa from London as part of a bomber squadron during the war, but he was from an Irish background in Cork. He met my mother in South Africa.'

They went to London when he was a child but his mother didn't like the weather so they returned and his father joined the Department of Water Affairs in the high plains of the Free State. 'They were building a water-supply scheme to supply water to the Free State goldfields, which were just opening up,' he says. 'I actually grew up in this tiny village – I don't think there were 20 houses. Bothaville was a big town: it had about 30 houses. My mother was Afrikaans but we actually spoke English at home; my father never learned Afrikaans, but schooling was in Afrikaans.'[5]

The young Gilbertson was fortunate to have had a great mathematics teacher who spotted his aptitude for science. After matriculation, he studied physics and mathematics at Rhodes University on a bursary from the Council for Scientific and Industrial Research (CSIR). He did the fourth year – the honours year – in physics and then joined CSIR to repay his bursary. 'They posted me to the Institute for Rocket Research – great stuff for a young man,' he says. At the time, South Africa was under siege internationally for its apartheid policies. 'Nobody would sell any weaponry to the country except the French. There was a joint project with the French Government to build a rapid-reaction surface-to-air missile system.

'To my great good fortune, instead of being sent to the army I ended up in the team that was posted to Paris to work on this missile system. I had one of the best times of my life. Instead of marching up and down with a gun on my shoulder in South Africa in basic training, I was in Paris with the bright lights, and they actually paid us a very generous salary. I was able to save enough to buy my first car. I was in Paris for not quite a year and then went back and worked with CSIR.'[6]

While Shell was acquiring Billiton in 1970, Gilbertson married his fiancée, Rensche Fouche, and accepted a job offer from the South African mining group Johannesburg Consolidated Investment Company (JCI),[7] which wanted to use his scientific expertise to find new mineral deposits. 'I became a minor expert in a field of mathematics called pattern recognition,' he says. 'If you are in a fighter plane and you want to launch a missile at another fighter plane, your missile has to recognise its target. So it looks at the very hot exhaust pipe if it's an infra-red-guided missile and it then goes after that. But if the Sun gets in the way, it might get confused, so the pattern it's got to recognise is the exhaust pipe and not the Sun. The mathematics are fairly advanced when you move from my simple example to more complex examples. I became a minor authority in South Africa in that field.'

Some of his work could be applied to looking for geological features. 'JCI had a visionary mining director called Bernard Smith, who had heard of this technique from an American professor and wanted to see whether you could use these techniques to discover mineral deposits,' he says. 'They placed an ad and I think I was the only person in the country who understood it. I applied for the job and asked for an exorbitant salary and a motor car; and because I was the perfect match I got everything I asked for. We didn't find any mines. It just didn't work terribly well in that application – it was better trying to put a missile up the tail of a fighter.'[8]

One of Gilbertson's first projects at JCI was to prospect for uranium in an old gold mine that Bernard Smith was keen to reopen. He didn't succeed in finding any uranium but was soon flying around the wilds of South Africa with the exploration unit searching for mineral deposits using a technique called multi-spectral remote sensing. 'We were trying to identify whether particular vegetation or rocks had signatures which would indicate gossans, for example, which would indicate there was copper down below,' he says. 'This was becoming a very topical area of research, and NASA launched what was called the Earth Resources Technology Satellite No. 1 which flew around with scanners imaging like a television set but in very narrow parts of the spectrum so they wouldn't look like pictures that you would normally see. Vegetation, for example, would come out as bright red or whatever colour you wanted it to be. NASA was looking for scientists around the world to join them and to put forward proposals which would demonstrate the power of this new technology as applied from space.'

Gilbertson persuaded JCI to submit its proposals to NASA and was appointed one of 70 NASA investigators around the world. His little laboratory received the first data transmitted from the new satellite. 'We got the first pictures of the Great Dyke[9] and I took them along to a symposium in Washington,' he says. 'The geologists were gobsmacked – they'd never seen anything like this from space – it was very exciting.'[10]

After 16 years in exploration and finance, Gilbertson joined the JCI board on taking over as managing director of Rustenburg Platinum Mines, which operated on South Africa's famous Merensky Reef in the Bushveld Igneous Complex, one of the most heavily mineralised areas in the world. 'JCI was owned 30 or 40 per cent by Anglo American,' Gilbertson says. 'It was allowed to play around in mining but essentially it was there to house two things: platinum and some diamond shares. The platinum division was on the fourth floor, very secretive, very competitive – you didn't have access unless you were in the division. My first important presentation – I was horribly nervous having to do it – was to the Anglo American Corporation – for that, read Mr Oppenheimer – an idea to consolidate the platinum holdings in the eastern limb of the Bushveld Igneous Complex.

'I had put together a consolidation that would lock it away for the great-great-grandchildren. We didn't realise black economic empowerment was coming ten years down the line. I was put in the library with some other executives to wait for his arrival after lunch. He arrived a few minutes late apologising profusely to me. I took him through it and he approved it and we did it.'

Bernard Smith, JCI's heir apparent to the chairmanship, was devastated when the top job went to Gordon Waddell, a rugby player who happened to be Harry Oppenheimer's son-in-law. 'There was a bit of a power struggle up at the top,' Gilbertson says. 'You can't have two bulls in the same china shop. It wasn't going to work.' Smith joined JCI's rival Gencor, the group that had emerged from General Mining's hostile takeover of the twice-as-big Union Corporation in 1980.

General Mining had been founded on 30 December 1895 – the day after the launch of the notorious Jameson Raid in the Transvaal – by George and Leopold Albu, who controlled gold mines on the Witwatersrand. The Union Corporation's founder was Adolf Goerz, a mining engineer who, like the Albu brothers and the mysterious Charles Rasp at Broken Hill, was German. Goerz, a Protestant, and the Albus, Sephardic Jews, were among the least known of the 25 Randlords, the European emigrants who sailed to South Africa in the late nineteenth century and trekked across the veld after the discovery of gold on the Rand in 1886.

When it became clear that the Boers had found 'an endless treasure of gold' (the line of lode was 280 kilometres long and 3.6 kilometres deep in places), Cecil Rhodes, the Kimberley diamond magnate and imperialist prime minister of Cape Colony, paid Dr Leander Starr Jameson and his gang of 500 Rhodesian troopers to incite an uprising among the British prospectors – *uitlanders*, or foreigners, to the Boers – in Johannesburg, with the aim of seizing control himself. The Jameson Raid was a rank failure – the miners simply refused to be incited. Jameson was arrested and Rhodes forced to relinquish his prime ministership.

In the aftermath, Paul Kruger's Transvaal government set up a commission of inquiry into the Rand's gold mines at which George Albu was star witness for the mine owners. His address to the commissioners could have served as a blueprint for apartheid: the wages of indigenous workers should be slashed, he said, to prevent 'kaffirs' from accumulating sufficient funds to retire to their kraals after a few years' labour; they would then have to work in the mines indefinitely to support their families. He added, 'I, as an employer of labour, say it would be a good thing to have forced labour.'[11]

During the Anglo-Boer War (1899–1902), George Albu fled to Cape Town, even though his sympathies were with the Boers' struggle for independence; Boer commandos had threatened to blow up or flood the mines and it was no longer safe for him to remain in Johannesburg. After the war, General Mining recruited Chinese labourers, who, while not actually treated as slaves, were generally regarded as subhuman. His efforts on behalf of cheap labour did not go unrewarded in the new Union of South Africa: in 1912, he was awarded a baronetcy by King George V and became Sir George Albu of Johannesburg.

By now, the shape of race relations in an industrialised South Africa had been established: the blacks had been driven off most of their lands by legislation that reserved 87 per cent of South Africa for the white minority and confined the vast majority of black South Africans to 'native reserves';[12] a strict colour bar was already in force on the diamond fields, where black workers were compelled to live in compounds, carry pass books and undergo humiliating body searches.

Mining was the making of South Africa: it transformed an economy based on beef, wheat, maize, tobacco, citrus fruits and cotton. Huge dividends flowed to shareholders in Britain, Germany and the United States, where no one questioned the Randlords' mining methods or the conditions of their workers. The Zulu and the Pedi ('kaffirs') were dispossessed in the same way as the Aboriginals and Native Americans.

When the National Party won the 1948 election, it enacted laws to enforce apartheid, or 'apartness' (later defined as 'separate development'), which legalised racial segregation and political and economic discrimination. From the 1960s, 'Grand Apartheid' enforced territorial separation by creating the so-called homelands. Faced with growing hostility from Britain and other Commonwealth members, South Africa became a republic and quit the Commonwealth on 31 May 1961.

The government of Hendrik Verwoerd, the 'architect of apartheid', was determined to give the politically dominant

Afrikaners a greater share of the mining industry. However, British corporations continued to enjoy the lion's share of South Africa's mineral wealth. Easily the biggest and most prosperous miner was the Anglo American Corporation of South Africa, founded in 1917 by Ernest Oppenheimer, a cigar merchant's son from Friedberg, Germany. The company had started with authorised capital of £1 million, raised mainly from British and American sources, hence the company name. In 1926, Oppenheimer made his greatest acquisition when Anglo American became the largest single shareholder in one of Cecil Rhodes' old companies, De Beers Consolidated Mines (motto: 'A diamond is forever'), the diamond miner with a virtual world monopoly on the sale of the precious stones through the London Diamond Syndicate.[13] During the late 1940s and '50s, Anglo American's labour-intensive mines in the Free State goldfields and the Vaal Reefs thrived on cheap black immigrant labour.

In 1957, Sir Ernest Oppenheimer died and was succeeded by his only surviving son, Harry, who had represented Kimberley in the South African Parliament since 1948 and was the opposition's spokesman on economics, finance and constitutional affairs. Splitting his time between Parliament House in Cape Town and Anglo's headquarters on Main Street, Johannesburg, Harry Oppenheimer dominated the gold and diamond businesses to such an extent that rival Afrikaner politicians tagged him 'Hoggenheimer', an anti-Jewish reference to an extremely rich character in the Broadway musical comedy *The Girl From Kays*.

Verwoerd had got nowhere with his attempts to break up the Anglo American empire, but General Mining, in which Anglo owned a 23 per cent stake, became vulnerable following the death of Sir George Albu's son in 1963. The main bidder was Federale Mynbou (Fedmyn), an Afrikaner coal-mining company that had recently moved into the diamond business. The deal with Fedmyn was done with the blessing of Harry Oppenheimer, who ostensibly wanted to give the Afrikaans business community a larger share of the mining industry. By showing that Afrikaners and English-speaking South Africans could cooperate in business, he hoped to prevent the further separation of these groups within South Africa's fractured society.[14]

Oppenheimer 'facilitated' Fedmyn's takeover of General Mining to the great joy of the ruling National Party. Fedmyn's two senior executives, William Coetzer and Tom Muller, both members of the Afrikaner Broederbond (Brotherhood), a secret society dedicated to Afrikaner nationalism, became chairman and managing director respectively of the vastly enlarged group.[15]

Anglo American, however, retained a substantial minority interest and insisted on a contract that restricted further Afrikaner expansion in diamonds. Thus the wily Oppenheimer, while achieving his political purpose, had also protected his stranglehold on the diamond business by deflecting Fedmyn away from diamond mining.[16]

The merger created the Federale Mynbou–General Mining group, producing coal, gold, uranium, platinum and copper; it also made consumer goods and asbestos fibre, which would later lead to thousands of claims for compensation from victims of asbestosis. 'Federale Mynbou' was dropped from the group's name in 1965, but the merger had firmly established General Mining as an Afrikaner house, dominated by members of the all-male, all-Protestant Broederbond.[17]

In 1970, the new chief executive, Dr Wim de Villiers, set about growing the company. De Villiers was a big, burly Afrikaner from the Free State, a member of the Broederbond who had worked for both Anglo American as an engineer and for the huge Afrikaner life-assurance company Sanlam as industrial adviser. Sanlam, founded in 1918 and one of the National Party's mainstays, was General Mining's largest institutional investor; with its backing, de Villiers sold off its consumer interests and invested the proceeds in gold-mining stock that then rose dramatically to provide him with a bulging war chest.

In 1974, he swooped on South Africa's fourth biggest miner, the Union Corporation, acquiring 29.9 per cent in the first stage of a hostile takeover bid. Union was a rich prize. Its first big success had been the Modder Deep Levels mine on the East Rand, an asset that founder Adolf Goerz had called 'the jewelbox of the Reef'.[18] Union had then founded the first gold mine in the Free State and had later discovered the Evander goldfields and established four mines there. It had also bought Impala Platinum, operated the Beisa uranium mine south of the Sand River, and extracted titanium, ilmenite, rutile and zircon from sand mining at Richards Bay, a fishing village on the Indian Ocean coast of Zululand.

General Mining and Union Corporation were united under the name Gencor when the takeover was completed in 1980. Wim de Villiers, however, was swept away in a boardroom clash between Sanlam and Gencor's other major stakeholder, the tobacco-based Rembrandt group. Following a period of stagnation, Derek Keys, a 55-year-old accountant, was drafted in as chairman in April 1986 with a brief to give Gencor a complete overhaul.[19] 'I started with a very clean slate in terms of knowledge of mining,' he says. 'But I had been a management consultant then for about 20 years, so it wasn't strange terrain in that respect.'[20]

Keys knew he would have to separate Gencor's manufacturing and mining interests into two separate divisions, hack away at costs and reduce staffing levels. But first Gencor, steeped in apartheid, needed a new image and new blood. He asked Bernard Smith, head of operational services, to suggest a new head of mining operations. Enter Brian Gilbertson of JCI.

'It was the first time I was fired from my job,' Gilbertson says. 'I was the head of the glamour [platinum] division of JCI and thought I was probably in the running for a top post in some years. I wasn't hugely ambitious – I had a rather modest view of my capabilities – but I was seeking some assurance from the hierarchy that I would at least be in contention.

'I knew enough to know the decision would not be made in JCI but in Anglo American, so I asked for the opportunity to get some feedback from Anglo. The new chairman of platinum [Pat Retief, a South African-born former British Army officer] went through the roof and effectively said, "Walk the plank." He was going to put me in some junior post in finance.

'I went across to Derek and said, "If that offer still stands – here I am." So I moved to Gencor. It was the first time I got my picture on the front page of the newspaper, because I was leaving to join the competition. Sad, really – I'd been there 18 years. Anyway, it was the first time I was fired.'[21]

Gilbertson joined Gencor in 1988. Derek Keys had cut a deal with the JCI management that his new recruit would have nothing to do with platinum until he became head of the whole mining division. 'Brian had six months in coal, then six months or more in one part of base metals, then another six months in another, in every case as chief executive of those divisions,' he says. 'In every one of them, he achieved dramatic improvements and came up with new initiatives.'[22]

Dave Munro, who joined Gencor's coal division Trans-Natal in March 1981 and then moved to the marketing department in Johannesburg four years later, recalls Gilbertson's impact. 'Gencor had hired Mike Salamon from Shell, and he was an important figure in marketing when Brian Gilbertson arrived and needed somebody to think through how things should be structured,' he says. 'Mike and one or two others were co-opted by Gilbertson to design the structure of the group.'[23]

Gencor was a great, sprawling conglomerate, and to tighten their control over it Keys and Gilbertson created General Mining – Genmin – to house the mining arm, which included 14 gold mines, the base-metals group Samancor, the platinum-producer Impala, the coal-group Trans-Natal and a big minerals division.

Meanwhile, Wim de Villiers, Gencor's ousted chief, had

joined the South African Cabinet at the request of his friend, President P. W. Botha, to shake up the economy. In line with Britain and Australia, de Villiers had begun to privatise state assets, a move that allowed Derek Keys to grab a controlling interest in Alusaf, operator of an aluminium smelter at Richards Bay. One of the poorest areas in South Africa, Richards Bay had been part of the government's policy to remove industries from the Transvaal and place them in the ten theoretically sovereign bantustans. Alusaf's Bayside smelter had begun operations in 1971, using power from Eskom, the state-run electricity company, to process imported bauxite.

Keys decided Gencor should seek new opportunities offshore, even though it would have to operate covertly through third parties, usually Australian or British, because of his country's pariah status. So Gilbertson and other key executives were sent abroad to study new technologies and to seek out possible mining prospects in South America and Australia.

'That's the question of not pulling on the bridle,' Keys says. 'We used to discuss things, and if I had any points that were worth bearing in mind Brian took them on board. I'm certain I'm not the only chairman he could have worked with, but in fact our styles fitted together.'[24]

Politically, times had never been worse. Africa's winds of change reached tornado strength in Cape Town later that year when F. W. de Klerk seized the presidency from P. W. Botha and called for a non-racist South Africa and for negotiations to decide the country's future.

On 2 February 1990, de Klerk announced the epochal decisions to lift the ban on the African National Congress (ANC) and other proscribed organisations, end the state of emergency and release Nelson Mandela from prison, thus signalling the end of apartheid and opening the way for a new constitution based on the principle of one person, one vote. The liberation of the 72-year-old ANC leader nine days later, after 27 years' incarceration, was widely seen as a symbol of the white regime's surrender.

Derek Keys and his young team judged that the time was now ripe to plan Gencor's international expansion. But first, the group had to be slimmed down by 'unbundling' – demerging – around half of its assets to raise funds and to make it attractive to foreign investors who had so recently scorned everything to do with the republic. Keys had not moved far in that direction when in January 1992 President de Klerk approached him on the first tee at a presidential golfing day. 'I was called into government by de Klerk to make sure the finances didn't go wrong during the transition to majority rule in South Africa,' he says. 'Brian had to make the speech when I departed from Gencor, and he said that he'd worked with me for three and a half years and he'd never actually seen me work. I took that as a great compliment.'[25] Keys joined the Cabinet as minister of trade and industry and shortly afterwards was appointed to the crucial role of finance minister.

There were five contenders for the top position at Gencor, and Gilbertson says he was surprised to be chosen. He had been promoted to chairman of Genmin in 1990 but had been with the group for less than four years. In the goldfish-bowl world of South African mining, he was still regarded among his more conservative rivals at Anglo American and De Beers as something of an upstart.[26]

Nevertheless, he found himself at the age of 48 in charge of a successful, decentralised group with a solid base from which to tackle international growth. One of his first acts was to stop expensive deep-level gold mining, which had reached 3.5 kilometres in parts of the Reef. 'They wanted to go down to four kilometres but I put a stop to that,' he says. 'I wanted to expand into other areas of mining.'[27]

Aluminium was top of the list – and it was the need to secure supplies of bauxite and alumina for Richards Bay that put him on Billiton's trail. 'Richards Bay had cheap electricity and very little industry,' he says. 'It was the ideal place to build a new aluminium smelter but we needed to raise the funds.' He also needed to locate a cheap overseas source of bauxite and then negotiate a low rate with Eskom for the huge volumes of electricity needed to produce alumina that would be smelted in electric pots to produce aluminium.

The Gencor board approved the Hillside smelter project for Richards Bay at a meeting in November 1992, estimating the cost at R6.3 billion. Equity funding was set at R2.7 billion, with Gencor committing R1.125 billion in order to defend its 40 per cent holding in Alusaf. But there was a problem. 'The aluminium price suddenly slumped when a Russian glut created a tsunami of aluminium around the world,' Gilbertson says. 'The Soviet Union had just broken up and they weren't building aircraft and missiles any more – they were just selling aluminium as cash in metal form. There was this wall of metal coming out and hitting Western markets.'

Meanwhile, South Africa edged ever closer to majority rule. The last major apartheid laws, the Group Areas Act and the Population Registration Act, had been rescinded, convincing many countries to end their cultural, economic and sporting boycotts of South Africa.

It was in the middle of these momentous events that Brian Gilbertson turned to Sanlam, Gencor's Afrikaner godfather, to invest in his new smelter at Richards Bay. He invited the Sanlam directors, a bunch of mostly elderly conservatives, to a meeting in Johannesburg. After the morning session, he was about to take them to lunch when his mobile phone rang and his secretary warned him, 'Don't come out!' It was too late. The group walked outside the Gencor building and found themselves in the middle of a huge demonstration of black Africans singing and dancing down the street.

The Sanlam group looked askance. 'The blacks were going to run the government and now they were demonstrating in the middle of Johannesburg,' Gilbertson says. 'Their whole world was crumbling.' There was a break in the crowd and, like a scene in an *opéra bouffe*, the group dashed across the street to their restaurant. All through the meal, Gilbertson feared that the Sanlam people would baulk at investing in Richards Bay.

Yet after lunch, against the odds, they agreed to provide their share of the funding.[28]

The 1990s ushered in what has been called the Magnetic Age, in which the producers of natural resources were drawn together in voluntary alliances to avoid takeover or were swallowed up by even bigger predators. Fuelled by massive profits, self-interest and hugely escalating demand, the mergers-and-acquisitions frenzy witnessed the formation of mega-mining companies as BHP, Rio Tinto, Anglo American and CVRD took over weaker rivals, while in the oil-and-gas industry it gave birth to the super-majors ExxonMobil, ChevronTexaco, TotalFinaElf of France and British Petroleum, which became plain BP after devouring Amoco and Arco.

At the same time, more than 70 countries changed their mining laws to make themselves more attractive to foreign investment. From Argentina to Zambia, governments that once treated mining groups with suspicion now competed for their favours. Many loosened or abolished restrictions on foreign ownership and relaxed punitive taxes that previously discouraged companies from exploring or mining in many parts of the globe. With the death of apartheid, Gencor could go pretty much where it liked.

In 1993, Brian Gilbertson sold off Gencor's non-mining assets and went hunting with a small team of trusted colleagues to find a suitable vehicle in which to make what was being called in the South African press 'the great trek to the outside world'. One of his team was Miklos 'Mike' Salamon, a forceful, fair-complexioned man with a drooping moustache who had been born in Hungary in 1955, the year before the Uprising. When Soviet tanks rolled into Budapest, his father, also Miklos, fought in the resistance, was sentenced to death and fled with his wife and baby son to neighbouring Austria.

Trained as a mining engineer, Miklos Salamon Sr emigrated first to Britain to work for the National Coal Board at Newcastle upon Tyne, then to South Africa, where his son's extraordinary career began in 1975 at De Beers, followed by Anglo American.

After taking his MBA in London, young Mike served in various management jobs at Shell Coal and Gencor, eventually rising to chairman of the Gencor subsidiary Samancor, the world's biggest chrome and manganese business.

'Brian kissed many frogs,' Salamon says, 'to see if they would turn into a prince. We were looking for a partner to get us out of South Africa and into a global business. Eventually, he landed on Billiton.'[29]

CHAPTER 16

Out of Africa

Proving one of his favourite maxims that 'mining is all about timing', Brian Gilbertson made an unsolicited bid for Billiton International in May 1993 in what would turn out to be one of mining's great international coups. Commodities had experienced a tough time in the 1980s and '90s, and Billiton had not lived up to expectations – in fact, there had been periods of considerable loss. 'Shell decided to retreat to its core businesses of oil and chemicals and sell off metals and coal,' Paul Everard says. 'That resulted in Billiton becoming available.'[1]

The credit for identifying Billiton as a worthwhile prospect went to Alusaf chairman Fred Roux, who was looking for sources of bauxite and alumina for his new Hillside smelter. Shell's mining arm not only operated a large bauxite mine in Suriname but had bought into the integrated bauxite/alumina project at Worsley in Western Australia as well as acquiring a 40 per cent stake in the Alumar alumina/aluminium project in Brazil. As a further bonus, it was a partner in the Cerro Matosa ferro-nickel mine and smelter in Colombia, which gave the company access to the lucrative stainless-steel market.

Throughout the 1980s, Shell had endured a blistering

anti-apartheid campaign in Europe, the United States and Australia to drive it out of its self-funded operation in South Africa. The directors had refused to bow to boycotts, violent protest and sabotage, although at times they came close to caving in. Now that apartheid was dead, they expressed interest in Gilbertson's bid but – as usual in the oil industry – negotiations had to be conducted in great secrecy, with Gilbertson and Bernard Smith representing Gencor[2] and Evert Henkes, Billiton Metals coordinator, leading the Shell team.

'Shell didn't want it known that they were even contemplating selling their assets,' Brian Gilbertson says, 'so we met at some hotel stuck away in the forest in Holland.'[3]

News of the negotiations, however, found its way into the pages of *The Economist*, where it was read with great interest by a young South African living in the Netherlands. Marius Kloppers, a 30-year-old scientist who had studied in the United States and France, was working for McKinsey in Amsterdam. He wrote to Brian Gilbertson at Gencor's headquarters in Johannesburg.

'I started talking to Brian Gilbertson somewhere in 1993,' he says. 'I thought that Gencor was a company that was growing internationally and I thought I had something to offer.'[4]

Kloppers had been born in Johannesburg on 26 August 1962. His father, Neville, an executive with the Old Mutual life-assurance company, had died when he was 12, leaving his mother, Marinda, to raise him and his younger brother, Pierre, as a single parent. She sent Marius to the all-male Helpmekaar High School in Johannesburg, where he starred academically and on the rugby field, once representing his country at under-19 level. He met his future wife, Carin, at a school function and, after he had completed two years' national service in the South African Army – including a stint in war-ravaged Angola – they were married during the second year of his chemical-engineering course at the University of Pretoria.

After graduation, he moved to the Massachusetts Institute of Technology on a Fulbright scholarship, gaining his doctorate on

'The Photo-electric Chemistry of Iron and Chromium Alloys'. His thesis explored electronic models for species propagation through thin films, with a view towards developing models for resistivity of stainless steels – a fundamental explanation of why stainless steels remain stainless. Gilbertson, a scientist himself, was impressed. He offered Kloppers a job on the aluminium side of Gencor at Richards Bay. Kloppers and Carin had left South Africa at the height of apartheid more than a decade earlier and were overjoyed to be going home at such a propitious time.

Billiton had never sat comfortably in the Shell portfolio. It survived the tin-price collapse in the 1980s – the London Metal Exchange actually suspended tin trading in October 1985 – because of its strength in bauxite, alumina and nickel. But it had been starved of exploration funds by a parent company that was struggling to stay on top of the fluctuating oil market. In common with Jack Welch of General Electric, Shell was anxious to divest itself of all its mining interests in favour of stable investments with steady, predictable cash flows. 'Many companies have to get rid of certain parts of their business which are not making enough money,' John Loudon mused in 1989. 'I can see a group like ours at a certain stage saying "Well, we might as well sell our Billiton interest."'[5]

Mike Salamon says, 'Shell had decided it wanted to get out of mining but it wanted to do the right thing socially, particularly in Holland, so it didn't want to decimate its mining business. We, on the other hand, wanted to get a global mining business and we wanted a global management team to complement our management team. We also wanted somebody to bankroll it because we didn't have enough money offshore to pay for it.'[6]

Gilbertson's main problem in clinching the deal – and it seemed insurmountable – was that the governor of the South African Reserve Bank, Dr Chris Stals, refused to permit Gencor to export funds abroad. Assuming Gencor and Shell could agree on a price – and Shell were asking for a hefty US$1.8 billion – the money would have to be raised offshore, a Herculean task for a newcomer to the international money markets.

The talks had been progressing slowly for four months when in September 1993 Gilbertson hired Mick Davis, a 35-year-old accountant, after hearing he had been passed over for the chief executive's job at Eskom. 'Derek Keys and Mick Davis had the all-time highest results for chartered accountancy in South Africa,' Mike Salamon says. 'Derek knew Mick and vice versa. He was a very young lad but an outstanding intellect; we needed a CFO and he needed a new job.'[7]

Mick Davis agreed to join Gencor as finance director, with the added incentive of the chairmanship of its vast Trans-Natal coal division. Davis wanted to start work at once, but Eskom asked him to remain *in situ* until the end of the year. Gilbertson short-circuited that plan with a telephone call that the Shell talks had reached a critical stage and his services were required immediately. Davis packed his bags and flew to London that night.[8]

Davis was born in Port Elizabeth on 15 February 1958, the youngest of three brothers. After majoring in accountancy at Rhodes University, he worked in the Johannesburg offices of Peat Marwick, where he astonished everyone with his handling of the important Barclays Bank account while still an articled clerk. When the firm refused to make him a partner at 28, he joined Eskom as chief internal auditor and was given the daunting task of raising new money in the international markets at a time when South Africa was in the depths of its unpopularity.

Davis had been abroad only once in his life and knew virtually nothing about international finance. One French banker refused to invite him into his office and kept him standing in the banking hall. Nevertheless, Davis got the funds that transformed Eskom's fortunes and won him plaudits from some of industry's senior executives.

Mick Davis is a big man – over six feet tall and heavy – yet he speaks with a surprisingly soft and well-modulated voice.

At 50 and now chief executive of the booming Anglo-Swiss miner Xstrata, he wears glasses and his hair is turning grey. He has strong features and a full beard in the manner of his Hasidic faith. He is dressed in navy-blue trousers and a blue shirt with silver cufflinks and an orange-spotted tie. There is an inscribed silver band on his left wrist and he plays with a gold letter opener in the shape of a shepherd's crook. There is a chromium-plated spade leaning against one wall of his London office – a farewell gift from Eskom. Mick says he sometimes picks it up and makes a shovelling motion 'if someone is talking crap'.

'I spent the best part of a year on a plane, sometimes travelling to London and back the same day, then back the next day,' he says, recalling the Billiton acquisition in his London office, a few steps off the Haymarket. 'It was a very hectic time. Although the transaction in today's terms was not that big – it was about $1.8 billion in total – South Africa's exchange controls at the time made it very difficult to raise the money because we couldn't use the Gencor balance sheet.'[9]

Gencor, however, had interests worth some US$300 million in Europe, mostly in London property and North Sea oil-and-gas assets. Gilbertson had also found an ally at Shell in Cornelius 'Cor' Herkströter, who had become chairman of Royal Dutch Shell's committee of managing directors the previous year. Unlike John Loudon, Herkströter was not a 'from the cradle' oil man – he was an economist and an accountant who had been a member of the Billiton staff from 1967 until 1980. 'He was the most senior guy around,' Gilbertson says. 'But he stayed in the background and didn't get down into the dirt with us.'

Even with a great deal of goodwill on both sides, the talks dragged on into the New Year. 'We went through a very long-winded process – Gencor had no cash, so we had to structure the deal very carefully,' Gilbertson says. 'It was also at a time when aluminium prices were falling and Shell had made the fundamental decision to get out. They tried to run an auction but no one came; we were the only ones hovering around. Shell has a process for buying or selling things, almost a manual you had to work your way through to make sure all the boxes were ticked. The Gencor Group was much more fluid and flexible – I was the chairman and chief executive, so essentially if I could bring my two shareholders along – Sanlam and Rembrandt – then I could settle.'[10]

Meanwhile, the political convulsions in South Africa gave birth to the Rainbow Nation. In the country's first universal democratic elections on 27 April 1994, Nelson Mandela was elected president. He invited foreign investors to support South African industry and urged South African companies to expand abroad. Gilbertson was only too anxious to oblige but not even presidential backing could alter the Reserve Bank's intractability. 'No one can appreciate how precariously balanced this whole Billiton transaction was,' Mick Davis says. 'We were coming to the party without the capacity to do the deal.'[11]

Gilbertson acknowledges the help he received from Shell after it discovered during the negotiations that it actually wanted the deal to go ahead as part of its own restructuring plans. This realisation was his ace in the hole. When the Gencor team suggested Shell come in on the financing side, Shell proposed a loan. The South Africans said they couldn't afford it and, after explaining their Reserve Bank problem, Shell put up $300 million in bonds.

'Shell came to the party – that was the brainchild of Bernard Smith,' Mick Davis says. 'He negotiated that with Shell, a very smart piece of work on his part. It gave them a potential equity participation and then my smart move, after raising the finance, was a year later buying up that equity participation at a very reasonable price.'[12]

By now, the purchase price had been reduced to US$1.14 billion and the question was whether Davis could bank the transaction. Once again, he tramped through the banking halls of Europe. 'I had a very good colleague, Willy Murray, one of the most outstanding people I've ever worked with – he's now treasurer of BHP Billiton,' Mick Davis says. 'He and I did the financing. It was tough but we got through. The assets we had to sell were falling in value and it was knife-edge stuff as to whether we could finance it. One of the French banks, Paribas, pulled out at the last minute, which irritated me no end. I remember seeing the then chairman of Paribas three or four months later and his only explanation for why they pulled out was a Gallic shrug and "Pooh!"

'The lead bank was UBS and the lead person there said to me, "You know, Mick, it's all in the compensation," so we structured a very expensive tranche of money to bridge that gap.'[13]

It wasn't until the end of October 1994 that everything was in place. Gencor put up $300 million in offshore assets (a figure that rose to $335 million); the banks (UBS, Barclays, Credit Suisse and Dresdner) contributed $510 million of debt financing and Shell put in $300 million in exchangeable bonds, which amounted to a three-year interest-free loan.[14]

The deal took effect on 1 December. Gencor acquired the larger part of Billiton's operations, ranging across the mineral spectrum from bauxite and alumina in Australia, Brazil, Suriname and New Guinea to the Cerro Matosa nickel mine in Colombia, gold mines in Ghana, Indonesia and Brazil and copper and zinc in Canada. The portfolio was heavily weighted towards aluminium. Gilbertson says, 'As the ink was drying on the document we had signed with Shell, Paul O'Neill, the head of Alcoa, did an industry settlement with all the key players under the guidance of United States Government anti-trust lawyers and came to some reasonable way of reducing the flood from the former Soviet Union in return for some investment from the West into modernising the Russian plants.

'Instantly, the metal price turned and what appeared to have been a very risky acquisition strategy on our part turned out to be hugely successful. We repaid all the debt in less than two years. We had acquired a set of assets which internationalised us and we had acquired a set of people who knew the industry. We were on a roll.'[15]

Alusaf's Hillside smelter, equipped with state-of-the-art Pechiney AP30 technology, was completed at a cost of R5 billion – R1.3 billion below budget. 'It was French technology, so the French were involved very intimately, but we did the construction,' Gilbertson says. 'Up till then, that technology had not been used much outside Pechiney itself and we put it on the global map. For a decade, it became the preferred technology.'

Alusaf was geared to break even if the price of aluminium fell as low as $850 a ton, but when Hillside began production in June 1995, the price had topped $1600 a ton and went on to climb above $1900 later that year. 'Nobody had ever built a smelter that quickly and that cheaply before,' Gilbertson says, 'and to have done it in darkest Africa where there is no history of doing that was incredible.'

Gilbertson's gamble had paid off: Billiton bauxite and alumina would feed the Hillside smelter, while Gencor's new joint venture in stainless steel at Columbus in the Transvaal would use Colombian nickel. The deal also brought all of Gencor's divisions under the umbrella of Billiton's sophisticated worldwide marketing operation.

Marius Kloppers, meanwhile, had been sent to the old Bayside smelter to learn the aluminium business. He found a mentor in a Scot named Rob Barbour. 'I joined the Hillside smelter as human-resources manager just after the elections. They had set out as a new material investment to change the demographics of the people they wanted to employ,' he says. 'That was a fairly challenging task. The guy who was there before me didn't make it, so I was drawn in from an operational job into that role. We had the opportunity to recruit a completely new workforce and that's what we did: 65,000 applicants, 10,000 psychometric and assessment tests, 5000 interviews and a thousand people recruited. It was a new operation, so we could recruit who we wanted. When our technology provider departed, I ran the Hillside operation.'[16]

Sir David Barran, the former chairman of Shell Transport,

confessed that Billiton had never achieved the desired synergy under Shell management. 'We were looking around for what was to be the next thing,' he said, 'and it didn't go quite as much hand-in-hand as we had hoped.'[17] For Brian Gilbertson, Billiton was more than 'the next thing'; it was the answer to his corporate prayers. Its purchase instantly gave Gencor a presence in 15 countries. The first of South Africa's mining companies, long in thrall to their British, American and Australian competitors, could now make its entrance on the world stage.

The timing could not have been better for South Africa, which was emerging from 20 years of decline. Battered by sanctions, hit by drought and drained by recession, the country was at the point of financial and economic meltdown. While the ANC-dominated Cabinet wrestled with the problems of dismantling the apartheid bureaucracy, Mandela retained Derek Keys as finance minister in his Government of National Unity to tackle the crisis of low productivity and high unemployment. Keys prepared the new South Africa's first budget, a cautious document that demonstrated a commitment to fiscal discipline.

'Brian Gilbertson mentioned to me on one occasion that if my enforced political career were suddenly to end he would fancy my taking the chairman role of Billiton while he and Gencor got themselves into a position to go for a listing in London,' Derek Keys says. 'That point duly arrived after six months with the new government and that's the first time that I made direct acquaintance with Billiton itself.'[18]

Keys' appointment was announced at Gencor's annual general meeting at the end of October 1994. Shortly afterwards, he moved to London to manage the corporate context of the acquisition from the Gencor office at the Aldwych end of the Strand. Dave Munro, who had been appointed managing director-designate of Billiton, joined him there for a few months, then moved to The Hague to run Billiton's day-to-day operations.

Paul Everard says, 'Derek visited the key operations – the aluminium, the nickel – and he was certainly active in developing strategic initiatives for the businesses. But he was also looking with Brian and Dave at how the group was going to move forward in the future.'[19]

The following year, Gencor celebrated its centenary by moving into a swanky new head office, complete with helicopter pad, at 6 Hollard Street in the heart of Johannesburg's business district. TV cameras rolled as President Mandela unveiled a plaque outside the building in front of hundreds of staff and invited guests, including his predecessors F. W. de Klerk and P. W. Botha. Everything was going according to plan until Mandela suddenly digressed from his speech notes and launched into a tirade against South Africa's former regime. At first, de Klerk and Botha seemed stunned, but by the time Mandela had finished speaking both men were clearly furious. 'It was with some difficulty that I persuaded them to enter the building for the rest of the celebrations,' Gilbertson told the authors.

Says Mike Salamon, 'We slowly welded Billiton into a global business but as a company we were quite clumsy: the company was listed in Johannesburg, it still had exchange controls, there was a very limited array of things we could do. The next thing was to get a global listing.'[20]

Mick Davis and Willy Murray prepared a strategy document called 'The Road to Irian Jaya' with the intention of developing Gencor into an international company.

'We had exploration properties almost adjacent to Freeport McMoRan's great copper mine in Irian Jaya[21] and if they were prospective there was no way that a company constrained by exchange control in South Africa could build a $1–2 billion mine there,' Davis says. 'The question was, how could we take Gencor into a position where we could actually build it? We attached a second document to it called "The Seven Steps" to what we wanted to achieve. One of those steps was to reverse the company into another company offshore.

'Between 1995 and 1997, we tried three times to find companies we could actually reverse into but none of those worked. I sat down, musing to myself. I said, "Well, if we can't sell ourselves to somebody, we'll sell ourselves to ourselves. Why don't we list those former Shell assets and then use that company to buy Gencor?" It didn't quite happen that way because Billiton bought both those assets and the Gencor assets, but that was purely for structure.'[22]

One balmy evening in the summer of 1995, Brian Gilbertson was due to meet Jerry Ellis at the Melbourne Club at the Paris end of Collins Street. There was only one problem: Qantas had lost his luggage. 'I had this vision of appearing in my jeans, T-shirt and running shoes,' he says. 'I had to rush out and buy new suits before I met Jerry and some of his colleagues. I took the bill to Qantas the next day and they nearly fainted when they saw what I'd bought.'[23]

Jerry Ellis recalls that night. 'We entertained Brian Gilbertson to dinner at the Melbourne Club, but that was just mining people getting together,' he says. 'I happened to have all of my team in Melbourne – because they were scattered around the world – and Brian happened to be in Melbourne or it might have been by arrangement because I certainly wanted him to meet them.'[24]

Gilbertson and his team spent the next 18 months integrating Billiton's assets into Gencor with the intention of making Billiton its offshore investment subsidiary to be listed on the London Stock Exchange – the first South African company to make such a move. President Mandela approved the plan and kept in touch with the company's progress. Meanwhile, Derek Keys kept Billiton on an even keel. 'I had to work with the Billiton people, some of whom had come out of Shell,' he says. 'I had the great good fortune to have Dave Munro as my chief executive. He's a grand fellow. Somebody was looking to hire him as chief executive of another company and I came up with a perfect phrase: "We haven't yet discovered what he can't do." My first task as the chairman was to get on the best of terms with Munro. It turned out to be a very happy partnership.'[25]

The Gencor board then divided the group's assets between a Johannesburg-based precious-metals company and a London-based international commodities group. The non-precious metals (aluminium, titanium, steel, ferro-alloys, nickel, coal and base metals) plus its marketing, trading and exploration arms were transferred to Billiton in exchange for nearly 80 per cent of Billiton's shares, which were distributed to Gencor investors. Gencor then retained its gold and platinum holdings – Gengold and Impala Platinum – on the Johannesburg Stock Exchange.[26]

'We decided we would list the industrial businesses – aluminium, copper, coal, nickel – and we chose the Billiton name because it goes back to 1860 and had a long tradition and history,' Mike Salamon says. 'We left Gencor behind in South Africa controlling the two businesses which were very South African, the gold and the platinum. Subsequently, the Gencor gold business merged with Gold Fields and platinum with Impala Plat.'[27]

Brian Gilbertson explained to reporters in June 1997 that he needed access to international capital markets. 'Mining has long lead times and swallows up large amounts of capital,' he said. 'For us to be in the first league, we have to be able to access capital.'[28] He described Billiton plc as a first-class investment with a list of impressive assets, including Samancor's ferro-metals and the aluminium smelters and mineral sands of Richards Bay. In coal, Trans-Natal bought Randcoal to create Ingwe Coal[29], which then acquired Coal Mines of Australia in 1996. The base-metals segment was smaller but growing and the nickel business would take a huge leap to fourth place in the world league if a proposed merger between Queensland Nickel and Cerro Matosa in Colombia was successful.[30]

Gilbertson expected Billiton's market capitalisation to be among the top 60 companies on the London Stock Exchange, which would guarantee it a place in the FTSE (Footsie) 100 Index. The company would then secure between US$1 billion and US$1.5 billion through a rights issue – a greater amount of fresh capital than had ever been raised by a mining company anywhere in the world. He would be chairman of both Gencor and Billiton, although he would step away from Gencor over time.

The Billiton board was slimmed down and internationalised, with Gilbertson replacing Derek Keys as chairman. Keys, Mick Davis, Mike Salamon and Dave Munro all became executive directors, and key staff appointments were made. Having completed his assignment at Hillside, Marius Kloppers and his family – he and Carin had two children of their own and had adopted an African child – headed back to Europe. 'I moved into marketing and was back in the Netherlands,' he says. 'I was actually working for Dave Munro when the Billiton listing took place.'[31]

Gilbertson engaged the British merchant bank of Flemings to help him find two British non-executive directors. In early June, Roddy Fleming phoned John Jackson, non-solicitor chairman of the London-based law firm of Mishcon de Reya.

'John,' he said, 'we've got something coming up which might interest you. Could you have a chat with Robin Renwick?'

Robin William Renwick had been British ambassador to South Africa during the tumultuous period from 1987 to 1991. A tall, slight, good-looking man with a thatch of brownish hair, Renwick was 'old school' – St Paul's School, London, and Jesus College, Cambridge – but neither snobbish nor particularly conservative: he succeeded in making friends with both de Klerk and Mandela.

After his stint in South Africa, Renwick was posted to Washington as British ambassador to the United States and, on his return to London, was ennobled by Prime Minister Tony Blair as Baron Renwick of Clifton. 'I then privatised myself and joined Flemings,' he says.[32]

'Billiton, a mining company presently listed in Johannesburg, is coming to London,' Lord Renwick told Jackson when he visited the Mishcon offices. 'The institutions want two independent British directors. I'm one of them; would you be interested in being the other?'

The listing of Billiton would be the first of the big mining initial public offerings (IPOs). Billiton did not have stellar assets but it had an outstanding management team.

'That's very interesting indeed,' Jackson replied. 'First, it's interesting to have South African companies coming to London; second, it seems to me the investment community has got mining completely wrong and that the shares of these companies are hugely undervalued.'[33]

Then, in the middle of Royal Ascot, Jackson – who was at the racecourse in his capacity as chairman of the bookmakers Ladbrokes – received a call to meet up with Mick Davis at the Hilton Hotel at Heathrow airport, where Davis was catching a plane back to South Africa. 'We were quite close to the launch and we really needed these directors in place,' Davis says. 'John was all dressed up in his morning coat – it was quite hilarious. I met him and immediately liked him very much – I thought he would be an outstanding non-executive director.'[34]

Jackson was also impressed. 'It wasn't a long conversation but I took to Mick hugely – he struck me as being a very interesting and highly intelligent man,' he says in the Mishcon boardroom at Red Lion Square. 'The next thing was that I met Brian Gilbertson via a videoconference link: I was in Flemings' offices and he was in the Billiton offices in Johannesburg. I agreed to join the board and it went on from there.'[35]

Cor Herkströter would also become a director after retiring as president of Royal Dutch Petroleum and chairman of the Royal Dutch Shell Group the following year. 'One of the important things in a London listing is that you should have a board composed of directors who have sufficient gravitas and industry knowledge,' Gilbertson says. 'You can't just take some of your shareholders and put them on. We had some but you needed a better balance than that, and Cor struck me as the ideal director because he had been at the top of one of the world's great companies and he was an international businessman of stature. I went with some trepidation to his office to ask him whether he would be willing to come on to the board. And he was – he came on; he was a great director.'[36]

As the countdown began to D-Day on 27 July, Mick Davis and Mike Salamon arrived in London to join Dave Munro, who had moved from The Hague with most of his executives. Gilbertson shuttled between his home in Pallinghurst Road in Johannesburg's exclusive Westcliffe area, the Hollard Street headquarters of Gencor and Billiton plc's new London address: the top floor of the Grand Buildings in the Strand overlooking Trafalgar Square.

'This was the first South African listing outside South Africa; it was a bellwether event,' Mike Salamon says. 'The guys running Gencor were Brian, Mick, Dave Munro, myself and a guy called Mike McMahon. The five of us were called "the Gencom" – the Gencor executive committee. We left gold and platinum in Gencor under Mike McMahon. Brian, Mick, Dave Munro and myself ran the new business. We were called "the Billicom".'[37]

The Billicom Four held the new company's inaugural board meeting in its new London office and then hit the road in European and American cities to stimulate demand among investors for Billiton's offering of 375 million new shares. Gilbertson and Salamon flew to the States, while Davis and Munro covered Europe. Their efforts paid off. On Billiton's first day of trading, the share price hit £2.28, slightly higher than the £2.20 listing price.

After flotation, the Billiton team focused on broadening the company's base-metals business by enlarging its existing mines and expanding elsewhere. Shareholders in Queensland Nickel (QNI) voted in favour of the $2.3 billion merger with Billiton to create one of the world's top nickel groups. QNI chairman Max Roberts said the merger would make QNI the fourth-largest nickel producer in the world, with a production capacity of about 60,000 tons. Mike Salamon, Mick Davis and Chris Pointon joined the QNI board. It was a fractious acquisition and Mike Salamon was greeted with some hostility when he went to Brisbane, but he says in just three weeks he won them over.

Billiton's shares had hit £2.49 when things started to go wrong. First, South African investors sold their Billiton shares to raise hard currency, then metal prices collapsed following economic turmoil in Japan and South East Asia and the bottom fell out of mining stock.[38]

Billiton desperately needed a good head of investor relations to handle press inquiries and calm shareholder fears, and they found one in Marc Gonsalves, a 37-year-old former Catholic priest who had been working for JCI and had resigned because he and his family wanted to return to the United Kingdom.

'I was born in West Africa, my father was South American, my mother is French and I lived in Britain and Australia,' says Gonsalves, a large, tousled-haired rugby player who now lives in Yorkshire. 'Brian and Mick interviewed me. Here was this gung-ho bunch of South Africans coming to London, setting themselves up against one of the icons of the industry, Rio Tinto – a fantastic company that was the paradigm of an international mining company in the minds of the London investors. I'm sure Brian and Mick were advised by their banks to get a patrician, florid-faced, Establishment person connected to the London Stock Exchange. My appointment was relatively brave of them.'[39]

Gonsalves' fire-fighting skills were immediately put to the test. 'Brian's chairman's statement in the annual report for that year was published two days after I joined,' he says. 'There were two big cock-ups. It was released at 4.30 in the afternoon, which in London is an absolute no-no: you give the market no time to respond, there's no time to get your message out, no time for analysts to brief their sales teams. The timing was almost designed to flag it as something which shouldn't be looked at. It was complete ignorance on behalf of those who were then responsible.

'The second problem was there was a sentence in Brian's statement, and it is indelibly marked on my brain, "If the downturn in the Asian economies proves to be of extended duration, Billiton, like other companies, will not escape its impact." Looked at in cold terms, it's a statement of the bleeding obvious. However, it was widely interpreted as a profits warning. I walked into a maelstrom the following morning, with our share price down eight per cent.'

Mick Davis was in Australia as part of his mission to raise US$1.2 billion from a consortium of 13 banks, the largest capital-raising then made in mining. There was huge sensitivity about Billiton, and the banks were all nervous. 'Marc came on board at exactly that time,' Davis says. 'The market said, "Ahh – a profit warning," and our share price collapsed. Banks were calling me up saying, "What's going on?" Quite honestly, we never intended it to be a profit warning, we didn't think of it as a profit warning and it wasn't a profit warning. It was simply a logical comment on the market.'[40]

In London, an emergency meeting was called and a delegation of grim-faced bankers trooped into Billiton's office at 11 am. It was Gonsalves' third day in charge of investor relations. 'I wandered into the meeting – I had the foresight, thank God, to bring in my financial PR people and the brokers who at least had some market gen,' he says. 'The company's deputy treasurer began the meeting by saying, "Ladies and gentlemen, we've clearly got a crisis in respect of the statement made yesterday and the market's response to it. I'd now like to hand over to Marc Gonsalves to tell us what's going on." I got home that day and said to my wife, "I think we've made a mistake."'[41]

Another of Billiton's problems was that the directors of Sanlam, now at the forefront of black economic empowerment in South Africa, had what Brian Gilbertson describes as 'a Damascene conversion' and started to unload their stakes in various companies.[42] 'South Africa had undergone a sea change with the transition from the old South Africa to the new democratic South Africa,' he says. 'The institutions – companies which had previously seen their role as being to control the

South African economy – became much more conventional, and one of those decisions was that as an insurance company you shouldn't have all your eggs in one basket, and Gencor and Billiton had been a very big basket for them. The right thing to do was what other international insurance companies had done, and that was to spread your investments in line with Markowitz portfolio theory.[43]

'So they made that transition under Marinus Daling who, incidentally, had been one of the driving forces in the Gencor unbundling – he was on the board of Gencor. Somewhere at the top of Sanlam, they made the decision that they should reduce their holding, and that coincided with a crisis in Japan and South East Asia when all of the shares fell off a cliff.'[44]

When Billiton plunged to £1.53, Gilbertson received heavy flak from the 'suits in the City', who questioned his many trips back to South Africa on Gencor business and talked of him as being 'an absentee landlord'. 'We were criticised quite a bit in the press about how Billiton was the first South African company to come to London and look what a pup they'd been sold,' Gilbertson says. 'We actually dropped below £1 and were heading for 90p, and this at a time when we had cash in the bank of 80p – all these great assets scattered around the world were viewed as having no value at all. It was a perfect illustration of the folly of investors in falling markets. We just couldn't believe this was happening.'[45]

In fact, there had been no cause for panic. Gilbertson had reported a profit of US$481 million in Billiton's first financial year on the London Stock Exchange – a 44 per cent increase over the US$335 million, excluding exceptional items, earned in the previous 12 months. It was a record performance compared with results under Gencor.

'In a perverse way, what Brian had signalled was the weakness coming out of Asia following the Kyoto Treaty and all the rest of it,' Marc Gonsalves says. 'So we all went into the doldrums between the end of 1997 and when the commodity markets started to pick up again in 1999.'[46]

The end result was that Billiton acquired a much more diversified shareholder register. Gilbertson says, 'The market started to recognise that this was crazy – we were sitting on 80p in cash, with the share price trading at 90p – so the share price came back and did very well and the shareholders were happy.'[47]

Billiton and its management emerged from the uncertainty of its launch as a publicly listed company with a reputation of being resilient, aggressive and ambitious.[48] 'Brian was very aggressive in the positive sense of the word in terms of developing the business,' Paul Everard says. 'He was always willing to lead from the front and at the corporate level he was looking at making quantum changes to the Billiton business.'[49]

Gilbertson and Davis recognised that market credibility and access to capital were absolutely critical to Billiton's future success. Even before the company fully recovered, Gilbertson sketched his master plan to Ian Fraser, who joined Billiton as human-resources director in March 1998. 'This is what we're going to do,' he told the 37-year-old Glasgow-born psychologist. 'We're going to sort out this portfolio, we're going to de-list the South African assets to get access to the direct cash flows, we're going to reinvest those cash flows into these businesses and expand them internationally, and then we're going to merge with BHP, and when we've got that sorted we're going to take over Rio Tinto.'

Fraser said it seemed like a great plan. 'What do you want from me?' he asked.

Gilbertson replied that he might not be around for the whole exercise. 'The first thing I want you to do is find the man who's going to succeed me,' he said.[50]

CHAPTER 17

The Cruellest Blow

On John Prescott's watch as chief executive, BHP became such a diverse and powerful operator that its footprint covered the globe. Foreign assets increased from 28 per cent of total holdings in 1991 to more than 40 per cent in 1996. The company developed 90 separate operating units and businesses in oil, petroleum, steel and minerals across 50 countries.

Emblematic of the company's return to its roots as a supplier of natural resources, a new section, 'World Minerals', was added to the BHP portfolio under Tim Winterer, a 61-year-old veteran of the Utah purchase. 'World Minerals contained projects that didn't fit in nicely anywhere else,' he says. 'It was a lot of odds and sods around the world: a gold mine in Mali, a platinum mine in Zimbabwe, iron in Brazil, diamonds in Canada, steam coal in New Mexico, a silver mine in Queensland.'[1]

No amount of spin, however, could disguise the fact that profits peaked in 1995 at $1.216 billion, fell to a still highly respectable $1.046 billion in 1996 but then took a catastrophic tumble in 1997, the year that would become BHP's *annus horribilis*. Investors looked askance at the dwindling share price of a company that had so recently stood for security, solidarity and a particular brand of Australian flair.

'The 1991–95 period wasn't too bad – we made a huge profit in '96,' John Prescott says. 'I remember saying to the board, "I'm sorry, but this will be the last record profit for a while. Things are getting pretty difficult." And then they got very difficult in 1997.'[2]

Just 18 months after the purchase of Magma Copper, BHP took a $550 million charge against that asset, accounting for much of the 61 per cent decline in profits to just $410 million in the year to the end of May 1997. In his message to shareholders in the BHP annual report, Prescott reasserted the company's dedication to diversity. 'We have six groups of businesses that we are confident will continue to perform strongly against our criteria,' he said. 'These include the oil-and-gas activities in Bass Strait and the North-West Shelf, Escondida copper mine, our various iron-ore businesses and most of our coal and flat-products steel activities. These are the businesses we know best, where we see our major comparative advantages and where we achieve great results.'

Brian Loton stepped down as chairman and that month – May 1997 – Jerry Ellis, godfather of the Magma project and now deputy chairman, took control of the bridge. It marked the start of a dismal time for John Prescott, who had been one of the prime candidates for the top job and must have been disappointed. He had been a BHP director since 1988 and, although three years younger than Ellis at 56, had been his boss from 1991 to 1996.

'John Prescott was asked by the board to stay on as CEO and not look to the chairman's position,' says a BHP insider. 'But they didn't have a solution as to who the new chairman should be and they came up with this idea that they should put Jerry Ellis in that job because they thought it was more appropriate for him to be a chairman than a continuing executive. They asked Prescott to accept that situation, which was somewhat difficult for him.'[3]

There had been friction between Ellis and his beleaguered chief executive prior to Ellis's appointment as chairman. Prescott now found himself beavering away at an array of seemingly insoluble problems under the man who could fairly be said to have been responsible for creating the biggest one. Even allowing for the copper price slump, Magma had performed badly. The $550 million write-down confirmed what some stock analysts had suspected all along: that $3.2 billion was an astronomical amount of money to have paid for Magma, especially when BHP owned a far richer, more productive copper mine in the massive Escondida project.[4]

Nor was Magma the only big loss-maker. Another $124 million was written off the value of the Pacific Resources oil refinery in Hawaii, renamed BHP Hawaii. Chip Goodyear found himself on the other side of the table representing Pacific Resources in 1989 when BHP bought the refinery for more than $500 million.

'The oil business had expanded dramatically but also faced an uncertain future because Bass Strait wasn't going to go on forever and the North-West Shelf, while it was a pretty useful asset to have in conjunction with Bass Strait, wasn't enough to satisfy our ambitions in the oil-and-gas industry,' John Prescott says. 'We did a fair bit of other exploration in Australia for oil and gas and had some success but come the mid-'90s we were desperately keen to find a new Bass Strait, or some substitute for it, and at the same time we had successfully expanded our minerals business. We had seven or eight consecutive years of record profits in minerals, iron ore and copper, in the main.

'We also started to look seriously at whether we could shed the steel industry. I'm told that a number of directors had been keen to get out of steel from the early 1980s and they'd never found a way. We set out to find a solution to that and at the same time to continue to expand our minerals and petroleum businesses.

'We had more opportunities to expand the minerals business than the oil-and-gas business: probably the best thing that happened to help us with petroleum was exploration in the Gulf of Mexico. We'd made a number of acquisitions in petroleum prior to that, including the Hamilton Oil Company. They were useful but they weren't a Bass Strait.

'We went into the Gulf of Mexico in a fairly substantial way in very deep water before the world oil industry had worked out how to produce oil at those depths. Companies like Shell and BP, and probably Chevron, were learning how to go into much, much deeper water and we had actually done some pretty useful work ourselves but we weren't a Shell or a BP in the oil industry. However, we took that punt into the Gulf of Mexico and we had some significant discoveries in conjunction with others – in some cases, we were the operator; in some cases, we weren't.'[5]

The Hamilton acquisition enabled BHP to move into the booming North Sea, where it had a 16 per cent interest in the Bruce field. In South East Asia, BHP moved one of Hamilton's vessels off the coast of Vietnam to explore the Dai Hung field, a venture that never looked like fulfilling its promise. After spending $260 million, BHP abandoned its 43.8 per cent operating interest in the project.

Meanwhile, the petroleum division – still under the lively command of Irishman John O'Connor – doubled its profits to $676 million in the year to the end of May 1997, a performance that prevented BHP from slipping into the red. To galvanise his troops to even greater effort, O'Connor had watches and little clocks stamped with the BHP insignia and the slogan, 'A billion dollars by '98'.

In July 1997, an edict went out from BHP Tower that the company's 90-odd operating units would henceforth be judged against the world's best companies in their respective industries. Any unit that failed to maintain the highest standard would face liquidation. But although it seemed the Jack Welch philosophy of 'Fix it, sell it or fold it' had taken root in BHP, it was already too late to halt the haemorrhaging.[6]

'We had three years of pretty significant write-offs of a number of investments that went wrong,' Graeme McGregor says. 'Magma was the major one, then we had problems with the HBI plant at Port Hedland, the titanium sands at Beenup and the Hartley mine in Zimbabwe: there was a series of them that unfortunately all came together, but Magma was the cruellest blow.'[7]

Jim Curry, the former head of BHP Minerals, became a director of Newmont, Magma's one-time owner, after retiring from the BHP board. 'I don't really know what brought the company to the point that it had so much trouble, except that they made a couple of bad decisions,' he says. 'The company was still solid, it had good people and good operations, but the Magma thing was a disaster and they got into a couple of other investments that weren't too good either. One of the differences between BHP and Utah was that BHP did not do the level of digging or analysis that we did. Utah was "study it, study it and study it again". Having big overruns or overpaying for something or misestimating reserves were things you couldn't afford to do.'[8]

The recession-plagued copper industry just couldn't shake itself out of the doldrums. 'We had to constrain some of the development of Escondida because not only the price dropped but world consumption dropped,' John Prescott says. 'Stage II and Stage III had gone ahead pretty quickly, and they'd been hugely successful. The board had approved Stage IV in principle but Stage IV didn't advance quite as quickly as we'd originally envisaged.'[9]

Then, in August, three key executives departed in the space of 72 hours, sending shock waves through the company and alerting the stock market to the fact that heads were starting to roll. First was Dick Carter, boss of the minerals division, who was pushed into retirement on 6 August following cost overruns and delays that had inflated the price of the Boodarie HBI plant at Port Hedland to $2.6 billion.

The following day, Geoff Wedlock, BHP's general manager of iron ore, joined Carter in early retirement over the same issue. The direct reduction of iron had been successfully executed in different ways around the world, most notably at a HBI plant on the Orinoco River in Venezuela in which BHP had a 50 per cent stake. 'We tended to use the technology that the Venezuelans had used – which I think was Austrian technology – to develop the plant in the Pilbara,' John Prescott says, discussing the HBI disaster that would, over time, rival Magma Copper in terms of red ink. 'It would have enabled us to sell an extra five or six million tons of lump a year, which we really wanted to do; if we produced five or six million tons of lump, we got five or six million tons of fines with it. The alternative to putting the fines on the ground was to put them through a direct-reduction iron plant. We believed we'd negotiated markets for that direct-reduced iron.

'However, the plant didn't develop and commission as well as had been envisaged. It was an engineering problem, partly because the engineers changed some of the technologies that had been utilised in Venezuela. There were some other difficulties that were quite unusual in BHP: there was some concealment of overspend, for which some people were removed.

'BHP had a culture where that sort of thing didn't happen, but these two things combined to make that project a very substantial disaster at the same time as the copper industry was going south. And there were a couple of nasty fatalities. It was a big hit; it was a project that had overspent to hell, and so it was a substantial knock to BHP at the time.'[10]

Prescott's problems escalated when John O'Connor publicly promoted the flotation of BHP Petroleum as a separate entity on the stock market to unlock shareholder value. Seizing on this possibility, analysts estimated that flotation could produce up to $18 billion, about half of BHP's capitalisation at that time. 'I was with the head of investor relations at a lunch for analysts in Sydney,' O'Connor explains. 'I was fairly honest in responding to questions to the extent I could but I was careful not to run counter to the board. The background was we had had a project [Project Leopard] to evaluate whether or not it would have been better for BHP to have floated some or all of the petroleum business six or so months before this particular lunch. For about three months, all the analysis right up to Christmas 1996 had been very encouraging, to the extent that I remember John Prescott saying to me, "This is great. By the time the New Year comes in, you'll be well on the way to having a separate enterprise."

'Then it was the Australian summer for January and February and there were no board meetings, best I can tell, and a sort of hiatus developed. At the next board meeting, which seemed to me to be March of 1997, it was quietly said that Project Leopard was no longer going to proceed; there needed to be further evaluation; it wasn't necessarily a good thing. It just faded away, ran into the sands – there was never any rationale put forward as to why it should not go ahead but it was clear it was not going to go ahead.

'So, fine, that was that. I was asked about that at that lunch [in Sydney] and I said, "Look, the board has made this decision. If I didn't support the board's decision, I'd have to resign from the board. I support it." It was subsequently reported that I had been critical of the board. In answer to some hypothetical or other, maybe I'd said that it would be better if they had some petroleum knowledge. I didn't think it was very controversial at all, but be that as it may. I remember waking up on the Friday of that week. I had a TV in my bedroom and the news was saying, "Second major thunderclap at BHP. Dick Carter, head of minerals, has been fired and now O'Connor is criticising the board."

'Rubbish – but I think it was just a culmination of everything: the HBI thing, the sacking of Dick Carter. It was all done very quickly and discreetly, with no questioning of what really happened. I tried to explain what had happened – nobody wanted to hear. I got called out to the managing director's office. There was an opportunity to go quietly and I thought, "Okay, why not?"'[11]

On 8 August 1997, O'Connor was shown the door for his temerity. Jerry Ellis made it clear to investors that BHP had not rejected spin-offs as a strategy but did not believe that floating its petroleum division would be in the best interests of the group at that time. Unconvinced, many shareholders abandoned BHP, and its share price dropped by almost six per cent to $16.99.[12]

As we have seen, Phil Aiken, who had joined BHP just five months earlier from the automotive-parts group BTR Nylex, stepped into O'Connor's role. His first tasks were to restore public confidence in BHP Petroleum and to convince his disenchanted executives to stay with the company.[13]

'The spin of the whole thing at the time was necessary for Ellis and Prescott to retain credibility in the markets, so it was perfectly understandable from a business point of view,' O'Connor says. 'I thought it was distasteful, but I'm a big boy and that's the way things work. They don't like anybody flying in the face of received wisdom or being in any way implicitly critical of the whole thing, but the reality was that BHP was a provincial enterprise run by provincial people – well-intentioned people but simply not up to the task of managing effectively a global company. This is not hindsight, it's what I was alluding to at the time. The fact they could bring in someone from the outside world like me and have a significant difference made to what was up to then a sleepy business I think gave some credibility to the justified criticism of the way the business was being run.

'It was an old boys' club. The leadership had been handed down from Sir Ian McLennan to Sir James McNeill to Brian Loton and then Jerry Ellis – it was like one hand rubbing the other hand along the way. There was never any real attempt while I was there to get to grips with the cost basis of the corporation.

'The same cosy companionship pretty much prevailed on the board. It's interesting now to see the composition of the board because I was always concerned that there was no other person who knew the oil-and-gas business, yet we were projecting making a billion dollars of earnings. Who could argue about oil things brought to the board? For that matter, there weren't many mining experts on the board either.'[14]

John Prescott admits life became extremely difficult. In February 1998, BHP laid off more than 400 workers at its Pinto Valley mine in the Miami/Globe area of Arizona when the copper price fell to 72 cents a pound, close to what it cost to get out of the ground. Production at the Ok Tedi mine, the company's lowest-cost copper producer, had already been halted since mid-August 1997 when, for the second time since the company had taken it over, the Fly River had fallen so low during a drought that it was impossible to navigate.

'It seems to be a feature of minerals development that the weather changes while you're in the development phase,' Prescott says. 'Whereas you would have expected to have all the water in the world to build the mine, we ended up having to fly most of the gear in.'[15] Even the price of oil was down to $14 a barrel, compared with $25 early in 1997, while gold was selling for just under $300 an ounce, compared with $376 at the end of 1996.[16]

Steel prices were steadier, but Asia provided markets for half of the output of BHP Steel and no one expected demand to be sustained during the financial troubles that had devastated the Tiger economies. Furthermore, South Korea's steel industry would shortly benefit from the fall in the value of the won, threatening BHP exports to the region.[17]

Brad Mills had four months to go on his BHP Copper contract in San Francisco when he received a phone call from Prescott. 'Would you like to come down to Melbourne and become the vice president of strategy for BHP?'

Mills was astonished. 'Are you really sure you want me to?' he said. 'You know I don't really think a lot of what's going on inside BHP is the right stuff – there's a lot of problems and a lot of bad decisions have been made and there are some real tough issues that you're facing. Are you really sure you want me to come down and take that on?'

There was a long pause at the other end of the phone. Then Prescott replied, 'Brad, actually that's the reason I want you to come. You're one of the few people in the last two years who's really been telling the truth about what the issues are in the business. I really would like you to come down and help me try to fix what's not working.'[18]

Mills moved his family to Melbourne – to a house on the beach at Brighton – and worked with Prescott to put together a strategic reorganisation of the company. 'We told John, "You have to break the company apart – you have to spin out the steel business,"' he says. 'John agreed with us. He decided to tackle the board and propose the spin-out of the steel business as a whole – take the whole thing out.'[19]

'One of the things that hasn't yet emerged publicly is that I recommended the removal of the steel company from the company's assets,' John Prescott says. 'I recommended that we quit the steel business and developed a scheme to do that which solved all the tax issues associated with it that had plagued the removal of steel from the company's portfolio for about 15 years. We came up with a solution to that tax problem and when it was taken to the board I was told it was an absolutely brilliant concept. A couple of directors said to me they had been on the board for many years and never thought they'd find a solution. We were to be congratulated on coming up with that solution, but when it finally went to the board they didn't bite the bullet.'[20]

It was Prescott's last throw of the dice. 'When it came down to the final presentation to the board,' says Brad Mills, 'where it was go or no-go in terms of the reorganisation of BHP and splitting the steel company off and a bunch of other structural issues that we wanted to tackle, I very much got the sense from talking to the different directors that John didn't have the votes, didn't have the support.

'John didn't want to hear that. He was confident he could carry it. They said to John, "Your strategy is fine but you're asking us to tear apart the company that you have built over the last seven years. We don't think you're the right guy to do this, so we're going to make a change and you're leaving." He was quite surprised by that decision of the board.'[21]

Enmeshed in problems, the last thing John Prescott wanted to hear was that his embattled company had attracted the attentions of the rapacious South Africans at Billiton, who had coveted BHP's assets for some time. Mick Davis recalls that the first time he started thinking about BHP was during the roadshow for the flotation of Billiton in 1997. 'It was on one of the flights between cities that Dave Munro and I started saying, "What's next?"' he says. 'We spoke about merging with BHP; that was the first time we started thinking about that idea, and it germinated for a period in the company. When the market started picking up, we looked at it again and again. From the Billiton perspective, we thought it would be a major step forward into some world-class assets – and we thought for BHP, perhaps rather arrogantly, it would be a major step into world-class management.'[22]

Says Dave Munro, 'Mick Davis was quite an extraordinary finance director. There was no transaction which he wasn't confident he could fund if the story was right. He liberated the thinking within the Billiton organisation. He was always ready to think of a way to make things possible.'[23]

In March 1998, Billiton made the first serious approach. Davis and Salamon flew to Melbourne and met with John Prescott. 'Unfortunately, that was the very day he was fired,' Davis says. 'So we had a meeting with him and an old-timer who is no longer there. They said, "Yes, fine, terribly interesting," and of course nothing happened. BHP then went into hibernation to look for a chief executive.'[24]

John Prescott resigned as chief executive on 4 March 1998, effective from April. The master plan had been to create a low-cost, diversified miner capable of withstanding the vagaries of the commodities market, but it had spectacularly misfired. Prescott acknowledges that strategic mistakes were made. 'You can't blame the board, you have to blame the management of the day for not being able to convince the board to go in a certain direction,' he says. 'I'm not trying to pass the buck to the board. It was a difficult period.'[25]

The stock market recoiled in horror when BHP reported a whopping operating loss, after tax, of $1.474 billion in the year to the end of May 1998 (compared with a profit of $410 million the previous year and considering it was only the second loss in BHP's hundred-year-plus history). BHP's share price plunged to a historic low of just over $10, little more than half the previous year's high. Embarrassingly, BHP lost its prized top position on the stock market, slipping to fourth place.

The list of new write-downs – the losses from failed projects – looked as though someone had thrown red ink at the balance sheet. It made nightmarish reading: $620 million for the San Manuel smelter; $868 million for the Arizona copper mines; $129 million for the Tintaya copper mine (Peru); $378 million for the Boodarie HBI project at Port Hedland; $357 million for the Hartley platinum mine (Zimbabwe); $99 million for the Beenup titanium minerals operation (Western Australia), and so on.

'No doubt Mr Prescott (with Mr Ellis's help) has made a few errors,' *The Economist* editorialised. 'But, to be fair, he has also been desperately unlucky. BHP has four operating divisions: minerals, copper, steel and petroleum. All of them have been hurt by falling prices.'[26]

Asked whether he rated himself unlucky, Jerry Ellis replies with another rueful laugh, 'I don't rate myself – that's what others did.'[27]

Lance Hockridge thought the reversal of fortune was symptomatic of a widespread malaise. 'Magma and the HBI project alone represented write-offs of somewhere between $6 and $7 billion,' he says, 'in addition to which there were some much smaller issues around the company – but it had developed an extraordinary level of things going wrong.'[28]

Brad Mills had been in Melbourne for only a couple of months when the chief executive who had hired him disappeared from BHP Tower and Ron McNeilly, former chief executive of BHP Steel – 'a steel man who loved the steel business', according to Mills – was asked to step into the breach as chief operating officer at the head of an interim management group to run the company's affairs. 'It was difficult: Ron knew that

I'd supported the spin-out of the steel business,' Mills says. 'He was very committed to trying to become the chief executive of the company; he wanted it. I thought strongly that it wasn't necessarily a great outcome for the business. We were tackling a lot of turnaround issues at that time: what to do with HBI, what to do with Beenup, what to do with Magma – all these failed investments that were littering the shop floor needed to be addressed. Market confidence was shattered and there were still big structural issues that needed to be sorted out because we still hadn't completely cleaned up things like the old Foster's cross-shareholding. Lots of messy structural things were holding back the reforms and consuming a lot of time.'

As described in Chapter 8, there had been a defensive cross-shareholding between BHP and Elders IXL, as Foster's was then named, during the Holmes à Court takeover battles of the 1980s. To recoup the $1 billion debt now owed to BHP, Graeme McGregor found himself in the brewing business to sell off some assets and restore market confidence in Foster's Brewing Group. 'I joined the Foster's board in 1992 and was there until '96 when I became a BHP director and it was inappropriate that I was on both boards at that stage,' he says. 'After retiring from BHP, I became a director of Foster's again. We're just wrapping up the last of the deals, which was a land development in Houston called Trinity Park. It will be wrapped up this year [2008] but it just shows how long it takes to finalise some of these matters.'[29]

Brad Mills had very definite ideas about what was needed to restore confidence in BHP itself. 'We convinced Craig Mudge, the chief of human resources, to convince Jerry Ellis that they had to go outside and do a full external search for the new chief executive of BHP,' he says. 'It wouldn't be fair to shareholders or the business if you didn't look at who was available in the marketplace. He agreed to that – it was a key decision, probably one of Jerry's best decisions.'[30]

Jerry Ellis saw this as his chance 'to break from the old BHP mould, which was a formula that no longer worked'. He explains, 'All of us were insiders – it was the way we were brought up. I'd spent 30 years with the company and was full of its traditional ways of doing things. We needed fresh air. And John Prescott was the same. The people who were incumbent at that time in the '90s were essentially insiders – by then, even the Utah fellows were insiders – so it was necessary to break the mould.'[31]

BHP hired an international executive-search firm, Heidrick & Struggles, to find the most suitable candidate, a move that would have been unthinkable a few years earlier in a company that prided itself on its Australian roots and its culture of internal succession.

'Our businesses have been adversely affected by the combined effects of lower commodity prices and the impact of the financial situation in Asia,' Jerry Ellis admitted in a message to BHP shareholders. 'Difficulties in bringing some important capital projects online have also impacted on our results.'

One mining executive, who heard Jerry Ellis speak to shareholders at a meeting in Brisbane, recalls, 'Jerry's presentation focused on all the negatives. He was explaining and apologising for the problems and I remember thinking to myself, "His shareholders don't want to hear that. They want to hear the bad news in context." The fact was that BHP at the time was not at death's door; it had made some huge mistakes but it could withstand them. The presentation to shareholders should have been a balanced presentation about the strengths and weaknesses of the company and it was all about the weaknesses.'[32]

World Minerals, however, had recorded a loss of $111 million. Its major assets fell into two categories: projects such as the Hartley platinum mine in Zimbabwe and the Beenup mineral sands project in the north of Western Australia that had failed or, at the other end of the scale, mines such as the $1 billion EKATI diamonds project in Canada and the Cannington silver, lead and zinc operation in Queensland that would be much more valuable in the hands of their competitors.[33]

'There had been a number of successes which people tend not to reflect on, like Cannington and like EKATI diamonds in Canada: that was brought on in remarkably quick time,' John

Prescott says. 'It's not as important to BHP today as it was in 1998 because BHP is a much larger company.'[34]

Prescott's departure did nothing to alleviate BHP's misfortunes. In June 1998, BHP wrote down the estimated value of its North American copper assets by a further $931 million. It also decided to suspend operations at the Hartley mine because it could not achieve the required quantities of ore or the anticipated grades.

BHP owned 67 per cent of Hartley and managed the project on behalf of its partner, Delta Gold. 'It has done so with extraordinary ineptitude,' Matthew Stevens noted in *The Australian*. 'Very little has gone right. The original mine design has proved to be substantively wrong. Mining the deposit has proved very difficult and the refinery has twice needed redesigning.'[35]

While the hunt for a new chief executive was being conducted around the globe, BHP launched an asset sale as part of an attempt to regroup its business around 'established profit centres'. Finance director Graeme McGregor, who had been put in charge of disposals, denied he was running 'a fire sale or a garage sale', but it was clear from the list that a further $4 billion to $6 billion of assets were not regarded as core to BHP's future. 'The BHP which emerged from the takeover challenges of the 1980s allowed too much freedom to its senior executives,' Matthew Stevens wrote in *The Australian*.

> The silo mentality undermined accountability by creating fiefdoms and a culture of transferable accountability. BHP management is rightly suffering for its errors. Some have been sacked, some fallen on their swords, with the survivors left to find a way of cleaning up the mess and accepting the scorn of the owners of the business, the shareholders. But those owners could well now ask themselves, just what was BHP's board doing as the expansion juggernaut propelled out of control? No directors have resigned. And Jerry Ellis, who was an essential player in the silo game, remains chairman.[36]

But not for long – in August, the board announced that Ellis would step down as chairman in the first half of 1999. His replacement would be fellow director Don Argus, the gritty, no-nonsense, 60-year-old chief executive of National Australia Bank Limited.

At the annual general meeting in September 1998, Ellis apologised to investors for the group's disastrous $1.5 billion loss in the previous financial year. He gave investors little hope of a quick recovery and rejected suggestions that value could be realised by spinning off the company's various divisions. 'I don't see BHP breaking up just because analysts and brokers and others out there think it is a good idea,' Ellis said, adding that BHP was still under pressure from the Asian financial crisis, which had devastated commodity prices. Lower prices, particularly for oil and copper, had cost the group $521 million in profits. 'Almost all of our commodities are at the bottom of the cycle, a situation we have not encountered before,' he said.[37] Clearly, BHP was heading in the same direction.

To add to Ellis's concerns, he received a visit from his erstwhile dinner guest at the Melbourne Club. 'South Africa has very great mining assets but many of them tend to be quite difficult to mine – for example, the gold is at deep levels through hard-rock mining – and we always thought that BHP had among the finest assets in the industry,' Gilbertson says. 'BHP was going through some difficult times and normally in those circumstances people are more willing to talk than they might otherwise be if they are up on a crest or on a high. I must have gone down two or three times to see Jerry Ellis. I remember going back to his office and floating the possibility of some kind of transaction. At one stage, we actually got fairly close.'[38]

Jerry Ellis recalls that Gilbertson was accompanied by James Graham, head of Gresham Partners. 'The proposal they put to me was essentially to merge BHP Minerals, as it then was, with Billiton,' he says.

'I said, "Now is not a good time for us to consider that, mainly because our share price is in the doldrums as the result of some poor investment decisions we made in the minerals business, and so why don't you come back at another time?'"[39]

It might have come as a surprise to the harassed BHP chairman that his utterances were regarded with great respect inside Billiton. 'There was a quote from Jerry Ellis which was a mantra within Billiton that in the years of the new century the mining industry would come to be dominated by two or three large global players diversified in terms of their spread of assets, currencies and commodities,' Marc Gonsalves says. 'We believed that absolutely; it was one of the articles of faith. Right from the start, we knew we had to get Billiton to a position where through marriage or takeover we found ourselves one of those large groups that was going to dominate global mining. The belief in Billiton was absolutely core that the era of smaller, single-plane miners around the world was over. We knew the endgame was going to be some form of marriage or takeover with Anglo, Rio, CVRD or BHP.'[40]

CHAPTER 18

Easy Rider

Top of Heidrick & Struggles' list of candidates to replace John Prescott were Brian Gilbertson, chairman and chief executive of Billiton, and Paul M. Anderson, a pragmatic, results-orientated, motorbike-riding American. Gilbertson was the man with a proven track record in mining. The headhunter told him that BHP was like a plane flying on one engine and he was the industry's choice to fix it. Gilbertson found it a tempting prospect – either joining BHP or, alternatively, taking it over – and he discussed the matter with some of his directors.

'In late 1998, Brian told us privately outside a board meeting that BHP was sniffing at him,' John Jackson says. 'I thought that although this would be quite tricky if Brian moved to BHP, it might open up some very interesting possibilities for the future.'[1]

In fact, we can reveal that Gilbertson was actually offered the job. He asked his colleagues on the Billicom, 'What do you think we should do about it? Should I take the offer?'

He was told, 'If it's a way of creating a merger between Billiton and BHP, then yes. If not, it's up to you.'[2] Gilbertson went back to Melbourne and told BHP he would be interested in the job if it were seen as a precursor to a merger. 'They couldn't swallow it,' says a Billiton source. 'The reason was BHP had a lot of mess to clear up and they didn't want to go into a merger and let us do it. It was not in the interests of Australian shareholders, so they said no to Brian and he said, "Sorry, I'm off."'[3]

Over in Charlotte, North Carolina, Paul Anderson was contemplating early retirement from his role as president and chief operating officer of Duke Energy. In a 20-year career in the oil-and-gas industry, he had masterminded two multibillion-dollar mergers and was still young enough, at 53, to enjoy riding his Harley-Davidson around the United States with his wife, Kathy, or going yachting and scuba-diving with his two daughters, both in their twenties.

Born on April Fool's Day 1945, Anderson grew up on the west coast of America and gained a degree in mechanical engineering from the University of Washington (1967) and an MBA at Stanford University (1969). He worked for the Ford Motor Company until 1977 when he switched to oil and gas, starting as director of corporate planning at Texas Eastern. When Texas Eastern merged with Panhandle Eastern in 1995, he became chief executive of PanEnergy. Then, in 1997, he 'engineered himself out of the job' with the US$7.7 billion merger between PanEnergy and Duke Power, although as president and chief operating officer he was second in command of Duke Energy.

But then came the offer from BHP, a job regarded by the *Financial Times* as 'the most compelling challenge for any executive in the resources industry'.[4] 'From a financial standpoint, I would have been better off to stay with Duke,' Anderson says. 'But I was familiar with BHP, and when they explained the situation and the challenge, I said, "Well, one more campaign can't be bad – I'll take this one on."'[5] With Anderson's appointment, the BHP caste system was decisively broken. Not since General Douglas MacArthur had taken control of the Australian Army during the Pacific War in 1942 had such an important Australian position been handed to an American. 'It was a brilliant move and I do claim that as mine – no one else does, but I do,' Jerry Ellis says. 'I led the mission that found Paul Anderson. We had a small committee of the board, which included, of course, Don Argus, because by then we had decided that Don would take over from me and the candidate had to be agreeable to Don. Yes, it was an opportunity to break from the old BHP mould, which was a formula that no longer worked.'[6]

Anderson's arrival was keenly awaited by investors, stockbrokers, reporters and employees alike. He flew to Melbourne in November 1998 and started work on 1 December on what was described as 'a fundamental restructuring of BHP'.[7]

The first Paul Anderson knew that the phone at his new Toorak home was connected was a call from Brian Gilbertson, who was sitting in a Billicom meeting in London. Not one for idle chit-chat, the South African said, 'Hello, Paul, you don't know me. I'm Brian Gilbertson. I run a company called Billiton. Our two companies belong together and we need to put them together.'

Paul Anderson replied, 'Well, thanks for saying hello. I've literally walked into my new home. I didn't even know my phone was working. I've got a lot to do at BHP to sort things out, but thank you for your call.'[8]

Back at BHP Tower, Anderson called in the senior leadership team. 'I explained who I was, why I was there and what my expectations were,' he says. 'I told them I was going to meet with each one of them for an hour or more and listen to what they had to say. I asked each of them to put together a two-page paper: the first page was a little introduction – who they were, their background, job responsibilities, the issues they were facing in their job and whether they required any major capital expenditure in the next six months; then, on the second page, I asked them to put down what they would do if they were CEO of this company. I said, "That one will be between you and me. It won't go any place. But I'd like to know if you ran the company, what would you do – no holds barred?"'[9]

Anderson seemed unnervingly receptive to fresh ideas, telling staff to call him by his first name. Graham Evans, then director of external affairs, says that for the first few weeks back at headquarters, 'He really didn't do anything. He just went around talking to people and listening to what they had to say. He regarded that as an important characteristic of a good leader, listening and understanding what drove people in terms of attitude and so on.'[10]

When he did act, he was decisive. 'He was quite strong on demonstrating by his own behaviour that he was serious about the things he wanted to do in the company,' Evans says. 'He started eating in the general cafeteria. He made a number of changes that flagged a different sort of company. He introduced "casual Friday" in terms of dress and subsequently moved to a position where people could dress casually every day. But within sensible bounds. If it made others uncomfortable if you weren't wearing a suit, then he expected you to wear one, and he did so himself.

'He tried to interface a lot more directly with staff. He used to hold regular staff briefings. He'd encourage people if they had issues to send him an email and he'd respond to that. If there was one characteristic of Paul's style which was typically striking, it was that he was a very good listener.'[11]

Discovering that each sector had become a little enclave that enjoyed considerable financial independence, he pulled everything into a centralised system of rigorous analysis and budgetary control. He shook up BHP's corporate culture by changing the company's idiosyncratic June–May fiscal year to bring it into line with the rest of the Australian business community and even renamed it from the cumbrous Broken Hill Proprietary Company Limited to BHP Limited.

He trimmed the executive ranks, tied two-thirds of their pay to performance, eliminated the company car as an automatic perk and ripped out the en suite office bathrooms.[12] Many of BHP's traditional titles disappeared. 'We really only need three titles,' he told executives. 'If you've got board responsibility, you're a president, and if you report to a president, you're a vice president, and if you report to a vice president or you're somewhere else in the organisation, you're a manager. If that doesn't make sense, come see me.'[13]

One employee was moved to express his feelings in an anonymous message in BHP's intranet chatroom: 'Yankee go home!'[14]

One of Anderson's most trusted advisers was his wife, Kathy, who had been in charge of public and investor relations for Enron, the United States energy group that bought most of BHP's copper concentrate (but later crashed in one of the biggest financial scandals of all time). Kathy attended analyst meetings and offered advice, all with the blessing of the BHP board.[15] 'She was a great unpaid consultant,' Anderson says. 'I would take her around with me on tours of plants or mines and it was a second set of eyes that was very helpful. She would get input from people who were reluctant or afraid to talk to me. Where a plant manager was stifling everybody under him and I don't get to see that because he's managing me, Kathy would say, "Go visit this part of the operation."'[16]

She was also valuable through her background in investor relations. 'We didn't have a US investor-relations program, so we cranked that up quite a bit,' he says, 'and the percentage of shares owned in the US went up fairly dramatically.'

At Brad Mills's suggestion, Anderson moved all the portraits of former chairmen, 'glowering from the walls on the executive floor – the 49th – to the conference-room floor – the 50th – and put some nice art on the executive floor. It changed the symbology of this ancient way of history that was dragging the place down.'[17]

Jerry Ellis found Anderson to be 'a straight talker, down to earth, with a great set of values. He was universally accepted as an excellent person for the job,' he says. 'Paul had lived in some pretty tough environments, so he knew how to look after cash. I don't ever remember anything said negatively about his predecessors. He never had a bad word. He only spoke about what he needed to do in the future. I didn't come under any criticism from him or any of his staff at all.'[18]

For the vital role of chief finance officer, Anderson placed his faith in a fellow American with the appointment of 40-year-old Chip Goodyear, who had first been approached in September 1998 when he received a telephone call from a New York headhunter who asked him, 'Any interest in being the CFO of BHP?' Goodyear replied, 'Until you get a CEO, it doesn't make any sense to be talking about a CFO.'[19]

Descended from an immensely successful American lumber baron, Goodyear was born in Hartford, Connecticut, and raised in Houston, Texas, where his father worked for Exxon. After graduating from Yale in 1980 with a degree in geology and geophysics, Goodyear began his career as a geologist at Mobil. He left to complete an MBA at the Wharton School of the University of Pennsylvania, then moved into investment banking in 1983 with the Wall Street firm of Kidder Peabody. Six years later, he joined Freeport McMoRan, the copper-and-gold producer based in New Orleans, as chief financial officer. At the time of the BHP approach, he was president of Goodyear Capital Corps, his family's private investment company.[20]

Then, in November 1998, he heard that Paul Anderson had been appointed chief executive of BHP. They had met when Goodyear was at Kidder Peabody during the merger between Texas Eastern and Panhandle Eastern. Anderson says, 'I pulled up the names of everybody who had been suggested by the headhunters. Chip was made for the job: his background was perfect, including his experience with Freeport McMoRan and Kidder Peabody. I put him at the top of the list.'[21]

The headhunter called Goodyear again: 'Okay, we've got the CEO, now what do you think?' Goodyear flew to Melbourne for an interview. 'He was from central casting – when he walked in the room, he looked like he should be the CFO,' Anderson says. '[His wife] Elizabeth got along with Kathy. It wasn't very hard to make the decision; it was mainly hard to convince him that he wanted to leave the United States and come over to Australia.'[22]

Says Brad Mills, 'I interviewed Chip to come down to work with us; I was one of the interview panel. I like Chip – he was a modern American finance guy, a confident character, and he worked well with Paul.'[23]

Goodyear accepts he joined BHP at a difficult time but it was a challenge that he relished. 'I like restructuring opportunities, I like rebuilding and I had known the company probably a lot longer than Paul had known the company. My experience covered everything from oil and gas and minerals – not steel, admittedly – but then you had that finance side of it, so it was really an excellent fit in terms of my background and interests,' he says. 'So we worked together, not only with Paul but with Don [Argus], the board and the management team, and we set up a strategy that first of all Paul felt was righting the ship and bringing it back on an even keel to tap the quality of the assets and the business so that the bad decisions from HBI, Beenup, Hartley, Magma didn't sink the company. Those things would have sunk any lesser organisation.'[24]

The tall, softly spoken Ivy Leaguer said in the press release that marked his arrival in June 1999, 'My joining the management team will drive a new era of value creation and growth at BHP.' There were some who might question that estimation: in the first two years, the dynamic duo of Anderson and Goodyear would shed 2000 jobs and $6.9 billion worth of assets in 30 deals.[25]

'One thing I've found is that no matter what I do, there'll be people who disagree with it,' Anderson told the *Financial Times* in an interview at that time.[26] This was certainly true of his attempt – at Graham Evans's suggestion – to develop a mission statement in the form of a company charter. 'The first thing Graham did,' he says, 'was to put together a cross section of about 30 people in the organisation. I gave them the skeleton outline of what I wanted it to have – a purpose and some imperatives, what are our values and how do we judge success?

The group finally came up with a charter and we circulated it to about a thousand people and the general reaction was, "This is bullshit. This is something clearly written by a committee." So I took everything we had and locked myself in a room over a weekend and hand-wrote the charter, which is very similar to the one that's in the annual report now.

'It was a very useful document, a touchstone – whenever you had major decisions, it was a good thing to refer back to.'[27] Anderson wrote:

> We are BHP, an Australian-based global company founded in 1885 which is undergoing fundamental change as we adjust to a highly competitive global business environment.
>
> Our purpose is to create shareholder value through the discovery, development and conversion of natural resources.
>
> To survive and prosper we must:
>
> Re-establish a foundation for future growth by eliminating underperforming assets and rebuilding margins.
>
> Create a high-performance organisation in which every individual accepts responsibility and is rewarded for results.
>
> Earn the trust of employees, customers and shareholders by being forthright in our communications and consistently delivering on commitments.
>
> We value:
>
> Integrity – doing what we say we will do.
>
> High performance – the excitement and fulfilment of achieving superior business results and stretching our capabilities.
>
> Win–win relationships – having relationships which focus on the creation of value for all parties.
>
> The courage to lead change – accepting the responsibility to inspire and deliver change in the face of adversity.
>
> Respect for each other – the valuing of diversity, enriched by openness, sharing, trust, teamwork and involvement.
>
> Safety and the environment – an overriding commitment to safety and environmental responsibility.

We are successful when:

Our shareholders are realising a superior return on their investment.

Our customers are benefiting from the use of our products and services.

The communities in which we operate value our citizenship.

Every employee starts each day with a sense of purpose and ends each day with a sense of accomplishment.

Anderson found a willing ally in his compatriot Brad Mills. 'Paul came out of the same school of business that I went to, the Stanford School of Business. [He was] a pragmatic, competent American businessman who understood the structural issues and the strategic issues,' he says. 'When he landed, we had the complete map for what needed to happen to the company. Paul picked it up and said, "Okay, let's execute it." Over the next three years, there was the execution of that very substantial corporate turnaround, a clean-up plan.

'We spun the steel business in two bits instead of one: we chopped off the long products and then the flat products. Paul was a good politician – he took his board with him. Once that happened, we were able to sort out the Foster's thing, write down all the bad assets – the HBIs and the Beenups – clean up the operating structure, and the business started performing much, much better in terms of having the focus at the right time. But it was very tough on the corporate culture of BHP. The metric I often look back on: if you look at the top hundred executives in BHP at the time Paul Anderson started, 60 of them left over the next three years. So it was when the culture changed to being an international mining company.'[28]

As foreshadowed the previous year, Jerry Ellis had departed on 31 March 1999 and Don Argus, the feisty Queenslander recruited to the board from National Australia Bank, had become chairman. As a young man, he had represented his state as a hockey player and coach for ten years. Indeed, as the only Australian with international coaching qualifications, he had considered making it his career before turning to banking. Nothing, however, could prevent The Big Australian plunging $2.31 billion (US$1.14 billion) into the red in the year to the end of May that year – Australia's worst-ever corporate loss. Paul Anderson told the ABC, 'The good news is that while the financial results are deplorable, and I use that word carefully, in part they reflect the fact that we've taken a number of difficult but very necessary steps to provide a solid foundation for the future.'[29]

Anderson had also authorised a makeover of the company's image. 'We were already preparing to change the identity of the company,' says Michael Spencer, BHP's then vice president communications. 'We were very keen to move away from The Big Australian. The whole company rested on this image. The problem was that big meant not being nimble; being the Australian constrained you. In the States, it was seen as being quaint but not global. We had to position ourselves as a global player; the days of national entities were passing.'[30]

Spencer engaged a local company to do 'pilot testing' of concepts that would underpin the new identity. The crowd favourite – particularly with staffers – was 'being resourceful': *a resourceful resource company*, that said it all. He was off and running.

The first opportunity that Paul and Kathy Anderson had to explore Australia for themselves came six months into the assignment, when they took off on his Harley-Davidson motorbike to see some of the country. With the saddlebags packed and Kathy riding pillion, they headed down Victoria's Great Ocean Road. 'We'd heard a lot about it, so we took the bike and rode down to Port Campbell and back – it was a great ride,' he says.[31]

On his return, BHP shut down its loss-making titanium project at Beenup, pulled out of freight shipping between Australia and New Zealand and sold its power generation and transmission assets for $509 million to Anderson's previous employer, Duke

Energy. It also banked around $650 million for the sale of its manganese twins, GEMCO and TEMCO, to Billiton plc, whose manganese arm, Samancor, had been restructured as a joint venture between Billiton (60 per cent) and Anglo American (40 per cent). As a result, Samancor became manager of BHP's manganese mine on Groote Island and smelter at Bell Bay, Tasmania. The sell-offs enabled BHP to cut its debt-to-equity ratio from 52.5 per cent to around 49.5 per cent.[32]

'Paul is a great guy and a wonderful businessman with a distinguished record,' Lance Hockridge says. 'He was very focused, knew with a remarkable degree of precision what he wanted and, equally importantly, what he didn't want. He set about rebuilding the company out of what were, to say the least, very troubled times.'[33]

In late June, with copper averaging just 64 cents a pound – the lowest price of the century in inflation-adjusted dollars – Anderson made his biggest decision so far: he closed the San Manuel mine and smelter indefinitely, throwing almost 2200 people out of work. An additional 400 employees were laid off elsewhere in Arizona and Nevada, representing the company's almost total withdrawal from the American copper industry.

BHP spokesman Jay Rhodes said the company was forced to stop most production in the United States because it was unprofitable at such low prices. Closing mines and laying off workers, while unfortunate, was hardly unusual in the industry. 'Copper is a cyclical business,' Rhodes said. 'It's been one where when the price increases, the players holding low-grade deposits open them for production. When the cycle is down, they have to put them on hold.'[34]

Paul Anderson told an ABC news reporter on 25 June 1999, 'The spot price of copper today is down another six/seven cents versus the average of last year, but I would be surprised if we didn't see some movement as a result of the closure of our south-west properties.'[35]

The effect on little San Manuel was cataclysmic. According

to one former resident, 'an entire community lost its identity and lifeblood in the blink of an eye'.[36] 'BHP didn't pull the plug on San Manuel because the ore was gone,' says Richard Ducote of the *Arizona Daily Star*, published in nearby Tucson. 'Nearly two billion pounds of copper remains entombed in the lower reaches of the San Manuel and Kalamazoo ore bodies that were in production when the lights went out.'[37]

'The San Manuel operation had been shut down but the smelter was still in place and could have been started in a couple of months,' says Dave Lowell, who had discovered the Kalamazoo deposit back in the 1970s. 'The copper price had to rise about five cents. San Manuel and Kalamazoo had a big flow of water and it was terribly expensive to keep the mine, so they made the decision to turn the pumps off and flood the mine. Within two months, the price of copper had risen to their target price and were the mines in operation now, they would be making billions of dollars a year.'[38]

Paul Anderson maintains that the Magma operation was refocused on ways of maximising the value without developing the mine further. 'We switched over to an exit plan to do some acid leaching of some of the ore piles that were already there and get some copper out of what had already been taken out of the mine, and we would see if we could find a home for the smelter in a deal with Phelps Dodge or somebody like that,' he says. 'Ultimately, we got some leached copper out, but the smelter – there was a lot of games-playing between ourselves and our competitors, and they realised that they had the upper hand and they would be better off if the smelter got shut. It could have made sense to do something with one of the competitors but we would have benefited a lot more than they would have and they realised that.'[39]

So the mines were stripped of equipment, sealed and allowed to flood. The huge smelter disappeared, as did the rod plant and electrolytic refinery. The twin smelter stacks, more than 500 feet tall and each weighing 10,000 tons, were demolished by explosives – an event that provoked a new wave of anguish and resentment among the people of San Manuel.[40] Women wept as the giant chimneys, landmarks in so many facets of their lives, crashed to the ground in clouds of brick-dust. To many, it seemed like an act of corporate vandalism.

'There are three-generation families in this area that worked there – I worked there, my son worked there, my grandson worked there and there were many families like that. If you were in the family, it was easy to get a job there,' Taffy Tafoya says. 'I mean, hell, while you were in high school they were already training you. You could get jobs in the mine. If you go look at that area now, you're not going to believe what you see – nice rolling hills. They planted grass and smoothed out all the gullies and made it beautiful – it looks like beautiful parkland. It's not open to the public. They erased everything off the top of the earth.'[41]

With the price of copper hitting $4 a pound, Lance Hockridge says, 'A lot of it was timing. If the Magma Company had been bought today, it would have been superb – but life as a manager is as much about getting the timing right as anything else.'[42]

Hockridge was singing the same tune as Brian Gilbertson, who was looking around for a partner to consolidate Billiton's position and protect it from the predatory lions that were systematically devouring the weak in the 'victor or victim' dismemberment of the mining industry. 'We'd sorted out Billiton and we wanted to take the next step,' Mike Salamon says. 'We were still in this world where mining was bad news; the mining industry was dead. You needed to be much more efficient. The way to do that was to take bigger businesses and merge them. We looked around the world and said, "What's doable?" The list wasn't very long: you had the national champions like CVRD, which you couldn't do; then you had Anglo American, which would, in a sense, have been back to the future; Rio Tinto, a dominant number one; and then BHP, which was going through a lot of issues but had a fantastic resource base, in particular iron ore, coking coal, Escondida – those were outstanding franchises.'[43]

Paul Anderson finally met Brian Gilbertson some six

months after their telephone conversation when the two chief executives ran into each other in London in June 1999. Once again, Gilbertson raised the question of a possible merger. 'We've got a strategy we're pursuing and I don't want to divert the attention of the troops,' Anderson told him. 'We've got so much stuff going on that the idea of even talking about a combination or anything like that wouldn't be appropriate.'[44]

Once again, Gilbertson said he was prepared to bide his time. 'One of Brian's greatest strengths is a huge persistence and a total inability to know when he's being unreasonable and a complete refusal to take no for an answer,' Dave Munro says. 'He'd approached BHP on several occasions, and had it not been for his persistence there would have been no deal.'[45]

Gilbertson called his vision of a merger 'Project Bardot' after his favourite film star. He'd had a crush on her since seeing her in *Viva Maria!* when he was working in Paris during the 1960s. 'I've always said Project Bardot was creating the most desirable company in the world,' he says, 'That was our internal name for it on the Billiton side.'[46]

Back in 1998, it had taken Ian Fraser three months to find Gilbertson's heir apparent. 'I met all the senior people, dug about and came back to Brian with a huge pile of CVs,' he says. 'Brian hated paper, so I did it deliberately. He said, "What the hell's all that paper?" I said, "Don't panic – you only have to look at one." I pulled out a CV and he said, "What's that?" and I said, "That's the guy you need." He read it and, of course, it was Marius Kloppers. He'd recruited Marius but he didn't really know him. Marius had built the Hillside smelter and it was running brilliantly. He'd just moved to Holland and was doing aluminium marketing. We then had to test him and grow him into this role. Brian went about designing his career.'[47]

CHAPTER 19

Project Bardot

Paul Anderson's strategic-planning group had a system for analysing potential merger-and-acquisition targets in the mining and oil sectors. Once a month, they updated a bubble chart with BHP in the centre and various targets circling it 'like a solar system, with the planets going around the sun'.[1] The chart ranked companies by price-earnings ratio relative to BHP, their current market price relative to their net asset value and their growth potential relative to the price premium on assets. Month by month, any particular target became more or less attractive to the analysts according to the changes in these variables.[2]

'There were three deals that were pretty much always in play: the Western Mining acquisition, Woodside to acquire the bit of Woodside we'd sold the first time round, or Billiton,' Brad Mills says. 'And then the fourth one, which we always thought about but never could figure out how to do anything about, was Rio Tinto. Those four were always being worked on in some fashion from the sublime to the ridiculous.'[3]

BHP started talking seriously to Billiton later in 1999 when Chip Goodyear, Brad Mills and Marcus Randolph met with

Mick Davis, Dave Munro and Mike Salamon. 'We worked through all the structural issues, worked out the DLC [dual-listed companies] structure, worked out the logic and the business combination,' Mills says. 'The strategy – which was always the right strategy from the BHP perspective – was: China's going to happen. We just want to build a storefront in front of China. It was a simple strategy, but it was clearly the right one. We had the iron ore, we had the copper, we had the coking coal, we didn't have the aluminium. Billiton was a very good fit for that with their aluminium assets and more copper assets. The mineral sands were also fine, so it was a very good fit for the overall strategy.

'Everybody saw the industrial logic, everybody liked the deal. Mick Davis and I were the two principals who worked like dogs on this thing, with the rest of the negotiating team as backers. We got to the point where everybody was happy, and so we put the two chief executives and two chairmen together. Their job is to sprinkle holy water over all that we have done and then work out some of the social issues, basically who is going to be chief executive and chairman of the company.'[4]

In late October, John Jackson received a summons in London from Brian Gilbertson to fly to Melbourne. 'Sure – what's it about?' Jackson inquired.

'I'll tell you when you get here,' Gilbertson replied. 'Mick will be here as well.'[5]

Jackson booked his ticket. After decades in the corporate world – his business career included electronics, engineering, pharmaceuticals, biotechnology, hotels, property, racing, mining and retail – very little fazed him. He had been born in a little Devon village called Membury but raised in London and educated at The King's School, Canterbury, and Cambridge University. He had also gained extensive experience of the media industry, having worked in television broadcasting (terrestrial, cable and satellite – with Rupert Murdoch, whom he admires).

Jackson arrived in Melbourne at around 7 pm on Saturday, 30 October and checked into the Grand Hyatt in Collins Street.

Over lunch the following day, Brian Gilbertson explained that he'd been having discussions with Paul Anderson about the possibility of Billiton and BHP getting together. That evening, Gilbertson, Mick Davis and Jackson met for dinner with Don Argus, Paul Anderson and Chip Goodyear. 'We had a cordial enough dinner,' Jackson says, 'but you could see some tension already starting to develop between Brian and Don.'[6]

It was agreed that the following day – Monday, 1 November – Gilbertson would spend the morning with Don Argus, Mick Davis would spend it with Chip Goodyear and Jackson would spend it with Paul Anderson. They would all then adjourn upstairs for a sandwich lunch with other BHP directors and executives. 'This was absolutely fascinating because we were already starting to talk about the possible merits of a dual-listed company structure,' John Jackson recalls. 'Paul and I talked a fair bit about that and possible complications, but Paul was inquisitive as to what Brian would bring to the party. "Why does this chap insist on being chief executive?" I said, "You just judge him for yourself but my experience of him is that he's very able and he's a good team leader."

'Towards the end of the morning, we all foregathered in Don's office and again the conversation focused very much on Brian's wish to be chief executive. This was plainly exercising the mind of Don Argus, who effectively said, "Why the hell?" I remember Brian saying, "It won't necessarily be forever. I wouldn't necessarily regard this as my last job." Which may not have gone down with Don in the way that Brian intended.

'We went upstairs and had a very nice sandwich lunch with very nice BHP chaps who plainly knew that something was up. We were all sniffed at by these good Australian dogs.'[7]

As the Billiton trio left BHP Tower, Jackson said to Gilbertson, 'You see that enormous building? I promise you that in the woodwork there are Australian gentlemen, long dead, who'll come out of it to stop the young people doing what they want to do. We would be mad to do this – we will get eaten alive. We are in the heart of Australia!'[8]

Gilbertson recalls, 'We thought there was the possibility of a deal but we got there and walked into a brick wall: it just didn't work at all – there was a complete misunderstanding.'[9] Paul Anderson thought 'the stars weren't aligned', while Chip Goodyear agreed 'there was never a meeting of minds'. Some useful contacts were made, though. 'I spoke to Chip and we established a very good relationship, which has continued to this day,' Mick Davis says.

Don Argus believes that one of the obstacles was how Brian Gilbertson would be positioned in the new entity. 'I think there was an element of that,' he says. 'I'm only surmising that; it was never said to me. When I reflect on those days, I think that probably was part of it because Brian was very keen to become the CEO of the company and I think all we were offering was the deputy chairman's role.'[10]

Gilbertson says he never placed personal ambition before a good deal for his shareholders; the chief executive's job was never an issue. 'He certainly didn't push it,' Mick Davis says. 'In fact, it was a deliberate strategy on our part that we wouldn't push because we knew that Paul wanted to exit, so it was then just a matter of time.'[11]

One of the things Paul Anderson had attempted to sort out was the troublesome Ok Tedi copper mine. The company was facing yet another court battle, this time over its failure to meet the terms of the 1996 settlement. No tailings dam had yet been erected and the dredge could not keep up with the waste pouring into the river from the mine. Environmentalists and sociologists from around the world had turned the disaster into a classic case study; whatever the return from the copper, the damage to BHP's reputation was incalculable.

Anderson visited the mine in December 1998, his first overseas journey since joining the company. 'It was a very impressive engineering feat but the river was silting up and there was a possibility it would become acidic,' he says. 'There were a lot of risks with the way the mining was being pursued.'[12]

He met with Papua New Guinea Prime Minister Bill Skate and told him they should consider closing the mine. Skate wouldn't hear of it. It was the biggest employer in the province and the country needed the export income. He told Anderson, 'I would have more unrest from shutting it down than from environmental issues.'

Another possibility was returning the waste to the pit. But that would mean only 75 per cent of the ore could be mined, and OTML's Canadian partner was not in favour. He could have sold BHP's controlling interest on the open market, but a less responsible miner would make things worse. 'That was inconsistent with our charter and with the way we wanted to run this company,' he says.

His solution was to put BHP's shares into a trust on condition that they would continue with the dredging of the river and minimise the environmental damage. Don Argus says, 'Paul came to the decision pretty quickly. He's a man of great integrity. He saw the damage and he went to the [PNG] government and said, "We can't continue to mine like this." Then he came back and said, "We've got to get out of here." That was a pretty ballsy sort of a statement to come to a board and say, "We've done bad here; we've got to get out. And we're going to give it to the people on the river."'[13]

A laudable sentiment, but much easier said than done. Anderson established a group to negotiate with the stakeholders; the venerable European banking house Rothschilds would act as 'mediator'. He announced on 9 February 1999 that in order to cut its losses, BHP had 'transferred its 52 per cent stake in OTML' to a new entity, the PNG Sustainable Development Program Limited (PNGSDP). Incorporated under Singapore law, the PNGSDP would join the PNG Government (30 per cent) and the Canadian Inmet Mining Corporation (18 per cent) as OTML's major shareholder. OTML would continue to operate the mine but the new arrangement, he said, 'protects BHP shareholders from liabilities arising from the mine subsequent to our exit'.

PNGSDP would be chaired by the respected academic, economist and Australian Government adviser Ross Garnaut,[14] who would also become a director of OTML. Its brief would be to invest one-third of its income from the mine in 'current sustainable-development projects' in PNG and the remainder in a long-term fund to finance projects for up to 40 years following the closure of the mine. In addition, its funding could be drawn upon for OTML capital calls, contractual obligations including indemnities, and operating expenses.

Keith Faulkner, who had successfully managed mines in Australia, Armenia and South Africa, was engaged by OTML as managing director. 'The place was well run, well organised and in very good shape,' he says. 'I think the arrangement BHP came to with the other partners was a good structure. It had checks and balances to prevent the misuse of funds.'[15]

However, it would be another three years before the company was finally able to free itself from the Ok Tedi tar-baby, and even then – as we shall see – it would carry with it dark trails of opprobrium from social scientists and the international media.

The most immediate task was to redress some of the malaise that had crept into BHP's business practices. In early 2000, Anderson and Goodyear applied the Markowitz portfolio theory to all of the company's assets and, at the same time, tackled the touchy question of whether its managers should continue to hedge its exposure in currencies and commodities.

'Traditionally, the company had been a hedger and it had allowed that to occur at the asset level, which was insane,' Goodyear says. 'There was no way the individual businesses could assess the impact and the relationship between commodities and currencies. Secondly, the management teams which sit around and for a third of their time say, "Should we hedge today or not?" instead of working on those things which are within their control: the efficiency of mining activities, where they should be mining, etc. The third thing was that they didn't even hedge based on a view of the fundamentals of their market; what they really did was say, "Is this a price above the budget I agreed to commit to at the beginning of the year? If it is, we are going to lock that price in and increase the probability that we will meet our budget."'[16]

When Anderson and Goodyear studied the portfolio model and the cash-flow risk, they realised that while individual commodities were indeed volatile, an aggregation of BHP's assets across numerous commodities, markets and currencies was actually rock solid. 'It was like the Rosetta Stone,' Goodyear says. 'It created the foundation for the decision to move forward. There were operating decisions that needed to be made, but the financial strategy kicked off those as well as numerous other discussions, including getting rid of hedging, which we did. And that made all the difference.'

BHP turned its attention to Rio Tinto in 2000 when Don Argus and Paul Anderson met with Bob Wilson in Singapore to try to merge their respective iron-ore divisions. 'It was quite an interesting meeting in the context of the future of both the companies because I was very conscious of how Rio acquired CRA – how they pinched it – and I think the CRA board need to be challenged pretty hard about how that transaction was done,' Argus says. 'I'm pretty fired about that. There's a lot of people need to look at their careers over that.' The talks, however, foundered on some basic points. 'Bob didn't like petroleum and he didn't like the HBI plant,' Argus says, 'and he didn't like the steel division, so it didn't go anywhere.'[17]

Bob Wilson explains, 'I didn't relish the idea of getting back in a big way into businesses where we didn't have long-term sustainable competitive advantage.'[18]

Meanwhile, Billiton's anointed wunderkind Marius Kloppers had been given one challenge after another to mould him as Gilbertson's successor. Through a company initiative called 'Extracting value from our businesses', Kloppers came up with the idea of consolidating Billiton's marketing operations by creating a commodity-trading business. Gilbertson told him, 'It sounds like a good idea – go and do it.'[19]

Kloppers was put in charge of an entity called B Mark – Billiton Marketing – based in The Hague. Once again, he did a brilliant job. 'This guy is good,' Gilbertson told Ian Fraser. 'Let's see what else we can do with him. He's run a smelter but he hasn't run a mine. What's our toughest job?'

The most troublesome part of the Billiton portfolio was manganese, so Kloppers was sent back to Johannesburg to run Samancor, and he did it well. 'He'd done smelting and built a refinery, he'd done marketing and commodity trading, and now he'd proved that he was also an operator,' Fraser says. 'He'd moved his family four times in as many years and was okay with it. This guy was special.'[20]

Kloppers was still in South Africa in November 2000 when the entire acquisition landscape dramatically changed after Brian Gilbertson, the former rocket scientist, spotted a heat-seeking missile heading straight for him.

The Dulini Game Lodge in the Sabi Sand Reserve near the Kruger National Park was one of Billiton's showpieces. It had been bought by Gencor when South African companies had big internal cash flows and were looking for things to buy with them. The lodge, built in the style of Karen Blixen's 'farm in Africa', had luxurious suites for visitors and observation platforms to view the wild animals.

'It was very useful because the first thing a new customer would ask you was to see the animals, so you could be a gracious host and give them a unique experience,' Gilbertson says. 'We had added CVRD to our list of potential partners and we had a very senior delegation there. I had to leave them to go and receive some news about the Anglo American Corporation.'[21]

Later that day, Marius Kloppers and Roger Agnelli, CVRD's chief executive, arrived by helicopter for a tour of the Koornfontein coal mine. Billiton had already bought a small stake in the Brazilian company and it was thought the talks of a merger would progress over dinner that evening. Having showered and changed after emerging from the coal mine, Kloppers was heading towards the helicopter when Gilbertson walked over. 'Brian put a single piece of paper in my hand,' Kloppers says. 'It was a fax from Matthys Visser, who was the Rembrandt director on the Gencor board. Brian said to me as he handed me the piece of paper, "I guess dinner is going to be somewhat difficult tonight."'[22]

The fax disclosed that Anglo American had disposed of one of its non-mining assets, a 15.3 per cent stake in the financial-services group First Rand, to the Rembrandt Group in exchange for two mining assets: 7.1 per cent of Billiton and 11.3 per cent of Gold Fields. As of that day, Anglo was a seven per cent stakeholder in Billiton. Gilbertson regarded Rembrandt's move as rank betrayal – it flew in the face of assurances given over many years. 'I was given an hour's notice of the news,' he says. 'Anglo ended up with a substantial holding in our shares and we thought that was the precursor to a takeover bid.'[23]

Mick Davis was in Cape Town about to start a vacation with his family when Gilbertson phoned. 'We had a conversation with a lot of pregnant pauses,' Davis says. 'There was much rage between us as to how these people could do it. But it gave us a thing which we could reflect back to BHP that if they didn't act now they might not get the company.'[24]

At that time, however, Anglo American was intent on privatising De Beers, in which it had a large holding, so the feared takeover bid did not eventuate. In fact, Anglo gave an undertaking that it would not make a hostile bid for Billiton or increase its share to more than 15 per cent before 2002 unless another company made a bid for Billiton.[25]

'That created a very interesting situation because there were three big players in the industry: BHP, Rio Tinto and Anglo American,' Gilbertson says. 'Each was of the order of a $20 billion company, while Billiton was just less than a $10 billion company. So we were the kingmaker: whoever got Billiton would automatically become number one in the world.'[26]

There followed 'an interesting set of meetings' with Rio Tinto's chairman, Bob Wilson, and a 'flirtation' with Paul

Anderson at BHP in September 2000 when Gilbertson attended the Sydney Olympics as Anderson's guest. 'I had no huge aspirations to be an independent company or to be in control and run the thing; my aspiration was to get the maximum value for my shareholders,' Gilbertson says. 'Harry Oppenheimer had retired and Julian Ogilvy Thompson was in the chair at Anglo American. I thought if Anglo took us, we would be stifled and just disappear into their revenues. By then, Billiton was already a plc, we'd twice raised money, we'd started acquiring things internationally, but BHP always seemed the natural partner.'

Three months after the Olympics, Gilbertson and Anderson met again. 'Paul had gone to Morocco to look at some oil opportunity and on the way back to Melbourne for Christmas he said he'd come through Johannesburg,' Gilbertson says. 'I flew up from my holiday home at Plettenberg Bay and we met for an hour or two in the hotel at what was then Jan Smuts airport and essentially agreed the merger. I went back to Plett and Paul flew off to Melbourne and I wrote it in longhand on a sheet of paper – two sheets if I remember correctly – faxed it across to Paul and he came back and said yes, he thought that was okay. As far as I was concerned, and as far as Paul was concerned, the deal was done – without any lawyers around or without any corporate advisers. We saved a lot of money and when they came back from their vacations in early January we said, "Here's the deal – just get it done."'[27]

John Jackson was on holiday in California when Gilbertson telephoned. 'Just to let you know: it's started up again,' he said. 'Paul and I have had a meeting in Cape Town and we think there really is something in this.'

According to Marius Kloppers, 'things then moved quickly'. Gilbertson wrote to his senior executives saying that Gencor in its present form would have ceased to exist in 12 months' time; that all of their preparations had to be geared towards that objective. He also appointed investment bankers to analyse the various options that were open to him and then, in the

New Year, summoned Kloppers and the rest of his team to a meeting in London.

'We reviewed the various combinations that were possible: Alcan [the Canadian aluminium firm], CVRD, BHP,' Kloppers says. 'The review was started with a view towards consummating one of those transactions in short order. BHP was the one that was most attractive to the management team – [it was] more upstream than Alcan perhaps. It was also felt that there was a precedent in the Rio Tinto/CRA dual-listed structure which probably made that a little bit easier to think about. And there had been some earlier discussions between Brian and Paul in June of the previous year.'[28]

Gilbertson circulated copies of the fax to the Billicom group, which now included Marc Gonsalves, Ian Fraser and Marius Kloppers. 'We all knew what this was about, whereas my counterpart at BHP found out ten days before the merger was announced that this was going on, so there were very different cultures,' Gonsalves says. 'When I think back to that fax, it *was* the deal. After that, there was an intense period when the advisers and the bankers came in and gilded the lily and refined the whole thing. Mick talks about momentum, and this started to get momentum from that December. There was a clear business logic to it that was so strong that it prevailed against the political sensitivities and the weighting of the various companies, all of which were potential deal-destroyers. Those two months before the deal was announced were a great deal of fun.'[29]

Paul Anderson had sensibly resisted the merger until the pendulum had swung in his favour and BHP could negotiate from a position of strength – impossible even a few months earlier. After a series of write-offs, the company had gone from recording the largest corporate loss in Australian history to posting a record profit of $1.43 billion in the six months to December.[30]

Says Brad Mills, 'We'd done all the work, we'd done all the evaluations and so everybody was ready: we knew the structural issues, we had the legal documentation finished. Even though it had been on the shelf for six months, we were able to just dust it off.'[31]

It seemed to John Jackson that the BHP ghosts were no longer going to be able to keep the South African outsiders at bay. 'The more one looked at it from the point of view of Billiton, the more attractive it looked,' he says. 'But there were still some issues around. Brian was insisting that within a measurable time Paul Anderson stepped down as chief executive and he took up the position.'[32]

Lord Renwick, who was involved in the merger discussions, was enthusiastic about the prospects. 'The rationale for the merger, as conceived by Paul Anderson and Brian Gilbertson and his team, was to create a truly global mining company in virtually every metal in virtually every geography,' he says. 'You would have tremendous diversification of opportunity and also tremendous diversification of risk – you wouldn't need to do hedging for these various metals because you were automatically hedged already. The power of this combination would be hugely effective and the combination would throw off a lot of cash, enabling you to both develop huge long-term projects and make further acquisitions. Obviously, we were very optimistic about metal prices, but what happened exceeded our expectations.'[33]

The Billiton merger, however, was only one of BHP's options. After the Billiton deal fell apart in November 1999, Anderson became serious about buying Western Mining, moving in and out of Western Mining shares and talking to the Western Mining Corporation (WMC) board. When the BHP board met to decide on the BHP merger with Billiton, directors found themselves looking at *two* deals: the Billiton merger or the acquisition of Western Mining.

'We gave them an alternative: which one did they want to do?' Brad Mills says. 'We were prepared to execute against either deal coming out of the board meeting. We felt we had to do one or the other. At the end of the day, the Billiton deal created the bigger, more exciting platform of the two. We'd had tortuous negotiations with Western; it wasn't going very well. They were resisting us with great vigour. Part of the problem was that we would have had to go hostile. They just wouldn't accept a friendly deal – they wanted us to bid for the company. We really didn't want to get involved in a big auction at that point. Paul felt there was too much at risk and he'd rather do a friendly transaction. He talked through the issues with the board and the board selected the BHP–Billiton merger. The rest, as they say, is history.'[34]

'There were a number of issues that had to be gotten through to make it work,' Mike Salamon says. 'There were all the FIRB [Australian Foreign Investment Review Board] issues: we wanted to retain both listings – London is the mining finance capital of the world but in order to retain a listing there we had to live by a whole lot of Stock Exchange rules; there were different accounting interpretations and there was obviously the merger ratio. All of that came together.'[35]

The next time Brian Gilbertson arrived at Melbourne's Tullamarine airport, he was on his way to meet BHP's senior manager in advance of the public announcement of the proposed merger. 'I met Brian at a private meeting of executives,' says Lance Hockridge, who was running the Port Kembla steelworks. 'It was at Paul Anderson's house in Toorak the day before the announcement – an early-morning meeting and very much a business meeting. We were given an opportunity to meet Brian and then we were dispatched back to our respective realms of operations to be prepared to deal with the announcements and the repercussions.'[36]

On 19 March 2001, Paul Anderson publicly revealed plans to merge BHP with Billiton as dual-listed companies. If consummated, the deal would create a diversified mining colossus with a market capitalisation of $60 billion. BHP shareholders would have the upper hand, controlling about 58 per cent of the combined group's equity, compared with Billiton's 42 per cent (a ratio that, despite its Australian bias, has been the subject of great controversy in Australia ever since). Anderson would serve as chief executive until the end of 2002 when he would hand over to Brian Gilbertson. 'This is a sensational fit,' Anderson told the press. 'The companies balance each other well, with an exceptional breadth of assets and capabilities which have taken many years to develop.'

Gilbertson was equally fulsome. 'We're creating the best company in the industry and I look forward very much to working with you,' he told staff at an introductory meeting before heading back to London. 'We're going to do great things.'

The merged company, provisionally known as BHP Billiton, would instantly become the world's second-biggest mining and metals group after America's Alcoa and would be quoted on the Australian and London Stock Exchanges.[37] There would also be a secondary listing on the Johannesburg Exchange and an American Depositary Receipts listing in New York. The effect on BHP's market value was immediate: its shares jumped more than five per cent in early trading in Melbourne and touched a high of $22.05. The deal was seen as the latest in the frenzy of consolidation that had gripped the global mining and metals industry.[38] Paul Anderson said he had examined every possible merger combination in the mining sector before deciding to link up with Billiton. 'We were at a crossroads,' he said, 'and we had to move or just watch the sector consolidate around us.'

Nigel Boardman, one of the leading solicitors from the London mergers-and-acquisition specialists Slaughter & May, was consulted about the contracts. If either company pulled out of the deal, it would have to pay a $100 million break-up fee. UBS Warburg acted for BHP; J. P. Morgan for Billiton. Paul Anderson insisted that rapid integration was of the utmost importance. 'I've learned with mergers,' he said, 'that no matter how fast you move, you didn't move fast enough.'[39]

Indeed, the merger announcement had put Billiton into play and had thus ended Anglo American's freeze on increasing its stake.[40] The boards of both BHP and Billiton waited apprehensively to see whether Anglo would make a counter-bid but, although Gilbertson expected a move from that quarter, 'for reasons to this day that I do not understand it never materialised', he says. However, Brad Mills reveals, 'Under London Rules, Anglo American were frozen until they had completed everything to do with the De Beers merger. We were able to sequence the timing of the BHP Billiton transaction such that it closed inside that merger window so that Anglo American couldn't act on their shareholding and couldn't compete with the deal.'[41]

Not surprisingly, perhaps, given the iconic nature of BHP, financial journalists – and some shareholders – lambasted the merger. The barbarians weren't exactly storming the gates but a bunch of South Africans were seen climbing into a large wooden horse. The financial press was seeded with scary headlines, such as 'Is BHP being suckered?', 'Billiton assets might be a liability' and 'Merger data still too murky'. The 'Trojan horse' mentality persisted when the Australian Securities and Investments Commission insisted that the companies specify the key assumptions used in valuing the bid. Critics claimed that the BHP stake was undervalued, whereas supporters maintained the bid must be assessed on the combined strength of BHP and Billiton. The taboo words 'reverse takeover' were whispered in the holy of holies, the Australian Club.[42]

BHP directors were accused of metaphorically dropping their pants – an allegation that led to a touch of low humour in BHP Tower when a bulletin board called 'Merger Update' was renamed 'Takeover Update' by some wag and then altered to 'Bendover Update'. Marc Gonsalves says, 'That was in that period when there was so much angst because the press in Australia were stirring it up that this was a fifth column of Billiton people who were doing a reverse takeover of BHP and the BHP guys were screwed.'[43]

Brian Gilbertson thinks the merger was regarded as a reverse takeover because most of his colleagues survived the inevitable cull. 'Normally, the victors come in and those who lose the takeover are put to the sword and are gone, and that didn't happen,' he says. 'I had some very gifted colleagues working with me. Mike Salamon went on to become a board member of BHP Billiton, Marius Kloppers became chief executive and Dave Munro was a senior executive until he left [to join platinum-miner Lonmin].'[44]

The deal was complementary largely because BHP had a strong balance sheet but a weak range of projects, whereas Billiton had lots of new projects that urgently needed finance. It would yield $270 million in savings, mainly from increased purchasing power, but Anderson played down the importance of cost savings. 'We would have done the deal even without the synergies,' he said.[45]

BHP's shareholders gradually familiarised themselves with Billiton's assets prior to voting on the merger. Billiton, they learned, was a major producer of aluminium and also the world's biggest producer of chrome and manganese ores and alloys, with operations in Australasia, South America and Africa. 'The Australian media were essentially very hostile, not so much towards me but to Don Argus and Paul Anderson,' Brian Gilbertson says. 'They felt that great BHP assets had been sold into the merger too cheaply in return for assets in funny countries that they really would prefer not to be in.'[46]

Some of the names, however, were all too familiar. 'By merging with Billiton,' Lance Hockridge says, 'BHP was effectively buying back a number of operations which it had sold over the years: for example, GEMCO and TEMCO were ex-BHP businesses which had been sold to Billiton and then came back into the business as part of the merger.'[47]

Shareholders were invited to an extraordinary general meeting in the Melbourne Concert Hall at the Victorian Arts Centre on 18 May to vote on the matter. In advance of the meeting, Paul Anderson gave an interview to Alan Deans of *The Bulletin*, published on 25 April under the headline 'Speak Softly, Carry an Iron Bar', in which he disclosed the threat looming over BHP if it became a marginal player in the mining industry. 'We have to participate or become a victim,' he said. 'If we don't, Rio [Tinto] will get together with a big oil company and break up BHP.'[48]

There had already been an aborted attempt to put BHP's iron-ore assets together with Rio Tinto's, while copper producers had inquired about buying Escondida. However, BHP had conducted strategic studies about diversifying into aluminium, nickel and steaming coal and discovered that these were all key Billiton assets, making the South African company the perfect fit.

On 18 May, shareholders had to run a gauntlet of 3000 trade unionists standing shoulder-to-shoulder and blocking the city-bound lanes of St Kilda Road to reach the Concert Hall. Greg Combet, the ACTU secretary, claimed that the deal with Billiton would disadvantage Australian workers and eventually move control of the company offshore. 'We don't want a deal to go ahead until our concerns are satisfied,' he said. 'We are going to make sure that the people here are going to be held to account for the decision they make today.'[49]

Inside the Concert Hall, Don Argus reacted sharply when one of the 1500 shareholders raised the reverse-takeover spectre. 'The share price was down to $11 and now it's $22.85, which is a testament to the focus we have,' he said. 'So to say this is a reverse takeover is nonsense – it's not a reverse takeover. As far as my position is concerned, if it got voted down then clearly I would have to reconsider my position.'[50]

After several hours of sometimes heated argument, a majority of the Australian shareholders finally raised their hands in support of the merger. In Johannesburg, Billiton's shareholders had already given their approval with unconcealed jubilation. In the final analysis, 88.2 per cent of BHP shareholders were in favour, compared with Billiton's 91.5 per cent.

Referring to the 32 per cent added to the pre-merger share price for Billiton investors, Brian Gilbertson says, 'We had held out for a premium and we'd got a generous premium in the process. My shareholders were very happy and they still are. I go down to Cape Town and see some institutions and they still thank me for getting them into some of the world's finest assets.'[51]

Don Argus says the Billiton team handled their options extremely well. 'We get criticised for perhaps overpaying for the opportunity,' he says. 'You could argue that the quality of the assets were not the tier-one assets that other companies had, but what it did was it provided a stable of people with actual mining skills and that's one of the strengths that emerged from that merger – and it's one of the strengths underpinning this company now because I would say that BHP did not have the practical mining skills that Billiton had.'[52]

Lord Renwick thought that Don Argus understood the need to change things 'because old BHP had a reputation for very good assets but not the greatest management and very poor project execution: there were problems in Papua New Guinea, Zimbabwe and so on. The Billiton team was an exceptionally talented one,' he says. 'We did pride ourselves on the fact that we never had a project which didn't come in on time and on budget, including the huge aluminium smelters in Mozambique which nobody thought we could build. This was a very highly motivated bunch of people who wanted to do deals.'[53]

Discussing the personalities in both companies at that time, Paul Anderson said to Renwick, 'There will be some cultural differences.'

'How would you describe the Billiton culture, Paul?' Renwick asked, to which Anderson replied: 'Full steam ahead and damn the torpedoes!'[54]

CHAPTER 20

Hunters and Skinners

The difference between executives in the mining world was neatly summarised by one Billiton veteran who classified them as 'hunters or skinners'. 'The hunters are mainly guys who go into the jungle and kill the beasts,' he was fond of saying. 'The others stay at home and make things from the skins.'[1]

BHP's executives, many of them from a steelmaking or manufacturing background, fell mainly into the skinner category. 'The Billiton team had been together for years and we suddenly encountered a management team that had just been thrown together,' Dave Munro says. 'They were still in the process of working out the structure of the group and the strategy. They were happy to sit down and work out how to run this big new company.'[2]

Even before shareholders had given their consent, a team of senior executives from both companies was burning the midnight oil to solve the prickly question of staff integration. 'In these exercises, you've got the deal team and you've got the merger team,' says Mike Salamon, who had moved to Melbourne at the end of March and was living in a penthouse in one of the tower blocks at Beacon Cove, overlooking Port

Phillip Bay. 'The stuff that the bankers get excited about is the deal – they get their fees, and then you've got to make it work. The finance guys have been very involved in the transaction but it's the operating guys who've got to make it work. My counterpart, Brad Mills, and I sat down and over the course of a few days essentially designed a new organisation. Then his team and my team met and we worked out the integration plan. First of all, there were no consultants – we agreed we were going to do this ourselves, which was unheard of.'[3]

Salamon, Mills and Ian Fraser, who took over as head of BHP Billiton's human-resources department, spent a year putting the integration together. In the beginning, they could only do the planning because the Competition Commission[4] had yet to give its approval. 'When the commission finally said yes and the green lights were all in place and the deal consummated, the actual execution was very easy,' Mills says. 'The teams had worked it all out and we knew exactly what we were going to do with the people. They were thoroughly professional people – I liked the Billiton guys; it was a good group.'[5]

Paul Anderson admitted in an interview that BHP had become dysfunctional and entangled in red tape, that although executives wanted to progress they ended up taking grander titles but with few added responsibilities. 'BHP has a good culture in terms of managing a large organisation and having procedures and practices, well-defined systems, to institutionalise efficiency,' he said. 'Billiton has a very entrepreneurial culture of finding an opportunity and grabbing it, but they do not necessarily follow it up and get the best out of it. There is no centralised procurement activity. They do not have a well-developed shared facility for back-office functions. Billiton is ready, fire, aim. We are ready, aim, aim. We find it hard to pull the trigger.'[6] He had been successful in moving BHP's culture about 20 per cent down the desired path, but Billiton would get it the rest of the way in one bound.

On 4 June, the federal treasurer, Peter Costello, announced the government's blessing of the merger, although it was accompanied by a string of conditions designed to uphold the national *amour propre*. To retain an Australian identity, the Australian FIRB demanded that BHP Billiton's headquarters be located in Australia; that the chief executive and chief financial officer have their main residence in Australia; that a listing be retained on the Australian Stock Exchange; and that most board meetings take place in Australia.[7]

The treasurer was clearly exercised about this South African incursion into Australian big business. 'Costello wagged his finger in my face when I went to pay my respects,' Brian Gilbertson recalls.[8] And for understandable reasons: Billiton's top team – Gilbertson, Davis, Munro, Salamon, Kloppers and Fraser – would make a powerful impact.

But then Mick Davis, chief development officer-designate of BHP Billiton, sent shock waves through the industry when he suddenly resigned to become chief executive of Xstrata, a relatively unsuccessful Anglo-Swiss mining company. In his farewell message, Davis said his time at Billiton had been 'replete with invaluable and rewarding experiences' but he now had the opportunity to take a leadership role in a smaller company. He added, 'As it is smaller, there is more room for growing it – the job I enjoy most.' This was an understatement: Xstrata was mired in US$500 million of debt.

The real story of Davis's departure from the BHP Billiton scenario, however, is told here for the first time. 'The view among my colleagues was that essentially it would be the management team of Billiton who would be running the new company,' he says. 'I didn't take that view. I said to them, "I think this is a very Australian-centric organisation. I do not think that they are going to allow a management takeover. By comparison, BHP is an organisation with a huge amount of process and bureaucracy, and process is almost more important than the outcome."

'Billiton was relatively light on that and there was no doubt whose process would win out. I didn't think that was an organisation that I wanted to battle through.

'I was still happy to stay on. I was not convinced it was going to be the seamless deal that everybody thought it was going to be but I did everything I could to make sure that the deal would happen because I thought it would be very good for our shareholders.

'There were some incidents. The first was when Don Argus and Paul visited London shortly before we had meetings with all the management team. Paul said to me, "So why are you against the deal?" I wasn't happy with that approach. I didn't appreciate somebody attacking me in that way. That was the first negative.

'The second negative was the fact that the chief executive officer and chief financial officer had to be resident in Australia – that had been negotiated between BHP and FIRB. I had no doubt that it was something that BHP engineered, and I didn't take very kindly to that.

'Thirdly, I had no intention of moving my family to Melbourne. I think it's the wrong place to be running an international mining company. I still think it's the wrong place. However, when Brian went over for the penultimate meeting things were about to fall off the rails. The BHP board took the view that Paul had been out-negotiated and outmanoeuvred by Brian and ourselves. He was accused by one of his directors of "dropping his pants".

'Brian came back to South Africa and told me that I was seen to be the "touchstone" of this sense of concern. Because of my insistence on remaining in London, I was going to be the guy who eventually moved this company to London. So I said, "Brian, if that's the case, I'm happy to step back. I'll see the transaction through and go off." Initially, that seemed to be acceptable, but then a few days later they said could they not take the job of chief financial officer and split it between myself and Chip, where Chip becomes the chief financial officer and I become what's called the chief development officer and I could reside in London?

'We did all those things: we split the job up and how it was going to work. Chip and I would have worked fine together.

But I just sat back and thought to myself, "Now is a good time to make a break. There clearly is concern about me. There's going to be tensions going forward." I didn't appreciate Paul's approach; in fact, I never appreciated Paul's management style at all, and I thought he and I would clash going forward. I thought, "You know, I've had a great time in Billiton. This is a great transaction for shareholders. What a good time to move on and do something else." And that's why I took the decision to leave. I communicated that decision prior to the announcement of the transaction [in March 2001] but said I would keep it quiet and do all the roadshows. Paul and I did the roadshows together, and that was fine."[9]

Brian Gilbertson was sorry to lose Davis but appreciated that he would have found it difficult working in a more bureaucratic environment, which the Billiton executives perceived BHP to be. 'It had a big head office with one or two thousand people, whereas we just sat in a little office in the Strand with 50 people, so Mick felt that wouldn't work out for him,' Gilbertson says. 'He also wanted to go out and sail his own ship, and he's done some great things at Xstrata. He was the only member of my team who didn't come along with me. All my key members got key positions, but they generally got them because they were very good. I would take over from Paul in two years, under the original plan, and I would be his deputy for the initial period so I could learn the bit of the business I didn't know and get to know the Australians.

'I guess that's part of the reason it was perceived to be a reverse takeover. Paul and I didn't have any issues that I was aware of – we worked well together; I respected what he was doing. He'd come in from outside the industry and had changed the culture greatly and given BHP a sense of pride back.'[10]

In Gilbertson's opinion, Anderson had secured a good transaction for BHP's shareholders, but the press didn't share that view. It was unforgiving. 'They flogged Don Argus and Paul for months; even now, you hear echoes of it: at least two or three times a year, some journalist or analyst will put out a set of figures that show what BHP had effectively paid,' Gilbertson says. 'Given what iron ore has done, what oil has done, given what copper mines have done – we didn't have copper in Billiton[11]: we had the smelters and coal mines in South Africa – if you do the sums that way, it really does look as though they paid a high price.

'But at the time I thought it was a very sensible deal: it put BHP Billiton at the top of the pile; it gave them a new sense of pride; it really ignited the BHP interest in the world of mining as opposed to the narrower focus on Australia. They had withdrawn after the Magma thing, an experience that had branded them. The merger made them number one, and whereas before BHP didn't feature in the reviews of the mining companies published by London stockbrokers because they were down there in Australia, they were suddenly top of the list.

'As we'd created it as a dual-listed company, it had the following both of the London analysts and the Australian analysts, and that way we kept the internationalisation and a much wider and more intensive exposure among international investors. I think it was a great deal – look what the company has done since then.'

But first, there was a great deal of corporate engineering to complete. 'Very sensibly, they put the two boards into two much bigger boards,' Derek Keys says. 'You had to have a BHP Billiton plc board and you had to have a BHP Billiton Limited board in Australia. Both those boards were the same and they consisted of all the directors of both companies.'[12]

The new boards had 17 all-male members – almost a full Australian Rules football team. Ten were from BHP and seven from Billiton: Don Argus, 62, chairman, BHP; John Jackson, 72, deputy chairman, Billiton; Ben Alberts, 61, BHP; Paul Anderson, 56, managing director and chief executive officer, BHP; David Brink, 61, Billiton; Michael Chaney, 51, BHP; John Conde, 52, BHP; David Crawford, 57, BHP; Brian Gilbertson, 57, deputy chief executive, Billiton; Cornelius Herkströter, 63, Billiton; David Jenkins, 62, BHP; Derek

Keys, 69, Billiton; Ron McNeilly, 57, executive director global markets, BHP; John Ralph, 68, BHP; Lord Renwick of Clifton, 63, Billiton; Barry Romeril, 57, Billiton; and John Schubert, 58, BHP.

Don Argus decided that some new-age bonding in a traditional setting would help the integration process among such diverse personalities. He scheduled a board meeting for New York, and Kathy Anderson helped organise the trip. On the afternoon of Tuesday, 19 June 2001, the directors and their wives met at the St Regis Hotel on East 55th Street at 5th Avenue. 'That evening, we split up into small self-selecting groups either to dine together or to go to the theatre,' John Jackson says. 'The following two days, the "boys" worked (I chaired the first meeting of the new remuneration committee) and the "girls" socialised largely on shopping trips. On the evening of Thursday, 21 June 2001, we had a major celebratory dinner with speeches. We dispersed gradually in the course of Friday, 22 June.'[13]

The following Friday – 29 June 2001 – all of the preliminaries had been completed and everything was in readiness when Australia said goodbye to BHP and put out the welcome mat for the merged company. BHP Billiton Limited and BHP Billiton plc existed as separate entities but would operate on a combined basis as BHP Billiton. The headquarters of BHP Billiton Limited and the global headquarters of the combined BHP Billiton Group were located in Melbourne, and BHP Billiton plc in London. Both companies had identical boards and were run by a unified management team.

'I knew from the start that would only be a 12-month thing as far as I was concerned,' Derek Keys says. 'I'd already retired but I did the 14½-hour flight to Melbourne several times. They take the Great Circle route, which involves going south, so you're over the ice for something like three hours.'

Asked how the South Africans and the Australians interacted in those early days, Keys varied the 'like poles repel' analogy. 'Well, you know,' he tactfully replied, 'we're very alike, so it's not so easy to get along.'[14]

Nevertheless, BHP Billiton established an inner cabinet of all the talents, a seven-person executive committee, known as ExCo, comprising Paul Anderson, Brian Gilbertson, Chip Goodyear (chief development officer following Mick Davis's defection, and also acting chief financial officer), Mike Salamon (president and chief executive officer, minerals), Philip Aiken (president, petroleum), Kirby Adams (president, steel) and John Fast (chief legal counsel). When a new chief financial officer had been appointed, he or she would also join the executive committee.

Bob Kirkby was put in charge of carbon steel materials – iron ore, coking coal, manganese – Dave Munro would run aluminium, Brad Mills got the job of running copper and there were two senior operating roles: Phil Aiken became president of petroleum and Mike Salamon president of minerals.

There were a number of innovations, such as the setting up of two marketing hubs run by the thrusting young South African Marius Kloppers – one at Singapore to focus on the Asian energy market (energy coal, oil and gas) as well as carbon steelmaking raw materials, and one at The Hague, built around aluminium, base metals and the European energy-coal market. 'Marius's role in the new BHP was marketing,' Dave Munro says. 'We took the Billiton model of centralised marketing which we'd established after Billiton had come to London, and Marius took that up and for a couple of years refined and developed it hugely.'[15]

However, the centralised decision-making process, established by Paul Anderson following the poor investment decisions of the 1990s, was scrapped in favour of a decentralised structure under which the mineral, petroleum and steel divisions could decide on capital allocation, mergers and acquisitions up to US$1 billion.

Seven customer-sector groups (CSGs) were formed to reclassify the company's business units. For example, coking coal, manganese and iron ore – all ingredients of steelmaking – were placed in the same division, while steaming coal, used in generating electricity, was in another, a departure from the usual practice of putting all of the coal assets in the same category. 'We invented a number of things to try to make sure it didn't look like BHP and it didn't look like Billiton but it would be BHP Billiton,' Mike Salamon says. 'The job was to deliver this business with the customer-sector groups that had a common look and feel, a common understanding of what the company strategy was, a centralised marketing organisation.'[16]

The biggest breakthrough had been the final resolution of the steel issue. Over time, Anderson had made the bold strategic decisions necessary to engineer the company's exit from the business that had for so long been its proudest possession. 'At the time of the Newcastle closure, BHP Steel was still part of BHP,' Lance Hockridge says. 'Then, in 2000, the company separated the long-products business, so having closed the steelworks part of Newcastle the long-products business was reconfigured around the Whyalla steelworks and the Rooty Hill mini-mill, and it was spun off into a separate company named OneSteel.

'At the time BHP merged with Billiton, the decision was taken to separate the flat-products part of BHP Steel, and that has now become BlueScope Steel.[17] From that time forward, the old BHP and what is now BHP Billiton has had no steelmaking operation whatsoever. The only connection with BHP Billiton is that BlueScope buys pretty much all of its coal and 60 per cent of its iron ore from BHPB.

'Given that the announcement of the separation of BHP Steel was made at the same time as the announcement of the merger, I wound up spending my time on the steel demerger side and was very little involved on the merger side of the business. The company wanted to concentrate on resources, and in that context the manufacturing operations of BHP Steel really didn't fit the strategy.'[18]

On 20 August 2001, BHP Billiton released its first combined result, a remarkable profit of US$2.18 billion ($4.07 billion) for the 12 months to 30 June. There was, however, a US$1.1 billion bill for exceptionals related to the writing-off of BHP's 50 per cent interest in the troublesome HBI plant in Venezuela and the Ok Tedi copper mine in Papua New Guinea, where millions of tons of mine waste had polluted the Ok Tedi and Fly Rivers, devastating two thousand square kilometres of forest and destroying the fish stocks.[19]

Don Argus told investors, 'In Western Australia, we decided to continue to operate the HBI facility within strict technical and financial parameters. An exit or closure would have resulted in the destruction of shareholder value to a greater extent than we believe can be preserved by improving the performance of this asset.' It was an important decision and one that would rebound spectacularly in the months ahead.

Paul Anderson introduced a BHP Billiton charter, a mission statement that committed the merged company to deliver value to its shareholders through the exploitation of natural resources, while at the same time maintaining 'an overriding commitment to safety, environmental responsibility and sustainable development'. The annual report was peppered with references to the charter, which, Anderson said, was 'the foundation stone of the entire operation' – a prudent move in view of the Ok Tedi disaster.

'Paul Anderson had spent a lot of time with BHP designing the charter, while we in Billiton were a little more buccaneer about life,' Mike Salamon says. 'We didn't get carried away with this formal stuff, because there were so few of us. I could look you in the eye and we could work out what our mission was: I didn't have to get too bureaucratic about it. But we recognised we had this huge company; we had to play that game. We changed one word in Paul Anderson's vision statement: we took out the word "Australian" and put in the word "global". That was the only thing we changed. We liked his values and everything else.'[20]

According to Graham Evans, '[Anderson] found it quite important to define the values in which the company worked, that there needed to be real clarity around the business strategy and around how the company did business.'

'It was basically as a consequence of BHP doing business across a whole range of countries that it hadn't previously done business in. There was uncertainty on the part of some of the employees on what they could and couldn't do. There was clarity around the legal issues but much less clarity around what attitude the business took to issues that were in the grey area – for example, facilitation payments.

'There are certain issues that are clear-cut, issues that are illegal and improper, but there are plenty of others which are judgmental issues and what the company tried to do was to expose employees to the framework of global business conduct and get people to think about and talk about what that meant in their workplace. John Prescott started this and Paul Anderson followed it through.'[21]

It was, however, merely the forerunner of many good intentions and ecological initiatives which were open to question. Anderson was on more solid ground when he promised investors that the company would announce a new strategic framework early the following year, with an emphasis on return on invested capital and a strong customer focus. The following month, he announced that the new chief financial officer would be the burly 46-year-old former Australian Rules player Christopher J. Lynch, who had joined BHP from Alcoa the previous year and was currently chief financial officer of BHP Billiton's minerals division. Chris Lynch was educated at the Marist Brothers College at Forbes, New South Wales, and gained a commerce degree, accounting, and MBA at Deakin University, Melbourne. His appointment freed Chip Goodyear to move to London at the end of 2001 in his new role as chief development officer.[22]

Meanwhile, Brian Gilbertson moved his main domicile from London to Melbourne. 'I stayed in hotels,' he says, 'but then I did a deal with Don Argus and the remuneration committee that I would get an apartment – a very nice apartment overlooking the Botanic Gardens and the Eternal Flame. I could actually see the office in Bourke Street. My building was an old hospital once – I lived right at the top of that.'[23]

It was at this point that he started a bumpy relationship with the Australian press that continues to this day. 'When Brian had his first meeting as deputy chief executive around the table with senior Australian journalists, he made the point that he now had an apartment in Melbourne and was living there,' Marc Gonsalves says. 'The first question was from some hack who said, "What colour are the sheets on your bed?" I wanted to get rid of this ridiculous spotlight that was on us in Australia, where you couldn't fart without someone writing a story. I wanted the freedom we had in London to get on with the business of the company and take control of the communications around it, so that when we had something to say, we'd tell them.'[24]

Gilbertson, however, appeared unconcerned. He and his wife, Rensche, sampled the city's culinary delights and declared that Melbourne had 'the best chefs in the world'.[25] He attended a couple of Australian Rules football matches but, although he enjoyed the spectacle and the passion, his favourite sports remained squash and cycling. As a symbol of his successful campaign, he had a picture of Brigitte Bardot – 'the famous pouting one' – hung on the wall of his office in BHP Tower.

'I really have been very fortunate,' he says, looking back at that remarkable period. 'The purchase of the Billiton assets was perfectly timed; when Anglo made its move on us and bought the Rembrandt shares, we were ready; Paul Anderson came through at the right moment; we got it just right – we got the right deal for Billiton. And for BHP the timing was terribly important, too, to make the next step.'[26]

However, John Jackson, the wise and emollient deputy chairman, saw trouble ahead. 'It became clear pretty quickly that Don Argus was not looking forward to the day when Brian Gilbertson would take over from Paul Anderson,' he says. 'There was uneasiness in Don's mind about how he saw the proper relationship between a board and its chairman and chief executive, and how Brian might see it. It emerged that before Paul and Brian had ever met, but at about the time we'd heard that BHP might be interested in Brian, BHP had made inquiries about Brian and been advised that he was – I think the exact expression used by Don – "strong-headed".

'One could see winding up a pretty familiar conflict which I've seen in other companies where you get a very capable and powerful leader of the executive team – which Brian had undoubtedly shown he was at Billiton – and a strong non-executive board chaired by a very determined person who had clearly got in the back of his mind the interests of Australia plc. There was going to be the most enormous explosion.'[27]

PART IV

The Power

CHAPTER 21

Life with Brian

The Big Australian expired with the start of the new millennium at the venerable age of 116 years. In this brave new world, BHP Billiton, the lusty offspring of the union, was gifted with a new nickname, courtesy of chairman Don Argus: 'The Big Fella'. 'I've never referred to the company as The Big Australian – that's something I'm very careful about,' Argus says, leaning forward in his chair in the Copper Room at BHP Billiton headquarters.[1]

With 40 per cent of the shareholder base offshore under the dual-listed company structure, the important thing for Australia then, he said, was to look after its national heritage in terms of natural resources – 'and what grows off that is to me the big advantage for a company with sovereign assets of the quality that we have'.

Nations that did not protect their export income had been 'hollowed out' in similar circumstances. Australia had to be careful or it would finish up like Canada, 'where their endowment is lost; they don't have a national champion as such'.

So The Big Fella encapsulated the Argus philosophy: the new company would be progressive and global – still Australia's champion but less parochial than The Big Australian of yesteryear.

On the 49th floor of BHP Tower, Paul Anderson and Brian Gilbertson worked on a new strategic framework that would lead the dual-listed entity into a promised land of reliable cash flows and high dividends, thereby justifying their faith in the controversial merger and silencing the BHP grumblers who were still complaining that the equity ratio had favoured Billiton shareholders.

At the same time, the integration process was completed. 'We'd set ourselves a number of metrics such as, "What does success look like?"' Mike Salamon says. 'One thing you don't want to do is to miss on the synergies you thought you'd had and you also don't want to constipate the business. You can have a lot of infighting and then decisions stop being made. We had five metrics and we reported against those metrics every month. In February 2002, we delivered it to the board. We then got out of integration mode and went into running mode.'[2]

Brian Gilbertson says, 'We had promised the shareholders that the integration would be smooth, that we would achieve a variety of economies, and then perhaps above all, because of the diversity of this new company, that the shareholders could rely on our cash flows.

'Chip Goodyear and his team built a big model which simulated what the new company would look like if prices fluctuated or if the exchange rate between the US dollar and the South African rand changed. He used the past ten years' worth of quarterly data, and the amazing thing is that it came out with a continuous cash flow: no matter what you did to something, there would be an offsetting change which would keep it stable.

'That was not new – it was just applying Harry Markowitz's portfolio theory to the merged entity. We made it a key platform of our strategy that our shareholders could rely on stable cash flows and we could do our planning properly because we wouldn't be crippled in some years when the cash flow dried up; we'd have a stable cash flow and we could sensibly expand.'[3]

But before Gilbertson could present his vision to shareholders, the Boodarie HBI jinx returned with a vengeance. In March 2002, a tube burst in a gas-generating unit at the West Australian plant. The mishap affected only one of four production lines, but the other three were shut down pending an inspection to determine the cause of fractures that had mysteriously developed in the gas pipe.

Since BHP Billiton was unable to meet demand for the plant's output of feedstock, mostly from Asian steel mills, Anderson was forced to declare *force majeure*, a legal move that releases suppliers from contractual obligations owing to unforeseen events.[4] It was the first indication that reprieving the plant might not have been such a good idea.

On 8 April, the Paul and Brian show took to the stage in Sydney. 'Brian and I have worked jointly on this framework and share a common vision of the future,' Anderson told an audience of investors, many of them diehard BHP shareholders. 'However, it is only appropriate that Brian, as the incoming CEO, should present this framework, as he will be responsible for building on it and taking it to the next level.'

Anderson sat down without revealing that he intended to step down a lot sooner than anyone expected. 'The handover [to Gilbertson] happened at the time we declared the integration complete,' Mike Salamon says. 'Paul had a few projects he personally took on board, like the steel spin-off, and Brian started to run the go-forward business from January/February 2002.'[5]

When Gilbertson started speaking, his objective was to make the 'Old BHP' stakeholders feel a little more reassured that their national treasure had ended up 'not in the hands of a crazy gunslinger but a serious shareholder-sensitive corporate executive'.

'It was but a year ago that Paul Anderson and I announced the intention to merge BHP and Billiton,' he began. 'It was the culmination of a process of consolidation that had been underway in the metals and mining industry for a decade. The consolidation drivers were numerous. Important among these was the generally poor investment performance of the single-commodity corporations. With only one outlet for their cash flows, "one-trick ponies" tend to over-expand when the relevant commodity price is high, and then face cash starvation and capital write-offs when prices inevitably decline. This boom-to-bust pattern, typical of the resource industry of old, drove shareholders to distraction.

'A second factor was the escalating cost and complexity of implementing large resource projects – size being increasingly characteristic of the most efficient assets – and particularly so in relation to environmental and "sustainable development" pressures.

'A third driver was the desire of portfolio managers for large, liquid stocks, which permit major changes in portfolio weightings without significantly affecting the ruling share price. I am often told by the major investors that companies with market capitalisations of less than US$10 billion do not even show up on their investment radar screens.

'Finally, I think that the past few years have seen the emergence of a new generation of resource executives, driven to achieve shareholder value, rather than by emotional attachments to particular assets.'[6]

The extent of that consolidation had been remarkable, Gilbertson said. The top five metals and mining companies in 1990 had accounted for less than 25 per cent of the industry's US$150 billion total equity value. The then-largest company, BHP, had a market capitalisation of around US$9 billion. Now, the top five companies accounted for almost 50 per cent of the resource equity value of $US250 billion, 'effectively a doubling for the top five over the decade'. BHP Billiton was still the largest company, four times bigger than BHP in 1990, and as large as the top five aggregated in that earlier year.

The merger created not only the industry leader but also

one unlike any other that the industry had seen before. 'My colleagues and I believe that our company has unrivalled potential to bring shareholder value in the years ahead,' Gilbertson said, 'so that it will have a strong claim to being a core holding in major international portfolios.'

The generation of stable cash flow was one of the group's major strengths, he said, enabling it to meet dividend expectations and to fund growth opportunities on the basis of merit, without concerns about short-term cash-flow disruptions. 'Our decisions to sell down our interest in the Columbus stainless-steel plant, to exit the Arutmin coal deposit [in Indonesia] and to exit Ok Tedi were driven by the desire to improve the portfolio, to reduce its volatility, to stabilise its cash flows, and to eliminate problem areas,' Gilbertson said. 'Even the spin-out of our high-quality BHP Steel business (on schedule for 1 July 2002) will leave a portfolio better matched to our desired structure. I must pay particular tribute here to Paul Anderson, who, as chief executive, has dealt decisively with a raft of problem assets to restore the quality of the overall portfolio.'[7]

This 'strategic framework' presentation was generally well received among investors, analysts and financial journalists. It looked as though BHP Billiton had cast off the sackcloth and ashes of the 1990s and was thrusting ahead into the new decade. On 1 May, however, the company revealed that its third-quarter net profit had slumped 33 per cent to US$406 million. A reduction of US$260 million in revenues from lower prices for base metals, oil, steel and aluminium was only partially offset by an improvement of US$80 million in coking and thermal coal prices. Sales had fallen 8.4 per cent to $4.28 billion and showed few signs of recovering.[8]

'We see little evidence of a strong pick-up in many markets,' Chris Lynch told a videoconference of journalists and analysts in Melbourne and London. 'Inventories remain high in several of the LME [London Metal Exchange] commodities. Our profit of US$406 million despite this lower-price environment is a very solid result.'

At the same time, it was announced that Paul Anderson would relinquish his job five months earlier than expected. 'I got the distinct impression that he was very proud of what he had done but he wasn't sad to say goodbye either,' Mike Salamon says.[9] In fact, Anderson now refers to his term in Melbourne as 'my favourite time'.

'We worked well together but it made sense [to shorten the two-year period],' Gilbertson says. 'The integration had gone as well as we thought it would and I became chief executive on 1 July 2002. I had to be sure I didn't drop the ball.'[10] In an official company statement, Gilbertson was described as 'very much the architect of Billiton's success'; Don Argus said he looked forward to working with him in his expanded role.[11]

'It was smooth,' Lord Renwick says. 'Paul was very happy to step back – he's a very classy person and he handed the reins to Brian. What then happened was in a sense almost inevitable. Brian is a very hard-charging CEO and Don is a tough and experienced chairman.'[12]

'Don and Brian were headed for a very early test of strength,' John Jackson says. 'The test of strength emerged in relation to a proposition that Brian was very keen on, and that was merging BHP Billiton with Rio. He thought that would create a world leader in the mining industry and in a world in which the demand for commodities was going to take off.'[13]

There seemed to be no doubt that Gilbertson, both in his background and style, represented a radical departure from the BHP norm. In London, Neil Collins, city editor of the *Daily Telegraph*, cast a seasoned eye over events in Bourke Street. 'BHP used to encapsulate everything the Australians believed was best about themselves,' he wrote.

> It was big, brash and butch, as mining companies are supposed to be Down Under, and it was the centre of corporate Australia. As miners do, the muscle started turning to flab, the directors started falling out among themselves and BHP turned from a

> national champion to a business protected from takeover only by Australia's xenophobic domestic-preference laws.
>
> Mr Gilbertson was lucky enough to be in charge when BHP was reviving under Paul Anderson, a man who saw the limitations of being based on the far side of the world.
>
> Following the path pioneered by RTZ in its takeover of its Aussie associate, the pair locked BHP and Billiton together, into two companies with identical boards and pooled profits. Australian sensibilities were thus dealt with, at the price of Mr Gilbertson (and Mrs Gilbertson) agreeing that he liked Melbourne so much he would move into a flat there.
>
> Yesterday he got his reward, with promotion to chief executive of BHP Billiton when Mr Anderson retires in July. The cumbersome dual structure does not seem to have caused too many problems, and looks stable enough, although both the market in the stock and the real base of the business is overwhelmingly in London.[14]

The strategic framework was indicative of the good working relationship between the incumbent chief executive officer and the heir apparent. 'Brian and I got along just fine on a personal basis, but you might imagine in a setting when you've got a transition going between a fairly headstrong CEO to another soon-to-be CEO that it would create some tensions in terms of arbitrary things,' Anderson says. 'Our basic strategy and our view of the industry and how to run a company were identical – we had no disagreement – but there are always little fine-line things as simple as what should the new logo look like.'[15]

To the delight of communications man Michael Spencer, the new merged management team cast their eye towards a more 'market focused' image. He combined with Billiton's marketing specialist Marius Kloppers to work on BHP Billiton's 'branding' and had 'very comprehensive' interviews with senior management, particularly Brian Gilbertson.

'Marius felt we should be a new-generation resources company which values the intangibles (resourcefulness) as well as the tangibles (stuff in the ground). So we wanted to symbolise this adaptive thinking. Tangibles and intangibles hadn't been tried in a resources company before. We wanted a fluid, emerging, evolving symbol; organic rather than physical and structural; no rigid lines; a sharp break with the past. We're not just digging up rocks; we were building and creating something – so it should emphasise our intellectual horsepower.'[16]

With the general concept settled, they contacted international branding houses and one group flew a team from London to make a pitch for the contract. In the event, they chose a local firm, Future Brand, which produced two designs, one in traditional style with a circular theme and the other – the successful one – depicting a large liquid-metal blob (representing BHP) merging with a smaller blob (Billiton) to become a perfectly integrated entity, while the name 'bhp billiton' was spelled out in lower-case lettering (informal, intellectual, adaptive).

At a total cost of $800,000, the new logo at least had the virtue of being easily adaptable to accommodate Rio Tinto should the need arise.

With his star irresistibly in the ascendant, it was taken for granted in analyst circles that Brian Gilbertson would soon head for 'elephant country', home of the big mining beasts, in search of fresh quarry, although Rio Tinto was surely too big for him to bag. The most obvious targets were WMC and Woodside Petroleum, both severely undervalued. However, WMC was in the process of selling its 40 per cent interest in the world's largest alumina production business, Alcoa World Alumina and Chemicals (AWAC), to its partner Alcoa, while Royal Dutch Shell held the whip with a 34 per cent stake in Woodside after acquiring BHP's interest.

At one of the regular weekly meetings of the executive committee (ExCo), Gilbertson tabled a one-page note arguing that BHP Billiton should consolidate its position by becoming the industry's first US$100 billion company – three times its value at that time and a figure that raised the bar to seemingly impossible heights. It was, he conceded, an ambitious goal and one that would have to be pursued while running the existing businesses and expanding them when necessary. However, there was one opportunity that stood out as a tremendous prize: putting BHPB together with its greatest rival, Rio Tinto.

'Ever since I've been there, we've had some discussions – some more detailed than others – with Rio,' Chip Goodyear recalls. 'Certainly, 1999 was a pretty active discussion. Brian is a very smart guy but also very transaction-oriented and he would certainly have been looking around the industry for the next set of opportunities to create a true industry champion. He would have been the one who took direct ownership of that, no doubt.'[17]

Indeed, in the northern summer of 2002 Gilbertson took his proposal to the next level. The Danesfield House Hotel, a whitewashed neo-Tudor mansion, is set on the site of a prehistoric fort in the Chiltern Hills overlooking the Thames in Buckinghamshire. It was here that the board of BHP Billiton and members of ExCo gathered in June 2002 to discuss strategy. And it was within these crenellated walls, surrounded by Italian gardens and plied with the very best in cuisine, that they first heard about Project 6.

There was a big turnout of directors and most, if not all, of the senior executives: Phil Aiken (petroleum), John Fast (legal), Ian Fraser (human resources), Bob Kirkby (carbon steel materials), Marius Kloppers (marketing), Chris Lynch (finance), Brad Mills (base metals), Dave Munro (aluminium), Mike Oppenheimer (energy coal) and Mike Salamon (minerals). Not all of these, however, attended all of the meetings, including the board's deliberations.

One absentee was Paul Anderson, who would remain a director until November. 'It was to set the budget for the upcoming fiscal year and I said, "I'm not going to be responsible for this budget." There was not a lot of benefit to having me there, and there could be some real downside, so I thought the best thing was not to attend.'[18]

As befitted the surroundings, the itinerary was a combination of work and pleasure. 'We met for dinner at Danesfield House on the night of Tuesday, 11 June,' John Jackson recalls, consulting his diary. 'We had a photo session at 8.30 in the morning on 12 June; we were at Danesfield House the whole of 12 June and we were there the whole of Thursday, 13 June. I had to peel off in the morning to meet the British Government on the Hunting Act issue, but I rejoined them in the evening. We had an excellent dinner on the evening of 13 June at Waddesdon Manor, one of Lord Rothschild's country homes [just outside Aylesbury, Buckinghamshire], and on Friday, 14 June the board met at the Versailles Suite at Danesfield House at eight o'clock in the morning.'[19]

Brian Gilbertson was in his element. He had a list of bullet points that spelled out his vision as the incoming chief executive. 'Danesfield was really Brian's first opportunity to address the board on a strategic vision for the company,' says Chip Goodyear 'And he presented something that he called "125", and it was meant to be $100 billion market value and a 25 P/E [price/earnings ratio]. And he talked about trying to create an entity that looked like that. At the time, the market value would have been around $30 billion, maybe a little bit more, so it was quite an aggressive vision for the company that needless to say would have required some significant acquisition to get there. I would say there were some sceptics around the table about whether or not that was really something that was achievable – and certainly achievable quickly after the combination of BHP and Billiton.'[20]

Gilbertson did indeed have a significant acquisition in mind: a merger between BHP Billiton and Rio Tinto. As Rio's London address was 6 St James's Square, the merger became known as Project 6.

'Brian gave his assessment of where the industry was going, with particular reference to the huge emerging economies in China, India and South America,' John Jackson says. 'He thought Africa, if it could get its act together, would eventually be important but would lag somewhere behind. He presented a very interesting picture of where the mining industry was and reckoned there should be further consolidation, that BHP Billiton was very well placed to participate in that, and one of the things that leapt out as being theoretically obvious was Rio.'[21]

'Oh gosh, yes,' says Marius Kloppers, who attended the ExCo meetings. 'I remember the vision thing. [It was] for a combination of Rio Tinto. Certainly, there was a discussion, if I recall. Perhaps, yes, it was Danesfield. I recall talking about the Rio issue, but I also recall talking about Russia's resources, and we talked quite extensively about how we step up our activities in marketing product to China.'[22]

Mike Salamon saw Project 6 as the next logical step on the consolidation ladder. 'The Billiton way of doing things was to keep moving,' he says. 'So having built one platform, you were immediately thinking, "Well, where's the next one?" We were in an environment where you still had Enron and much, much bigger companies than us and so we were not competing against mining businesses, we were competing for a place in the sun, [where] size actually does matter.'[23]

That a merger between BHP Billiton and Rio Tinto would create the biggest entity in the energy-and-resources universe was self-evident; it was also true that in financial wunderkind Chip Goodyear, Gilbertson had the perfect man to work out the numbers.

Did the merger have his support at the time?

'That's one of the things about the way I run my business,' Goodyear says. 'I do the analysis and then reach the conclusion, as opposed to reach the conclusion and then do the analysis. So I'd say the most that was going on at that time was an assessment of the opportunity. I wouldn't probably have got to the point at that time where you reach the conclusion on whether it made sense. It's always been an intriguing strategic question – the value of a combination. I look at any transaction, any investment: 1, does it make strategic sense? 2, is there a value proposition? And 3, can you deliver it? And you have to have a positive answer on all of those things in order to push the button. So at that point, where on the surface the strategic issues are where people would say, "Of course!", the opportunity to investigate that was yet to come in the 2002 conference.'[24]

'Chip Goodyear did a major part of the presentation on US125,' Gilbertson says. 'The board endorsed these initiatives, including Project 6.'[25] In principle, the possibility of a merger with Rio Tinto had been given the green light. Realistically, though, could Gilbertson pull it off? And would it bring him into conflict with Don Argus, a former chief executive skilled in takeovers?

'Don felt very strongly that matters of that sort should be firmly in the hands of the board, which should determine both tactics and strategy,' John Jackson says. 'Brian strongly disagreed with that and felt that this was fundamentally a matter that should be handled by the executive team, keeping the board informed – but with it being fundamentally a matter for the chief executive and his team to take the initiative on. That was the origin of their big falling out.'[26]

CHAPTER 22

Road to Rio

Rio Tinto takes its name from the famous red river of Andalusia whose mines had supplied the Phoenicians, Greeks, Carthaginians and Romans with copper and iron since time immemorial. According to local legend, they even supplied the empire of King Solomon and could justifiably claim to be the fabled King Solomon's mines.

By 2002, Bob Wilson had risen to the chair at Rio Tinto after a golden run as chief executive. Born in suburban Surrey, Wilson studied economics at Sussex University. He began his career in 1966 as an economist at Dunlop – a move he later described as 'my first career mistake' – but soon moved to Mobil Oil. He then joined RTZ in 1970 as a financial analyst before switching to operational duties, running the European zinc and lead smelting subsidiaries.

Wilson played a key role in all of Rio Tinto's major strategic developments, recognising the potential of the Escondida copper mine and negotiating RTZ's 30 per cent stake in 1985, and then acquiring BP Minerals in 1989. As chief executive, he orchestrated the dual-listed merger between RTZ and its Australian subsidiary CRA in 1995, which created the modern Rio Tinto.[1]

'I became chief executive of RTZ in 1991,' Bob Wilson says, speaking for the first time about the controversial merger that had so infuriated Don Argus. 'RTZ owned 83 per cent of CRA in the early 1970s but had agreed with the Australian Government to dilute that percentage over time to 49 per cent. RTZ had traditionally been a bit more of a mining finance house than a mining company, but following the acquisition of BP Minerals it suddenly owned a lot of directly controlled operations. From that, it was going to be clear – clear to me, anyway, and getting increasingly clear to some people in CRA – that we were going to be treading on one another's toes a bit because RTZ was now a mining operator and a mining company focused particularly and solely in that sector with global aspirations. Basically, we needed to work through what this meant for RTZ and CRA and how they would work together and how that relationship was going to work in the future.

'A few of us had been thinking about it and talking about it for a little while. Then, fairly early 1995, RTZ did a deal to get into the other major copper discovery of the last 50 years. It had already got into Escondida, so the next one was Grasberg, which Freeport McMoRan had in Indonesia.'[2]

In early 1995, Rio Tinto and Freeport established a joint venture under which Rio Tinto became entitled to 40 per cent of additional production as a result of the expansion of the Grasberg mining project in West Papua. 'We did a very attractive deal which in a way served to crystallise the potential issue between RTZ and CRA,' Wilson says. 'The operation was up there in West Papua, traditionally CRA's doorstep – they'd never even had a look-in at a deal there. It became clear from both sides that not only were we heading for a potential conflict of interest but it was also going to be a problem for CRA's aspirations, certainly outside Australia, if we couldn't find a constructive way to resolve this.

'It was also clear that, as RTZ and CRA were both substantially focused on mining, it would make sense in terms of rationalising the areas of overlap where we were wasting effort in terms of some of the overall research effort in identifying opportunities.'

Discussions about a merger began after the then CRA chairman, John Uhrig, asked Wilson if RTZ were prepared to make a takeover offer for the minorities. 'He wasn't saying he wanted that to happen but were we prepared to do that?' Wilson says. 'My answer was no. I actually wanted to retain the best of both companies, including Australian quotation of CRA and CRA management. We then spent six months between us, looking at various ways of how we might proceed, and we came up with a modernised version of the dual-listed structure that Shell and Unilever had used before; it had some characteristics of both of those, but we also said, "Surely they wouldn't design them quite that way if they were designing with a clean sheet of paper today. What would they do differently?" We said, "Surely there has to be one head office, rather than multiple head offices, otherwise you don't get a coherent management. Surely there has to be the same members of the boards of both companies or potentially you get a rather chaotic decision process, or a very bureaucratic or politicised one. So let's have the same directors of both companies."

'We looked at what's a modern-day version of the way those guys set things up 80 years ago in those companies. I think we did get it pretty well right. The issue then was if we are going to merge these companies on a non-premium basis, I – Wilson – don't have a problem selling this to my shareholders. The problem is going to be selling it to the CRA shareholders and the Australian Government.'[3]

The burden of that argument wasn't actually carried by Wilson – the hard work was done by John Uhrig, who was chairman, and Leon Davis, who was chief executive of CRA, in persuading those constituencies that this was the right thing to do in the interests of Australia and the Australian shareholders. 'They bore the brunt of carrying the argument, which they did very effectively,' Wilson says. 'Hindsight has shown them to have been right because the benefits to shareholders that flowed through in subsequent years were very, very considerable.' However, Wilson agreed that national self-esteem had suffered 'in the eyes of people like [Peter] Costello' from moving the head office from Melbourne to London.

'There was a famous cartoon which had the lion carrying off the kangaroo in its jaws,' Marc Gonsalves recalls. 'Reference was made repeatedly to me about it. On every one of Billiton's forays into Australia, which weren't without controversy, that was dusted off and metaphorically pushed into our face.'[4]

The merged company started off with a name that both Leon Davis and Bob Wilson detested. 'We found it pragmatic to compromise and call the company RTZ-CRA – a ridiculous name, and we knew it was ridiculous, but there were sensitivities about retaining individual names and the link with the past,' Wilson says. 'We moved away from that as soon as we could and called the two companies Rio Tinto plc and Rio Tinto Limited.'

Wilson was due to retire in 2003 after reaching Rio's mandatory retirement age of 60. In London on 4 July 2002, just four days after he had officially assumed full powers as chief executive, Brian Gilbertson made contact with the veteran miner (designated 'C6' – chairman of Rio Tinto – in Gilbertson's code) about a possible merger.[5] According to insiders, his unsolicited overture was well received at Rio headquarters in St James's Square, providing a happy augury for the new BHP Billiton regime and its ambitious chief executive. It was not, however, a scheme that could be announced to the markets, where there were gloomy predictions, following the disappointing third-quarter figures, that Gilbertson would preside over a poor profit performance for the year ended 30 June 2002, the merged company's first full-year results.

In the event, Gilbertson astonished the doomsayers by unveiling a net profit of $US1.7 billion net ($3.18 billion), a rise of 10.5 per cent over 2001. In briefings beamed by satellite from Melbourne to Sydney, London and Johannesburg, he declared that BHP Billiton had overcome the worst economic conditions in a decade to record steady cash flows of US$3.9 billion after paying all interest and taxes.

These figures had been achieved despite a commodity-price slump – notably in oil, aluminium and copper – that alone slashed $US665 million off revenues. As outlined in his strategic-framework speech, the merged company had demonstrated its extraordinary resilience by coming through the economic turbulence relatively unscathed.[6]

Gilbertson had also been lucky. He had merged Billiton with BHP before the stock market slumped in the wake of the 9/11 terrorist attack on the World Trade Center and in advance of a new Mineral and Petroleum Resources Development Act that almost halved the value of South African mining assets. 'Due to his excellent timing, shareholders in the company that Gilbertson formerly headed ended up owning 42 per cent of the merged group,' analyst Ivor Ries declared at the time. 'Yet the 2002 accounts revealed that the operating-profit contribution from the former Billiton assets amounted to just 34 per cent of the group total. Given the plunge in the value of South African mining assets over the past 18 months, BHP today would be able to buy Billiton for significantly less than the $19 billion it agreed to pay early in 2001.'[7]

The dark mutterings of the old boy network about the 'unfair' equity split rumbled anew in the saloons of clubland. 'Some people live in the past. Once it's done, it's done,' the pragmatic Mike Salamon comments, 'but there are people who try to keep the score.'[8] Don Argus concedes that the deal left 'some pretty bad scars'. 'When the merger was done,' he says, 'there was a certain investment bank in London walking around saying, "This is a reverse takeover." The reality was it was a 60/40 split and it's still a 60/40 split.'[9]

There were also murmurings about Brian Gilbertson's 'autocratic' style of management. At Billiton, he had been chairman and chief executive, answerable only to his shareholders – a set-up that appealed enormously to his entrepreneurial instincts. BHP Billiton, however, had a hands-on chairman in Don Argus, who was naturally determined to avoid the meltdown that had occurred through the slew of bad offshore investments in the 1990s. 'The challenge for Gilbertson will be in translating his entrepreneurial and fast-moving management style into a much larger company with a very different governance structure than the one he grew up with,' Ivor Ries noted. 'If he succeeds, other mining houses had better watch out.'[10]

Gilbertson maintains he had no difficulty making that adjustment, despite later assertions in the press to the contrary. 'The company was very well run,' he says. 'We were organised into production units and each one had a very good chief executive running it. Chip Goodyear and I were sitting in the centre of the organisation like the conductor leading the orchestra, but the orchestra didn't need much leading. The iron-ore business was running very well; the copper business was running very well. We made a couple of key decisions from the centre, but essentially the company was in great shape. It didn't need fixing; it wasn't broken.'[11]

Gilbertson reported to shareholders that savings of $500 million had been identified and were being achieved, while Chip Goodyear confirmed that the vision of a diversified, cash-flow-generating machine had become a reality.

One of the things that symbolised the difference between BHP and Billiton attitudes was air travel. Gencor had maintained a fleet of aircraft that were used to fly staff to its mines scattered throughout South Africa. When the company moved further afield into Mozambique, Australia and South America, Gilbertson procured a long-range jet, starting with a Falcon and then a Global Express. BHP, on the other hand, dispensed with the company Gulfstream during its period of austerity.

'Don Argus made a point of never flying in the company jet – he'd use commercial airlines,' Gilbertson says. 'The impression was created that this was there for my convenience. In fact, that wasn't true – my usage of the plane was relatively low compared with people such as Mike Salamon, for example, who had a very broad portfolio. He could do a tour of South Africa and South America in two or three days rather than two weeks by having his own plane on tap. Anyway, the furtherest it got in my day was a request as to whether we really should have these planes and whether they were justifiable.'[12]

Mike Salamon, who had an apartment in Melbourne, a house in Johannesburg and a third home in Surrey, where his wife and children lived, was an outspoken advocate of corporate jets. 'I was living in three countries,' he says. 'I slept on planes for a hundred nights a year for years. When we did the integration, I used our big plane like a bus. I went all over the place to talk to the management teams because I was writing the integration. I'd be in Melbourne on Friday, all over South America for Saturday, Sunday, Monday and back to Melbourne on Wednesday for a board meeting.

'In any event, the directors – in particular the ex-BHP directors – felt that it was inappropriate for companies to have such accoutrements, so we had to sell them all. Because BHP had gone wrong, they went through this period of cutting costs, [yet] to do our jobs properly you had to show your face in the trenches regularly.'[13]

By now, Project 6 was already well advanced. Despite later claims about a lack of consultation,[14] Gilbertson says he kept key executives apprised of his every move. 'There were follow-up meetings [after Danesfield],' he says. 'Minutes of these meetings went to members of the board.'

Asked whether Gilbertson had discussed the Rio merger with him at any point during 2002 following the Danesfield meeting, John Jackson replied, 'Yes. Brian never had any doubt about the industrial logic [of a merger]. I think he was pretty certain that it would be strongly blocked by Don, partly because of The Don's Australian blood.'[15]

Meanwhile, Gilbertson was spending much of his spare time keeping in shape. 'I bought my most expensive bike in Melbourne and I used to go cycling,' he says. 'They had an around-the-bay race which happens once a year [in October]. It's 200 kilometres, which is a serious bike ride, at least for me. I agreed to do one leg of it – 100 kilometres – and get someone to come and take me back. But it didn't work that way. There was supposed to be a bus that brought me back but when I got there the bus was going to be another six hours, so I cycled back. I did the whole bloody 200 kilometres and I nearly died.'[16]

On 23 October, there was a farewell party in Melbourne for Paul Anderson. Then, a week later, Gilbertson gave an address entitled 'Investing in Risky Geographies' to members of the Melbourne Mining Club in which he turned conventional wisdom on its head by demonstrating that investing in politically stable places such as the United States (Magma) could be more dangerous to shareholders than investments in countries that apparently epitomised risk, such as Mozambique (the first Mozal aluminium smelter) or Chile (the Escondida copper mine).

'I was still trying to dampen investor and press concerns that the merger had traded good, safe BHP assets for risky Billiton ones,' he says. 'The strategy was to direct BHP's hard cash into Billiton-generated projects with the goal of achieving a 15–25 per cent return on a capital investment of US$10 billion and thus double the company's earnings.'

There were many clues in Gilbertson's exposition to his thinking and it set the hares running. BHP Billiton's balance sheet and cash flows had been so healthy that he could afford to mount a US$10 billion takeover bid without raising a sweat. The question was: which way would he jump – acquisition or merger?

There was also the question of the composition of the board, which had been slimmed down from 17 directors to 12, just two of whom, Gilbertson and Goodyear, would be executives. Derek Keys, having turned 70, had already departed, and John Jackson, who was three years older than Keys, was the next to go. 'The last thing I did for Billiton,' Jackson says, 'was on Monday, 4 November 2002 when we had the AGMs and we ran them with a video link. BHP was meeting in Melbourne; Billiton was meeting in London. I chaired the London meeting.'[17]

The following day, the Gilbertsons were at Flemington to watch Media Puzzle win the Melbourne Cup. There were no visible squalls on the horizon, but a few short weeks hence the media would be puzzling over what exactly had happened to cause a sudden and traumatic breakdown in the relationship between the South African chief executive and his Australian chairman. For in that short period, Project 6 would hit the rocks and sink, leaving wreckage scattered through the corporate surf.

It had all seemed so hopeful.

There was agreement between the negotiators that one of the iron-ore assets owned by the BHPB and Rio might have to be sacrificed if government regulators raised objections; that would bring the value of the merged entity down below the US$100 billion mark, but it would still be close to it.

In the early stages, Bob Wilson talked about bringing in a third party to take the oil-and-gas assets; indeed, Lord Renwick still believes 'that in the event of a combination Rio would have wanted to see the oil-and-gas business spun off'.[18] However, Brian Gilbertson maintains that BHP Petroleum would have remained an integral part of the merged company's diversified portfolio.

Gilbertson says he was willing to stand down as chief executive, but it was agreed that he would become chief executive of the merged company, with 55-year-old, Adelaide-born Leigh Clifford of Rio Tinto nominated as his successor: a nice compromise in that the chief executive officer's job would revert to an Australian for the first time since John Prescott had stepped down in 1998.

Clifford trained as a mining engineer before joining CRA in 1970. In 1995, he was seconded to London to work on CRA's merger with RTZ. Clifford returned to Australia with Rio Tinto for several years but found himself back in London in 1999 and in 2000 was promoted to chief executive.

The question of Gilbertson's successor was decided at a meeting between the parties in Melbourne on 18 November 2002. There were, however, governance issues about the composition of the board to be finalised. The scene then switched to London, where, on 27 November, Brian Gilbertson and Bob Wilson held a crucial rendezvous prior to the BHP Billiton board meeting the following day.

According to Gilbertson, Wilson saw the merger as an attractive opportunity and felt that if it could not be done now it would never be done. As he planned to retire shortly, he would not seek the role of chairman of the merged company, which raised the question of who would become chairman. Not Don Argus, apparently: his strident view – that RTZ had 'pinched' CRA – would not have endeared him to Rio's upper echelons in St James's Square. 'The chairmanship was an issue,' Gilbertson says. 'And the Rio directors were also concerned to see that the synergies we had promised would be delivered.'[19]

That night, Gilbertson told Don Argus, who had just arrived in London, that Rio Tinto was prepared to return to Australia, or, in his emotive phrase, 'the prodigal son comes home'.

Project 6 was still extant the following day – 28 November – when Chip Goodyear reported to the board at its meeting at BHP Billiton's ultra-modern London headquarters at Neathouse Place, Victoria, on the shareholder value that would be released in a merger with Rio Tinto. Gilbertson told the meeting that Gresham Partners had been retained to report on financial issues. Bob Wilson's points of concern were listed under four headings:

- Petroleum.
- Anti-trust.
- Synergies.
- People.

The board agreed that Project 6 had merit. 'Brian reported to the board that he'd talked to Bob Wilson about a combination,' Lord Renwick says. 'But I think he triggered this discussion of merging with Rio too soon and also on a basis which wasn't going to be acceptable to the Australian side, and that led to this eruption.'[20]

Renwick confirmed that Rio Tinto had wanted a new chairman. 'This was unattractive to Don; it was unattractive to the Australian directors,' he says. 'The rest of us were not against a merger with Rio – we could see the benefits – but it was raised in a very abrupt way. There was nothing wrong intrinsically with the Brian vision. Raised in the way it was, I thought there was an inevitable difference of opinion which was bound to develop because the non-Australian directors for the most part could see the attractions of this thing, [but] everybody is influenced by where they come from, so the Australian directors naturally were less impressed, and, of course, there was a long history of not-very-good-relationships between BHP and Rio over the Rio acquisition of CRA and also tussles about iron ore in Western Australia. There was a feeling in Australia that CRA was supposed to be in a merger with Rio but it ended up effectively being a Rio takeover. I did hear from both sides that there had been a fair amount of friction between old BHP and Rio.'[21]

That evening, Gilbertson and Argus came face to face again when the directors attended a farewell party for John Jackson at the Design Museum on the Thames, opposite the Tower of London.

'We'd had the board meeting,' Gilbertson says, 'and the major issue was the top two posts in the merged company: CEO and chairman. Bob Wilson was not looking for either position, and I was prepared to step down but Don said he was not prepared to be traded.'[22]

The man most favoured to take the chairmanship, we can reveal, was 52-year-old BHP Billiton director Michael Chaney, the Perth-born son of Sir Fred Chaney, a navy minister in the Menzies government and later administrator of the Northern Territory. Michael was educated at Aquinas College and the University of Western Australia, and had completed the Harvard Business School's advanced-management program before working in the finance and petroleum industries in

Australia and the United States. Concurrently managing director of Wesfarmers and a director of Gresham Partners, he was one of the stars of the Australian business community.[23]

At the Design Museum, amid the clink of champagne glasses and the buzz of social chatter, Gilbertson and Argus agreed to meet the following day to discuss how to conduct the negotiations with Rio and to define the boundaries of future negotiations.

However, Argus had not been a party to the talks to date and he made it clear to Gilbertson that he had no intention of yielding his position. As he had said at the board meeting, 'Why not make the CEO the lightning rod and not the chairman?' He also wanted to see BHP Billiton properly bedded down before making any more big plays. John Jackson recalls that Gilbertson seemed 'unhappy' at the party, although he was unaware of the reason.

Without informing Gilbertson, Don Argus then called Bob Wilson. 'I suggested to Bob that in the world I come from, normally chairman to chairman sit down and talk about any proposed merger,' Argus says, 'and I thought it would be a good idea if he and I sat down and talked about this particular initiative.'[24]

On 29 November, Argus met Wilson. 'That's when the thing all started to unfold,' Argus says. 'Then I had a phone call with Mr Gilbertson, and it probably would have been one of the most unpleasant phone calls I've ever had in my life.'

Asked to describe the content of the call, Don Argus leans back in his chair in the Copper Room. 'Oh, I won't go down that path,' he says. 'Clearly, there had been some discussions about a potential merger with Rio and BHP Billiton at the time, but not many of the board members were privy to those discussions.'[25]

Brian Gilbertson says he had always been conscious of the need to take board members with him in every mergers-and-acquisitions situation. 'I briefed Don Argus after every meeting with Rio and the board at every board meeting,' he says. 'I also did the occasional note for the board – maybe I should have phoned every board member after every meeting with Bob Wilson.'[26]

Says Mike Salamon, 'The most challenging part of these big deals is what they call "social issues". The social issues are the key board members and the key executives. What happens to them and how are they perceived in history? Those are very important things at the time of doing a deal. You had some pretty big personalities around the table who were not always going to agree about things.'[27]

Gilbertson then phoned Bob Wilson, who told him that Don Argus did not have much enthusiasm for a deal, that he wasn't up for it and that he felt the whole thing was too hard. The biggest merger in the industry's history had effectively been torpedoed. 'It was in the bag – we would have been heroes in Australia,' Gilbertson says. 'We hadn't written the agreement, but everything pointed in the right direction. Under different circumstances, I think Don would have been in favour of the deal.'[28]

By 2008, time and geography had not quite succeeded in merging the endeavours of Brian Gilbertson and Sir Robert Wilson but physically they were indeed very close. Wilson was working as chairman of the BG Group (formerly British Gas) at 108 Jermyn Street, just a couple of blocks from Gilbertson's Pallinghurst Resources at no. 54 in the same street, a fluke that both men found amusing.

The smart but totally anonymous offices of the BG Group are sandwiched between a men's outfitters and a shoe shop. Wilson's spacious sixth-floor office overlooks Piccadilly. He is of medium height, a dapper dresser with neatly brushed grey-flecked hair, blue-checked shirt, autumnal tie, light tweed suit. He had vowed not to talk about BHP Billiton but, aware of his role in these momentous events, he relents and discusses them for the first time.

Asked whether Brian Gilbertson had approached him in July 2002 about the possibility of a merger between Rio Tinto and BHP Billiton, he replies yes.

Gilbertson seemed to think those talks were going quite well. Would that be your take on it?

Yes.

There was a crucial BHP Billiton board meeting in London in November 2002 when Don Argus was apprised of the fact that possibly a change of chairmanship was in the offing. We understand he contacted you and was somewhat abrupt.

Wilson laughs heartily.

Is that a fair summary?

That's a fair summary.

There was another name mentioned in terms of the chairmanship: Michael Chaney. Would that also be a reasonable thing to say?

Not as a part of any discussions I had. [Brian Gilbertson insists Chaney's name was in fact discussed.]

But a new chairman would have been a requirement if the combination had proceeded?

Umm, I'm not sure that the conversation had really got that far, quite honestly.

How far had it got?

I think that it was beginning to touch on some of those questions. Who's going to be doing which jobs? It was fairly close to when I intended to retire. I told both Brian and my own board that I didn't intend to have this become the basis for me staying on if it went ahead. And that caused some problems with my own board. 'Well, we don't think you should be doing this unless you commit to staying on to see it through' was the view of some of them. This was not a discussion I'd had with Brian at that point and there were also issues . . . If it is going to be a BHP condition – a Don Argus condition, not a Brian Gilbertson condition – about where the head office of this company should be located, I think that was going to be a problem. The head office should be where the head office should be.

The Rio board would have preferred it to be in London?

Not necessarily. I'd spent quite a lot of time thinking about a number of alternatives, one of which was Sydney, none of which was Melbourne. One of which would have been the west coast of the States. Basically, in my view, there were three options: one would have been Sydney, one would have been London and a third would have been somewhere like San Francisco. I don't think I'd had that discussion with Brian. I can't be certain whether I did or not, actually, because it's quite a long time ago.

Brian Gilbertson seemed to think there was scope for movement: that the head office could move from London.

For me, it's a pragmatic decision: where is going to be the best place to run the business?

Why Sydney not Melbourne?

I see Sydney as being more outward-looking, better communications also to the outside world.

Melbourne would be considered to be the traditional home of the mining companies.

Yes, but it's not particularly well connected to the rest of the world. There is now a notably different quality of transport availability out of Sydney compared with Melbourne. It hasn't always been quite as notable as it is today. Also, I think if the two companies were to get together there was some merit in an entirely new location.

It seems the idea was that Brian Gilbertson would stay for a little while if this happened and that Leigh Clifford would then take over as chief executive.

That was most likely.

Do you recall discussing Leigh's name at all in this context?

Yes.

Was there a chance of a merger between Rio Tinto and BHP Billiton in 2002?

Chance? Yes, there was a chance. I wouldn't say it was a strong likelihood.

Back in Melbourne, Brian Gilbertson mulled over what had happened in London and decided in early December that he had to resolve the governance issue. But first, he phoned his former boss Derek Keys to seek his advice. It was unequivocal: 'Just put up with it.'

Gilbertson could not. He sat down at his computer and wrote a 'back me or sack me' memorandum to the board, detailing the events leading up to the curtailment of Project 6. He saved the memorandum without sending it to give himself time to consider Derek Keys' advice.

'Headstrong' and 'unpredictable' were two of the adjectives used to describe Brian Gilbertson in the aftermath. Derek Keys, who knows him better than anybody in the business world, says, 'I won't say unpredictable, and headstrong would be the wrong term. He's a highly entrepreneurial chap and he doesn't sit on his ideas – he gets on with them.'[29]

Don Argus does not believe he is an overbearing chairman. 'I've had my day in the sun [as chief executive officer] and I'm very protective of the space a CEO needs,' he says expansively. 'If I start to overstep the mark, I always challenge myself and say, "Would I have liked that?" And if the answer is "no" then I step back out of it very quickly. Now I believe in adult conversations. If I see something is going on, I'll go and sit down with the CEO and say, "I'm sure this is the way to go." Not everyone likes adult conversations, but I don't hesitate.'[30]

Gilbertson had spent the previous 30 Christmases at Plettenberg Bay, South Africa, and he saw no reason to change that enjoyable routine. However, there had been some criticism the previous year about South African employees going to South Africa, so he and Rensche decided to spend the second half of the holiday in Tasmania. On 16 December, sitting in front of his computer, with Brigitte Bardot smiling down from the photograph on the wall behind him, Gilbertson re-read his memo and considered the consequences.

Then he pressed the 'send' button.

CHAPTER 23

Test of Strength

The fifth and final Ashes Test was about to swing England's way on 4 January 2003 when The Don went in to bat for Australia. Brian Gilbertson had arrived in Melbourne from South Africa the previous night with his wife Rensche for the showdown. When he got to 600 Bourke Street around nine o'clock that Saturday morning, Don Argus asked him to wait in his office while the board considered his memorandum.

Donald Robert Argus had been born in Bundaberg in the cane-cutting, rum-distilling region of Queensland on 1 August 1938. His father was a linotype operator who bought the *Gympie Times* and became its proprietor, and his brother became a journalist. The family moved to the bayside Brisbane suburb of Redcliffe and, as a teenager, Don attended Church of England Grammar School,[1] where he distinguished himself as a cricketer. And while the drama of the Test match unfolded at the Sydney Cricket Ground[2] (SCG), he was to be found defending his position on his own turf high above Bourke Street.

Argus was accustomed to tight situations. 'In Australia, you've an element of people who play the man,' he once explained to a British interviewer. 'It does not matter who you are, directors are maligned.'[3] Argus had followed Jerry Ellis into the BHP chair in 1999 when commodity prices had hit their lowest point of the decade and the company had recorded a loss of $1.5 billion. Environmentalists had brought dead fish to that year's annual general meeting and Argus faced 1200 angry investors voting against the re-election of the directors. 'Don had been mercilessly attacked in the Australian media over the merger,' Brian Gilbertson says. 'But he was rock solid in defence of it at the AGMs. He'd stand there for hours answering the critics.'[4]

At 9.30 am that day, BHP Billiton's Australian non-executive directors and one English director – the former head geologist at BP, David Jenkins – assembled in the boardroom on the 50th Floor of BHP Tower. None of the Billiton directors – Lord Renwick, Cor Herkströter and David Brink – was present but they would come online via the company's teleconferencing system. Argus had made careful preparations. He had circulated a rebuttal to Gilbertson's 16 December memo and he had engaged Nigel Boardman from Slaughters to steer the directors through the difficult hours ahead. Boardman had flown to Melbourne and was available for consultation, in Don Argus's words, 'about a potential separation'.[5] Described as 'enigmatic and self-contained', the tall, slim, silky Englishman had the reputation of being 'the City's best merger lawyer, bar none'.[6]

Chip Goodyear, the 44-year-old heir apparent to Gilbertson's mantle, had been holidaying with his family at a mining site, albeit a luxurious one. The ski resort of Sun Valley had been developed by the wily American diplomat Averell Harriman above the old silver-and-lead mining town of Ketchum, Idaho. Goodyear was topping up his snow tan on the runs that curved through the conifer forests down Baldy, the 3000-metre-high Bald Mountain, when he received an email from Don Argus alerting him to the storm breaking over Melbourne.

'There was no indication what it was about,' he says. 'Clearly, there was some stress and strain regarding Brian in the CEO role vis-à-vis the board.

'Brian is a very bright guy, certainly a big thinker, and he was certainly more focused on the big deal than the day-to-day operations of the business. He was dealing with quite an aggressive travel schedule that certainly would be challenging for anybody, so there was a lot of angst in the last months of 2002. Having said that, I still didn't get a sense of what would happen in early January because in Australia that's kind of a dead time. I said, "Can we do this on the phone? What are we going to be talking about?"'[7]

Don Argus gave nothing away. Goodyear headed for the airport.

With the Sword of Damocles hanging over his head, Brian Gilbertson finished some paperwork in his office and switched on the TV to watch the cricket at the SCG. Since sending his memo on 16 December, he had consulted the British law firm of Cameron McKenna about his position. Friends-at-court had always been essential to success among the higher echelons of BHP Tower, and Gilbertson knew from his own soundings that he lacked the support of sufficient board members to carry the day.

While he could count on Lord Renwick and Cor Herkströter and possibly David Brink, his two greatest allies, Derek Keys and John Jackson, had both retired from the board. Jackson's replacement, John Buchanan, former chief financial officer of BP and designated as senior independent director, was not due to join the board until 1 February.

Don Argus called for order. Recalling the event, he is typically succinct. 'It was a specially convened board meeting to establish how we were going to run the organisation going forward,' he says.[8]

In fact, the proposition before the directors was not about the Rio Tinto merger at all but rather that the chief executive should be dismissed. Considering the issues at stake, it was a fairly low-key event: there was no loss of temper, no intemperate language.

David Brink, who followed the proceedings at the end of a telephone line, says the meeting addressed the issues that had given rise to the differences between Gilbertson and the board – differences that first became evident at the November board meeting in London – in a cordial and professional manner.[9]

'I could understand perfectly well that the board didn't want to do the Rio transaction in this way,' says Lord Renwick, who was in Cape Town. 'But I thought that rather than simply dismiss the CEO, the board should say to him, "This is what we want and you now have six months to prove yourself to us." He'd only been there six months. Cor Herkströter and I took the view that rather than dismissing Brian, there should be a conversation with him about what the board expected.'[10]

When it came to a vote, Renwick's and Herkströter's were the only voices raised in opposition to Gilbertson's dismissal; David Brink sided with his chairman. 'The Aussie directors were all very much in the same position and no doubt had talked to each other beforehand, as was David Jenkins, who was the English director on the old BHP board,' Lord Renwick says.

Don Argus and another director, John Schubert, went down to Gilbertson's office and told him the directors had read his memorandum and, although the board was not unanimous, he did not have the support of the majority. Gilbertson says he had the feeling that Argus was inviting him to 'jump ship or be pushed'. He insisted on seeing the directors himself, so at 1.45 pm the trio trooped up to the boardroom, where the South African came face to face with the men who had sealed his fate.

Nobody seemed to want to add anything to the bland statement that the board did not support his position, in effect dismissing him as the company's highest-paid executive.

Don Argus then invited the chief executive to address the directors. Gilbertson had prepared a little speech. He told them that he had acted in the best interests of the shareholders and had kept the board fully informed about Project 6. They had created a great company together and he was very sorry to be leaving; he wished them well in the future and wanted them all to remember that he personally held more shares in BHP Billiton than the rest of them put together. He hoped they would continue to work for the success of the company. He was then asked to leave the room and returned to his office.

Next, the board sent a message to Chip Goodyear, who had been waiting in his office. When he reached the boardroom, he says, 'I was informed that Brian had decided to leave the company. They asked me if I would take the CEO role. I said, "If I may ask one question – I need to understand that this is not about the strategy." And they said, "No, it is not about strategy. We support the strategy that the company has." Then I said, "Well, fine, I'll do it."'[11]

Ian Fraser, vice president of group human resources, says, 'Brian had called me during the Christmas break and said he'd been called to a board meeting and he thought it might be his last meeting with the board. He was right. He saw the board and the next thing he phoned me up and said, "That's it – it's over."'[12]

Gilbertson also phoned Lord Renwick in Cape Town to seek his advice and was persuaded that resignation was the wisest course of action. 'He resigned,' Renwick says. 'He did the right thing. He was asked to resign effectively and did resign.'[13]

As a reminder of that day, Gilbertson keeps two photographs in his London office: one shows him giving one of his presentations to BHP Billiton investors, while Don Argus sits stony-faced in the background. Somewhat more metaphorically, the other shows the Politbureau sacking of Gromyko as chairman of the Soviet Presidium on 1 October 1988. Gromyko looks decidedly gloomy, while his comrades sit shell-shocked at what they have done. Gilbertson evidently sees some parallels with his own situation, although unlike Gromyko he is smiling.

The smile, however, quickly faded when the company's investor-relations officer, Robert Porter, presented him with a statement that he intended to circulate to the media. It said words to the effect of 'Now that the merger has been completed, Mr Brian Gilbertson wants to move on and do some other things'. Gilbertson took exception to the wording, describing it as nonsense and pointing out that the markets were not going to believe it. Either they should explain the true reasons for his departure or they should say something like there had been 'irreconcilable differences and therefore we have decided to part'.

After some discussion, Don Argus agreed to make the change: Gilbertson's sudden exit from BHP Billiton would be attributed to 'irreconcilable differences' – a phrase that neatly encapsulated the spirit of the rift without actually providing any details of the execution that had just taken place. Gilbertson then retired to his office, where he made some phone calls and sent emails to his 'direct reports' – the executives within the chief executive officer's orbit – about his departure. He thanked them for their efforts and wished them well.

Dave Munro, who had taken up sailing the previous year, was on the dockside in Cape Town about to step aboard the yacht *Indaba*[14] for the annual Cape Town to Rio de Janeiro race when his mobile phone rang. 'I got a call from Brian Gilbertson at eight o'clock in the morning telling me about the board meeting and what had happened,' he says. 'Then Chip Goodyear rang to get my reaction and ask me where did I stand. It was quite bizarre standing there with everybody rushing around getting our boat ready. I offered to step off the boat and come and help bail things out. Chip and I were both based in London, and I got on very well with him. I like Chip a great deal, and he was feeling quite exposed at that stage. He said it wasn't necessary and I said I'd call him when I got to Rio. We were at sea for 28 days and I had no further contact with the office – we had an SSB radio and that was it.'[15]

Gilbertson had also spoken to Chip Goodyear about his appointment and discussed a couple of matters pertaining to the handover. He then took his wife to the movies.

'Boy, then the alarm bells went off,' Goodyear says. 'It

was basically 48 hours or more with zero sleep because I had to communicate with all the senior management team that Brian had moved on and I was going to take over, which was going to be a challenge with a number of the people that were there.

'The Billiton people could have thrown up their hands and said, "Our guy's gone and this is not what we want to do." But they took a very professional approach to it and everybody put their shoulder to the grindstone.'[16]

The Gilbertsons were due to go down to Tasmania the next day – Sunday, 5 January – but postponed the trip for 24 hours because Gilbertson still had to submit his letter of resignation and the final version of the press release had to be formalised. He was also anxious that his sudden exit from Melbourne should not be construed as running away.

BHP Billiton's statement, released in Australia early Monday morning (Sunday evening in London), said that Gilbertson had left the company 'due to irreconcilable differences with the boards' of the Australian and British arms of the company. 'In order to resolve this situation, and in the best interests of the company and its shareholders, Mr Gilbertson decided to resign,' it said.[17] Gilbertson was quoted as saying, 'During my time at BHP Billiton, it was a privilege to lead an experienced and talented management team as we created the leading player in our industry. I have every confidence in the future success of the group under Chip Goodyear's leadership.'[18]

Don Argus said Chip Goodyear had the full support of the board in continuing the strategy that the group had announced in 2002. 'During his time at BHP Billiton, Mr Goodyear has shown real leadership skills, financial acumen and a great ability to get things done,' Argus said. 'He is widely respected throughout the company and is highly regarded by the investment community.'[19] Both sides agreed to say nothing further to reporters.

On that Monday morning, news of Gilbertson's departure hit BHP Billiton stock like a bombshell. In the first two minutes of trading, it fell more than three per cent and finished the day four per cent down. Astonishment gripped trading floors across the country as analysts sought to understand the significance of the crisis that had so unexpectedly enveloped BHP Billiton just six months into Gilbertson's tenure.

'I was actually sorry to see Brian go – I liked his style and the way he thought about the metals industry,' Brad Mills says. 'I was on the other end of a phone call saying, "Brian's gone and Chip Goodyear is the new chief executive." That was the first time I realised there was a problem. When Chip became chief executive, I was surprised. He wouldn't have been my first choice. I wasn't completely convinced that Chip was the right guy.'[20]

The ABC, after interviewing the usual analysts, decided that Gilbertson was 'arrogant' and 'difficult'. 'Apparently after ten years with no boss,' Zoe Daniel said on *The 7.30 Report*, 'the independently minded Brian Gilbertson just couldn't adjust to the rigorous board process applied to the merged company.'[21]

The only director to voice an opinion to the media was his fellow South African, David Brink. 'Obviously, something such as a chief executive's resignation is regrettable and carries a measure of surprise,' he said.[22]

In the absence of an alternative view, the public were led to believe that Gilbertson had meekly resigned from the biggest job in Australian mining, a notion that made nonsense of his gritty character and enthusiastic presentations about the company's glowing future over the previous months. The true nature of the events at BHP Tower on 4 January remained clouded in rumour and conjecture.

John Curry of the Australian Shareholders Association upbraided BHP Billiton for simply making a bald statement that one chief executive had gone and another had taken over. 'It's not really good enough to say that there are irreconcilable differences,' he said. 'Those differences should have been explained to some extent.'[23]

Throughout Monday, BHP Tower was under siege as

the management was put under increasing pressure by the Australian Securities and Investments Commission, the stock-exchange watchdog agency, to explain in greater detail why Gilbertson had resigned. The company was forced to issue a further statement to reassure the market that his departure was 'not related to any concerns by the board about the financial performance of the group'. The statement added, 'Mr Gilbertson's resignation will not result in any change in the company's strategy nor in initiatives previously announced.' But, despite the clarification, the inveterate intriguers of the bourse continued to speculate as to why the South African had stepped down so abruptly.[24]

Under these circumstances, it was not surprising that the nationalist element should surface. *The Economist* sagely noted:

> Australians and South Africans love to scrap. South Africa's cricket team was officially named the world's best this week, to great fury in Australia, whose team had just suffered an embarrassing loss to England. Rugby matches, surfing competitions and the world barbecue (or *braai*) championships are always hot-headed affairs. South African newspapers keenly plot the Ozzie dollar against the rand. Each January, statisticians grimly compare Christmas road-death rates in the two countries. But nothing gets southern-hemisphere blood boiling more than gold, diamonds and other minerals.[25]

The *Financial Times* pointed to Brian Gilbertson's 'insatiable appetite for deals and his autocratic management style' as the reasons for his departure. One analyst told the newspaper, 'Brian has an ego the size of a planet. He is very headstrong and used to getting his own way rather than living under the shadow of a strong board and chairman.' Tensions were understood to have been simmering for weeks between Argus and Gilbertson because the latter was keen to make large acquisitions while other directors, led by Argus, wanted to concentrate on synergy savings and the group's strong list of projects.[26]

Meanwhile, the press had tracked down Gilbertson and his wife on their bush-walking safari in Tasmania. As they strolled into one of the hotels on their itinerary, the check-in clerk informed him, 'Mr Gilbertson, there's a journalist waiting – do you want to see him?' Gilbertson knew it was futile to hide but, as agreed, he declined to make any comment. Instead, he posed for a photographer. The snapshot shows him sitting on a boulder on a sandy Tasmanian beach. As a man who once said he had spent a lifetime in search of the perfect beach, his broad smile seemed to indicate that he might have found it.

Don Argus, however, appeared on TV and made several comments that upset Gilbertson's Tasmanian idyll. He rang his former colleague and found himself talking to his voicemail, so he left a message to the effect of 'If this is the way you want to play it, that's fine with me. I'll give similar interviews, but otherwise I want silence.'

'They just shut up shop completely,' Gilbertson says. 'They didn't say anything further.'[27]

By now, however, the newshounds had picked up the scent of blood and were following the trail. Reuters quoted 'a source close to the company' as saying that Gilbertson had quit after proposing a major international transaction that could have meant a change in the chairmanship. Though details of the proposed deal, dubbed Project 6, were still shrouded in secrecy, the source said it had been under discussion internally for several months and chairman Don Argus had finally moved against Brian Gilbertson after it became clear the chairmanship was at stake. 'A lot of people in the company think Argus should explain the extent to which Project 6 and in particular his potential removal from the chairmanship really lay behind his move against Gilbertson,' the source said.[28]

The source further revealed that the proposal was for a 'very significant, single transaction' that had been analysed by Chip Goodyear and was due to go to the board in February. John Buchanan, the new, British-based, non-executive director, was due to take his seat at that board meeting, perhaps giving

Gilbertson another ally on the BHP-dominated board. 'The meeting on Saturday was a stitch-up,' the source said. 'Argus had already prepared the groundwork, even flying in one of the top labour lawyers from the UK before the meeting.'[29]

There was no let-up the following day when Adele Ferguson let rip in *Business Review Weekly*, accusing Don Argus of putting his reputation on the line and betting the future of the company by making 'a personal crusade' out of his differences with Brian Gilbertson. She wrote:

> This is the second chief executive that Argus has seen off in less than three years. Since BHP Billiton announced the shock departure of Gilbertson on 6 January, shareholders have seen more than $2 billion wiped from its market capitalisation. The losses are mounting because the company has failed to adequately explain why Gilbertson lost the backing of the board. The official explanation – 'irreconcilable differences' – can mean anything. As long as investors are assessing whether the abrupt change of chief executive indicates further underlying management problems, the short-term negative sentiment will continue to hang over the shares.[30]

However, Mike Salamon, who was appointed to the BHPB board as an executive director the following month, says, 'I got on very well with Don Argus. He understood the difference between the CEO and the chairman. There's a quaint concept in Australia that the boards run businesses, which is total crap. They really don't. A lot of directors have very little idea of what actually goes on in the company. Don thoroughly, because he'd been a CEO – not in the mining industry but in a bank – understood that very well: that as a chairman or a director you should try to work out what your real role is and make sure you do that very well. Don't try to get into the game or try to second-guess management.

'The fascinating thing which again demonstrates just how important boards and CEOs are, or are not, is that the business was going gangbusters all the way through that, despite what was going on, with Paul going, then Brian going, then Chip coming. What it demonstrates is that the board and the CEO in such a big company are irrelevant in the short term. It's like a battleship: the big decisions turn the battleship but it takes miles for that to happen. In big companies, you measure it in years not months or quarters. So all of that was going on and the business kept on doing what it was supposed to do.'[31]

Salamon's appointment as BHP Billiton's senior minerals executive was made as the company presented a relatively optimistic outlook for the rest of the year and reported a solid set of interim results. 'The appointment of Mike will strengthen the depth and breadth of operational experience on the BHP Billiton board,' Don Argus said in a statement, allaying fears that Billiton could become under-represented following Gilbertson's departure. 'He has wide international business experience and is well known to the United Kingdom and South African investment community.'

Two other former Billiton executives, Dave Munro and Chris Pointon, along with Marcus Randolph, formerly of Rio Tinto, were also appointed to Chip Goodyear's executive committee. Munro succeeded Goodyear as chief development officer responsible for group strategy, mergers and acquisitions and business evaluation; Chris Pointon became president of stainless-steel materials, while Marcus Randolph took over as president of diamonds and specialty products.[32]

The ABC's *Inside Business* program quoted Don Argus as suggesting 'the board had concerns Mr Gilbertson, who was used to having sole control over Billiton, was having trouble adjusting to Australian corporate-governance requirements'.[33] However, the biggest issue quickly became the size of Gilbertson's payout, which was rumoured to be anything up to US$25 million. After months of legal wrangling, Gilbertson received US$8.5 million for the six-and-a-bit months he worked as chief executive, $6.7 million of which was as a termination payment.

On 21 May, Don Argus announced, 'We have resolved this

matter on the terms specified in our contract with Mr Gilbertson. The delay in settling the matter reflected differences between us about the contract.' Despite his entitlement to options on more than 760,110 shares at the time of his departure in January, Gilbertson agreed to retain rights to a maximum of 228,685 shares. Argus was also keen to emphasise that Gilbertson's pension fund – a touch under $15 million – was unrelated to the termination; rather, it reflected his 32 years with Gencor, Billiton and BHP Billiton. Gilbertson had been on a three-year contract, which BHP could terminate by giving 24 months' notice; that right, however, only applied after the expiry of the first year.

Even so, the payout attracted bitter criticism from the Labor opposition in federal parliament, who saw it as a clear-cut case of corporate greed. 'It is just unacceptable,' Shadow Minister for Financial Services Stephen Conroy told the parliament. 'The board is out of control and shareholders are being played for mugs.' Prime Minister John Howard, a friend of Don Argus's, was provoked into instructing the boards of Australian companies to put their houses in order. 'You want to keep the capitalist system free of too much government regulation, well you've got to deliver,' he told them in a radio broadcast, without actually naming BHP Billiton. 'And one thing you've got to do is stop entering into absurdly generous payout arrangements in the first place.'

Gilbertson pronounced himself relieved that the issue had been settled but said the experience had made him reluctant to take another post as chief executive. 'I don't think anyone particularly enjoys seeing their private affairs splashed across the newspapers,' he said. 'I've been astonished at the amount of interest that's been shown in the settlement.'[34] He was back in harness as a consultant advising the London-listed platinum group Lonmin on its black-empowerment obligations in South Africa.

As though to symbolise the beginning of a new era, BHP Billiton moved from BHP Tower to its present address in the

QV building at 180 Lonsdale Street in September 2003. The board was careful to inform its investors that Chip Goodyear would receive an annual-remuneration package of up to US$6 million, consisting of a base salary of $1.9 million, another $1 million in lieu of superannuation contributions and bonuses of up to $3 million. Goodyear brought his children to a company briefing to demonstrate to them that their father did more at work than watch television.[35]

Goodyear, who had become known to analysts for his economical, easy-going style and his ability to preach prudence even in the boom times, got off to a flying start by unveiling a record net profit of US$1.879 billion for the year to the end of June 2003, up 18.9 per cent over 2002 – a profit that owed a considerable amount to his predecessor. The result was even more laudable in that it had been achieved despite a number of major economic shocks and significant price volatility, with oil prices fluctuating from $18 to more than $30 per barrel and copper swinging from a low of 58 cents per pound to a high of 80 cents.

In his address to shareholders in the 2003 annual report, Don Argus declined to 'play the man' – in fact, Gilbertson was lucky to get a mention at all. 'During the year, Chip Goodyear succeeded Brian Gilbertson as CEO of the Group,' Argus wrote. 'Chip has settled into the position extremely well and, with an outstanding executive team and first-class organisation, is continuing the strategic direction outlined to the market in April 2002.' And that was it: no recognition that the 'strategic direction' had been largely Gilbertson's creation, as had been BHP Billiton itself.

The snub did not go unnoticed in Johannesburg. 'Despite their well-publicised differences of opinion, a word or two of thanks from Argus might have helped show the man possesses statesman-like qualities required of someone in a position of such great trust,' journalist Alec Hogg commented. 'Instead, his enemies have been given further ammunition to brand him as the small-minded and parochial mediocrity they suggested he was after the battle with Gilbertson.'[36]

Perhaps realising he had made a strategic error, Argus made amends at the annual general meeting on 24 October. 'While it is not my practice to dwell on the past,' he said, 'it is fitting that I pay tribute to Paul Anderson and Brian Gilbertson, who shared the vision for the merger of BHP and Billiton, and to whom we can attribute the outstanding success of the integration process.'

The company's operational performances had indeed been going gangbusters through all of these internecine battles – a fact that was confirmed when Chip Goodyear replaced Argus at the microphone to list the performances of each of the company's seven CSGs. The full scope – and strength – of BHP Billiton's assets, so carefully compiled by exploration, merger and acquisition in the four corners of the globe and of which he and his executive team were but custodians, then became apparent. The following is a summary of Goodyear's report on the seven groups:

Petroleum (Philip Aiken): Oil and gas – an area that made BHP Billiton unique among the big miners – had provided around a third of BHP Billiton's profits. This was mainly due to higher average prices, even though production had declined by nine per cent to 122 million barrels of oil equivalent from Bass Strait, the North-West Shelf, Liverpool Bay, Laminaria/Corallina, Typhoon/Boris, Griffin, Bruce/Keith, the Americas and Zamzama. The group had had excellent exploration successes and had sanctioned two major projects during the year at Atlantis in the Gulf of Mexico and Angostura off the coast of Trinidad. The benefits of deep-water exploration would show through in higher production from the end of 2004 with the commencement of the Mad Dog field in the Gulf of Mexico and Angostura.

Aluminium (Mike Salamon): This group had produced a profit of US$581 million, up 18 per cent. It owned the world-class alumina refinery at Worsley in Western Australia, and two large smelters in southern Africa: Mozal and Hillside. The Mozal smelter in Mozambique had been expanded seven months ahead of schedule to produce an additional 250,000 tonnes per year, and a 150,000-tonne expansion was planned for Hillside.

Base metals (Brad Mills): Profits up by 50 per cent, through higher prices for copper and increased production from Escondida and a full year of operations from Antamina, Peru. The Tintaya operations would start up again shortly and shipments of concentrate would reach the market early next year. The 200,000-tonne Spence copper project in Chile would also go into production.

Carbon steel materials (Robert Kirkby): Iron ore from Mt Newman, Yandi, Mt Goldsworthy, Jimblebar and Samarco (Brazil), coking coal from the Bowen Basin and the Illawarra and manganese from Samancor made the sector the second-largest contributor of the year. Despite record iron-ore production, profits were slightly down as a result of the lower prices and the impact of the strong Australian dollar and South African rand on costs.

Diamonds and specialty products (Marcus Randolph): This group included the EKATI diamond mine in Canada, mineral sands in South Africa and the Integris Metals business in the United States. Diamond production was up and costs down.

Energy coal (Mike Oppenheimer): Ingwe, New Mexico, Hunter Valley and Carrejon (Colombia) had experienced a very tough year owing to the so-called 'perfect storm' conditions of lower coal prices, a strong rand and high inflation in South Africa. Together with the loss of US$124 million of profit the previous year from the PT Arutmin operations in Indonesia, profits had slumped 65 per cent lower than the previous year at US$190 million.

Stainless-steel materials (Chris Pointon): Nickel (Cerro Matosa and QNI Yabulu) and chrome (Samancor) had a complete turnaround, with profit up from US$3 million to US$150 million. Plans for the Ravensthorpe/Yabulu nickel project, capable of producing 45,000 tonnes per year, were due to be approved in the first half of 2004. Once completed,

BHP Billiton would be the third-largest nickel producer in the world.

Not everyone, however, was singing the new chief executive's praises. 'Chip and I didn't always see eye to eye on certain issues,' says Brad Mills, who had already clashed with him in Brian Gilbertson's time over the wisdom of cutting back copper production to avoid swamping the market with the metal and to foster a higher price – a tactic that had contributed to a 50 per cent increase in the copper group's profit. 'I tend to be more aggressive and bolder on strategic issues than Chip. Chip is a little more finance-oriented, a little bit more conservative perhaps, so sometimes we crossed swords on certain key issues. I had to report to Chip and found it difficult. There was huge pressure on costs in the copper business against the price environment, which was extremely difficult to operate in.'[37]

The fall in copper prices to a 14-month low in November 2001 had brought matters to a head. In order to end the cyclical, boom-to-bust pattern of the past, Brad Mills had argued that copper output should be curtailed at Escondida and the company's other copper mines. 'We can't just keep pumping copper out into this marketplace,' he said. 'I don't care if we're the world's top producer: 58 cents a pound! We're making no money. There's no point in making excess amounts of copper – it's in our interests to curtail production.'[38]

Brian Gilbertson grasped the point but Chip Goodyear was opposed to such drastic action. The company, however, announced a significant cut in output. 'It was done without disrupting the industry or dismissing staff, but simply by moving the machines to banks where you could extract ore but of lower grade,' Gilbertson says. 'The impact of that decision was astonishing in the speed at which it hit the market. I actually plotted the graph day by day of what the price of copper was doing, and in the course of the next week to ten days the price went from about 58 cents to the high 60s, dropped back a bit from there and went back up again when some of our competitors announced similar actions.'[39]

Brian Gilbertson finally broke his silence in public about life in Australia and his erstwhile employer in an interview with a reporter from South Africa's *Business Report* on 22 October 2004 – but remained tight-lipped about the events that had catapulted him out of the chief executive's chair. He had found Australians very friendly, he said, and Melbourne's restaurants were excellent; he and his wife had been working their way through a long list of them. 'Clearly, the company has been a great success,' he added. 'The deal that Paul Anderson and I delivered was a great deal. Everyone benefited from it. It's the greatest company the world has ever seen. In our industry, it really is! Go and look at their results.'[40]

CHAPTER 24

Digging Deeper

Staying true to BHP's Nietzschean *Strength through diversity* motto, Chip Goodyear moved smoothly to cement in place the company strategy he had developed with Gilbertson and the management team. He worked closely and amicably with Don Argus and the board. 'Chip realised the value of the capital that he was working with,' Don Argus says. 'He allocated it wisely; he had good capital discipline and he understood the company, which was good from a financial perspective. Chip would be the first one to say that his skills in operations were a bit limited, but he grew very quickly and he grew into a quality CEO.'[1]

As his enthusiastic publicity team would have it, Goodyear cut an impressive figure as the epitome of a robust, young chief executive. He cycled to work and shared the lift with employees in his biking shorts. He was a family man who enjoyed travelling abroad whenever possible with his wife and two children, both of whom were encouraged to study Japanese and Mandarin. His own daily regime was a model of self-discipline. Rising at 5 am, he would work out, then watch the financial news on CNN. After a quick breakfast of bagels – 'If you gave me my choice, I'd eat a stack of pancakes' – he would be at his desk by 7 am.

He hit the phones first and then did his emails before checking his diary with his PA. 'People try to schedule meetings with me, but I try to avoid scheduled meetings,' he said. 'I like to do management by walking around, getting down to the people who are actually doing the work.'[2]

With offices round the world in different time zones, there was always someone, somewhere trying to get hold of him – staff, customers, investors and bankers – but he tried to get home by 7.30 pm to put his children to bed. He then hit the phones again before retiring at 11 pm. He didn't get enough sleep. 'But you don't want to get used to sleep,' he said. 'If you do, it's a hard habit to break.'[3]

However, beneath Goodyear's clean-cut Ivy League image, the company was convulsing as it struggled to transform itself from within. And Goodyear's qualities would be tested to the limit. 'Early on in the CEO role, one of the executives said to me, "What's your vision for this company?"' he recalls. 'I thought about it for a while and I said, "I see an entity that creates a return on capital that is the highest of all our industry peers," and the guy said to me, "That's wonderful. What are you going to tell the other 99.9 per cent of the people who work here?"' It brought him up short. Suddenly, he realised that he had not been trained for the role. 'When you get to be CEO, you've got to put away what you know on most skill sets – somebody else has to do that.'[4]

'He found people management tough early, as most CEOs do,' Don Argus says, 'but he was able to get around that and he developed a rally call and people started to follow him very well. Paul tried to set up an open-door culture and tried to get people to engage, and Chip followed that, and I thought that was a good sign of a potential leader of the future.'[5]

He was fortunate to have Mike Salamon, who, according to Lord Renwick, was 'the best operations guy in this business. Mike was very complementary to Chip Goodyear because Chip has a first-class financial brain and risk-evaluation but is not the guy who's going to fix problems on No. 6 shaft,' he says. 'Mike is a real hard-hat character who goes to the mine and sees what's wrong with it and fixes it. He's a legendary figure in the industry as a hands-on manager.'[6]

However, there were casualties along the way. After three years in Houston grappling with the vagaries of the copper industry, Brad Mills handed in his resignation in February 2004 to become chief executive officer at platinum miner Lonmin. 'I don't think Chip was ever comfortable with me and I don't think I was ever comfortable with Chip,' he says. 'So when the Lonmin opportunity came along, I felt I had done everything for BHP and BHP Copper. With Brian leaving and Chip sitting there in the chief executive role, I didn't think I had a career path in BHP any more, so it was an easy decision.'[7]

In March 2004, Goodyear simplified the company's structure yet again by reorganising operations into three broad areas: non-ferrous materials, carbon steel materials and energy. The diamonds and specialty-products sector was handed over to the company's new rising star, chief marketing officer Marius Kloppers.[8]

Then, at midnight on 20 May, an explosion ripped through the Boodarie HBI plant at Port Hedland while a group of maintenance workers were cleaning a reactor. The gas flare-up turned the reactor into an inferno and four men were severely burned. The Royal Flying Doctor Service mobilised four aircraft to evacuate the injured to Royal Perth Hospital, where one of them, James Wadley, died the following day.

The West Australian Government demanded an urgent meeting with BHP Billiton to discuss safety issues, while the Australian Workers Union called for a wide-ranging audit of the plant. BHP Billiton suspended its HBI operations – again – and replied that it would have to consider closing them down permanently.

It was a serious blow to both the company's safety record and its public image. Indeed, for much of his five years at the helm Goodyear would be confronted with a series of 'perception' issues – many of them hangovers from the 1990s – and the growing spectre of climate change. This struck home in 2005 when news broke that BHP Billiton had participated in the biggest international kickback scandal in the country's history. Until then, the activities of Norman Davidson Kelly in the BHP Petroleum division had been a closely guarded company secret. Now, Australians were shaking their heads in disbelief. It was bad enough that a pillar of the agricultural establishment, the AWB, could have orchestrated a $290 million undercover deal with Saddam Hussein's egregious regime; the involvement of The Big Australian seemed almost incredible.

The federal opposition quickly turned the imbroglio into a political *cause célèbre*.[9] Prime Minister John Howard responded with a commission of inquiry with closely defined terms of reference, headed by Terence Rhoderick Hudson Cole QC. Cole had been at the University of Sydney Law School at the same time as Howard in 1961 and had previously presided over a royal commission into the building industry for the prime minister. Now, he would investigate allegations that the AWB paid massive 'trucking fees' on its wheat shipments that found their way to Saddam's 'loathsome'[10] regime.

Goodyear said, 'This is never a pleasant situation for any company and it's certainly not for this one,' and announced that BHP Billiton would launch its own internal inquiry. 'You can't necessarily judge the organisation on the impact or the event that happened, but you can judge the organisation on how it reacts to those things.'[11]

When Commissioner Cole reported on 24 November 2006, press coverage concentrated overwhelmingly on the findings against the AWB figures most deeply entwined in the deception. Cole found that 11 AWB executives may have broken Australian law. He made no adverse findings against BHP Billiton. However, the commissioner found that NDK – who refused to appear at the commission – and Charles Eric Stott – who worked for the AWB before and after his time with BHP – 'may have broken Australian laws'. 'On the evidence before me,' Cole concluded, 'Mr Davidson

Kelly is a thoroughly disreputable man with no commercial morality.'

Astonishingly, when Goodyear released the internal review into the affair in November 2006, it revealed that BHPP 'is currently a party to two cooperation arrangements, which include [Davidson Kelly's company] Tigris, in relation to Iraq'. However, it said, BHP Billiton was 'reviewing both arrangements in the light of the findings of Commissioner Cole'.

The internal review found that John Prescott 'had made a prudent and sensible decision on how to proceed' with the wheat shipment. Moreover, 'no individual acted in breach of his or her duties to BHPP in connection with the making of the 1996 wheat shipment by breaching a particular policy, or by breaching standards of business conduct'. Nevertheless, in the interim BHP Billiton had made 'a considerable number of enhancements to its practices and processes that it believes better protect the company from the risk of this kind of reputational damage'. These included the establishment of a global-ethics panel and a forum for corporate responsibility.

In January 2004, Tom Harley had been promoted to BHP Billiton's president of corporate development. He was also chairman of the Australian Heritage Council and chairman of the Menzies Research Centre, the Liberal Party think tank. In November 2008, he left BHP Billiton to take up an appointment with Dow Chemicals in Melbourne as senior adviser to the Executive Leadership Committee. He retained his positions with the Heritage Council and the Menzies Centre.

Then, on 19 December 2007, the Australian Securities and Investments Commission (ASIC) launched civil penalty proceedings in the Supreme Court of Victoria against Charles Stott and five other directors and executives of AWB. ASIC chairman Tony D'Aloisio said, 'We have commenced these actions as we believe that the conduct of the directors and officers in these circumstances fell short of what the law requires in relation to the management and supervision of corporations.' In July 2008, an ASIC spokesperson said that Norman Davidson Kelly was 'not party to any ASIC proceeding at this time'.[12]

Meanwhile, BHP Billiton was on the verge of securing a $500 million contract to develop – with Shell – the prized Halfaya oilfield, one of the cooperation agreements the company had retained with Tigris in 2006. However, Goodyear said that in 2007 BHP Billiton and Shell had 'bought out' Norman Davidson Kelly. 'There's a clause in the agreement that said if anybody was doing something illegal, we could buy them out,' he says. 'We had to go through a process to do that and there were time periods to do it.' He could not remember how much they paid him. 'It would have been a pretty nominal amount of money. I don't know that we paid him anything.'[13]

Paradoxically, while BHP's wheat-for-oil efforts had collapsed with the downfall of the Saddam Hussein regime, Australia's participation in the so-called Coalition of the Willing at the behest of the Liberal Party's John Howard had helped secure the merged company's selection to the shortlist of oil developers by Saddam's American-backed successor. BHP's investment in the Liberal Party – a constant of its political modus vivendi – had paid off once again.

It was no coincidence that one of the Baghdad buildings to survive America's 'shock and awe' bombing raids virtually intact was the ministry of oil. American troops who liberated the capital in March 2003 also had orders to preserve the ministry's storehouse of blueprints of the country's oilfields and contracts relating to oil deals with companies from France, Russia and China.

Once Iraqi oil started flowing at full capacity, it would be quick and extremely cheap to extract. Current proven reserves are 115 billion barrels, but the oil multinationals knew that further exploration would lead to huge additional discoveries. For, despite Iraq's long history as an oil producer, only 2300 wells (for both exploration and production) had ever been drilled there (compared with one million in Texas). And only 21 of the 80 known oilfields had ever been developed.

Furthermore, 70 per cent of current Iraqi production derived from just three old fields: Kirkuk, discovered in 1927, and North and South Rumaila, discovered in 1951 and 1962 respectively. Western oil companies were gambling that Iraq had far larger oil reserves than documented so far, possibly an extra 200 billion barrels.

J. Michael Yeager, a Texas-born former United States Marine who became chief executive of BHP Billiton Petroleum in 2006, had the perfect background to tackle the Halfaya challenge in partnership with Shell. After five years in the Marines, Yeager joined Mobil (where he met John O'Connor) and then, after its merger with Exxon, he'd worked for ExxonMobil on the upstream side. 'I've never done anything except the drilling, the production, the engineering, the operations,' he says. 'I did catch BHP Billiton where we were in the midst of executing major new projects. Quite clearly, we were changing from a little, sleepy non-operating company to one where we operate really big projects around the world – that's my speciality and that's what I've tried to bring to this business.'[14]

These projects include the large Scarborough gasfield and the Griffin oilfield off the coast of Western Australia, and the Neptune and Shenzi oilfields in the Gulf of Mexico. BHP had first gone into partnership with Shell in the North-West Shelf, where natural gas is brought onshore, liquefied and then shipped to markets throughout South East Asia. The two companies then joined forces to pursue the Halfaya objective in Iraq. 'We've got a split [in Iraq] where it's 60 per cent Shell and 40 per cent ourselves, and we would work things jointly,' Yeager says. 'We're waiting for the Iraqis to establish the rule of law so that if we invest in certain ways then we will be remunerated. So, right now, the hydrocarbon laws and the entire framework for the oil-and-gas business are being reworked as a result of the new government.

'The other major obstacle is the security on the ground. [When that] is good enough, we can send people in and feel confident they'll be safe. We view Iraq as a substantial opportunity but one that quite clearly could be a number of years away, depending on how things go. We visit with the Iraqis all the time and we continue to show our interest, but obviously we're waiting for the rules to get clarified and the security to get better.'[15]

Shell is an enthusiastic partner in the project. Chief executive Jeroen van der Veer told his annual general meeting in The Hague in May 2008, 'We are keen to work in Iraq and I fail to see what's wrong with that.' Linda Cook, the Shell director in charge of gas and power, added that Iraq was a major resource holder – the third biggest in the world. 'We understand the concerns,' she said, 'and we are looking for the opportunity to bring technology to the Iraqi oil industry. But we will only do that if it is in line with Iraqi law and safe for our employees.'[16]

'There's never any shame in saying that you're keen to get access to a resource,' Marius Kloppers says with reference to his participation in Iraq. 'I'd be keen to get access to the platinum resources in Zimbabwe. However, just not under the current set of circumstances. So I wonder if Jeroen doesn't talk about the prospectivity of the resource as a whole, but I'm absolutely sure that a company like Shell would like to do that in the proper way.'[17]

Meanwhile, on 19 January 2007 at 3.47 pm, the Australian Associated Press news agency reported from Port Moresby: 'Mining giant BHP Billiton and the operators of the Ok Tedi copper mine in Papua New Guinea are being sued for civil damages exceeding $US4 billion ($5 billion) by villagers on the Ok Tedi River.' Less than a minute later, it was on the computer screens at BHP Billiton's Melbourne headquarters, sending a tremor of anxiety through the building. 'The nightmare was back,' one company insider said. 'No one mentions Ok Tedi, not even as a joke.'[18]

The sensitivity is understandable. By now, the gold-and-copper mine in Papua New Guinea's remote Western Province abutting the border with Indonesian Papua – and which Paul

Anderson had cut loose – had cost BHP Billiton billions in lost revenue. More importantly perhaps, it had savaged the company's international environmental reputation. The report continued:

> PNG lawyer Carmellus Narokobi lodged the lawsuit in the National Court in Port Moresby on behalf of 13,000 villagers. They are seeking compensation for the destruction of their traditional lands along 38 kilometres of the river.
>
> 'The Ningerum people have suffered from tonnes and tonnes of arsenic, copper, zinc and other heavy metals dumped into this once pristine habitat where they had lived since time immemorial,' Narokobi said. 'Experts predicted it would take 300 years to clean up the toxic contamination,' he said.
>
> Narokobi represents six Ningerum clans who are not signatory to the Community Mine Continuation Agreement (CMCA) between landowners and Ok Tedi Mining Limited (OTML) . . .

OTML communications manager Jane Mills responded the next day that the lawsuit was 'old news' and 'without merit'. Tim Offor, the public-relations operative hired by BHP in 1999 to handle the OTML disaster, was publicly dismissive. The Ningerum had strange beliefs about spirits beneath the mine, he said. Moreover, 'BHP is very well insulated from any legal action.'[19]

The 'insulation' comes in the form of the CMCAs, which, in theory at least, ensure that those who signed them would not seek further compensation. However, in 2005, four years after the CMCAs were issued, a respected anthropologist, Nancy Sullivan, conducted a survey of the villagers of the region whose leaders had signed on their behalf. Commissioned by the Mineral Policy Institute in Sydney – an agency of Friends of the Earth – the survey's results were 'resoundingly pessimistic'.[20]

'We found that very few communities know any of the particulars of these CMCAs, whether as a result of OTML or their own leaders' negligence,' she said. 'Very few benefits have been realised from these agreements as yet and villagers are cynical about the prospect of much coming in the future.' She said an enormous amount of money and effort had been spent in the area. It had created an environmental disaster of overwhelming proportions, 'like the aftermath of a famine or a tsunami'. Millions more would need to be spent on rehabilitation before genuine development could begin.

A more recent review by an independent scientist, Dr Alan Tingay, in September 2006 was equally devastating. Much of it was based on research carried out by BHP and OTML over the past 20 years. In addition, he travelled to the region and visited more than 35 villages in the Ok Tedi and Fly rivers. 'Each year, the Ok Tedi mine puts 100 million tonnes of waste into the Ok Tedi and Fly River systems,' he said. 'Total waste disposed during the life of the mine will be more than 1.7 billion tonnes. About 70 million tonnes of the waste is carried down the river each year as suspended sediment to the estuary and the sea. This includes all of the tailings discharge.

'On the way, large amounts of this waste are deposited on the bed of the river system, up tributaries, into lakes and on to the floodplains. A large amount of the waste moves down the river on the river bed. A dredge on the Ok Tedi River at Bige [about 160 kilometres from the mine] has removed much of the bed load since 1998 and this is deposited on the river banks in large stockpiles. The dredge does not catch the suspended sediments.

'The bed load that was there before the dredge is moving down the Fly River at 8 km each year. This load is now in the central section of the Middle Fly; the amount on the bed is increasing due to deposits from the suspended sediments. The river bed in the upper-middle Fly has been raised by up to four metres by this process; the central-middle Fly is now being affected.

'The build-up on the bed of the upper-middle Fly will increase for at least the next 50 years. The build-up in the lower-middle Fly will take longer but will last for several hundred years.'[21]

The report paints a sad picture of the effects on flora and fauna, a summary of which is as follows:

- The final area affected by forest dieback in the Ok Tedi and Middle Fly may be as much as 3000 square kilometres. This is the entire forest area on lowland areas of the floodplain.
- Most of the middle Fly floodplains will be converted to swamplands.
- The number of fish species in the entire system has declined by 30 per cent; fish populations have declined by 95 per cent in the Ok Tedi, 85 per cent in the upper-middle Fly and 60 per cent in the lower-middle Fly.
- Over a million tonnes of copper has been discharged into the river system during the life of the mine. The CSIRO has suggested that the bio-available copper at present levels may impact 50 per cent to 80 per cent of all aquatic species in the long term.

Moreover, while the open-cut mine was due to be closed in 2010, this was later amended by the OTML board to 2013. Now, however, there are plans to continue deep underground mining thereafter.

By 2006, the mine was reporting an annual profit of K5 billion. The town of Tabubil, where the mine is headquartered, had a population of 25,000 with medical and other community services; downstream, the town of Kiunga had flourished as a small regional centre. OTML had created a services arm, the Ok Tedi Development Foundation, providing village health care to remote communities, assistance to small business and special projects for women.

The breach of contract case against BHP Billiton had dragged on until 2004, when it was settled out of court. Soon afterwards, OTML financed a major negotiation with the 50,000 residents of the 157 villages in the area, mediated through an American non-governmental organisation (NGO), the Keystone Center. After 18 months and more than 500 separate meetings, delegates from the nine affected regions along the river signed a Memorandum of Agreement that would eventually provide K1.1 billion (now worth approximately US$350 million) in cash compensation, projects and services.

The funds would come from OTML, the Papua New Guinea Sustainable Development Program and the Papua New Guinean Government. In the final report, the mediators said, 'We end our work with one worry: that the final agreement may not prove supple enough to respond to the wide-ranging needs and interests identified by the community leaders.'

Throughout the period, however, OTML had continued to dump all its tailings into the Ok Tedi and Fly river systems. In 2006, OTML designed and put aside US$150 million to build a 'special facility' to ameliorate the tailings problem – a pipeline from the mine carrying sulphur extracted from the tailings to the dredging area about 160 kilometres downstream near Bige, where it would be stockpiled. The project would begin commissioning in July 2008. Managing director Alan Breen says, 'The flotation plant is designed to remove sulphur from tailings in the form of pyrite concentrates (PCon), allowing the non-acid-forming tailings (NAF) to be used as cover for dumps at Bige.'[22] However, in December 2008 the ABC's *7.30 Report* revealed that the dredge at Bige had been out of operation for the previous 18 months. Alan Breen said dredging had now resumed and a second unit would come on line in 2009.

Dr Tingay says, 'The extracted wastes will be placed in dredged slots below the water table and buried below dredged sediments. OTML claims that the removal of [sulphur] wastes will make the sediment coming down the Ok Tedi suitable for covering the stockpile.'[23] His report foreshadows the following problems:

- Design life of the stockpiles is a hundred years. At some time in the future, the wastes will erode into the river.
- The environmental impacts on the Ok Tedi and Fly river systems will have profound and increasing social impact on thousands of people over many generations.

- Flooding will cause major changes to the whole floodplain ecosystem. These will be permanent.
- Dieback will severely deplete wild foods, forest animals and other forest products. Traditional garden areas and sago swamps will be destroyed. Sago supplies may not be adequate to feed the population.
- Water supplies will be affected by flooding and biological contamination. Clean water will be very difficult to get in the dry season.

Dr Tingay says it appears that at this stage 'nothing can be done to reduce these environmental impacts which in the future will cause very big impacts on human health and nutrition. [These] are the only things we can do anything effective about. The environmental impacts are the reasons for compensation.'

Nevertheless, former OTML managing director Keith Faulkner says that if the mine continued beyond 2013 as an underground operation, 'it would be a different arrangement. You're looking at essentially a quarter the scale of treatment and a fraction of the scale in waste.'[24]

PNGSDP chairman Ross Garnaut agrees. Moreover, he says the system to extract the sulphur from the tailings through a flotation process and transport it to the lowlands has not only been completed but 'PNGSDP is at an advanced stage of discussions with various potential users', which would 'remove the storage challenge'.[25]

In the last seven years, he says, the dredging operation had 'significantly reduced the river aggradation downstream and significantly eased the flooding problem in the middle Fly'.

Professor Garnaut says PNGSDP revenues 'are likely to support average annual development expenditures of around US$50 million (in 2007 dollars) in the years currently planned to mine closure. It is likely that the long-term fund will support continued development expenditure at this rate for at least 40 years after mine closure.'

Carmellus Narokobi's case on behalf of the Ningerum people was dismissed with costs in November 2007.

According to Marius Kloppers, BHP Billiton has adopted new standards of practice since Ok Tedi, which go beyond the operating boundaries set by governments, particularly in developing countries. These were put to the test with the September 2008 announcement of a nickel project on Gag Island in the environmentally sensitive Raja Ampat Archipelago off the coast of West Papua. Marine biologist Dr Charles Vernon said the archipelago was the international centre of marine diversity. BHP Billiton is in a 50/50 joint venture with the Indonesian state-owned company Antam to develop the deposit.

Kloppers says, 'We've got a specific set of policies on waste disposal, particularly tailings disposal, where we say we will not do any deep-sea placement of mining waste, we won't do any riverine disposal of mining waste. Those are two techniques that are absolutely permitted and condoned in a wide range of operating environments that we would find ourselves in, yet that is not something that we would do.'[26]

To reinforce his message, he later gave a categoric assurance at the 2008 annual general meeting in London. 'If Gag Island is gazetted as a World Heritage site,' he said, 'we will not go there.' Don Argus added, 'This company doesn't do silly things to the environment. We have a good track record.'

CHAPTER 25

Coal Climate

The faces flashed terror – and occasionally bravado – in the miner's lamps as the journalists reached the huge longwall monster in the hot, black belly of the earth. The 300-metre juggernaut roared as it advanced along its length, the journalists behind, a great sawtoothed mechanical drum feasting on the coal seam and vomiting the masticated lumps on to a pan line that took it to a conveyor belt and thence to the surface. They shouted – screamed – to make themselves heard above the thundering mechanical mole that endlessly devoured the 350-million-year-old remains of giant forests heated and pressured over the millennia into carbon-rich fuel for the world's industrial furnaces.

As it advanced, the overlying rock, no longer supported by the coal, slowly cascaded to the floor behind the operation. Sensors in the 'eyes' of the beast detected how much of the seam remained ahead, and robotic controls adjusted its course. Two miners 'rode' the monster with the journalists, and others emerged from the gloom to tend it through marathon six-hour shifts. Among the journalists, some of the screams took on a note of panic. The darkness was impenetrable, the heat unbearable, the noise insupportable, millions of tons of earth and rock poised to collapse on them, bury them.

Back on the surface in the clear, cool air with an open sky and a wide Queensland horizon, the journalists quickly recovered. The guide commiserated. 'You get used to it. The pay's pretty good . . . and you're doing something for your country.'

'Yeah?'

'Where would we be without our exports?'[1]

A rhetorical question, but it goes to the heart of the conundrum. Australia is easily the biggest coal exporter in the world, with about 30 per cent of market share, worth $24.5 billion in 2006–07. And BHP Billiton is the dominant producer. In Queensland, its vast Bowen Basin deposit – stretching 600 kilometres from Collinsville in the north, through the regions near Moranbah, Dysart, Emerald and Blackwater to Moura and Theodore in the south – holds an estimated 25,000 million tonnes.

To the Australian Government, this is a treasure trove that permits the country to import its needs for continued growth. And the tax on industry profits contributes to government services, from preschools to pensions. Yet coal is the principal polluter in the global battle against climate change.

The company's approach to the commodity illustrates the transformation that has taken place in the past century. In the early days, BHP followed the traditional practice of taking the iron to the coal in creating its steelmaking plant in Newcastle. But with the discovery of the Bowen Basin coking-coal deposit in Queensland in the 1960s – and the development of enormous bulk carriers by Japan and later Korea – the seas became a super-highway. The coal and the iron ore could be brought together anywhere on the globe that was accessible to the ocean-going leviathans.

When BHP took over Utah in 1984, it also clinched a Japanese partnership to form BHP Mitsui Coal, with big mines in the southern sector of the coalfield. Then, in June 2001, the company brokered a partnership with Mitsubishi, the BHP

Billiton Mitsubishi Alliance (BMA), which produced a massive 59 million tonnes annually. This made it Australia's biggest coal miner and exporter and the world's biggest supplier to the seaborne coking-coal market. New mines on the seam are continually being developed.

Similarly, in South Africa, Colombia, New Mexico and Indonesia, major BHP Billiton coal-mining expansion is underway. But just as coal has contributed to the company's rising profits – topping sales of $14 billion in 2006–07 – so too has it contributed to global warming. Australia's coal exports account for about 620 million tonnes of CO_2 emissions annually – compared with Australia's entire domestic emissions of 560 million tonnes. And, according to the Australian Bureau of Agricultural and Resource Economics (ABARE), coal exports will almost double by 2030. A new coal-fired power station is being built in China every two weeks. India is next in line for a massive expansion.

Against this background, BHP Billiton began a public-relations offensive under Chip Goodyear. In 2005, the BMA issued a charter 'to create value through the mining, production and marketing of high-quality coal resources, and the provision of innovative customer and market-focused solutions'.

A much wordier update on the Paul Anderson original, it continued with statements affirming its commitment to 'active management', 'high performance', 'integrity', 'safety' and 'a superior return on investment'. But the only mention of coal's devastating role in global warming came under the heading 'We value'. First on the list was 'Safety and the environment – an overriding commitment to health, safety, environmental responsibility and sustainable development'. This refers principally to mine workers and their surroundings. The larger issue of climate change was ignored.

In 2006, Goodyear initiated a sustainability report. It too is replete with the clichés and jargon of environmental concern. It states that for society to continue to grant the company 'a license to operate', it must fulfil its role as a responsible and ethical corporate citizen. Each year, it measures its performance in the areas of health, safety, environment and community (HSEC) and invites selected environmental organisations to 'interrogate' the results. 'I didn't find the interrogation particularly challenging,' Goodyear says. 'As the carbon issues came along, it just fitted into our business agenda like any other environmental, community or safety issue. I would say to our team, "The world has made its decision about the role carbon plays in the global environment, particularly around global warming. We can argue that, we can debate that, but the facts are that the communities in which we operate have made that decision. So how do we continue to create opportunities for ourselves? We must factor the environmental issue into our operations, particularly with carbon."

'We set targets very early on. Today, we've had 13 years in which we've had targets for energy efficiency and targets to reduce carbon emissions. And we've met those targets. We took a very strong leadership role, and the facts are we have done a tremendous amount.'[2]

Don Argus says, 'Two of the best meetings that I attend during the year are with the NGOs. The NGOs come in and they interrogate and critique our sustainability credentials. All the main NGOs, the noisy NGOs, that you would want.[3] [In 2007, the company] met or exceeded its HSEC targets in 19 of the 26 measured areas. Greenhouse-gas emissions generated from the business have been stable over the last five years, despite increased production.'[4]

In setting its targets, the company has adopted the criteria of the International Council on Mining and Metals (ICMM). And while good corporate and ethical governance and increasing shareholder value are not necessarily in opposition, the stewardship of the earth has never been the overriding priority for any mining company.

At the same time, the company declared its support for 'clean coal' technology. Indeed, the Australian industry has levied its coal exports $300 million over five years for research and development in the area. The industry also agreed to match the $500 million promised by then opposition leader Kevin Rudd during the 2007 election campaign.

The research is centred on carbon capture and storage (CCS), also known as geo-sequestration, designed to capture carbon-dioxide emissions from coal- or gas-fired power plants and carry it off via pipelines or haulage to be stored underground or in the ocean bed. The process has garnered some important scientific support. The Intergovernmental Panel on Climate Change (IPCC) said, 'With greenhouse-gas-emission limits imposed, many integrated assessments foresee the deployment of CCS systems on a large scale within a few decades from the start of any significant climate-change mitigation regime.' However, the IPCC warned that 'notwithstanding significant penetration of CCS systems by 2050, the majority of CCS deployment will occur in the second half of this century'.[5]

'We've contributed about $300 million into a lot of that research,' Don Argus says. 'I'd like to think we can get a solution. There's a commitment to it and we'll get a solution of some description.'[6]

Theoretically, it would be possible to capture 85–90 per cent of the carbon dioxide from a coal-fired power station, but the process would require the plant to burn 11–40 per cent more coal. This would result in greater emissions of other pollutants such as sulphur and particulates. And, of course, the increased coal mining required would bring its own environmental consequences to land, water and biodiversity. Modelling by the Massachusetts Institute of Technology in 2007 strongly suggested that even with widespread use of CCS, coal emissions would still be higher in 2050 than at present.

In March 2008, the federal energy minister, Martin Ferguson, opened a demonstration plant that would inject up to 100,000 tonnes of carbon dioxide into a storage site two kilometres under dairy-farm country in Victoria's Otway basin. At the time, it was the world's largest carbon-capture pilot project and was run by a consortium that included BHP Billiton, Rio Tinto and the federal government, among others.

Indeed, the political winds of change that would bring Kevin Rudd to power wrought profound changes to the climate-change issue. And ever alert to the political weathervane, chief executive officer Chip Goodyear issued a 'revised climate-change policy' on 18 June 2007. 'BHP Billiton has recognised that our company, as well as society generally, must make real behavioural changes and accelerate technological progress if we are to achieve a meaningful reduction in energy use and greenhouse-gas emissions,' Goodyear said.

He nominated four 'action areas':

- Understanding emissions from the full life-cycle of our products.
- Improving the management of energy and greenhouse-gas emissions across our businesses.
- Committing US$300 million over the next five years to support low-emissions-technology development, internal energy-excellence projects and encourage emissions abatement by our employees and our local communities.
- Using our technical capacity and our experience to assist governments and other stakeholders on the design of effective and equitable climate-change policies, including market-based mechanisms such as emissions trading.

These are high-sounding, if largely non-specific, aspirations. Undoubtedly, BHP Billiton is aware that it must be seen to conform to the zeitgeist of the day. Within the first week of his taking office, in December 2007, Prime Minister Rudd travelled to the United Nations climate-change conference in Bali, where he publicly signed on to the Kyoto Protocol. The Australian delegation took a leading role in developing the 'road map' for action leading to Copenhagen, the 2009 successor to Kyoto.

On his first major trip to the United States, in March 2008, Rudd told the US Chamber of Commerce in Washington DC, 'We must move to a low-carbon economy. That will mean a profound shift in the Australian economy and in the global economy. We will have to make that shift in a way that maintains our competitiveness. That is why we need a global approach to climate change.'

However, as a Queenslander with a highly developed political antenna, he was quick to support the coal industry. 'Australia is the world's largest exporter of coal,' he said. 'For us, developing clean-coal technology is a crucial part of our response to climate change. That's why we're investing in accelerating the development and deployment of these technologies – the government working with the private sector to find commercially viable solutions to climate change.'

It remains to be seen whether Rudd's faith in the private sector – or BHP Billiton specifically – is well founded or whether the industry is engaged in an elaborate public-relations exercise.

The company's appointment of its director of public affairs, Geoff Walsh, as Kevin Rudd led the Labor Party to victory at the polls in 2007 could hardly have been better timed. Walsh, a former journalist, was a senior adviser to prime ministers Bob Hawke and Paul Keating, national secretary of the Labor Party from 2000 to 2003 and chief of staff to Victorian Labor Premier Steve Bracks in 2006. 'The company has got a strong set of values,' he says. 'I was struck by how widely known and how frequently people reference them internally. This is ironic in a sense but from the outside people still have some outdated views about the way in which the company conducts itself. The company has commitments about its own energy use and has the view that action is needed.'[7]

Indeed, since the merger, BHP Billiton's public-relations unit, begun in the 1960s by Derek Sawer to 'open up' the company, had been transformed into a highly sophisticated operation under the aegis of Graham Evans's external-affairs department. He and his operatives developed extensive and intricate networks throughout successive administrations and the Canberra press gallery. They curried favour with journalists through lavish tours of the company's mining operations in private aircraft liberally supplied with culinary delicacies and a well-stocked liquor cabinet. The result was well worth the outlay, made through the Minerals Council of Australia. Journalists duly reported the massive developments and their manifest contribution to the economy and the welfare of all Australians.

However, the real strength of Evans's department was in the web of behind-the-scenes activity developed between lobby groups, the decision-makers in government departments and the Cabinet ministers they advised.

It was an operation conducted well below the public radar, and it would have remained so but for the revelations of a Liberal Party staffer and part-time lobbyist, Guy Pearse, who in 2007 published an exposé that revealed in detail the influence exercised by what he termed the 'Quarry Vision' cabal. Indeed, he quoted at length the key players in their successful campaign to reverse the initial Howard government support for the major climate-change initiative of the day – the ratification of the Kyoto Protocol.

Based on interviews conducted for his PhD from the ANU, his book, *High and Dry*, caused a brief sensation and inspired a *Four Corners* television program. But in the colour and movement of an election year, the real import of its 480-page exposure and analysis was not fully appreciated. The author and his work were dismissed or denigrated by former political colleagues; and the support he received from the then Labor opposition was muted in favour of their own 'positive' policies on the climate-change issue. However, it casts a deep shadow on BHP, before and after the merger with Billiton. And it calls into question the company's commitment to 'setting and achieving targets that promote . . . reducing and preventing pollution'.[8]

Pearse was born in Townsville the son of an engineer, and his mother had close family connections to BHP executive and Liberal Party enthusiast Tom Harley. After taking an Arts degree with combined honours in history and politics at James Cook University, Pearse became a member the Liberal Party in 1989. Soon afterwards, aged only 22, he joined Queensland

Senator Ian Macdonald as his research and media manager. 'For the next fifteen years,' he said, 'I was either literally or emotionally a servant of the Liberal Party of Australia.'[9]

A big, prepossessing man, he was soon marked out as a candidate for a safe passage into the federal parliament. 'I recall meeting with Tom [Harley] in Melbourne in the early 1990s and he was thinking out loud about the best [electorate] to slot me in.'

But when opposition leader John Hewson lost the 'unlosable' 1993 election to Paul Keating, Liberal Party morale was shattered and there was a widespread expectation that they faced an extended period in opposition. 'It was considered important that people like me who were looking for a long-term career used this time to develop their skills,' he said. So party elders organised a place for him at the conservative Washington think tank, the Heritage Foundation, and Pearse applied for graduate-school courses at the top American universities.

'I quickly discovered that mid-1990s US politics was far to the right of what I was used to in Australia,' he said. 'I had virtually no common ground with the Heritage Foundation.' However, he won entrance to the John F. Kennedy School of Government at Harvard University. 'It changed my life,' he said.[10]

His youthful experiences with his family at their rainforest holiday cottage had fostered a sympathetic interest in the environment. Now, at Harvard, he confronted the political nature of the issue:

> The [Liberal] Party's deep assumption was that the green movement was inherently and immutably biased against it, and that we should respond with similar vehemence. I decided I'd see what happened if I abandoned this prejudice: how could we work with the green movement to get something done? . . . The more I learned, the more excited I became about my mission.[11]

He even joined Al Gore's advance staff in the 1994 mid-term elections.

At home on holidays in Melbourne, he met with some of the BHP staff dealing with the environment. 'I was toying with the idea of having them as my master's thesis client, and possibly working with them when I graduated,' he said. 'Soon afterwards, Graham Evans flew me down from Boston for dinner in Washington DC to talk about possibilities.'[12] It was a congenial occasion and there was an assumption that they would continue to talk.

After graduation in 1996, he was offered the role of speechwriter for Environment Minister Senator Robert Hill and when, in 1997, Hill negotiated a good deal for Australia at the Kyoto conference, Pearse was pleased to be part of the team. Indeed, as Hill entered the Cabinet room on his return, John Howard and his colleagues gave him 'a standing ovation'.

Pearse chose to work from an office in the environment department rather than in the ministerial suite at Parliament House – a fundamental political error. He had not appreciated either the importance of propinquity to the source of power – the minister – or the paranoia of politicians under fire, as Hill soon was from his own side of the aisle.

When Hill asked him to write the Liberal Party's environment policy statement for the 1999 election, he said he needed to check public-service regulations on purely political work. Hill snapped, 'Forget about it.'

'Only six months later did I learn from others in the party that I'd had a major falling out with Robert Hill,' he said. 'Because Hill had cut me off, so did other friends and patrons. Much to my disappointment, it became clear that I would have to spend some time in the political wilderness.'[13]

However, he now had the opportunity to pursue consulting and lobbying work, and he turned to Billiton (and later the merged entity with BHP). He also began a PhD at the Australian National University on the climate-change issue. The research involved interviews with a wide range of stakeholders, and since it was an academic exercise with promises not to reveal sources, 'the lobbyists relaxed'. 'Some of them,' he said, 'had clearly been waiting years to have their vital role in the history of Australian greenhouse policy recorded, if anonymously.'

Easily the most influential group was the Australian Industry Greenhouse Network (AIGN), the country's biggest greenhouse polluters through industry associations and individual companies representing Australia's biggest fossil-fuel producers and consumers. BHP, both before and after the merger with Billiton, was one of the leaders of the group. And, according to Pearse, their power to influence policy was 'very unsettling'.[14]

AIGN personnel were all former federal bureaucrats or ministerial staffers from the industry portfolio. They were often called upon to assist in the development of environment policy. Pearse said, 'I was told that in at least two federal departments (industry and treasury), AIGN lobbyists had written cabinet submissions, ministerial briefings and costings on key greenhouse policy issues numerous times.

'Meanwhile, the same people in their capacity as lobbyists were writing very similar advice to government on behalf of the big polluting interests. So the government – particularly the Cabinet – was receiving the same message from both sides.'

Not surprisingly, perhaps, the results were spectacular. In short order:

- The Cabinet decided secretly not to ratify Kyoto without the United States.
- In 2001, the Howard government announced it would not pursue emissions trading until at least 2008.
- On World Environment Day in June 2002, Prime Minister Howard told parliament that Australia did not intend to ratify the Kyoto Protocol.
- In 2004, a government White Paper revealed no greenhouse-reduction targets post Kyoto, no emissions trading ahead of 'effective global action' and a hobbling of the renewable energy industry.

The final triumph for AIGN came in 2005 when the government announced the establishment of the Asia Pacific Partnership on Clean Development and Climate (AP6). Pearse said, 'The AP6 covered countries responsible for more than 50 per cent of global emissions, including China, India and the US, but did not require anyone to reduce emissions or even slow their increase.'[15]

At the same time, Pearse continued consulting work for BHP Billiton; and he and his wife shared a Canberra house with Senator Brandis – a classmate of Tom Harley's at Oxford – who had become a prominent supporter of Treasurer Peter Costello for the prime ministership.

'For a time, BHP Billiton HQ in Melbourne also sought my advice on the company's relations with the Howard government in general,' Pearse said. 'They were particularly interested in my good relationships with MPs close to Costello, obviously in anticipation of a possible leadership transition.'

One consequence was his introduction to the man Graham Evans had appointed the company's vice president of government relations and asset protection, Bernie Delaney. 'My first impression,' Pearse said, 'was that he was cluey but not half as intimidating as I would have expected.'[16] They frequently did the rounds of ministerial offices seeking government subsidies for company projects. 'More than once, I saw him bite his tongue and bide his time so as not to risk antagonising a petulant minister.'

They were paid on results. 'I sat with senior BHP Billiton people outside Aussie's Café in Parliament House one day and remember them explaining to me how they received personal bonuses on the basis of whether they secured government funding.'[17]

In 2002, Pearse accepted a retainer from Delaney to provide advice directly to him on the company's broad relations with the federal government. The focus of the company's continuing campaign, he says, was support for The Big Australian.

It was not always an easy sell. 'How do we convince the federal government that we are still The Big Australian even though anyone looking closely can see that we are nothing like as Australian nowadays?' he said. 'Most of the shareholders are overseas, most of the projects are overseas, most of the board, and if it weren't for the window dressing, HQ would probably be in London too.

'So, what can we do to maintain the political capital associated with being The Big Australian? That was my work: focusing on the financial contribution to regional Australia, the employment contribution, the indirect jobs created by the company's activities here, and the large indirect stake many Australians had in the company through their superannuation funds.

'My impression is that the company was completely accustomed to using The Big Australian moniker to their political advantage. They also weren't shy about ignoring it either . . . effectively threatening to take their business offshore unless government chipped in: sentiment when it suited, a whiff of economic blackmail when it didn't.'[18]

However, later that year the contract terminated 'very suddenly'. Delaney claimed the reason was a cost-cutting decree from chief executive officer Brian Gilbertson, but Pearse is not convinced. It came in the wake of a long conversation between Delaney and Prime Minister Howard's chief of staff, Arthur Sinodinos, at the Liberal Party's federal conference. 'I suspect it was to do with Bernie's assessment that "[Howard] is staying",' he said, so Pearse's Costello contacts were less important.

By then, he suspects, Delaney might well have begun to be concerned about his greenhouse views. However, the termination was 'relatively cordial' and he continued to lobby for government support of the company's Yabalu nickel refinery near Townsville and saw Delaney from time to time. 'Bernie Delaney is a seasoned political poker player,' he says. 'He knew what my PhD research was about and he knew my green-for-a-Liberal views on Kyoto. So, in hindsight, I think this flavoured our discussions on Kyoto and emissions trading.

'He gave me the impression that the company was ambivalent about these things and was far more ready than, say, John Howard to accept Kyoto and priced carbon. However, I also know that the aluminium side of the business was in the thick of the lobbying against both. And BHPB was also closely involved in most of the politicking by the Minerals Council of Australia [against them] too.

'Further, they were among those hiring Andrew Robb[19] to lobby against Kyoto.

'More recently, they have said they can slow the growth in their own emissions but that it's unreasonable for a company growing as fast as them to be expected to achieve absolute reductions in greenhouse emissions in the foreseeable future.

'On balance, for them to say something like that as recently as 2007 suggests that the moral imperative just doesn't register.'[20]

Geoff Walsh says that Bernie Delaney remained the principal in-house lobbyist to government: 'Bernie Delaney reports to me, but he's the person who principally looks after government relations at the federal level – all sides of politics and the federal bureaucracy.'[21]

When asked his attitude to carbon emission and climate change, Marius Kloppers pauses for a moment. 'We participate in the Coal 21 and Future Gen projects,' he says. 'I suspect, though, that the electricity-generation industry – which is multiple, multiple, multiple times the size of the energy-coal industry – will ultimately have the biggest vested interest to drive those changes. Changes in fuel-switching are largely made by generators, not by the people who supply them. The company's policy [on climate change] is pretty clear – it goes out from the premise that the science is real, that CO_2 concentration in the atmosphere is an issue and must be stabilised, so we favour policies that price the external cost of carbon-based fuels.

'What is important is to reduce the carbon content of the atmosphere. In reality, that will be driven by the large economies and any attempt that is not squarely aimed at building a global community to influence that is likely to have very little impact. Basically, the world is in a prisoner's dilemma at the moment on global warming – everybody is looking at everybody else because people are trying to set targets for something that is a hundred-year time frame.

'In my personal opinion, the real endeavour has got to be to get started across as broad a base as possible, not to out-cut each other, because in reality if one party makes a very aggressive set of cuts you're less likely to get international cooperation. You're more likely to get a global set of issues if you just get started in a modest way and continue to then build the broad base, and only after you've built the broad base do I think you can really start influencing for a hundred-year time frame.'[22]

Don Argus also measures his words carefully. 'I have a very strong view about the climate-change debate but I need to be careful that I don't pre-empt [the policy] the company has,' he says. 'I don't believe that you can go in isolation with emission trading.'[23]

He is concerned that the government would use the revenue from emission permits to 'pick winners' or subsidise renewable-energy initiatives that were not economic. If that occurred, Australia would not get the full benefit from the emissions-trading scheme.

'I read the science,' he says. 'I read all the articles and I read the sceptical environmentalists and there's enough data in there that would allow me to say "Yes, I query it", but intuitively, seeing stuff spewing up in the air I'm aghast that we're not bringing on the uranium debate here in Australia. I'm absolutely aghast. There's only one solution to save the ecosystems of the world and that's uranium.'[24]

CHAPTER 26

The Cakehole

In the 2007 federal-election campaign, Prime Minister John Howard proposed the use of nuclear power as a 'clean' alternative to coal-fired power stations. Opposition leader Kevin Rudd's Labor Party responded with a scare campaign that the Coalition would build 25 nuclear power stations around the country. At the same time, however, Labor reaffirmed its support for Olympic Dam – the world's biggest uranium mine – at South Australia's Roxby Downs and dropped its opposition to the development of additional uranium deposits.

In fact, according to Guy Pearse, 'Mining all that extra "clean, green uranium" at Roxby Downs will reportedly generate an estimated five million more tonnes of greenhouse gases annually – roughly adding one per cent to Australia's emissions, or the equivalent to about another million cars on our roads.'[1]

Such concerns were far from the minds of the two men meeting at London's Sheraton Park Tower at 101 Knightsbridge in mid-October 2004. The Sheraton is an undistinguished concrete-and-glass structure on the west London skyline, but its lack of architectural grace is more than redeemed in the eyes of some visitors by its proximity to the shopping mecca of Harrods and Harvey Nichols. And Mick Davis had shopping very much on his mind when he dropped in for breakfast with Andrew Michelmore, chief executive of WMC Resources.

Since walking away from BHP Billiton in search of new challenges in July 2001, he had performed something of a financial miracle with Xstrata. The bearded sage had persuaded Glencore, the Swiss trading and mining company that owned 40 per cent of Xstrata, to allow the coal assets contained in its subsidiary, Enex, to be passed to Xstrata. Enex's initial public offering (IPO) had failed miserably shortly after the 9/11 terrorist attack on the World Trade Center, but, with the help of Marc Gonsalves, who had departed BHP Billiton in October 2001, Davis successfully listed Xstrata on the London Stock Exchange in March 2002. Two years later, his extremely small team – initially just 17 people working from the basement of J. P. Morgan's offices near Blackfriars Bridge – had grown Xstrata into a US$40 billion company.

Over the croissants and coffee, Michelmore, scion of an old Melbourne family, and Davis, the hard-driving South African, sized one another up. 'That was the first time I spoke to Andrew,' Davis says, speaking about the WMC battle for the first time. 'I indicated to him at that stage that I was interested in putting the two companies together but I didn't table a transaction.'[2]

Since 2001, virtually every major mining company in Australia had been taken over by foreign interests. Indeed, Davis had stunned the mining world with his purchase of MIM Holdings for $3.44 billion in 2003 after a year-long battle with its recalcitrant shareholders.[3]

'Mount Isa Mines was one of the great corporate battles,' Davis says. 'Although the board supported us, the management didn't and the management found ways to fight us which used Australian corporate law very ingeniously. If you had 40,000 shareholders and 30,000 owned one per cent of the company and 10,000 owned 99 per cent, those 30,000 could stop the thing going ahead. So we nearly lost that. The whole of Australia was against Xstrata: it seemed to be Swiss gnomes backed by nefarious, shady people. I got emails to take my Nazi gold and go home.[4] It was really a very messy thing but we won that and that transaction actually made Xstrata. It was crucial.'[5]

Indeed, the deal had turned Xstrata into the world's largest exporter of coal for heat and power; now Davis yearned to join the biggest diversified miners at the industry's top table.

Western Mining, famous for its pioneering exploration and legendary characters such as Sir Arvi Parbo and Hugh Morgan, was the last of the big independents. And Davis wanted it – badly. In what Michelmore later described as a perfectly amiable manner, his guest raised the prospect of a merger between their two companies. Michelmore wasn't surprised. In December 2002, as foreshadowed, WMC had demerged its alumina business – a 40 per cent stake in the AWAC joint venture with Alcoa – into a separate company, Alumina, while WMC Resources retained the company's copper, nickel, uranium and fertiliser assets.[6] Although the demerger had been essential to sort out WMC's partnership with Alcoa, the simplified structures had made it easier for either arm of the old company to be taken over.

Two months previously, when reporting a tenfold leap in WMC's first-half net profits to $515 million (US$367 million), Michelmore flagged the dangers of a takeover by stressing the need for his company to diversify still further to generate a more consistent performance. 'We are heavily weighted to the [London Metal Exchange] and are therefore price-takers and subject to huge volatility,' he said. 'Iron ore, coking coal, alumina, mineral sands – these would give us a different product mix that also tends to run to a different cycle.'[7]

In Knightsbridge, Michelmore politely declined that first approach from Davis and their breakfast ended on a cordial note. The Australian, however, knew instinctively that this was not the end of the matter; on the contrary, it had just been a sighting shot prior to the launch of a hostile bid for WMC's prime asset: Olympic Dam.

Olympic Dam was the world's seventh-largest known copper deposit and its largest deposit of high-grade uranium ore. In 2004, it had produced 225,000 tonnes of copper, more than 4000 tonnes of uranium and nearly 90,000 ounces of gold.

The ore body takes its name from a modest excavation scooped out of the claypan on Roxby Downs station in 1956 – the year of the Melbourne Olympics. It remained nothing more than a watering hole for the stock that grazed among the spinifex until Western Mining began drilling for a copper deposit that geological modelling had located in the area. Once it had established the richness of the deposit, the company built Roxby Downs – a township of aluminium-clad, transportable houses – 16 kilometres south of the underground mine and started producing copper ore in 1988.[8]

WMC was also the world's third-largest nickel producer, supplying eight per cent of global demand. Even more enticing to a predator, it had recently signed a billion-dollar contract to supply nickel to China from its mines in Western Australia. Michelmore didn't have to wait long for the blow to fall. Before October was out, Xstrata slapped on the table a bid of $6.35 (US$4.98) per share – which valued the company at $7.4 billion.

Michelmore and his directors had no hesitation in rejecting the offer as too low, so Xstrata announced it would take it directly to WMC's shareholders. 'We made an approach to the Western Mining board, they rejected the approach, we then went hostile,' Mick Davis says.[9]

Davis's tactic was to force potential rival bidders BHP Billiton, Rio Tinto, Anglo American and Vale of Brazil into the open. 'I found out, because one of our advisers was conflicted, that BHP in fact had been studying Western Mining but hadn't done anything with it,' he says. 'I suspect that if we hadn't done anything, they still wouldn't have done anything. I take it as a great compliment that I've caused a number of companies to counter-bid against me. I'm always pleased when I can demonstrate that there's value when other people can't see it.'

As the quest for cheap mineral assets intensified to satisfy demand in China, each company had been studying the feasibility of mounting a bid for WMC. Under Australian takeover rules, however, Xstrata could block rival bids if it could acquire a stake in WMC of at least ten per cent. Chip Goodyear knew what Davis was trying to do and, although he coveted WMC's assets, he wasn't prepared to show his hand just yet. Despite booming commodity prices, he was painfully aware that the slumps of the past decade had almost crippled some mining companies, including his own: the spectre of Magma that had hung over the executive suite at 600 Bourke Street had followed The Big Fella to its new headquarters at 180 Lonsdale Street. But Goodyear was also conscious of the fact that while the rising Australian dollar made WMC an increasingly expensive target for foreign bidders, it meant the company was tailor-made for BHP Billiton. And he had a plan.

'We knew that whoever kicked the ball off with WMC, they were going to run the other way,' he says. 'That's the nature of acquisitions. You kick the ball off and it doesn't matter who you are, the guys hate you. So we wanted to be a friend and be somebody they could run to when that ball is kicked off. Sure enough, it did, and they said, "Anybody but Xstrata."'[10]

Marius Kloppers had moved to Melbourne in 2003 in a commercial role that involved him in mergers and acquisitions, in addition to business development and marketing. 'Marius and I developed a strategy that said we need to get close to this company,' Goodyear says. 'Marius developed relationships with the development team over there and so we got to know each other very well, recognising that there was a great fit here.'[11]

Kloppers concurred. 'We always thought that WMC would auction itself,' he says. 'The auction would conclude and it would be easiest for the party that had been friendly towards Western Mining to be in the best position to complete the transaction.' One of Kloppers' contacts at Western Mining was Mike Nossal, son of Sir Gus Nossal. 'We'd talked about the nickel business quite a bit because we felt our nickel business was a bit sub-scale and theirs was sub-scale, so there was an ongoing series of dialogues on how you could put the two nickel businesses together, but without reaching any fruitful outcome.'[12]

On 24 November, Andrew Michelmore raised the minerals reserve at Olympic Dam by 29.2 per cent to 3.8 billion tonnes as a result of recent test drilling. 'Based on these new estimates, Olympic Dam now contains the world's fourth-largest remaining copper and gold resources, up from seventh previously,' Michelmore told the stock exchange. 'Already the largest-known uranium resource, Olympic Dam now contains 38 per cent of the total global economic uranium base, up from 33 per cent.'[13]

Michelmore urged shareholders to ignore the Xstrata bid because it 'fails to recognise the current and prospective value of WMC's assets'. The statement warned shareholders against accepting calls from Xstrata, encouraging them to 'only accept calls which are officially endorsed by the WMC board'. He told the *Financial Times* that while he believed the company could deliver better value to shareholders by staying independent, he would be happy to talk to any bidder who was willing to offer a 'material improvement' on Xstrata's $7.4 billion. Michelmore said, 'I certainly don't blame Mick for coming along and trying to pick us up. He is ahead of the pack and he wants to pick us up before others recognise what our value is.' He described Olympic Dam as 'a ginormous ore body' and added, 'There is no question that we have the greatest suite of base-metal assets that exist certainly in Australia, but probably anywhere in the world.'[14]

The stalemate was still unresolved in the New Year when WMC produced a strong production statement for 2004 and an upbeat assessment of the year ahead. It had delivered record copper production, its nickel business had beaten targets and there had been a significant shift in the outlook for uranium. 'Continuing strong commodity prices, higher nickel and fertiliser production, and an accelerated program of growth and development projects position WMC for a strong 2005,' Michelmore said. 'All plants will be operating at or near capacity.'[15]

This bullish outlook forced Xstrata to raise its bid to $8.4 billion (US$6.5 billion) or $7.20 a share. WMC's board, however, still declined to endorse the revised offer and suggested it would seek a white knight prepared to offer an even higher price.[16]

Chip Goodyear still hadn't put his cards on the table on 16 February when he reported a record $4.1 billion pre-tax profit for the six months to 31 December 2004, more than double BHP Billiton's 2003 interim figure. He would not be drawn on whether BHP was considering a counter-bid for WMC, switching tack to discuss the uncertainty of investing in Russia's natural resources following President Putin's sudden tendency to renegotiate lucrative contracts signed in the past with Western oil companies or, in the case of the Yukos oil-and-gas conglomerate, handing its assets over to Russian rivals. 'What I would say is watch [Russia], put your toe in the water, but I wouldn't expect any significant investments there,' he said. 'The issues are going to be: what are your rights as the owner [of mineral deposits]?'[17]

By 8 March, Goodyear was confident the plan was working. It was time to throw the knockout punch. That afternoon, he announced a bid of $9.2 billion (US$7.3 billion) for WMC, easily trumping Xstrata's $8.2 billion (US$6.5 billion).[18] Deutsche Bank, acting for BHPB, had been buying WMC shares in the open market for several weeks and it had become clear to Mick Davis that the bank was trying to accumulate a 10.1 per cent stake of its own to foil Xstrata's offer under the takeover rules.

The bank had quietly offered a select group of WMC shareholders $7.85 a share in cash, well above Xstrata's offer of $7 and WMC's share price of $7.46, and was close to reaching its target. Once BHPB secured its 10.1 per cent stake, it would unveil a share bid for the rest of WMC.[19]

'I thought we played that one pretty well,' Don Argus says.

'I think having the support of the Western Mining board was a big plus.

'But I can remember one uncomfortable night when some of our whizz-kid advisers tried to encourage us to take up a part position in Western Mining, and that wasn't one of our smartest moves. We were very fortunate that the Western Mining board approved the transaction the next afternoon; otherwise, I reckon the UK market would have had our ears and everything for botching up a partial bid.'[20]

'Yes, it was stupid but there you are – they survived it,' Mick Davis says. 'Had BHP not come in, we would have won it at the price that we offered. I suspect they came in because it was incomprehensible to Don Argus that anybody other than BHP would own Western Mining. They would have paid any price, and the minute they came up with their price I knew the game was over and I thought the best strategy for me was to withdraw as quickly as possible. It took me by surprise – I didn't think they would come in. Thinking about it afterwards, Don decided nobody else was going to buy Western Mining, and with Marius and Mike Salamon quite eager to do something there were strong motivations. I don't think Chip was in favour of the deal at all, and that's what I was banking on, but the weight of Don, Marius and Mike won the day.'[21]

Chip Goodyear says, 'We worked through a process; we stayed in the weeds; and when we sprang out of the weeds, within 24 hours we had an agreed deal.'[22] The board of WMC Resources advised shareholders that in the absence of a higher offer, they should accept BHPB's bid. And once the deal was done, Mike Salamon replaced Tommie Bergman as chairman.

So how did Mick Davis take his defeat? Marius Kloppers flashes a smile. 'You know, I never really discussed that with Mick,' he says. 'I think Mick probably thought that he had it; they were very close. We waited until the last minute. Mick thought it was going to be all over in a day or two and I guess had mentally pencilled in owning the assets by then. I had quite a few discussions with his principal shareholder,

Glencore, afterwards and clearly Ivan Glazenberg [Glencore's chief executive officer] was keen for Mick to buy that set of assets.'[23]

Mick, however, holds no grudges. 'Chip came to see me a few months later to find out if I was still talking to him,' he says. 'I said to him, "I have no issue." It was entirely open to them to bid against me, and they were the bigger company and had bigger resources and that was not a problem for me. They could take a different view on risk and value than I could take, so I had no issue with that at all – that's the name of the game. You know what they say in the gangster movies, "It's just business – nothing personal."'[24]

Goodyear put the deal into financial perspective in an interview with Kerry O'Brien on the ABC's *7.30 Report*. 'It's a little over US$7 billion; our current market capitalisation is about US$85 or US$88 billion, so it's still less than ten per cent of BHP Billiton on an overall basis. It's a very good business, it fits well with us, but again, it's still relatively small in the scheme of the entire enterprise.'[25]

However, he knew that the real significance lay in the massive uranium deposit. He glowed when he said, 'In one step, we became the industry's main player in a critical resource.'

The glow became luminescent as the uranium price rose spectacularly from $10.10 per pound in 2003 to more than $56 five years later. Profits soared. The company planned a huge expansion.

'We had a different view of the future of Olympic Dam than they had,' Mick Davis says. 'We were going to expand and continue the underground mine. They were going to cannibalise the underground mine and go for a huge open pit. We couldn't do the open pit. We thought the open pit was highly risky. As it turns out, I think you'll find that for that open pit to make money it has to be bigger and bigger and bigger, so they are going to be sinking money into Olympic Dam for a long time.'[26]

But now, BHP Billiton found itself in the frontline of the

political debate on nuclear power, the nuclear non-proliferation treaty and an array of environmental and heritage issues surrounding the mine itself and its location in the Lake Eyre Basin. All had the capacity to take the shine off the acquisition.

From the beginning, the underground mine required vast amounts of water to process the ore, and all of it was drawn from the Great Artesian Basin. Ironically, Sturt's fabled inland sea had lain beneath his blistered feet as he and his party trudged endlessly through the red desert sands. One of the largest artesian groundwater basins in the world, it lies beneath nearly one-fifth of Australia with an estimated water storage of 65 billion megalitres. Individual bore depths vary up to 2000 metres, with the average being 500 metres; but around Olympic Dam it rises to the surface in unique mound springs formed over thousands of years. And as climate change and water shortage became political issues, BHP Billiton would soon find itself again in the environmental firing line.

The Labor Party had been split down the middle during the 1970s and '80s over the issue of mining uranium. At the 1982 federal conference, Victorian left-winger Bob Hogg[27] proposed that uranium mining should be allowed where it was 'mined incidentally to the mining of other minerals'. After a rowdy debate, Hogg's motion was passed, and when Labor won federal power in 1983 Prime Minister Bob Hawke used this precedent to approve exports from Roxby Downs, resulting in the 'three mines policy' that approved Narbalek and Ranger in the Northern Territory together with Olympic Dam but banned further uranium mining.[28]

Premier John Bannon officially opened Olympic Dam mine in 1988, and the following year his and the Hawke governments freed WMC from legislation requiring environmental and health reports unless agreed to by WMC and the government. This brought further protests from anti-nuclear campaigners, but without result.

Another part of the baggage BHP Billiton inherited was WMC's condescending – and at times bellicose – attitude to the Aboriginal people of the region. In developing the mine, WMC refused to negotiate with the Arabunna people, the traditional custodians of the Lake Eyre South region containing the mound springs, and by 2006 it was using 35 million litres of water a day. BHP Billiton's plans to expand the mine would triple the output, transform it to the world's biggest open-cut and create a massive reservoir of radioactive and highly acidic tailings.

'Uncle' Kevin Buzzacott, an elder of the Arabunna people, says, 'Since the late '70s/early '80s with the development of Roxby Downs and the Olympic Dam, it's sorta turned my life upside down.

'[They] made it a nightmare because of the destruction that these fellas done on us and on our country – desecrating and destroying the sacred sites, putting their pipelines in and their pump stations and taking very special sacred water from the Lake Eyre Basin.

'I think they take about 50 million litres a day to Roxby.[29] They've been doing that now for over 20 years and we been sorta monitoring our country the best way we can, and that's mainly from the highway. We haven't been able to go in off the road to check certain springs and waterholes and soaks. But the ones we have checked, we could see where some have been destroyed and we could see where the water level's gone right down.

'We used to use the water, but we only took what we need. And we washed and bathed and stuff in it as well. We've never expected, not in our lifetimes, that that amount of water that WMC and BHP Billiton – these people have been taking so much we've never see that before. Like I said, not in our Dreamtime.'[30]

Olympic Dam spokesman Richard Yeeles says, 'BHP Billiton regularly consults with Aboriginal communities claiming an interest in the Olympic Dam region. I am not aware of Aboriginal people in general being "deeply concerned" about the impact of BHP Billiton's consumption of water from the

Great Artesian Basin. This consumption is monitored by the South Australian Government under licence arrangements. BHP Billiton's consumption remains within all licensed limits.

'About seven years ago, Mr Buzzacott initiated action in the South Australian Supreme Court against the former owner of Olympic Dam, WMC, alleging genocide. The Supreme Court dismissed his action.'[31]

Chip Goodyear says he recognised the problems in dealing with communities surrounding controversial BHP Billiton operations, not least Roxby Downs. 'The most difficult ones to handle are generally community issues,' he says, 'particularly in operations that have long histories where perhaps there was a different view about relationships with communities – where they'll do what they're told or they won't be a factor. That's where we find our biggest issues.'[32]

Friends of the Earth spokesman Jim Green says the extraction 'has adversely impacted in the fragile ecology' of the area. 'BHP Billiton has a bore-capping program which, it claims, saves more water than the mine uses. But extraction for the mine is localised and the adverse impacts are all too apparent. BHP Billiton does not pay one cent for this massive water take.'[33]

Eileen Wani Wingfield, an Aboriginal woman from the area, said, 'Our sites are very valuable to us. That uranium is very, very bad. It gets into underground river and everything. It kills country.'[34]

In 1994, a massive leak from the radioactive tailings was detected. Over four years, some three million cubic litres of liquid leaked through the aquifer. Since then, there has been a series of incidents, such as on 20 March 2008 when a spill of 70 cubic metres of tailings resulted from a leaking pipeline. The waste was recovered and stored in the tailings-retention system.

A month earlier, BHP Billiton reported a spill of 270 cubic metres. According to the company press release, 'The tailings outflow was shut down immediately and the pipe section is being repaired. No employees had direct exposure to the material and there were no injuries associated with the spill. No material entered the general environment and there were no impacts on any worker or any member of the public.'

There are also concerns that the 4500 residents of Roxby Downs north of the mine may be affected by the waste. More than ten million tonnes of tailings are added each year to the 60 million tonnes already on the surface. According to Jim Green, 'The tailings-retention system (TRS) does not isolate the toxic wastes from the environment of Roxby Downs. They are subject to erosion by rain and wind, blowing across the mine site and the township where radioactive dust particles settle on rooftops, in gardens, gutters, streets, playgrounds, or are in the air the community breathes.'[35]

Not so, says the company. According to Richard Yeeles, 'The Olympic Dam hygiene-monitoring program shows that, in general, airborne contaminants are well controlled.

'Radiation exposure is one of the potential hazards encountered in the mining and milling of radioactive ores, and can be controlled through effective design and management practices. Olympic Dam uses international standards and Australian legislation as the basis for its systems of radiation protection. The results show that exposure levels for workers at Olympic Dam are consistently below radiation-protection limits.'[36]

Jessie Boylan, an organiser of tours to the mine for Friends of the Earth, says, 'There are no safe levels of exposure to radiation. Already, rare cancers are showing up in the Aboriginal people of the area.'[37]

Yeeles says there are now mutually beneficial relations between the company and the Aboriginal people in the region. The company recently concluded an agreement with three native title claimant groups as part of the big expansion plans. This would provide for annual company contributions to a trust that would be used for education, training and the development of Aboriginal businesses. He declines to say how much the company was contributing on grounds that, 'At this stage, the

Aboriginal groups have asked that the financial information remain confidential.'

In addition, he says, 'BHP Billiton has also employed three Aboriginal men to provide them with training in archaeology to help them record the Aboriginal heritage of the area. BHP Billiton regularly employs Aboriginal community representatives as consultants to undertake heritage surveys in the region.' [38]

Jessie Boylan says protesters and miners have reached stalemate. 'Richard Yeeles says the same old things, the same old lies. No one listens. People shout. It has become embarrassing. These people [at the mine] aren't evil; they're just doing their jobs. For the company, it's just about making money.'[39]

'Olympic Dam doesn't make a great deal of money,' Mike Salamon says. 'Look in the annual report. It's potentially huge; that's the important thing to recognise. But the potential has not been realised yet. In fact, the WMC management had not done a good job and that's why WMC was there to be taken. Olympic Dam was much too big an asset for that company. It was beyond their financial and every other form of capability. It will be a mine of the order of Escondida and it mines a million tonnes a day. That's a quotable truth. Escondida will produce more copper but Olympic Dam has also got the uranium and gold.'[40]

In June 2008, it was revealed that by 2013 Olympic Dam would be producing 730,000 tonnes of copper, 800,000 ounces of gold and 19,000 pounds of uranium.[41] Internationally, the market continued to grow exponentially. Until 2007, Australia opposed the sale of uranium yellowcake to India on grounds that it had refused to sign the Nuclear Non-Proliferation Treaty (NPT). Prime Minister Howard moved to relax the ban. When Kevin Rudd became prime minister, he reimposed it as part of an international campaign to revitalise the Treaty. Paul Keating says, 'The Indians are not signatories to the NPT, and until people want to play the game with the NPT then supplying countries like Australia should have their guard up.' However, it seems likely that a diplomatic formula will eventually bring down the export barrier.

At the same time, China, as a Treaty signatory, was importing increasing amounts of fuel for its nuclear power plants. By 2008, China had 11 nuclear power reactors in commercial operation, six under construction and several more about to start construction. Additional reactors were planned, including some of the world's most advanced, to give a sixfold increase in nuclear capacity to at least 50 GWe by 2020 and then a further three- to fourfold increase to 120–160 GWe by 2030. The country aims to become self-sufficient in reactor design and construction. Almost all of the yellowcake will be imported, the lion's share from Olympic Dam.

CHAPTER 27

Dragon Dance

Thérèse Rein noticed the change immediately. 'When Deng Xiaoping said you can sell your surplus product and keep the profit, overnight there were street markets; overnight you could buy silk nightgowns for one yuan – 50 cents; overnight you could buy unbruised apples.'[1]

It was a revelation for Ms Rein, the wife of the first secretary at the Australian Embassy in China, Kevin Rudd. Suddenly, in 1985, Beijing was on the move. And the future Australian prime minister was witness to the beginning of the greatest economic transformation in history. 'It was a good time to be there,' he said. 'The smart thing to do was to go to the countryside and the provinces and find out what was going on. So I travelled a lot.'[2]

What he saw had been a long time coming. The triumph of Mao Zedong's communist forces in 1949 ushered in three decades of disastrous economic repression and political manipulation. Only after the Great Helmsman's death in 1976 and the subsequent fall of the Gang of Four did Deng rise to the leadership and begin the process of opening up the economy and giving vent to the commercial and entrepreneurial instincts of his compatriots. In the mid-1980s, his 'socialism with Chinese characteristics' became the new national modus vivendi as the sleeping giant bestirred itself.

Rudd would develop his own business consultancy in the mid-1990s to assist Australian firms seeking to establish themselves in China at the time of the great awakening. BHP was not among them. At the time, BHP was preoccupied with the fallout from its disastrous acquisition of Magma, the US copper miner.

After the 2001 Billiton merger, the company reappraised the potential of China.[3] 'We saw what was going on in China, but China got delayed for two years because of 9/11,' says Brad Mills, who was one of BHPB's chief strategists at that time. 'Within one month [of the attacks], we saw a decline in consumption in the Western world across a whole variety of commodities by about ten per cent. Chinese growth just chugged along during that whole period and it consumed all of the excess capacity that had been installed but was no longer being used by the West. It pushed out the current price expansion by a two-year period. While there was excess capacity, the Chinese were able to consume everything at very low prices.'[4]

BHP itself had traded with the Chinese for more than a hundred years – even before the creation of the Republic in 1912. In the 1890s, the company had sold lead and silver bullion from the Big Mine at Broken Hill to the Ching Dynasty. According to Brian Loton, the Chinese were big customers who once saved The Prop from bankruptcy. 'There were disruptions in the United States and Europe, with people going off metallic currencies,' he says. 'But the Chinese stuck to their bargain, and if they hadn't the company wouldn't have survived.'[5]

In May 1971, before the Australian Government had recognised the People's Republic, BHP negotiated pig-iron sales to the country. 'Trade with China fluctuated over the years,' Brian Loton says, 'and in more recent times we started to put steel development there as a sole company [as opposed to a joint venture].'

In the early 1990s, Russ Fynmore was put in charge of BHP's China trade, mainly in iron ore and coal. 'We advertised for a Mandarin speaker, and a young man called Clinton Dines applied,' Fynmore says. 'He'd gone up there as a 20-year-old to learn Mandarin and was working in Hong Kong for a trading company. We liked him – he was a bit different: a modern style of person. He went to Beijing and did a great job for BHP.'[6]

In the new BHP Billiton, Mike Salamon was one of the most enthusiastic Sinophiles, along with the commercial chief Marius Kloppers, Brad Mills (copper) and Phil Aiken (petroleum). Salamon had first gone to China in 1992 when Samancor started to sell its chrome and manganese there. In 1993, the company hosted a major ferro-alloys conference in Beijing, for which it produced a ferro-alloy manual in Mandarin – nothing like that had ever existed. 'We realised stuff was happening there – and not just in Shanghai,' he says. 'I went to cities you'd never heard of – getting to them was almost impossible. You started to realise this was much more than just some ephemeral boom.'[7]

By the end of 2001, BHP Billiton had opened the company's biggest network office in Shanghai, and Clinton Dines moved down from Beijing to run it. 'We didn't shut the Beijing office, but Shanghai was the heart of China,' Mike Salamon says. 'It was one of the best strategic moves we made because by centralising everything we started to realise this was massive, and we saw that long before everybody else. We had source data which governments didn't have, nobody had. Consequently, we could think about a business model which was more analogous to the 1950s and '60s, when the world needed raw materials to rebuild Europe and Japan.

'From somewhere in the 1970s all the way through to 2000, that changed. All of us became fat and happy; that was how it was for 25 years until China got into its creation. We were already approving projects while other people were still in the old mentality, but it wasn't easy.'

In strategy meetings, Marius Kloppers maintained that BHPB's resources in the ground were now 'a hell of a lot more valuable' than they had been ten years earlier. Kloppers recalls leading a session on the subject at the Danesfield conference in June 2002. 'Because we had restructured our operations on the back of the merger, it gave us the opportunity to do a more holistic assessment of what was coming in terms of demand in China,' he says. 'Part of how we set ourselves up was to look at what we anticipated as demand pictures in China across the range of products.'[8]

China had already become the world's largest copper consumer and accounted for roughly a third of the world's steel exports. In 2002, BHP Billiton's sales to China were pegged at US$742 million, but they rose to US$1.2 billion in 2003 and in the first half of the 2004 financial year leaped to $1.1 billion, almost as much as in the entire previous year.

In March of that year, Chip Goodyear initiated an unusual equity deal with four big Chinese steel mills that locked them into an iron-ore contract worth US$9 billion over 25 years in return for equity in a new mining operation. The four mills – Wuhan Iron and Steel, Maanshan Iron and Steel, Jiangsu Shagang group and Tangshan Iron and Steel – each took ten per cent of Jimblebar mine, east of Mt Newman.[9]

One month later, the Chinese Government ordered banks to cut lending for iron, steel, aluminium and automobile manufacturing in an effort to cool down the red-hot economy. Commodity prices – and the shares of BHP Billiton and other resource companies – tilted sharply south.[10] Betting that China's demand for raw materials would survive the slowdown, Kloppers and his marketeers kept their nerve and pressed for more investment. The chief concern was still whether a lack of mine capacity would make it difficult to meet demand.

'Nobody had invested in development or reinvested in any new mines – there was no pipeline; all the exploration had been cut,' Brad Mills says. 'One of the big strategic arguments inside BHP was what was going to happen with the future of these metals? Would they really ever get back to some long-term normative number? In fact, would they start going to a real price appreciation? It was a huge battle inside BHP.'[11]

The board backed the strategists' confidence and agreed to invest US$5.4 billion over the next five years to expand production of its copper, nickel and alumina. 'In the long haul, we believe that China is a strong and robust story,' Chris Lynch, the chief financial officer, told the *New York Times*. 'We fully expect bumps and hiccups on the way.'[12] Investments included US$1.1 billion for a new nickel mine in Western Australia and US$300 million to expand the Queensland nickel refinery; US$870 million to enlarge Escondida yet again; US$192 million to increase the output of the West Australian alumina refinery; US$213 million to boost production at its iron-ore mines there and an additional US$351 million to expanding port and rail facilities.

The final sales figure for 2004 was US$2.4 billion, which meant that China had accounted for ten per cent of BHP Billiton's total sales and more than 20 per cent of its sales growth. Don Argus told investors at the annual general meeting in Sydney on 22 October, 'We expect China's economy to ease modestly from current near-double-digit growth rates, yet remain a large and sustainable consumer of raw materials and resources in coming years.'

China had rapidly become the leitmotif of Chip Goodyear's reign as chief executive and would remain so. 'We need to recognise there may be something different happening today than there was ten years ago,' he said in March 2005. 'And that is that 1.4 billion people in China and a billion people in India may be saying, "Hey, this is our century. This is our chance for a television set, a refrigerator, an air conditioner or ultimately an automobile." And when that population says that this is something they want to strive for, its consumption of raw materials will be quite significant, just as it was in the world that we see today as a developed economy. And when that happens, there's a great draw on the things that we produce. It will have its cycles just like every other economy we're involved in. So,

China is important to what we do, but we don't build it on the basis that it's going to grow to the moon.'[13]

Goodyear produced a chart of commodities prices going back to the Anglo-American War of 1812 that he called the '200-year view'. He argued that the Chinese bull market for resources was on a par with the Industrial Revolution and the rebuilding that had followed the Second World War. During both those periods, commodity prices experienced a 25-year increase. 'Do we think that China is going to be a place that's going to be a significant resource consumer for the next 20 to 30 years?' he asked. 'The answer is yes, we do.'

In February 2006, BHP Billiton announced it had broken the record for the highest six-monthly net profits at an Australian company for the fifth consecutive year. The US$4.36 billion profit for the last six months of 2005 confirmed the strength of demand from China, which was paying higher prices for iron ore, coking coal and copper. Iron ore alone rose 70 per cent. In 2005, China accounted for almost $3 billion in sales, 16 per cent of the company's income. Chip Goodyear said, 'We don't see much reason that [China] would be below eight per cent GDP growth, certainly for the next number of years.'[14]

The chief concern was that a lack of mine capacity would make it difficult to meet demand. 'You realise this is an entire changing of a massive society,' Mike Salamon says. 'The standards which the Chinese aspire to are yours and mine – they're not some second-class standards. They want nice apartments, decent airports, cars, then universities – and they want a clean environment. You look at modern Chinese buildings – they are *the* most modern, the most environmentally friendly. There's a lot of baggage there but they want to change it. Then you work out what does this mean in terms of materials and energy. If you add North America to Europe, it's much smaller than China, and then you've got India waiting in the wings.

'Visionaries like Andrew "Twiggy" Forrest[15] saw it and we saw it. And we had this incredible platform that we'd created for a different world, but it was the strongest platform ever in terms of its asset base and its global reach.'[16]

It was now apparent that China and India – 'Chindia' to the economists – had triggered a supercycle for commodities that would last for decades. Most of the economic activity in India, however, had been in call centres, computer software and the IT industry, none of which required huge infrastructure. But in China, airports, railroads, power stations and whole new cities – all big infrastructure projects – were being built on a massive scale.

In order to feed the voracious demands of the supercycle, Chip Goodyear had to swallow his reservations about Russia and compete for its largely untapped resources of copper, nickel, coal and bauxite. He took the first step in June 2006 by setting up a joint venture with two of Russia's oligarchs, Mikhail Prokhorov and Vladimir Potanin, controllers of Norilsk Nickel, Russia's biggest mining company. Ignoring his caution of the previous year, when he had described Russia as an 'immature' investment arena, Goodyear said during a visit to Moscow, 'This alliance with Norilsk is a win–win – it's an important step for BHP Billiton.'[17]

In fact, BHP Billiton was following the lead of Rio Tinto, which had completed a similar agreement with Norilsk just six weeks earlier to explore for base metals in remote regions of Siberia. President Vladimir Putin demanded that Russia retain control over core natural-resource assets, so the BHP Billiton venture was split 50–50 but Norilsk would own one extra share.[18]

After a meeting with Putin, Goodyear declared that Rosatom, Russia's atomic energy agency, would be a potential customer for its uranium when BHP Billiton increased mining at Olympic Dam. 'What Gazprom[19] is to natural gas, we are to uranium,' he told Reuters. 'We are about to go through a big expansion at Olympic Dam and make a decision to triple uranium production, so we need to find markets.'[20]

Back in Australia, the usually self-contained Goodyear could barely restrain himself when he reported BHP Billiton's third consecutive record full-year profit on 23 August 2006. 'What a year!' he declared during presentations to journalists and analysts in Sydney. 'We are clearly at an interesting time in our industry. The world has rediscovered resources and how critical they are to our daily lives. In developing countries, they are fundamental to economic development.' Net profit had risen 58 per cent to US$10.2 billion in the fiscal year ended 30 June, with revenue climbing 25.5 per cent to US$39 billion. Investors' expectations were now so high, however, that BHP Billiton's shares actually *fell* 36 cents to close at $28.30.[21]

With mines operating at full capacity, trade unions demanded higher wages for their members in several of BHP Billiton's operations. The most serious strike had begun on 7 August of that year when some 2000 workers at Escondida downed tools. Soon after the strike started, the company reported first-half profits for the mine of close to US$3 billion, more than triple its profits in the same period the previous year. Infuriated, the miners held their ground.

After a 25-day strike that cost the company about US$200 million in lost profits, the miners returned to work on 2 September, but only after reaching a deal that, according to union officials, made them the highest-paid workers in South America. It included a five per cent real-wage increase, new education, health-care and housing benefits, an end-of-strike bonus worth an after-tax $4600 and an unheard of bonus of $12,000 on account of high copper prices.[22]

Nothing, however, could interrupt the progress of the Chinese economic miracle. 'Once the genie is out of the bottle,' Goodyear liked to say, 'it is very tough to go backwards. Once people know you can have a fridge, education and so on, if you say, "Oh, I'm sorry, no more," then you have a problem.'[23]

No Chinese leader in the post-Deng era would volunteer for that problem. On the contrary, the Communist Party leadership showed themselves acutely aware that continued economic growth and rising living standards were central to their maintaining political control. And a significant element of that growth has been the raw material and energy supplies so abundant in the so-called Lucky Country.[24] Indeed, the complementary nature of the two economies was forging a new political climate within the respective leadership.

John Howard, who brought his conservative, anti-communist attitudes honed in the cold-war years to the prime ministership in 1996, would become an enthusiastic salesman for Australian mining groups. This culminated in a special 2006 trip to Shenzhen in support of a massive deal under which Woodside Petroleum would supply US$37 billion worth of liquefied natural gas to PetroChina over the next 20 years. Chinese Premier Wen Jiabao joined him in welcoming the deal. And by identifying himself so closely with the China connection, Howard opened the door for his successor to expand the relationship beyond the commercial boundaries.

Indeed, it provided opposition leader Kevin Rudd with a political coup in his quest for power in 2007. In the lead-up to the November election, Howard had planned a meeting of Asia-Pacific Economic Cooperation (APEC) leaders scheduled for Sydney in September as the perfect stage on which to parade his international leadership credentials. His friendship with the American president George W. Bush – a sure-fire electoral winner in the past – would contrast Howard the international statesman with the relatively young and inexperienced Rudd.[25] In the event, Bush's personal unpopularity and inept performance at the meeting (at one stage confusing the gathering with OPEC) neutralised the American connection. Then Rudd finessed Howard comprehensively at a luncheon for the Chinese president Hu Jintao when he addressed the visitors in perfect Mandarin. A clearly delighted Hu Jintao enthused, 'You know China inside and out,' while Howard squirmed in his seat. Suddenly, it seemed, it was Rudd who represented the future direction of Australia's commercial and political diplomacy.

However, Rudd's Chinese expertise, accumulated through an honours degree at the Australian National University, further language study in Taiwan and Hong Kong, the diplomatic posting to Beijing and his China consultancy, brought with it some unexpected constraints. His conservative opponents began a whispering campaign that Rudd was 'the Manchurian candidate',[26] suggesting that he was too familiar with the Chinese for Australia's good. This caused him to cancel a planned trip to Beijing prior to the election and to operate circumspectly in his dealings with the Chinese leaders.

By the time Rudd had swept to victory in November 2007, Chip Goodyear was in his last month as chief executive. The timing was unexpected, but Goodyear, still only 49, had always made it clear that he did not intend to stay at the company for a long term. He had presided over an incomparable boom that had made record profits almost the norm. Indeed, at the time he announced his resignation in February, the company posted its highest earnings ever for the second half of 2006. Led by soaring Chinese demand for copper and nickel, net profit rose 41 per cent to US$6.2 billion.[27]

'When I went down there, it was just to right the ship,' he says. 'I don't think this is well known, but the Sunday after taking the job I did tell Don [Argus] that it's a five-year commitment and that's essentially what it was.

'I'm a big believer in change. It's good for people and it's good for companies. You have a lot of good young people in the company and if they thought I was going to stay there till I was 65 they would have left – they should have left. We needed to move on.'[28]

Although headhunters scoured the global-resources industry for a replacement, it was generally thought that the two outstanding candidates to step into Goodyear's shoes were Marius Kloppers, a noted archer in his youth, and the former footballer Chris Lynch, both of whom had been elevated to the board in January 2006 and given new executive roles.

The smart money was always on Kloppers. At the time of the merger with BHP, he was Billiton's chief marketing officer and went on to develop a formidable reputation in all aspects of the business from mergers and acquisitions to copper, iron ore and alumina pricing. He was now president of non-ferrous materials.[29]

Chris Lynch, with his roots in Broken Hill, took over as president of carbon steel materials following the retirement of Bob Kirkby, and when Mike Salamon also retired he found himself in charge of the China office as well. At 51, he was seven years older than Kloppers.

The rivalry was intense but, according to insiders, the two candidates kept up appearances throughout the struggle. At the end of May, Don Argus announced in a press release that the contest had been won by 'Dr Kloppers, an achievement-driven individual', who would become chief executive on 1 October. Although Chip Goodyear would officially step down the day before, he would remain with the company until the end of the year to work on several projects. Chris Lynch promptly resigned.

'Marius is an extremely talented guy and was clearly the best qualified person to take over,' Lord Renwick says. 'He is very relentless and go-getting, and it took a while for the Australian directors to warm to him, but in the end they did. He's more of a deal guy than Chip. Western Mining was really done primarily by Marius and Don rather than Chip – Chip was more cautious: he's not an instinctive deal guy.'[30]

Don Argus dismissed suggestions that Kloppers' style was similar to that of his Billiton mentor Gilbertson. 'Marius is his own man,' he insisted. 'His vast experience in the resources sector and his demonstrated strategic capabilities provide the skills we need in the next leader of our great company.'

Gilbertson described Kloppers' appointment as 'an inspired choice'. 'He is a man of formidable intellect,' he said. 'He is a very good decision-maker. He can be tough and ruthless when he needs to be and he can be absolutely charming – which he is most of the time.'[31]

When Goodyear presented his last set of BHPB results in August, he unveiled a 21 per cent jump in pre-tax profits to US$18 billion for the year ending 30 June 2007. While

BHPB had benefited from higher commodity prices, especially in nickel, copper, iron ore and aluminium, Goodyear said the 'absolutely outstanding' results also stemmed from greater production from the company's mines, smelters and oilfields.

China now accounted for no less than 20 per cent of sales. 'We believe the industrialisation and urbanisation that have driven China's growth will continue for several decades as billions of people strive for a better quality of life,' he said. 'This growth is resource-intensive and it represents a steep change in resource demand.' Turning to his favourite metaphor, he added, 'Once people get visibility to a better way of life, and governments see that as a good thing, it's very difficult to put the genie back in the bottle.'[32]

Goodyear also sounded a clear warning to his successor. 'China now represents in excess of 45 per cent of global seaborne iron-ore demand, 22 per cent of copper, 25 per cent of aluminium and 17 per cent of nickel demand,' he said. 'While this represents a significant business opportunity, our exposure to China's economic fortunes and economic policies has increased . . . a slowing in China's economic growth could result in lower prices for our products and therefore reduce our revenues.

'China is increasingly seeking self-sufficiency in key commodities, including investments in other countries. These investments may impact future demand and supply balances and prices.'[33]

Goodyear's comment triggered speculation that the China Investment Corporation might use some of China's immense sovereign-wealth fund – then estimated at US$200 billion – to take a ten per cent stake in BHP Billiton, and perhaps Rio Tinto, in order to gain some measure of control over its supplies of iron ore, copper and aluminium. Kevin Rudd, still opposition leader, commented that a Labor Government would welcome Chinese investment, and even takeovers, if he won the November election. 'The Chinese are on a global-investment push,' he said. 'It is virtually impossible to kick through one [international] capital and not run into a Chinese investment team.'[34] However, as Rudd would discover when elected, it was not that simple. Chinese economic expansion would become a double-edged sword and he would soon have to contend with the disturbing consequences arising when, against all predictions, the Asian supercycle suddenly imploded and Chinese investors went shopping for bargains on the severely depressed Australian stock market.

CHAPTER 28

Meltdown

Investors had little doubt that Marius Kloppers would be more aggressive than his predecessor on the mergers-and-acquisitions front – BHP Billiton had made no big purchase since taking over WMC Resources in 2005, a deal in which he had been intimately involved. But no one outside the company anticipated just how quickly he would act. In less than six weeks, he launched an offensive that, if successful, would reshape the global-mining industry. On Thursday, 8 November 2007, he announced a massive bid for arch-rival Rio Tinto in a deal that would create a mining company worth US$350 billion in market capitalisation at that time.[1]

Kloppers' strategists had been laying the groundwork for several months before he took over from Chip Goodyear on 1 October, and the new chief executive fired off a merger proposal – over the signature of Don Argus – to Rio's chairman, Paul Skinner, who was visiting Sydney from his London base. As early as September 2006, Argus had an informal chat with Skinner about a negotiated combination, but that approach went nowhere.

Argus's letter set out what BHP Billiton believed to be

'a compelling and unique case' for a merger between the two titans, one that would deliver US$3.7 billion in annual cost-saving synergies. Most would come from the iron-ore operation in the Pilbara by combining Rio's Hamersley Iron with BHP Billiton's seven mining operations, including Mt Whaleback, the biggest single-pit, open-cut mine in the world. Both companies were planning to double production. Once combined, they could share rail and port facilities at Port Hedland and Dampier.[2]

But whether Rio Tinto's tough new American chief executive, Tom Albanese, would be tempted depended on how much of a short-term premium BHP Billiton was prepared to pay for Rio's proud independent heritage. That heritage ran deep. In one of the more extraordinary coincidences in the global-mining narrative, Rio Tinto could trace its beginnings back through Conzinc and CRA all the way to the Zinc Corporation, which mined its first paydirt at Broken Hill in the same ancient line of lode that gave BHP its start.

Albanese, fresh from a US$38.7 billion cash deal to acquire Alcan, immediately rejected BHP Billiton's offer of three shares for every one Rio share. Market analysts had a field day. Rivers of ink were expended, with a general consensus that while Kloppers would need to raise the bid before he could wrap it up, the international implications were epochal.

Analyst Ian Verrender said, 'This is not just another merger – this is a huge battle for control of vital and scarce resources, the sort of thing that has brought countries to war in the past, and it has coincided with an uprising of Chinese nationalism.'[3] Chinese Government spokesmen feared that the new mining behemoth would have the power to dictate prices to China's steel mills and power stations. The president of Chinalco (the state-owned Aluminium Corporation of China), Xiao Yaqing, said, 'A firm that owns too many resources is not good for the world. People do not want to see a company dominate the market in any industry.'[4]

More pertinently, perhaps, steeply increased prices for iron ore and coal would mean that Chinese manufactures would become more expensive, exports would be endangered, the great renaissance imperilled. Verrender added, 'Justified or not, the message from China was blunt: the West was jealous and fearful of China's ascendancy to its rightful position in the global community after a century of humiliation and poverty, and ordinary Chinese had had enough.'

Kloppers was quick to reassure his fastest-growing consumers. In November 2007, he visited Chinese steel mills to tell them the takeover would mean 'more iron and a more predictable pricing system'. 'For the Chinese economy that is growing very rapidly, the assurance they will get product at the market price and get more of that product is a very valuable proposition,' he said.[5] The Chinese kept their own counsel.

Word soon leaked that Marius Kloppers had dubbed his play 'Project de Bello' – *to do battle and vanquish.* He saw himself storming the City of London citadel and restoring Rio Tinto to the Australian fold. And he had no doubt that if anyone could pull it off, he was the man for the job. 'I've probably integrated more companies than any other executive in the industry,' he said. 'What I see before me is a deal absolutely without parallel.'[6]

In the New Year, BHP Billiton signed up China's biggest steelmaker, Baosteel, for an additional 94 million tonnes of iron ore from Western Australia, the first shipment scheduled for April. It was business as usual. But suddenly, on 30 January, in what was described as 'the biggest-ever dawn raid' on the London Stock Market, Chinalco joined with the US aluminium giant, Alcoa, to buy a nine per cent stake in Rio Tinto for US$14.05 billion. The consortium declared that it did not intend at that time to make a takeover bid for the company but reserved its right to do so later. Xiao Yaqing said in Sydney, 'Our acquisition of a significant strategic stake in Rio Tinto today reflects our confidence in the long-term prospects for the rapidly evolving global-mining sector.'[7]

Rio Tinto chairman Paul Skinner said he did not believe

Chinalco's motives were 'sinister'. On the contrary, he welcomed the emergence of a new player that would provide him with tactical leverage in the ensuing boardroom battle. Kloppers' reaction was swift. In February, he decided to go hostile with his all-scrip offer. And he backed his judgment by raising the bid to 3.4 shares to one of Rio's. Albanese and his board spurned that too.

To execute his battle plan, Kloppers detached the company's suave chief commercial officer, 48-year-old, Yale-educated Alberto Calderon, to lead no fewer than 100 BHP Billiton personnel in the Rio offensive. The charismatic Colombian, who lived in London with his wife, Marta, and two children, was soon on the warpath, describing Tom Albanese's claim to have increased the value of Alcan by US$30 billion as 'voodoo economics'.[8]

In April 2008, Calderon was joined by Nelson Silva, who had been running the aluminium division from company headquarters at Neathouse Place, Victoria. 'Nelson is very instrumental in looking at the iron-ore piece of the deal,' Kloppers said, 'and particularly the interaction with the EU, since he's had such an extensive history in the iron-ore business, having worked for CVRD [Vale] for many years.'[9]

Kloppers and his team were operating in a world of infinitely expanding markets for their major commodities and a stock-exchange bull-run powered by seemingly unstoppable Chinese growth. And when it began to slacken, India would come on line to drive resource companies along an endless path of rising prosperity. Their only concerns were the regulatory bodies, which seemed determined to guard against too great a market share falling to The Big Fella. And even there, the United States was making all the right signals and the Australian Consumer and Competition Commission (ACCC) under chairman Graeme Samuel could be expected to give the deal a tick. The European Union was another matter. On 4 July, the European Commission's competition regulator opened an in-depth investigation into the deal after issuing a tough statement that listed sweeping anti-trust concerns.

The new entity would have at least 36 per cent of the world's iron-ore market, and European steel mills would press their competition regulator to block the deal on anti-trust grounds. Japanese and Chinese mills were also likely to complain. Kloppers countered that while it would be a marriage of the second- and third-biggest iron-ore producers, it would still leave the world's biggest, Brazil's Vale, with a similar market share.

In his letter to Rio, Don Argus had been confident that regulators could be satisfied. Rio replied that it was sceptical about the chances of a mega-marriage clearing the regulatory hurdle. It also believed BHP Billiton was moving then because negotiations with Chinese and Japanese mills would result in commodity-price increases, and a big market re-rating for Rio, whose Pilbara mines were superior to BHP's.[10]

BHP Billiton's other main iron-ore asset was Samarco, an equal joint venture in Brazil with the mine's operator, Vale. The merger would mean that the company controlled close to 80 per cent of the world's seaborne trade in iron ore. But Vale would still be the biggest producer, with 300 million tonnes of ore expected in 2008, compared with 275 million for BHP and Rio.

Kloppers' new entity would have mines and oilfields in six continents, including an 87.5 per cent stake in Chile's massive Escondida copper mine. It also would have assets in uranium, diamonds, silver, lead and nickel. Rio Tinto had become the world's largest aluminium producer after acquiring Alcan, and a merger with BHP Billiton's enormous aluminium assets would make it bigger than the highly competitive Russians. The Alcan deal had saddled Rio with about $40 billion in debt, but in an expanding world market that was easily manageable.

The Rio battle – with fronts in many global time zones – meant longer working hours for Marius Kloppers and an even more fractured home life. 'I normally try to get a leisurely breakfast and a late start in the office – 10 am,' he told the authors. After a full day's work, he returned home 'for some sort of a break from six to eight or seven to nine' before the evening shift started with London coming into play. 'That goes through until whatever time it takes.'[11]

He spent half his time outside Australia, often travelling with his assistant, a Scot named Gordon Carlisle, 'one of the up-and-coming guys in the company, one of the young talents'. A South African and a Scot representing Australia's largest company at the highest levels no longer raised eyebrows. The Big Fella's cosmopolitan nature was now ingrained.

The Chinese, meanwhile, continued to defend their position in anticipation of Kloppers' success. Their Sinosteel made a $1.2 billion bid for the West Australian iron-ore producer Midwest. Sinosteel already owned 40 per cent of the Cannar mine, also in Western Australia. The bid was approved by the Australian FIRB. But Midwest directors recommended against acceptance and in March the bid turned hostile, the first of its kind by China in Australia.

With rumours flying of a Chinese counter-bid for BHP Billiton, Prime Minister Kevin Rudd's political antennae were engaged and his treasurer Wayne Swan announced a 'clarification' of FIRB criteria in a press release. 'The Australian Government welcomes foreign investment because it makes an important contribution to job creation and to our national economy more generally,' he said. 'Our job is to ensure that any given investment, regardless of its origin, is consistent with Australia's national interest.' Swan counselled a 'cautious' approach from Chinese investors. Bids would be examined 'on a case by case basis'. The key criteria for Chinese state enterprises were the extent to which the foreign investor operated at arm's length to the relevant government, and the extent to which the investment was driven by purely commercial objectives. But that still left substantial room for discretion.

Behind the political flummery, the Australian prime minister was acutely aware of two forces at play: first, public opinion, which still contained a measure of racial prejudice against the Chinese, having found its first expression in the riots against Chinese miners on the Victorian and NSW goldfields in the

1850s and '60s and led to the notorious White Australia Policy at federation in 1901. Sixty years later, during the Vietnam War, it erupted again in the form of the political canard – ruthlessly propagated by the conservative parties – of 'the downward thrust of Chinese communism'. Since then, it had simmered beneath the surface, erupting from time to time with the Beijing regime's excesses, most notably in Tiananmen Square in 1989.

The second force was a behind-the-scenes lobbying assault by BHP Billiton to defend itself against the rumoured raid on its own share register by a state-backed Chinese corporation. Jennifer Hewett, national-affairs correspondent for *The Australian*, said, 'BHP has been lobbying furiously in Canberra about the risks of allowing a Chinese company to block the prospect of a super resources company headquartered in Australia.'[12]

Don Argus was aggressively unrepentant. 'You have a look what's happening over in Africa, where the Chinese are actually going in taking Chinese people, trying to get countries, I suppose, to let them use their natural resources; they're actually buying banks – they bought a full bank – so you need to be careful,' he says. 'You've got the Russians setting up their major resources companies. You've got Brazil – these are all state-owned and you need a countervailing force to be able to take these people on. And I'm saying this is one of the benefits that comes with the BHP Billiton/Rio merger, because you are in there competing.'[13]

Moreover, he remained unabashed about pressing his case at the highest levels. 'I had a good working relationship with Bob Hawke,' he says, 'and Paul Keating – even though we disagreed on the four-pillars policy.

'I had a good working relationship with John Howard, and I like to think I've got a good working relationship with Kevin Rudd. I've never been afraid to say what I think, and it doesn't matter what side of politics is in. I'm very proactive in pushing Australia. I'm parochial when it comes to sport, and I'm very pragmatic about the way capital is used in an organisation, but I don't apologise for being a passionate Australian; patriotic is probably the word I'd use.'

Not surprisingly, Rio's Paul Skinner defended China's right to invest in Australian resources. The Rudd government, he said, had taken a 'very measured approach' to its FIRB rules. 'Japanese investment that was the key to developing Australia's resources industry in the 1960s and '70s also involved strong state direction,' he said.[14] In the event, at least ten Chinese companies subsequently withdrew foreign-investment applications to buy into Australian resource companies after Rudd had made it plain that he wanted more time to prepare the ground politically.

Inevitably, the battle with Rio Tinto became personal. Kloppers told the *Financial Times*, 'Tom Albanese has been comprehensively outperformed [by BHPB] in terms of volume growth, earnings per share growth, total return for shareholders and share-price performance.

'On every metric I can envisage, [Rio] have been beaten. They have missed the boat on China; they are missing the boat on energy. It must be terrible [for them] that every quarter BHP outperforms, and that has been the case for seven years.'[15]

Asked what it would mean for him personally and for BHP Billiton if Project de Bello collapsed, Kloppers said, 'If the deal did not happen – and it is a complex thing because there are many different angles – shareholders can take comfort in BHP having a great baseline strategy. We want to deploy $10 billion in capital on new projects and we have grown the company at eight per cent a year over the last seven years. We believe we are in a very sweet spot with our commodities mix.'[16]

That month – April 2008 – Don Argus was in China for an economic-development conference attended by Premier Wen Jiabao. 'The commerce minister [Bo Xilai] singled out eight people that were obviously irritants to them and we were one of them because of iron-ore pricing,' he said. 'The new minister for finance [Xie Xuren] gave us all a little lecture about our positions and we were given one and a half minutes each to respond.'[17]

International Harvester, Michelin and Toyota were all chastised for one reason or another. When it was Argus's turn, he gave vent to his feisty nature. 'Look, you tolerate a hundred steel mills that aren't efficient and that are setting the spot price,' he snapped. 'We'll always meet the contractual arrangements, but we'll have an eye on the spot price. And if you think you're going to have a benchmark price down here while there's a spot price up there, let me tell you, you will never get there. And not only that, iron ore is the only ore that you don't have an index on, and we're moving down that path, and we'll continue to move down that path.'[18]

Don Argus grinned. 'That was my one and a half minutes, and it didn't take me one and a half minutes to get it out, either. And as we were going out the door, this guy [Xie Xuren], who did everything through interpreters, said in the most beautiful English, "Oh, Mr Argus, we must keep talking." I said, "Very happy to talk about anything." They appreciate your candour, they do. I don't hold back. I don't leave anything on the table that they don't understand.'

The Rudd government's first Budget, delivered by Swan on 13 May 2008, underlined the reason for the prime minister's caution when it revealed the extraordinary effect the Chinese boom was having on the Australian economy. Swan announced a surplus of almost $22 billion – 1.8 per cent of GDP – provided overwhelmingly by rivers of Chinese gold that swelled the coffers of the Australian treasury. An even greater bonanza was in prospect – a 20 per cent increase in the terms of trade the following year – as BHP Billiton and other suppliers renegotiated the iron-ore price.

Marius Kloppers, however, said he saw China as only one element of the global strategy. 'We're in the extractive industries, and resources are viewed very much as an endowment of countries,' he said. 'We don't view China as very geologically endowed. We sell about 20 per cent of our product there but we look at the global market first in its entirety. If I look at coking coal, for example, that would be driven primarily by Indian development, because China has got quite a lot of coal and India is quite short of energy products.'[19]

In June, Rio Tinto announced it had secured an 85 per cent increase in the price of iron ore to the biggest Chinese steelmakers. Within weeks, BHP Billiton had matched the Rio rise by reaching a new agreement with Baosteel to almost double the price of its iron ore to March 2009. Ian Ashby, Melbourne-born president of the iron-ore division, said, 'Traditionally, prices only change once a year because the system was an annual negotiation. Things have changed slightly with the demand out of China because demand has outstripped supply.'[20]

On 8 July, Treasurer Swan revealed that the government would place limits on Chinese takeovers of Australian mining companies as it grappled with a $30 billion wave of Chinese foreign-investment proposals. Jennifer Hewett said that the move was likely to 'aggravate tensions' between the two countries. The Chinese ambassador to Australia, Zhang Junsai, told Hewett that Chinese firms were 'puzzled' by official delays in approvals. The Australian Government should encourage 'an attitude of welcome' to Chinese companies. Robin Chalmers, the only non-Chinese director of Sinosteel, said the government had recently asked a Chinese company to limit itself to 49.9 per cent of a target company as a precondition for granting its approval of a foreign-investment proposal.

By now, Clinton Dines, a fellow Chinese expert from Rudd's native Queensland, had become president of BHP Billiton China. He and his wife had even adopted a Chinese child and, at his urging, the company had been quick to appreciate the significance of the Olympics to China and became an official sponsor, providing the gold, silver and bronze for all the medals to be awarded. In August, Marius Kloppers spent ten days at the Games, welcoming a line of VIPs to the company's corporate-entertainment suite. 'We actually didn't have any formal investor discussions, or indeed customer discussions,' he said. Pressed at an analysts' meeting in London on whether there were any talks at all with Chinalco, he said there had been none, although 'for the avoidance of doubt, Chinalco was one of the guests we took to the opening ceremony of the Olympics, along with a whole slew of other people'.[21]

The takeover battle reached a new pitch of ferocity when, on 18 August, Kloppers reported net income of US$15.4 billion for the year ending 30 June, assisted by the jump in commodity prices, higher production and an ability to pass on higher costs. 'We're well set for the future,' Kloppers said in a conference call with analysts. 'We have a low-risk growth portfolio, we can contend with all sorts of headwinds and tailwinds and still turn in great results.'[22]

The results were staggering. No mining company had recorded such an astronomical figure before. But Rio was only briefly on the defensive. On 24 August, Treasurer Swan approved the acquisition of 14.99 per cent of Rio Tinto plc by Chinalco – about 11 per cent in the group, which included the Australian-listed Rio Tinto Limited. Any future proposal to increase its holding, he said, would require re-assessment at the time.

Two days later, Tom Albanese presented Marius Kloppers with an unwelcome present on his 46th birthday when, in reporting half-yearly pre-tax profits of $9.69 billion, he announced that Rio Tinto would pursue joint ventures with Chinalco around the world. And, in response to Kloppers' jibe that he had 'missed the boat in China', Albanese stated that Rio would even increase its presence there.

One of the most interested observers of the drama was Sir Robert Wilson, Rio's former chairman and chief executive. 'Things have moved on, of course,' he told the authors, 'and you have to say: do the advantages really still outweigh the disadvantages [of a prospective BHP–Rio merger]? Are those cost-saving synergies really that material?

'You shouldn't overlook the disadvantages of scale and manageability. We can already see companies, arguably in the oil-and-gas industry, which have become so big they can't really be managed. So I think there's a bit of a risk there. And what both companies would lose is actually the incentive to improve, because it would be daft to deny that for decades BHP and Rio Tinto have been sharpened by rivalry. Take that away and what have you got? You've got, potentially, a big stodgy vegetable.'[23]

Despite the Chinese manoeuvring and an announcement by the European Commission in September that a decision would not be made until January 2009, Kloppers and Argus maintained the pressure on Rio. Kloppers' campaign scored a major victory on 1 October 2008 when ACCC head Graeme Samuel announced approval of the takeover. Indeed, the ACCC comprehensively rejected the assertion that a BHP Billiton–Rio Tinto conglomerate would permit the new entity and its competitor, Vale, to manipulate the iron-ore market. 'This is because increasing demand, the heterogeneous nature of iron-ore production and infrastructure expansion projects, and the corresponding threat of non-compliance would be likely to destabilise any potential tacit or explicit consensus between the merged firm and Vale,' he said. 'Accordingly, the evidence provided to the ACCC did not establish that the proposed acquisition is likely to substantially lessen competition in the global seaborne supply of iron-ore lump and iron-ore fines.'[24]

So decisive was the ACCC finding that analysts judged the European Union would almost certainly follow suit. Until the announcement, Rio Tinto had been priced on the belief that the regulators might reject the deal. In the wake of Samuel's decision, the stock surged 12.4 per cent. And, in short order, the United States Department of Justice cleared the way without any objections.

But then, deliberately and hypnotically, the world of Don Argus, Marius Kloppers, Tom Albanese and the other metal men turned on its head. In October/November, the Wall Street financial crisis sent stock exchanges around the world into a state of chaotic disarray and the share market plummeted. Amid fears of an international recession, commodity prices slumped dramatically and mining stocks followed. The men at the top of the great extractive industries found their glorious certainties of six months ago crashing about their ears.

It was a new and unnerving experience. In many ways, the giant mining companies – BHP Billiton chief among them – had come to resemble medieval nation states, their rulers unencumbered by the demands of democracy and answerable only to an oligarchy of shareholders whose concerns rarely strayed from the bottom line. Not since the heady days of BHP in the post-Second World War years had the company enjoyed such a sense of supreme self-determination. It made its own rules of engagement with the governments of the day, developed its own ethical standards for its employee citizenry, created its own department of external affairs and set its own goals for nonstop expansion. Indeed, Chip Goodyear's famous analysis of 2000 had promised that this happy state of affairs would continue indefinitely whatever might befall the real nation states of the geopolitical world. Except, of course, if the world economy itself went into freefall.

The battle was in full swing when BHP Billiton's big guns gathered in London to show solidarity with their chief executive at the annual general meeting of BHP Billiton plc on 23 October 2008. As the ten o'clock chimes of Big Ben peeled across Westminster, Don Argus pulled up in a chauffeured sedan outside the Queen Elizabeth II conference centre on the northern side of Parliament Square. Clad in an overcoat against the autumn chill, he paused inside the car for a few moments, a mobile phone clamped to his ear, to finish a call and then alighted and threw one of his beaming smiles to the line of shareholders and reporters being frisked for cameras, recording devices and weapons by security guards in the foyer.

All the directors were present, including three new appointees: 60-year-old American Alan L. Boeckmann (chairman and chief executive of the massive engineering-and-construction giant Fluor Corporation), 61-year-old Australian David Morgan (formerly chief executive of Westpac) and 54-year-old South African Keith Rumble (formerly of Rio Tinto and Impala Platinum, with recent valuable experience in private-equity investments in Russia and India). There was also a good turnout of the group management committee – Alberto Calderon (chief commercial officer), Marcus Randolph (chief executive ferrous and coal), former company secretary Karen Wood (now chief people officer) and Mike Yeager (chief executive petroleum). Sitting next to Alex Vaneslow, the burly Brazilian chief financial officer, in the directors' line-up was Paul Anderson, sporting a new Hemingway salt-and-pepper beard and, in common with most of his colleagues, wearing a red Armistice Day poppy in his buttonhole.

Despite the economic downturn, it had been an exceptionally fine financial year for BHP Billiton, partly due to oil prices reaching US$145 a barrel. There was a lot to boast about, and Don Argus launched into paeans of praise for the company's record profit of US$15.4 billion – the seventh consecutive full-year profit increase – a 38 per cent return on capital and 41 cent per share dividend, up for the thirteenth consecutive year. 'As an old bank man, let me tell you this is a marvellous balance sheet,' he said. 'The current financial crisis will severely impact on the share price for some time, but our diversified portfolio and strong balance sheet put us in a good position in a cash-strapped environment.'

At 10.40 am, Marius Kloppers took the lectern to make his first report to an annual general meeting as chief executive (on a basic salary, the meeting was informed, of US$1,979,500). 'We are committed to a strategy of larger, long-life, low-cost, world-class assets diversified by geography,' he said. 'They are expandable and consistent in profit, and robust in a down cycle. Diversification reduces risk by not having all our eggs in one basket.'

Turning to Rio Tinto, he said, 'BHP and Rio Tinto are uniquely configured in the commodities we produce, in our geographies, in our customers and in the way we do business. But the synergies can only be unlocked through a combination of the two companies.'

Afterwards, Don Argus strolled upstairs to join shareholders over a buffet lunch. He asked one of the authors what the word was around London about the BHP bid. Told that Sir Robert Wilson thought the combined company might be too big to manage, The Don beamed and replied that while that might apply to some industries, 'mining is different'. He had told the meeting that he expected the takeover bid to be decided early in 2009 after all the regulators had reported their findings. BHP would send acceptance forms to Rio shareholders and an extraordinary general meeting would be held for BHP investors. But late that afternoon a spectre loomed over Westminster. For word swept through the BHPB hierarchy that Argus had been summoned to an urgent meeting with the European Commission's competition regulator based in Brussels. Something was up.

Coincidentally, rumblings about the international share market had begun at precisely the time Marius Kloppers was about to make his audacious bid for Rio. In September/October 2007, the New York Stock Exchange responded to a realisation that the United States housing boom was in fact a bubble inflated by 'sub-prime' loans, a euphemism that would disguise the true dimensions of the disaster for some time. Indeed, the early predictions from Wall Street – after the failure of Bear Stearns, a big United States stockbroker, in March 2008 and the bounce-back that followed – were that the losses from home buyers unable to meet mortgage repayments would represent little more than a 'speed hump' on that endless pathway of prosperity.

Only gradually did the world's share traders become aware of the complex financial instruments developed to market the mortgages. From 2000, as house prices rose, lenders had developed adjustable-rate mortgages (ARMs) with low 'teaser rates', no down payments and even the postponement of some interest monthly payments that were added to the principal of the loan. Then they added mortgage-backed securities (MBS) – the pooling of mortgages into packages for sale to investors who received pro-rata payments of principal and interest by the borrowers. Collateralised debt obligations

(CDOs) followed, in which some of the MBS were repackaged, often with other asset-backed securities, and sold even further afield to investors – including banks – around the world. And, as the regulators in George W. Bush's America turned a blind eye, these sub-prime derivatives multiplied like runaway cancer cells through the globe's financial body politic.

Even more reprehensible, perhaps, were the actions of the credit-rating agencies Moody's, Standard & Poors and Fitch, who encouraged the spread of the disease with their high ratings for the companies selling the derivatives. 'The story of the credit-rating agencies is a story of colossal failure,' Henry Waxman, chairman of the House of Representatives oversight and government-reform committee, said at a public hearing. 'Millions of investors rely on them for independent, objective assessments. The rating agencies broke this bond of trust. The result is that our entire financial system is now at risk.'[25]

Indeed, after the collapse of the 158-year-old Wall Street institution Lehman Brothers on 15 September, global credit markets simply froze as banks were unable or unwilling to risk lending to each other, let alone clients who relied on credit rollovers to maintain their businesses.

Government leaders responded by posting guarantees in an attempt to unlock the credit freeze but it quickly became clear that a major international recession was unavoidable. First, the United States and then Europe tumbled into the abyss. Even China was forced to recalibrate its growth forecast down from ten per cent to eight and then seven. Australia struggled to keep its head just above the recession waterline.

At BHP Billiton, Don Argus and Marius Kloppers watched as their share price slid ever downward from a high of $55 in May 2008 to hover around $24 by December. At the same time, Rio had collapsed from $155 in May to a low of $39. So, on one reading, the takeover bid of 3.4 for one was wildly overpriced, especially when Rio was carrying the US$40 billion Alcan debt to BHP Billiton's relatively modest US$6.5 billion. However, in early November the European Commission presented the

BHP Billiton team with a confidential 'list of objections' that would require the company to sell some major iron-ore and coal assets at a time when market conditions could hardly have been less favourable. Kloppers' war was suddenly being fought on an entirely new battlefield.

At the same time, Tom Albanese was feeling the strain. He had decided to press ahead with a $1 billion project in primitive Madagascar to mine ilmenite – used mainly in paint – and build a massive deep-water port in a cyclone-ravaged area to get it out to world markets. Progress was slow and the price was falling catastrophically. On his other flank, he was frantically trying to establish joint ventures with Chinalco to develop more iron-ore projects and make the takeover that much more difficult.

But for Kloppers, in the 28th-floor eyrie of his Melbourne headquarters, the real problem was the US$40 billion Alcan debt on the Rio Tinto books, plus a BHPB undertaking to buy back $US30 billion of its shares after the takeover. In a rising market, all of that could be incorporated into the balance sheet with relatively little discomfort. As share prices fell and mid-term-growth prospects evaporated, it became virtually indigestible.

Kloppers and his team worked day and night on the problem, approaching it from every possible angle. But, in the end, the young chief executive knew he had no choice. Throughout the process, he had kept Argus briefed on both tactics and strategy. Both men knew that they had to present a united front. And when Kloppers reached the terminal decision in the last week of November, he sat down with the hard-bitten Queenslander and laid out his reasoning.

Argus's banking background made the final decision inevitable, and when it went to the full board they made it unanimous. They would not meet the European Union conditions, and even if the European Union competition commissioner, Ms Neelie Kroes, then cleared the deal they would ask their shareholders to vote it down. The 18 months of Project de Bello – the planning, the tactical manoeuvring, the broadsides, the diplomacy and the expenditure (US$450 million in hard cash, plus an incalculable amount in the plunging share price and lost opportunities) – had gone for naught. The battle had been waged but only vaulting ambition had been vanquished.

Albanese scoffed at the US$40 billion 'excuse' for withdrawing the bid, claiming his company was well positioned. In his view, it was solely the actions of the European Commission that had scuppered the bid. Two weeks later, however, the precarious position of Rio became clear when he was forced to announce the shedding of a massive 17,000 jobs worldwide.

On 25 November, when BHP Billiton's board announced the withdrawal, they authorised a face-saver for their champion. It came in the form of a US$4.8 billion investment to increase production in their West Australian iron-ore holdings by 50 million tonnes to 205 million tonnes a year. It was an oddly contradictory gesture at a time when they were blaming future prospects for pulling out of the takeover, but Argus pressed the point home at a media conference with his repeated assurances that, 'Marius and his team have the full support of the board.'

He also took the opportunity to assert his own determination to stay as chairman for another full year, despite earlier suggestions that he would step down when the deal was concluded. So, was it really all over?

Kloppers: 'Obviously, we wouldn't like to speculate on anything that can happen going forward. We clearly have a balance sheet we believe is very robust, a balance sheet unlike any other in the industry. The management team here realises that as the effects of this ecomonic cycle become clearer, there might be other opportunities.'

In the longer term, he said, China's growth and urbanisation would return the mining industry to prosperity. 'We have changed nothing in our long-term view,' he said. 'If the non-China world – which consumes roughly 65–70 per cent of product – returns to trend and China continues to industrialise, the world is going to need our products.'

At BHPB's annual meeting in Melbourne on 27 November, Don Argus performed the funeral rites on the bid when he told shareholders that the 'almost unprecedented global financial crisis' would have meant forming a US$84 billion company with US$78 billion of debt.

Back in August, Kloppers had labelled his bid for Rio Tinto 'a deal for all seasons', inferring it could withstand all extremes of heat, cold and turbulence. But as the glowering winter skies descended on Brussels and New York, it shrivelled and died in the economic gloom. And at last the 'supreme realist' allowed himself a brief moment of remorse. 'There is a sense of loss,' he admitted.[26]

AFTERWORD

The Comeback

As all gamblers know, the game is never over until the last throw of the dice. And in the mining game, that day never comes. Players may retire from the table – voluntarily or otherwise – but the game goes on. And just when it seemed that BHP Billiton had overplayed its hand, the cards began falling its way.

By mid-year 2009, Rio Tinto was back in play after Chinalco decided to increase its controversial equity stake in Rio with a revised offer worth US$19.5 billion. Under British stock-exchange rules, Marius Kloppers was forbidden to launch another full-blooded takeover bid for Rio until November 2009 – 12 months from the time his first bid had been withdrawn – but there was nothing stopping him bidding for individual Rio assets, notably its enormous iron-ore operation in the Pilbara, where his team had identified synergies as high as US$525 million a year.

To counter Kloppers – or perhaps to do a deal with him – the Rio board brought in a heavyweight South African of its own, 55-year-old Jan du Plessis, who took over as chairman in April.[1] Described by colleagues as 'a politically astute and conciliatory chartered accountant', du Plessis had quietly emerged as a powerful figure in the City of London as chairman of British American Tobacco and a director of Marks & Spencer and Lloyds Banking Group.[2]

Born in Cape Town in 1954, du Plessis speaks with a strong Afrikaans accent and has spent most of his career in the Rembrandt Group, controlled by South Africa's breathtakingly wealthy Rupert family. He was charged with demerging Rembrandt's non-South African luxury-goods assets and listing them in Switzerland as Richemont (best known for Cartier jewellery and Montblanc pens).[3] More relevant to his looming match with Marius Kloppers and Don Argus (whom he met in a private room at the Sheraton on the Park Hotel in Sydney within 48 hours of taking over), his first big job was international finance manager at Rembrandt, whose transfer of its Billiton shares to Anglo American in 2001 had triggered Billiton's merger with BHP.

However, once ensconced as Rio's chairman his first task was to quell a shareholder revolt over his board's plan to offer a US$7.2 billion convertible bond to Chinalco as part of the US$19.5 billion package. The bond would raise the state-owned Chinese miner's stake in the company to 18 per cent while diluting the stock of other Rio investors. Aggrieved shareholders claimed that the Rio board was selling out too cheaply and complained that their influence would be restricted.[4]

As commodity prices began to recover, the share price rose and with it the ire of the shareholders. It became apparent that the China deal, conceived as a rescue package, no longer made financial sense. At the same time, BHP Billiton was making overtures both publicly and privately. With a resilient balance sheet to call upon, finance director Alex Vaneslow said his company's first rule was to invest in 'accretive business opportunities'.[5] And no company in the current economic climate satisfied that criterion better than Rio Tinto.

The secret talks between BHP and Rio about a new combination had been taking place for some months but were conducted below board level in order to circumvent a legal condition forbidding Rio from actively seeking alternatives to the Chinalco deal while it was still extant.[6] Chinalco was given the codename 'Colleen', which was changed as shareholder opposition strengthened, and elements of the deal were abandoned, to 'Colleen Lite'.[7]

Then, on 5 June, ten days before the Australian Foreign Investment Review Board was to rule on it, Rio Tinto and Chinalco suddenly announced that the deal had been scrapped. BHP and Rio then announced they had signed a non-binding agreement to establish a production joint venture encompassing the entirety of both companies' Western Australian iron-ore holdings. Jan du Plessis said that Rio Tinto would pay the Chinese an agreed break fee of US$195 million. And to ease the Alcan millstone from around its neck, the company would raise US$15.2 billion through a rights issue, enabling it to meet its debt-repayment obligations in 2009 and 2010.

But it was the joint venture that brought a smile to the face of Marius Kloppers, a face that appeared to have aged somewhat over the past six months but was instantly rejuvenated. 'While this deal has been more than ten years in the making, I believe it has been worth the wait,' he said.[8]

The Rio chairman spelled it out:

> The joint venture will include all current and future Western Australian iron-ore assets and liabilities and will be 50/50 owned by Rio Tinto and BHP Billiton. In order to equalise the contribution value of the two companies, BHP Billiton will pay Rio Tinto US$5.8 billion for equity-type interests. The establishment of the joint venture will be subject to execution of binding agreements as well as regulatory and shareholder approvals. The joint venture will establish an unrivalled iron-ore business with world-class assets and infrastructure. We believe it represents great value for shareholders and will create a business combination able to serve growing international markets with unparalleled efficiency.[9]

Marius Kloppers, the 'supreme realist', could be forgiven for savouring his triumphal moment. BHP Billiton and its advisers, Goldman and Gresham Partners, had secured a deal that embraced the very assets that were the main target of BHP's takeover bid for Rio Tinto in 2007. 'I am delighted that we have found a solution that works for both companies,' he said. 'This joint venture brings together world-class iron-ore resources, infrastructure and people, unlocks large synergies and is an outstanding outcome for all stakeholders.'[10]

His rival Tom Albanese, whose implacable opposition had stymied the BHP bid, bowed to the inevitable. 'We have long recognised the natural fit of our two iron-ore businesses and the industrial logic of bringing them together,' he said in the same press release.

Analyst John Durie reflected the view of his colleagues: 'Tom Albanese is clearly a dead man walking and the sooner he comes to that realisation, the better it will be for Rio shareholders.'[11]

The collapse of the Chinalco deal was greeted by Kevin Rudd's government with palpable relief. BHP Billiton lobbying and an outbreak of undisguised anti-Chinese xenophobia from sections of the political opposition had placed Rudd in an invidious position – unwilling to offend the Chinese yet facing a backlash in the polls if the deal was approved.

Rudd himself was overjoyed. When the prime minister, a devoted Christian, met Chinalco's new president, Xiong Weiping, in Canberra to reassure him that his government's attitude towards foreign investment remained unchanged, he looked as though his faith in the power of prayer had been reaffirmed. Describing the result as 'entirely a commercial matter between Rio on the one hand and Chinalco on the other', he said his government would consider foreign investment based on 'national interest' tests. 'I assume the Chinese Government makes decisions in the national interest about what foreign investment it welcomes in its country,' he said. 'We welcome Chinese investment in Australia just as the previous government approved some AU$15 billion worth of Chinese investment.'[12]

Rudd added that 'national interest' would also be relevant when it considered an application from BHP Billiton to combine its iron-ore operations with Rio's in the Pilbara, but his tongue was firmly planted in his cheek.

However, it was by no means a done deal. The BHP/Rio combination would create the biggest iron-ore supplier in the world, producing around 270 million tonnes of ore a year compared with Vale's 240 million tonnes. Together, the two groups would control 70 per cent of the iron-ore market, a nightmare scenario for all of Asia's steel industries in future negotiations to fix the annual benchmark price.[13]

The joint venture also angered the Western Australian State Government. Premier Colin Barnett, who had favoured the Chinalco deal, said the iron-ore venture was structured to avoid a $1 billion stamp-duty bill. He warned the miners there was a 'long way to go' for them to clear regulatory hurdles, including approval from his government.[14]

More pertinently, perhaps, the EU regulators would be under immense pressure from European steel mills to veto the deal, and it was this element of the original takeover bid that had most concerned them the first time around. That, however, was for the next hand in the great game.

As in so many of its corporate manoeuvres, the BHP–Rio Tinto alliance was no altruistic solution but one based purely on self-interest. There was no place in it for the revolution in attitude and action demanded by market domination or the niceties of politically correct international behaviour, much less the great dilemma of global climate change. Instead, it was rooted in that most basic of human responses to the world around it: to seek the planet's natural treasures ahead of the rest and fashion them to enrich their discoverer. It was a philosophy that inspired and incited Charles Rasp as he left his daub-and-wattle *gunya* and scrambled up the side of the broken hill in the blistering heat to stake his claim. It motivated the gamblers and the great builders who followed him – Guillaume Delprat, John and Harold Darling, Essington Lewis, Ian McLennan,

Brian Loton, Jerry Ellis, John Prescott, Brian Gilbertson, Chip Goodyear, Paul Anderson and Don Argus among them – as they took the corporation on an astonishing journey from miner to steelmaker, to manufacturer, shipbuilder, oil company and back to miner, but now on a vast scale.

As they built The Big Australian then extended it across the globe, their company served the host nation well. Indeed, it became an intrinsic element of the Australian story, bringing an economic maturity and an international perspective that transformed the country, its power and influence, and its self-regard. Now, it seems, the same philosophy would be employed to serve the company in the foreseeable future. And it has every chance of continuing its century and a quarter of outstanding success, for it does not stand alone. It has a second great incentive urging it forward. It is the innate desire of the human family to improve its living conditions, to build stronger shelters, better transport facilities, bigger and better factories and workplaces, new and innovative centres of leisure and entertainment. And those ambitions require the natural resources of the mining-industry giants to power and to sculpt them into humanity's future.

BHP Billiton – The Big Fella – though bruised from the blows of international economic turbulence, seems more than willing to meet all challenges and chart its own course forward. By trial and error, wise counsel and a goodly measure of luck, it has established a corporate persona that combines strength of purpose and tactical flexibility with the indispensable art of self-renewal. And these are the essential components of vigorous longevity. Its remarkable life is long past the end of the beginning, but it is much further, one suspects, from the beginning of the end.

ACKNOWLEDGEMENTS

The Big Fella: The Rise and Rise of BHP Billiton emerged from conversations between the authors after Peter Thompson attended the 2006 annual general meeting of BHP Billiton plc in London, where it became clear that the company had become as newsworthy as it was immense. It seemed extraordinary that there was no published account of the great drama surrounding BHP's merger with Billiton in 2001 or of the many astonishing events that preceded and followed that seminal event. Indeed, a check with library catalogues revealed that books about the history of BHP were few and far between and mostly company-sponsored, while the only texts available on Billiton were in Dutch.

This was the starting point of a complicated, labyrinthine and exhilarating two-year journey in Australia and the UK that took us from the boardrooms and gentlemen's clubs in both countries to Broken Hill, where it all began, then to the far reaches of the Australian continent, where new communities surround the great mineral deposits that fill the company's huge treasure chest to overflowing. We consulted what at times seemed an almost limitless number and range of people, from senior executives in the mining industry (not only of BHP

Billiton but of Rio Tinto, Xstrata, Shell and Mount Isa Mines) to astronomers, academics, miners, research scientists, politicians, lobbyists, public servants and intelligence operatives.

We would like to thank the following people (in alphabetical order) for interviews: Paul Anderson, Glen Andrews, Don Argus, Ian Ashby, Carol Austin, Max Banks, Jess Boylan, Alan Breen (by email), John Burton, Kevin Buzzacott, Harley Carey, Mick Carroll, John Clark, Tony Crook, James Curry, Mick Davis, Gary Dillard, Daniel Edelstein, John Elliott, Jerry Ellis, John Elliston, Graham Evans, Paul Everard, Keith Faulkner, Colin Filer, Matt Foraker, Ian Fraser, Russell Fynmore, Brian Gilbertson, Marc Gonsalves, Chip Goodyear, Stewart Greenhalgh, Geoffrey Heeley, Robert Hickman, Lance Hockridge, Juliana Hooper, Carrol Houser, Craig Hoyer, David Irvine, John Jackson, Paul Keating, Derek Keys, Marius Kloppers, Andy Kugler, Peter Laver, Charles Lineweaver, Brian Loton, Robyn Loughhead, J. David Lowell, Benjamin Macklin, Peter Maund, Dave McGarry, Graeme McGregor, Peter McLennan, Malcolm McMillan, Graham Menzies, Brad Mills, Aaron Minchin, David Munro, John O'Connor, Tim Offor, Guy Pearse, Ian Plimer, John Prescott, Pat Quilty, Kelly Quirke, Baron Renwick of Clifton, Gillespie Robertson, Mike Salamon, Stan Salamy, Graeme Samuel, Derek Sawer, Michael Spencer, Fred Stojich, Onofre Tafoya, Alan Tingay, Geoffrey Walsh, Robert Ward, Sir Robert Wilson, Tim Winterer, J. Michael Yeager, Richard Yeeles (by email). Our thanks to Tony Walker and the team at Mt Whaleback and Mt Newman, and to Professor Peter Spearritt of the University of Queensland.

We are grateful to the Geological Society (London) for access to their texts on mining and explanations of mining terms; to the BHP Archives, which are now, alas, disbanded, the documents distributed throughout the company's various divisions; the National Library of Australia (Canberra); the British Library (London); the State Library of New South Wales (Sydney); the State Library of Victoria (Melbourne); and the State Library of Queensland (Brisbane).

Warmest thanks to Macushla O'Loan, whose hospitality

during our travels was beyond generous. We are particularly grateful to Nikki Christer, our publisher at Random House Australia, and to Random House senior editor Kevin O'Brien for his splendid work; and to our agent, Andrew Lownie.

Regarding style, we have taken the liberty of using the present tense – for example, 'he says' or 'she recalls' – when a specific recollection may in fact have taken place years earlier. Our own interviews are clearly flagged in the References section.

APPENDIX I

Glossary of Mining Terms

Anticline: an upfold in rock strata, in this case on the seabed in Bass Strait, producing an arch or dome structure that provides a trap for hydrocarbons.

Barrel: 42 US gallons (159 litres).

Base metal: commercial metal such as copper, lead or zinc. The term was coined to indicate a metal 'inferior' to precious metals such as gold and silver.

Block-cave mining: an underground mining method in which ore is allowed to collapse due to its own weight. Block caving is usually used to mine large ore bodies of a consistent grade, but it also allows for the bulk mining of large, relatively lower-grade ore bodies.

Bore-capping program: a method of saving water and restoring artesian pressure through the capping and piping of old, uncontrolled bores. The Queensland Government's bore-capping program in the Great Artesian Basin, for example, saves 130,000 megalitres of water each year.

Briquettes: small blocks formed by pressing material together.

Cap rock: an impervious rock acting as a seal so hydrocarbons such as oil and gas remain trapped in a reservoir.

Carbon-capture project: a worldwide effort to capture and remove carbon dioxide and other greenhouse gases, particularly from coal-burning power plants.

Carbon steel: steel that has properties made up mostly of the element carbon and that relies on the carbon content for structure. Most of the steel produced in the world is carbon steel.

Coke: a hard, dry carbon substance that provides the basic fuel consumed in blast furnaces in the smelting of iron. It is produced by heating coking coal to a very high temperature in the absence of air. Metallurgical coal burns fitfully, whereas coke provides steady heat.

Direct-reduced iron (DRI): processed iron ore that is iron-rich enough to be used as a scrap substitute in electric-furnace steelmaking.

Electric-arc furnace: a steelmaking furnace in which scrap is generally 100 per cent of the charge and heat comes from electricity that arcs from graphite electrodes to the metal bath.

Farm-in/farm-out: a partnership or joint venture in which the incoming partner – such as Esso in Bass Strait – funds the costs of exploration to earn a stake in a property owned by the farm-out partner, such as BHP Billiton.

Fines: the fine-grained ore produced by crushing and processing.

Flat products (steel): the steel market is primarily divided into two main categories – flat and long. A flat carbon-steel product is a plate product or a (hot or cold) rolled-strip product. Plate products vary in dimensions from 10 mm to 200 mm and thin flat-rolled products from 1 mm to 10 mm. Plate products are used for shipbuilding, construction, large-diameter welded pipes and boiler applications. Thin flat products find end-use applications in automotive body panels, domestic 'white goods' products, tin cans and a whole host of other products from office furniture to heart pacemakers. Plates, HR coils and

HR sheet, CR sheet and CR coils, GP/GC (galvanised plates and coils), pipes, etc. are included in this category.

Flux: the material added to the contents of a smelting furnace or a cupola for the purposes of purging the metal of impurities and rendering the slag more liquid. The flux most commonly used in iron and steel furnaces is limestone, which is charged in the proper proportions with the iron and fuel. The slag is a liquid mixture of ash, flux and other impurities.

Hot-briquetted iron (HBI): a supplement for pig iron and scrap in electric-furnace steel mills. It is a compacted form of direct-reduced iron (DRI), which facilitates its handling, storage and use.

Leaching: a natural process in which ground waters dissolve minerals, thus leaving the rock with a smaller proportion of some of the minerals than contained originally.

Long products (steel): A long steel product is a rod or a bar. Typical rod products are the reinforcing rods made from sponge iron for concrete, ingots, billets, engineering products, gears, tools, etc. Wire-drawn products and seamless pipes are also part of the long-products group. Bars, rods, structures, railway materials, etc. are included in this category.

Longwall mining: an underground coal-mining method in which a steel plough or rotation drum is pulled mechanically back and forth across a coalface measuring several hundred metres long.

Mullock: mining refuse, muck.

Paydirt: rock that delivers a profit to the miner.

Pechiney AP30 technology: AP30 is the name of the design of the technology of the reduction line at the Hillside Smelter. The '30' stands for 300,000 amps. An aluminium smelter is made of four main parts:

- Electricity rectification to generate the direct current (300 kA) and high voltage (1200 volts) required for the reduction line.
- The anode production plant to make the carbon source for the electrochemical reactions that occur in the reduction line.

- The reduction line, where alumina, carbon and electricity react together at over 950 degrees Celsius to produce molten aluminium. Each reduction line has approximately 264 reaction cells, each producing over 100 kg per hour.
- The aluminium cast-house, where liquid aluminium is moulded and cooled into shapes for sale.

The technology of the AP30 essentially finds the right balance between the following: heat, mass, chemistry, power and the magnetic field of the cell. This balance allows reliable long-life operations, which minimises power consumption, maximising production and aluminium purity.

Porphyry copper systems: large quantities of hydrothermal solutions carrying small quantities of copper pass through fractured, porphyritic rock and over time deposit the metal in huge ore bodies. The largest examples are found in the Andes in South America.

Raises (in mines): vertical openings driven upwards from one level to connect with the level above. In the block-caving method of mining, copper ore – 'muck' to the miners – flows down from the ore body into transfer raises and is carried away in ore trains or on conveyor belts.

Rod plant: see 'long products' above.

Spot market: commodities such as iron ore and oil are sold on the spot market for cash and delivered immediately.

Spot price: the price being paid on the spot market as opposed to the negotiated benchmark price.

Spud in: to drill a new well.

Stopes: the openings made in the process of extracting ore are called stopes or rooms. As mining progresses, the stopes are often backfilled with tailings. Shrinkage stope mining, or shrinkage stoping, is most suitable for steeply dipping ore.

SX/EW: solvent-extraction/electro-winning.

Tailings: waste product remaining from a mining operation after valuable minerals have been extracted, sometimes containing toxic chemicals.

Wildcat well: a well drilled 'on spec' in unproven territory.

APPENDIX II

Glossary of Business Terms

All-scrip offer: shares only, no cash.

Asset stripping: the buying of a company in order to sell off its assets or businesses separately.

Balance sheet: one of the most important statements in a company's accounts, showing its assets and liabilities and how the business is funded by shareholders and debt.

Capital expenditure: 'capex' is the amount a company spends on buying fixed assets or investing in its own businesses.

Capitalisation: a measurement of corporate or economic size equal to the share price multiplied by the number of shares issued by a public company.

Depression: a severe economic downturn that lasts several years and adversely affects all economic indicators. The Great Depression of 1929 lasted for more than five years.

Hedging: a position established in one market in an attempt to offset exposure to the price risk of an equal but opposite obligation or position in another market – a strategy designed to minimise exposure to such business risks as a sharp contraction in demand for the business's inventory while still allowing the business to profit from producing and maintaining that inventory.

Initial public offering: an IPO, or flotation, is when a company seeking capital, or a privately owned company looking to become publicly traded, issues common stock or shares to the public for the first time.

Issue price: the price at which the shares in an IPO are issued to the public. Either the company, with the help of its lead managers, fixes the price or it is arrived at through building a book of investors with the help of a merchant bank.

Redeemable preference shares: shares that give the shareholder rights to dividends on specific dates, and often rights of redemption at the shareholder's request.

Recession: a general slowdown in economic activity over a sustained period of time, or a contraction in the business or commodity cycles.

Rights issue: a publicly quoted company can opt for a rights issue to raise capital from its shareholders. It is offered to all existing investors individually and may be rejected, accepted in full or accepted in part. Rights are often transferable, allowing the holder to sell them on the open market. Shares are generally issued on a ratio basis (e.g. a one-for-three rights issue).

Takeover bid: an attempt by one company to take control of another, usually by informing the board of directors that it intends to make an offer to its shareholders. If the board feels that accepting the offer is in the best interest of its shareholders, it recommends the offer be accepted.

A takeover is considered 'hostile' if the target company's board rejects the offer but the bidder continues to pursue it, or the bidder makes the offer without prior notification to the target company's board.

A hostile takeover can be conducted through a 'tender offer' where the acquiring company makes a public offer at a fixed price above the current market price to all stockholders to tender their stock for sale at a fixed price during a specified time, subject to the tendering of a minimum or maximum number of shares.

The bidder conducts 'due diligence' into the affairs of the target company to find out exactly what it is taking on in terms of financial, legal, labour, tax, IT, environmental and commercial matters.

In a 'reverse takeover', control goes to the shareholders (and usually management) of the company that is being acquired. A reverse takeover will almost always take place through a pure-equity acquisition or share swap.

Takeover premium: the temporarily inflated share price brought about by a takeover bid.

REFERENCES

Introduction: Global Australian

1 Authors' interview with Marius Kloppers, July 2008.

2 Authors' interview with Sir Robert Wilson, September 2008.

3 Authors' interview with Ian Fraser, November 2008.

4 Johanne Gray, 'Timing . . . It's That Simple Twist Of Fate', *Australian Financial Review*, 27 November 2008.

5 The commodities market goes in cycles. The Asian market is so big it is perceived to be a supercycle.

6 Steelmaking and other manufacturing enterprises are classed as secondary industry, while primary industry includes farming, grazing and forestry.

7 Authors' interview with Don Argus, July 2008.

8 Authors' interview with Mike Salamon, May 2008.

9 See Filer, Burton, Banks, pp. 1–3. Sir Robert Wilson told the authors of *The Big Fella*, 'Sustainable development was being talked about a lot in the late 1990s. None of the mining companies had made a serious effort to define what it meant to them. Then Hugh Morgan [chief executive of WMC Resources Limited from 1990 to 2003] gave me a call. He said, "Look, I'm worried about public perceptions about the mining industry. How about we convene a meeting with ten or a dozen other guys? How about we get together in your office and talk about some of these issues?" I said, "Fine, let's do that." It seemed to me that we were not going to

change perceptions of the industry unless we changed industry behaviour; that meant perhaps becoming much more open and allowing other people to express their views about us, as well as stating our position and trying to defend it. That led in due course to the Mining, Minerals and Sustainable Development Project, which was commissioned out to the International Institute for Environment and Development led by Richard Sandbrook [co-founder of Friends of the Earth]. We as an industry needed to define for ourselves what did sustainable development mean for us? What did it require of us? What did it imply? So that's why we started using that particular approach.'

10 Don Argus, speaking at the 2008 AGM in London.

11 Authors' interview with Paul Keating, September 2008.

12 Authors' interview with Marius Kloppers, July 2008.

Prologue: The Black Stump

1 Authors' interview with astronomer Dr Charles Lineweaver.

Part I: The Prop
Chapter 1: King Charles

1 Slave traders in the South Pacific for the Queensland sugar industry.

2 *Argus*, Melbourne, 19 August 1905.

3 Ibid.

4 Camilleri, *In the Broken Hill Paddock*, p. 16.

5 Trengove, pp. 9–10.

6 Archie Watson, quoted in Robinson, p. 32.

7 Ibid.

8 Ibid.

9 Ibid.

10 Ibid.

Chapter 2: Silver and Scabs

1 *Broken Hill Argus*, October 1888.

2 *The Silver City*, quoted in Trengove, p. 32.

3 Dale, p. 35.

4 E. B. Cotton, manager of the Australian Joint Stock Bank, was later fined three pounds for assault.

5 Roy Bridges, *Silver to Steel*, quoted in Trengove, p. 68.

6 Ibid.

7 Ibid.

Chapter 3: Blood and Iron

1 Dale, p. 118.

2 BHPBA CO66/M008/00092.

3 Ibid.

4 Ibid.

5 Ibid.

6 Ibid.

7 Official opening, Newcastle steelworks, 2 June 1915.

8 Kearns, *Broken Hill 1915–1939*, p. 10.

9 Trengove, p. 118.

10 To their credit, they eschewed the Adelaide mode of pie consumption – the 'floater', in which the pie is immersed in a green sludge of pea-and-ham soup, a culinary outrage that has caused horror-struck palpitations among visiting gourmands.

Chapter 4: Man of Steel

1 Turnbull, p. 5.

2 Trengove, p. 120.

3 Ibid., p. 60.

4 Ibid., p. 20.

5 Menzies, p. 11.

6 Blainey, *Steel Master*, p. 110.

7 Letter supplied to the authors by the Menzies family, February 2008.

8 The biggest family shareholders were the Darlings (68,000). Lewis and his family owned 20,205.

9 *Australian Dictionary of Biography*, Essington Lewis, Online Edition, http//:adbonline.anu.edu.au.

10 Blainey, *Steel Master*, p. 122.

11 BHP had an iron-ore mine at Cockatoo Island on Yampi Sound but the Japanese would probably have bought their ore from the nearby British company H. A. Brassert, as it was financed by the Nippon Mining Company of Japan.

12 Blainey, *Steel Master*, p. 146.
13 Ibid., p. 177.

Chapter 5: Supermac

1 Interviews with Sir Ian McLennan, 3 October 1978–5 February 1979. Reprinted with the permission of the McLennan family.
2 Ibid.
3 Ibid.
4 Robert Macklin was his press secretary from 1967 to 1971.
5 Interviews with Sir Ian McLennan, 3 October 1978–5 February 1979. Reprinted with the permission of the McLennan family.
6 Ibid. In fact, there was no commercial iron-ore deposit in Mt Newman itself, named in honour of A. W. Newman, an early explorer who died of typhoid just before reaching the area in 1896.
7 Authors' interview with Stan Salamy, July 2008.
8 McIlwraith, p. 15.
9 Interviews with Sir Ian McLennan, 3 October 1978–5 February 1979. Reprinted with the permission of the McLennan family.
10 Ibid., p. 50.
11 Don Argus, in response to a question at the 2008 AGM in London.
12 McIlwraith, p. 71.
13 Ibid., p. 52.
14 Ibid.
15 Authors' interview with Stan Salamy, July 2008.
16 Authors' interview with Jerry Ellis, August 2008.
17 Authors' interview with Dr Ward, August 2008.
18 Later, Hematite Exploration Proprietary Limited.
19 'History of Petroleum Exploration in Victoria', Department of Primary Industries, Victoria, www.dpi.vic.gov.au; Wilkinson, p. 89.
20 Wilkinson, p. 7 and *passim*.
21 Howarth, pp. 252–3; Yergin, p. 479 *passim*.

Chapter 6: Bass Strait Bonanza

1 Authors' interview with Russ Fynmore, June 2008.
2 The official BHP version of this event says that Norgard's trip to the United States was in early 1960.

[3] Weeks, p. 102.

[4] Lloyd, p. 5.

[5] Authors' interview with Dave McGarry, March 2008. McGarry left the Sydney Basin himself soon afterwards and went to Moonie in Queensland, where oil was struck in 1961–62.

[6] Weeks, p. 103.

[7] Weeks, p. 102 and *passim*.

[8] Authors' interview with Professor Patrick G. Quilty, March 2008.

[9] Professor Patrick G. Quilty and Dr Maxwell R. Banks, 'Samuel Warren Carey', *Historical Records of Australian Science*, Vol. 14, No. 3, School of Earth Sciences, University of Tasmania, 2003.

[10] In 1912, German scientist Alfred Wegener suggested that the close fit between the west coast of Africa and the east coast of Latin America was due to the fact that they had once formed a single supercontinent, which he named Pangaea (Greek for 'All Lands'), and had subsequently drifted apart.

[11] Samuel Warren Carey obituary, Geological Society of Australia, 2002, www.gsa.org.au.

[12] Greenhalgh, p. 57.

[13] Cockburn, p. 147.

[14] 'A Man of Great Vision', obituary of Eric Aroha Rudd (1910–1999), *Petroleum Gazette*, 1999.

[15] Cockburn, pp. 147–8.

[16] Authors' interview with Dr Maxwell Banks, January 2008.

[17] Letter from Professor Carey to his son Dr Harley Carey, dated 7 February 1996, reproduced with Harley Carey's permission.

[18] Professor Carey's unpublished memorandum on Lewis Weeks, reproduced with the permission of his daughter Robyn Loughhead.

[19] Authors' interview with Dr Andy Kugler, January 2008.

[20] Samuel Warren Carey obituary, Geological Society of Australia, 2002, www.gsa.org.au.

[21] Authors' interview with Professor Patrick G. Quilty, March 2008.

[22] Trengove, p. 208.

[23] Interviews with Sir Ian McLennan, 3 October 1978–5 February 1979. Reprinted with the permission of the McLennan family.

[24] In 1926, Standard Oil, playing on the 'S' and 'O' in its name, brought out a new blend of fuel under the trade name Esso. In 1972, Standard Oil of New Jersey

changed its name to Exxon Corporation, now ExxonMobil, the largest publicly traded petroleum and petrochemical enterprise in the world.

[25] Interviews with Sir Ian McLennan, 3 October 1978–5 February 1979. Reprinted with the permission of the McLennan family.

[26] Professor Carey's unpublished memorandum on Lewis Weeks, reproduced with the permission of his daughter Robyn Loughhead.

[27] Wilkinson, p. 44.

[28] 'History of Petroleum Exploration in Victoria', Department of Primary Industries, Victoria, www.dpi.vic.gov.au.

[29] Other oilfields at Moonie, Gidgealpa, Barrow Island, Moomba and Dongara also went on stream between 1961 and 1968.

[30] Authors' interview with Geoff Heeley, March 2008.

[31] Authors' interview with Russ Fynmore, June 2008.

[32] Ibid. Sir Howard Beale was visiting professor at Lewis Weeks's alma mater, the University of Wisconsin, in 1966 and 1969.

[33] Interviews with Sir Ian McLennan, 3 October 1978–5 February 1979. Reprinted with the permission of the McLennan family.

[34] The official residence of the prime minister in Canberra.

[35] Interviews with Sir Ian McLennan, 3 October 1978–5 February 1979. Reprinted with the permission of the McLennan family.

[36] Ibid., p. 66.

[37] Authors' interview with Paul Keating, September 2008.

[38] Interviews with Sir Ian McLennan, 3 October 1978–5 February 1979. Reprinted with the permission of the McLennan family.

Chapter 7: The Image Makers

[1] Interviews with Sir Ian McLennan, 3 October 1978–5 February 1979. Reprinted with the permission of the McLennan family.

[2] Authors' interview with Derek Sawer, March 2008.

[3] Authors' interview with Juliana Hooper, March 2008.

[4] Ibid.

[5] Authors' interview with Derek Sawer, March 2008.

[6] Authors' interview with Peter Maund, May 2008.

[7] Ibid.

[8] Authors' interview with Paul Keating, September 2008.

[9] Authors' interview with Peter Laver, May 2008.

[10] Authors' interview with Derek Sawer, March 2008.

[11] Authors' interview with Peter Maund, October 2008.

[12] Authors' interview with Carol Austin, June 2008.

[13] Ibid.

[14] Ibid.

[15] Authors' interview with Peter Laver, May 2008.

[16] Authors' interview with Graham Evans, July 2008.

[17] Authors' interview with Paul Keating, July 2008.

Part II: The Predator
Chapter 8: The Buccaneers

[1] Edwards, p. 145.

[2] Ibid., p. 146.

[3] Authors' interview with Brian Loton, April 2008.

[4] Nicholas Hasluck, *Quadrant* magazine, Vol. XXXV No. 4, No. 275, April 1991.

[5] Ibid.

[6] *The Financial Times*, 1 August 1987.

[7] Holmes à Court's father was the second son of the brother of the fourth Lord Heytesbury. The Holmes à Court name was created in 1833 when William Ashe à Court (son of the first Lord Heytesbury, the British diplomat and politician who had been ennobled in 1820) married Elizabeth Holmes at Calbourne, Isle of Wight.

[8] Sheryl Wudunn, 'Australian-Built Business Empire', *New York Times*, 3 September 1990.

[9] Hewat, pp. 102–5.

[10] 'By Chance I Became a Director of Elders', Sir Norman Young, MS, Adelaide, 1986.

[11] Authors' interview with John Elliott, October 2007.

[12] Patience Wheatcroft, *Sunday Times*, 25 April 1982.

[13] Haigh, p. 2.

[14] Authors' interview with John Clark, April 2008.

[15] Authors' interview with Jerry Ellis, August 2008.

[16] Authors' interview with John Clark, April 2008.

[17] Authors' interview with John Prescott, March 2008.

[18] In 2008, Samuel was chairman of the Australian Competition and Consumer Commission, one of the regulators deciding whether BHP Billiton would be permitted to take over Rio Tinto.

[19] Authors' interview with Graeme Samuel, September 2008.

[20] Samuel supplied the name off the record.

[21] Authors' interview with Peter Maund, October 2008.

[22] Haigh, p. 6.

[23] Authors' interview with John Elliott, October 2007.

[24] Hewat, pp. 128–9.

[25] Ibid., p. 129.

[26] Hugh D. Menzies, 'Broken Hill Outgrows Australia', *New York Times*, 25 August 1985.

[27] Authors' interview with John Elliott, October 2007.

[28] Haigh, p. 21.

[29] Ibid., p. 22.

[30] Authors' interview with John Elliott, October 2007.

[31] Haigh, p. 29.

[32] Authors' interview with John Elliott, October 2007.

[33] Authors' interview with Peter Maund, October 2008.

[34] Authors' interview with Paul Keating, September 2008.

[35] Authors' interview with Graeme Samuel, September 2008.

[36] Hewat, p. 131.

[37] 'Business Profile: The Corporate Wizard of Oz', *Daily Telegraph*, 4 November 2006.

[38] Authors' interview with Don Argus, July 2008.

[39] The brokers were Peter Lawrence's Roach Tilley Grice; John Baillieu's E. L. & C. Baillieu; and John McIntosh's McIntosh Hamson Hoare Govett.

[40] Hewat, p. 127.

[41] Authors' interview with John Elliott, October 2007.

[42] Authors' interview with Graeme Samuel, September 2008.

[43] Authors' interview with John Elliott, October 2007.

[44] Authors' interview with Graeme Samuel, September 2008.

[45] Geordie White was later elevated to the peerage as Lord White of Hull. Such was White's reputation as a corporate raider in the United States that he was written into the script of Oliver Stone's 1987 'greed is good' film *Wall Street* as Sir Lawrence Wildman, played by Terence Stamp.

[46] Authors' interview with John Elliott, October 2007.

[47] Haigh, p. 126.

[48] Ibid.

[49] Authors' interview with Geoff Heeley, March 2008.

50 Authors' interview with John Clark, April 2008.

51 Authors' interview with Brian Loton, April 2008.

52 Elliott and his first wife, Lorraine, had separated at Christmas 1985. The marriage was later dissolved.

53 John Elliott married Amanda Drummond-Moray at St John's Anglican Church, Toorak, in October 1987.

Chapter 9: Utah Unbound

1 Hugh D. Menzies, 'Broken Hill Outgrows Australia', *New York Times*, 25 August 1985.

2 Ibid.

3 Ibid.

4 L. J. Davis, 'Did RCA Have to be Sold?', *New York Times Magazine*, 20 September 1987.

5 Welch, p. 114.

6 Authors' interview with Tim Winterer, May 2008.

7 Welch, p. 115.

8 Authors' interview with Gillespie Robertson, May 2008.

9 Ibid.

10 1972 Cabinet documents, Queensland State Archives. The original Act was passed in 1968 and later amended several times.

11 Authors' interview with Tim Winterer, May 2008.

12 Welch, p. 115.

13 Houser, p. 7. General Electric produces television sets, aircraft engines, locomotives, kitchen and laundry appliances, lighting, electric distribution and control equipment, generators and turbines, and medical imaging equipment.

14 Authors' interview with Brian Loton, April 2008.

15 Authors' interview with John Prescott, March 2008.

16 The 1977 *Four Corners* report by Paul Lyneham won a Logie award despite fierce complaints from Utah.

17 Paolo Fresco became a member of the General Electric board in 1990 and was elected vice chairman and executive officer in 1992. After retiring from General Electric, he was chairman of Fiat SpA of Italy from 1998 to 2003.

18 Houser, p. 12.

19 Authors' interview with Graeme McGregor, April 2008.

20 Ibid.

[21] Houser, p. 21.
[22] Authors' interview with Brian Loton, April 2008.
[23] Authors' interview with Jim Curry, May 2008.
[24] Welch, p. 117.
[25] *New York Times*, 28 January 1983.
[26] *New York Times*, 9 April 1983.
[27] Authors' interview with John Prescott, March 2008.
[28] Authors' interview with Chip Goodyear, July 2008.
[29] Houser, p. 96.
[30] Ibid., p. 22.
[31] Authors' interview with Carrol Houser, August 2008.
[32] Authors' interview with Jim Curry, May 2008.
[33] BHP mined iron ore at Koolyanobbing, Western Australia, from 1967 to 1983.
[34] GEMCO (Groote Eylandt Mining Company) mined manganese ore for export to Japan and processing at TEMCO (Tasmanian Electro Metallurgical Company), a ferro-alloy plant at Bell Bay, Tasmania. Both companies were BHP subsidiaries until they were sold to Billiton in 1998.
[35] Authors' interview with Geoff Heeley, March 2008.
[36] Authors' interview with Sir Robert Wilson, September 2008.
[37] Ibid.

Chapter 10: The Hidden One

[1] Authors' interview with J. David Lowell, August 2008.
[2] Ibid.
[3] Authors' interview with Jim Curry, May 2008.
[4] Authors' interview with J. David Lowell, August 2008.
[5] Authors' interview with Robert N. Hickman, May 2008.
[6] Authors' interview with Sir Robert Wilson, September 2008.
[7] The owners of Japan Escondida Corporation are Mitsubishi Corporation, Mitsubishi Materials Corporation and Nippon Mining and Metals Company Limited.
[8] Authors' interview with Robert N. Hickman, May 2008.
[9] Authors' interview with Graeme McGregor, April 2008.
[10] Authors' interview with Robert N. Hickman, May 2008.
[11] Authors' interview with Graeme McGregor, April 2008.
[12] The Stoll Moss group, acquired through the takeover of Lord Grade's ACC and later sold to Andrew Lloyd Webber.

[13] Authors' interview with Brian Loton, April 2008.

[14] Carew, pp. 230–1.

[15] Authors' interview with John Elliott, October 2007.

[16] Terry McCrann, 'Colour Drains in Wall St Watershed,' *Herald Sun*, 13 October 2007.

[17] Authors' interview with Paul Keating, September 2008.

[18] Authors' interview with Jerry Ellis, August 2008.

[19] Authors' interview with John Elliott, October 2007.

[20] Authors' interview with Brian Loton, April 2008.

[21] Authors' interview with Paul Keating, September 2008.

[22] Authors' interview with Robert N. Hickman, May 2008.

[23] Authors' interview with J. David Lowell, August 2008.

[24] Authors' interview with Robert N. Hickman, May 2008.

[25] 'La Escondida', a *South Pacific Mail* survey, March 1991.

[26] Authors' interview with J. David Lowell, August 2008.

[27] David Elias, 'The Businessman, the NCA and the Tale of Lost Millions', *The Age*, 16 August 2002.

[28] In July 2007, John Elliott emerged from a ban on being a director and was free to pursue his business interests once again from his office at the 'big end' of Collins Street.

[29] Authors' interview with John Prescott, March 2008.

[30] Authors' interview with Lance Hockridge, February 2008.

[31] 2 August 1990–28 February 1991.

[32] Authors' interview with John Prescott, March 2008.

[33] Authors' interview with Lance Hockridge, February 2008.

Chapter 11: Mother Magma

[1] Authors' confidential source.

[2] Authors' interview with Graeme McGregor, April 2008.

[3] Authors' interview with Jerry Ellis, August 2008.

[4] Authors' confidential source.

[5] Authors' interview with Matt Foraker, April 2008.

[6] William Boyce Thompson (1869–1930) founded Newmont Mining in 1921 as a parent company for his extensive mining interests. At the time of Thompson's death, Newmont was the third-largest mining company in the world, after De Beers and Anglo American.

[7] 'San Manuel Facility: Site Visit Report', United States Environmental Protection Agency, Washington DC, 1992.

[8] Authors' interview with Onofre Tafoya, April 2008.

[9] Burgess Winter had worked on metals operations in South Africa for 17 years, had spent a further seven years as vice president and general manager of Inspiration Resources and five years as senior vice president of operations at Kennecott Corporation. Kennecott became a subsidiary of BP Minerals in 1987 when BP purchased an outstanding minority interest in Standard Oil in June 1989.

[10] Bradford A. Mills, Magma's executive vice president growth and technology, later president of BHP Base Metals and later still chief executive of platinum miner Lonmin, and Marshall H. Campbell, Magma's senior vice president human resources.

[11] Authors' interview with Matt Foraker, April 2008.

[12] Authors' interview with Brad Mills, June 2008.

[13] Joint presentation by John Champagne, president of Magma Metals, and Robert Gadiana, director of United Steel Workers of America, at seminar held by Work in America Institute, Washington DC, 10–11 July 1995.

[14] Authors' interview with Jerry Ellis, August 2008.

[15] Authors' interview with Robert N. Hickman, May 2008.

[16] 'Magma, Partner Pursue Chilean Project', *Arizona Daily Star*, Tucson, 23 June 1993; 'Other Companies Express Interest in El Abra Deal', *La Segunda*, Santiago, 14 March 1994.

[17] Authors' interview with Jerry Ellis, August 2008.

[18] El Abra is now owned 49 per cent by Codelco, Chile's state-run copper giant, and 51 per cent by Freeport-McMoRan, now the world's largest publicly traded copper miner.

[19] Class action in the United States District Court for the District of Arizona: Richard T. Hanley vs. Warburg Pincus Capital Company, Broken Hill Proprietary Company Limited, J. Burgess Winter and others: Summary of action 29 July 1997; Proposed settlement 26 January 2006.

[20] Stephanie Strom, 'Broken Hill of Australia to Buy Magma Copper', *New York Times*, 1 December 1995.

[21] Ibid.

[22] Kenneth N. Gilpin, 'Magma Copper Stock Soars 29% on Huge Takeover Bid', *New York Times*, 2 December 1995.

[23] *Mining Journal*, London, 8 December 1995.

[24] Authors' confidential source, September 2007.

[25] Authors' interview with Daniel L. Edelstein, April 2008.

[26] 'San Manuel Facility: Site Visit Report', United States Environmental Protection Agency, Washington DC, 1992.

[27] Kenneth N. Gilpin, 'Magma Copper Stock Soars 29% on Huge Takeover Bid', *New York Times*, 2 December 1995.

[28] Authors' interview with Peter Laver, May 2008.

[29] Authors' interview with Jerry Ellis, August 2008.

[30] Authors' interview with Graeme McGregor, April 2008.

[31] Authors' interview with John Prescott, March 2008.

[32] Authors' interview with Brad Mills, June 2008.

[33] Authors' interview with Matt Foraker, April 2008.

[34] Authors' interview with John O'Connor, May 2008.

[35] Authors' interview with Gary Dillard, April 2008.

[36] Authors' interview with Brad Mills, June 2008.

[37] Authors' interview with Matt Foraker, April 2008.

[38] Authors' interview with Lance Hockridge, February 2008.

[39] 'Is There Life After Steel?', *Economist*, 19 June 1997.

[40] Authors' interview with Lance Hockridge, February 2008.

Chapter 12: One Little Tremor

[1] Report of proceedings, OK Tedi mine-closure workshop.

[2] R. Jackson, p. 3.

[3] A US PhD student in anthropology working with the Ningerum people, and in 2008 the government minister for small business, independent contractors and the service economy and minister assisting the finance minister for deregulation.

[4] R. Jackson, p. 3.

[5] Authors' interview with Russ Fynmore, June 2008.

[6] R. Jackson, p. 3.

[7] Ok Ma led into Ok Tedi.

[8] Authors' interview with Russ Fynmore, June 2008.

[9] 'West Side Story: The State's and Other Stakes in the Ok Tedi Mine', *The Ok Tedi Settlement: Issues, Outcomes and Implications*, Research School of Pacific and Asian Studies, ANU, 1997, p. 49.

[10] Ibid.

[11] Authors' interview with Glen Andrews, June 2008.

[12] Metall Mining Corporation, the Canadian subsidiary of the remaining German shareholder (Metallgesellschaft), now held 15 per cent of total equity, the PNG Government 30 per cent.

[13] K = Kina. The PNG currency at the time was roughly par with the $.

[14] 'West Side Story: The State's and Other Stakes in the Ok Tedi Mine,' *The Ok Tedi Settlement: Issues, Outcomes and Implications*, Research School of Pacific and Asian Studies, ANU, 1997, p. 55.

[15] *The Times* of Papua New Guinea, 1 June 1989.

[16] 'West Side Story: The State's and Other Stakes in the Ok Tedi Mine', *The Ok Tedi Settlement: Issues, Outcomes and Implications*, Research School of Pacific and Asian Studies, ANU, 1997, p. 53.

[17] Ibid.

[18] Papua New Guinea *Post-Courier*, 5 October 1989.

[19] Authors' interview with Carol Austin, July 2008.

[20] The Ok Tedi Lawsuit in Retrospect, 1997.

[21] Ibid.

[22] The Eighth Supplemental Agreement.

[23] 'West Side Story: The State's and Other Stakes in the Ok Tedi Mine', *The Ok Tedi Settlement: Issues, Outcomes and Implications*, Research School of Pacific and Asian Studies, ANU, 1997, p. 67.

[24] *The Age*, 20 September 1995.

[25] Authors' interview with Graham Evans, July 2008.

[26] 'Offor Sharp 2006', quotes by Stuart Kirsch, *American Ethnologist*, Vol. 24, 2007, p. 309.

[27] World Bank Report, Executive Summary, p. 2.

Chapter 13: Black Gold

[1] Authors' interview with John O'Connor, May 2008.

[2] Ibid.

[3] Matthew Stevens, 'BHP Minerals Faces Break-Up', *The Australian*, 29 June 1998.

[4] The Zamzama gas field is located in Sindh Province, southern Pakistan. BHP Petroleum (Pakistan) has a 38.5 per cent interest in the field and operates it on behalf of its three partners.

[5] Authors' interview with John O'Connor, May 2008.

[6] Authors' interview with Don Argus, July 2008.

[7] Richard Baker and James Button, 'AWB Focus on Rogue Who Reaped Millions', *The Age*, 2 December 2006.

[8] Jamie Freed, 'A Desert Storm Threatens BHP', *Sydney Morning Herald*, 11 February 2006.

[9] Authors' interview with John O'Connor, May 2008.

[10] Richard Baker and James Button, 'AWB Focus on Rogue Who Reaped Millions', *The Age*, 2 December 2006.

[11] 'A Desert Storm Threatens BHP', *Sydney Morning Herald*, 11 February 2006.

[12] Established by the Howard government in 2006 to investigate alleged kickbacks of $290 million to Saddam Hussein.

[13] Leonie Wood, 'Scandal Claims Steady Hand at Helm of BHP Petroleum', *The Age*, 28 April 2006.

[14] Overington, p. 50.

[15] Statement by Tom Harley to the Cole Inquiry, p. 20.

[16] Ibid.

[17] Ibid.

[18] Ibid.

[19] Cole Inquiry exhibit, BHP.0001.0066_R.

[20] Alexander Downer, Foreign Affairs, and Tim Fischer, Trade.

[21] Cole Inquiry, p. 51.

[22] Authors' interview with John O'Connor, May 2008.

[23] Cole Inquiry, p. 57.

[24] Ibid., p. 58.

[25] Statement to the Cole Inquiry.

[26] Cole Inquiry exhibit, BHP 0008.0030A.

[27] Overington, p. 57. According to author Caroline Overington, he had attempted to contact the head of the Iraqi Grain Board, Zuhair Daoud, only to discover he had been killed, probably in a car accident: 'The driver was doing 160 kilometres an hour, not stopping for anything. The road surface was sizzling in the desert heat. The car blew a tyre and Zuhair – who, like most Arabs, just didn't get the whole seatbelt thing – was unrestrained. He flew through the windscreen and the air, and was decapitated on the steel barrier that separated inbound traffic from outbound. His head bounced for a mile along the sealed road.'

Part III: The Partner
Chapter 14: Billiton

[1] Raffles diary, quoted in *Gedenboek Billiton*, p. 75.

[2] *The Times*, 14 June 1824.

[3] Dictionary of Canadian Biography Online, www.biographi.ca.

[4] Loudon rhymes with howden.

[5] Broersma, p. 15.

[6] *The Times*, 6 June 1929.

[7] Quoted in Heidhues, p. 3.

[8] Ibid., p. 4.

[9] Ibid.

[10] Authors' interview with Paul Everard, August 2008.

[11] Jonker, Howarth et al., Vol. 1, p. 52.

[12] Yergin, pp. 118–19. The group was designated Royal Dutch/Shell until 2005, when Royal Dutch Petroleum and Shell Transport and Trading were merged into Royal Dutch Shell plc. For the sake of simplicity, the authors have used Royal Dutch Shell throughout when referring to the group.

[13] The Billiton Joint Mining Company: NV Gemeenschappelijke Mijnbouwmaatschappij Billiton (GMB).

[14] Heidhues, p. 12.

[15] Mining silver, lead and zinc, North Broken Hill Limited was formed in 1895 and incorporated in 1912.

[16] Heidhues, p. 19.

[17] Authors' interview with Paul Everard, August 2008.

[18] Royal Dutch Shell has never had an American-style chief executive officer. Its highest office is chairman of the committee of managing directors (CMD).

[19] 'The Diplomats of Oil', *Time* magazine, 9 May 1960.

[20] The Seven Sisters were Standard Oil of New Jersey (later Exxon), the Royal Dutch/Shell Group (later Royal Dutch Shell), British Petroleum (later BP), Standard Oil of New York (later Mobil), Standard Oil of California (later Chevron), Gulf Oil and Texaco (later merged with Chevron).

[21] Yergin, pp. 521–2.

[22] Agis Salpukas, John Loudon obituary, *New York Times*, 9 February 1996.

[23] Howarth, p. 310.

[24] *New York Times*, 9 February 1996.

[25] Jonker, Howarth et al., Vol. 2, p. 379.

[26] Authors' interview with Paul Everard, August 2008.

[27] Authors' interview with David Munro, October 2008.

[28] Authors' interview with Brian Loton, April 2008.

[29] Ibid.

Chapter 15: The Big G

[1] Now called Vale (pronounced varlay).

[2] Authors' interview with Brian Gilbertson, February 2008.

[3] Ibid.

[4] 'A South African Boss Goes Down Under', *The Economist*, 9 January 2003.

[5] Authors' interview with Brian Gilbertson, February 2008.

[6] Ibid.

[7] JCI was formed in 1889 by the British-born Randlord Barney Barnato to administer his gold mines.

[8] Authors' interview with Brian Gilbertson, February 2008.

[9] A geological feature that runs north–south through the centre of Zimbabwe.

[10] Remote sensing is now a well-established field of science and is used in monitoring crops and finding water resources.

[11] Jones, p. 129.

[12] Emilia Potenza, 'All that Glitters', South African History Online, www.sahistory.org.za.

[13] In 1871, the brothers Johannes and Diederik de Beer sold their farm Vooruitzigt, which they had bought in 1860 for £50, to Dunell Ebden & Co for £6300. The following year, Cecil Rhodes and his partner Charles Rudd brought an ice-making machine from England and sold ice to the diggers working under the hot African sun. The De Beers farm became the site of both the De Beers mine and the Kimberley mine. De Beers Consolidated Mines Limited was established on 12 March 1888, with Rhodes as its founding chairman. Its assets included the whole of De Beers Mine and three-quarters of Kimberley Mine.

[14] Jones, pp. 130–2.

[15] The Broederbond was described by former South African prime minister Jan Smuts as 'a dangerous, cunning, political fascist organisation'. Every prime minister and state president in South Africa from 1948 to the end of apartheid in 1994 was a Broeder.

[16] Fraser, quoting Dr Grietjie Verhoef's unpublished manuscript, 'The History of Federale Mynbou Beperk', in *South African Studies*, p. 464.

[17] Butler, p. 70.

[18] Jones, p. 11.

[19] Ibid., p. 205.

[20] Authors' interview with Derek Keys, May 2008.

[21] Authors' interview with Brian Gilbertson, February 2008.

[22] Authors' interview with Derek Keys, May 2008.

[23] Authors' interview with Dave Munro, October 2008.

[24] Authors' interview with Derek Keys, May 2008.

[25] Ibid.

[26] Rebecca Bream, 'A Miner of Many Resources', *Financial Times*, 2 September 2006.

[27] Authors' interview with Brian Gilbertson, February 2008.

[28] Ibid.

[29] Authors' interview with Mike Salamon, May 2008.

Chapter 16: Out of Africa

[1] Authors' interview with Paul Everard, August 2008.

[2] Jones, p. 235.

[3] Authors' interview with Brian Gilbertson, February 2008.

[4] Authors' interview with Marius Kloppers, July 2008.

[5] Howarth, pp. 310–11.

[6] Authors' interview with Mike Salamon, May 2008.

[7] Ibid.

[8] Jones, p. 236.

[9] Authors' interview with Mick Davis, September 2008.

[10] Authors' interview with Brian Gilbertson, February 2008.

[11] Jones, p. 238.

[12] Authors' interview with Mick Davis, September 2008.

[13] Ibid.

[14] Jones, p. 237.

[15] Authors' interview with Brian Gilbertson, February 2008.

[16] Authors' interview with Marius Kloppers, July 2008.

[17] Howarth, p. 311.

[18] Authors' interview with Derek Keys, May 2008.

[19] Authors' interview with Paul Everard, August 2008.

[20] Authors' interview with Mike Salamon, May 2008.

[21] The Grasberg copper mine in Irian Jaya (West Papua) is owned and operated by Freeport Indonesia, a subsidiary of Freeport McMoRan Copper & Gold.

[22] Authors' interview with Mick Davis, September 2008.

[23] Authors' interview with Brian Gilbertson, February 2008.

[24] Authors' interview with Jerry Ellis, August 2008.

[25] Authors' interview with Derek Keys, May 2008.

[26] Shares in Gencor ceased trading in September 2002.

[27] Authors' interview with Mike Salamon, May 2008.

[28] Julie Walker, 'Gencor Pops Champagne on Achieving its Ambitious Global Dream', *Sunday Times*, 22 June 1997.

[29] *Ingwe* means leopard.

[30] Julie Walker, 'Gencor Pops Champagne on Achieving its Ambitious Global Dream', *Sunday Times*, South Africa, 22 June 1997.

[31] Authors' interview with Marius Kloppers, July 2008.

[32] Authors' interview with Lord Renwick, September 2008.

[33] Authors' interview with John Jackson, August 2008.

[34] Authors' interview with Mick Davis, September 2008.

[35] Authors' interview with John Jackson, August 2008.

[36] Authors' interview with Brian Gilbertson, February 2008.

[37] Authors' interview with Mike Salamon, May 2008.

[38] Questor Column, *Daily Telegraph*, 8 September 1999.

[39] Authors' interview with Marc Gonsalves, October 2008.

[40] Authors' interview with Mick Davis, September 2008.

[41] Authors' interview with Marc Gonsalves, October 2008.

[42] Heather Formby, 'Leaner Sanlam to Focus on Financial Services', *Business Times*, 8 December 1996.

[43] Portfolio theory, which proposes ways for rational investors to use diversification to optimise their portfolios, was introduced by Nobel Prize winner Harry Markowitz with his paper 'Portfolio Selection' in the 1952 *Journal of Finance*.

[44] Authors' interview with Brian Gilbertson, February 2008.

[45] Ibid.

[46] Authors' interview with Marc Gonsalves, October 2008.

[47] Authors' interview with Brian Gilbertson, February 2008.

[48] Gillian O'Connor, 'Billiton Chairman Who Has Made Much of His Own Luck', *Financial Times*, 15 May 2001.

[49] Authors' interview with Paul Everard, August 2008.

[50] Authors' interview with Ian Fraser, November 2008.

Chapter 17: The Cruellest Blow

[1] Authors' interview with Tim Winterer, May 2008.

[2] Authors' interview with John Prescott, March 2008.

[3] Authors' interview with confidential BHP source, March 2008.

[4] 'Still Digging', *The Economist*, 14 August 1997.

[5] Authors' interview with John Prescott, March 2008.

[6] 'Still Digging', *The Economist*, 14 August 1997.

[7] Authors' interview with Graeme McGregor, April 2008.

[8] Authors' interview with Jim Curry, May 2008.

[9] Authors' interview with John Prescott, March 2008.

[10] Ibid.

[11] Authors' interview with John O'Connor, May 2008.

[12] 'Still Digging', *The Economist*, 14 August 1997.

[13] Leonie Wood, 'Bogged in Baghdad: Inside BHP's Nightmare', *The Age*, 15 April 2006.

[14] Authors' interview with John O'Connor, May 2008.

[15] Ok Tedi had suffered a similar problem during initial construction in 1983.

[16] 'Very Down Under', *The Economist*, 5 March 1998.

[17] Ibid.

[18] Authors' interview with Brad Mills, June 2008.

[19] Ibid.

[20] Authors' interview with John Prescott, March 2008.

[21] Authors' interview with Brad Mills, June 2008.

[22] Authors' interview with Mick Davis, September 2008.

[23] Authors' interview with David Munro, October 2008.

[24] Authors' interview with Mick Davis, September 2008.

[25] Authors' interview with John Prescott, March 2008.

[26] 'Very Down Under', *The Economist*, 5 March 1998.

[27] Authors' interview with Jerry Ellis, August 2008.

[28] Authors' interview with Lance Hockridge, February 2008.

[29] Authors' interview with Graeme McGregor, April 2008.

[30] Authors' interview with Brad Mills, June 2008.

[31] Authors' interview with Jerry Ellis, August 2008.

[32] Authors' confidential source, September 2007.

33 Matthew Stevens, 'BHP Minerals Faces Break-Up', *The Australian*, 29 June 1998. Cannington was commissioned in October 1997 and EKATI in October 1998.

34 Authors' interview with John Prescott, March 2008.

35 Matthew Stevens, 'BHP Minerals Faces Break-Up', *The Australian*, 29 June 1998. In May 1999, Zimplats entered into an agreement to purchase BHP's 67 per cent interest in the Hartley Platinum Joint Venture and its 61.3 per cent interest in the Mhondoro Platinum Joint Venture.

36 Ibid.

37 Simon Anderson, 'Broken Hill Chairman Apologises for Losses', *Daily Telegraph*, 23 September 1998.

38 Authors' interview with Brian Gilbertson, February 2008.

39 Authors' interview with Jerry Ellis, August 2008.

40 Authors' interview with Marc Gonsalves, October 2008.

Chapter 18: Easy Rider

1 Authors' interview with John Jackson, August 2008.

2 Authors' confidential source, November 2008.

3 Ibid.

4 Shawn Donnan, 'Profile: Paul Anderson', *Financial Times*, 20 March 2001.

5 Ibid.

6 Authors' interview with Jerry Ellis, August 2008.

7 Shawn Donnan, 'Profile: Paul Anderson', *Financial Times*, 20 March 2001.

8 Authors' interview with Paul Anderson, August 2008.

9 Ibid.

10 Authors' interview with Graham Evans, July 2008.

11 Ibid.

12 Becky Gaylord, 'American Accents in Australian Executive Suites', *New York Times*, 15 November 2000.

13 Authors' interview with Paul Anderson, August 2008.

14 Shawn Donnan, 'Profile: Paul Anderson', *Financial Times*, 20 March 2001.

15 Gwen Robinson, 'Paul Anderson, BHP's Quiet Achiever', *Financial Times*, 20 March 2001.

16 Authors' interview with Paul Anderson, August 2008.

17 Authors' interview with Brad Mills, June 2008.

18 Authors' interview with Jerry Ellis, August 2008.

19 Authors' interview with Chip Goodyear, July 2008.

[20] 'Call on the Slopes', *Mining Journal*, 16 February 2007.

[21] Authors' interview with Paul Anderson, August 2008.

[22] Ibid.

[23] Authors' interview with Brad Mills, June 2008.

[24] Authors' interview with Chip Goodyear, July 2008.

[25] Leora Moldofsky, 'American Who Reformed the Big Australian', *Financial Times*, 8 February 2007.

[26] Shawn Donnan, 'Profile: Paul Anderson', *Financial Times*, 20 March 2001.

[27] Authors' interview with Paul Anderson, August 2008.

[28] Authors' interview with Brad Mills, June 2008.

[29] Peter Martin, *PM* program archive, ABC, 25 June 1999.

[30] Authors' interview with Michael Spencer, November 2008.

[31] Authors' interview with Paul Anderson, August 2008.

[32] Michael Richardson, 'New Chief Has Work Cut Out as BHP Tries to Overcome Commodity Cycle', *International Herald Tribune*, 25 March 1999.

[33] Authors' interview with Lance Hockridge, February 2008.

[34] Verne G. Kopytoff, 'Tough Times in the Copper Pits: Excess Capacity and Sagging Prices Force Retrenchment', *New York Times*, 11 September 1999.

[35] Peter Martin, *PM* program archive, ABC, 25 June 1999.

[36] Former resident quoted in 'Remembering My Hometown of San Manuel, Arizona', www.theclosetentrepreneur.com.

[37] Richard Ducote, 'Town's Last Copper Relics to Pass into History', *Arizona Daily Star*, 17 January 2007.

[38] Authors' interview with J. David Lowell, August 2008.

[39] Authors' interview with Paul Anderson, August 2008.

[40] Richard Ducote, 'Town's Last Copper Relics to Pass into History', *Arizona Daily Star*, 17 January 2007.

[41] Authors' interview with Onofre Tafoya, April 2008.

[42] Authors' interview with Lance Hockridge, February 2008.

[43] Authors' interview with Mike Salamon, May 2008.

[44] Authors' interview with Paul Anderson, August 2008.

[45] Authors' interview with David Munro, October 2008.

[46] Authors' interview with Brian Gilbertson, February 2008.

[47] Authors' interview with Ian Fraser, November 2008.

Chapter 19: Project Bardot

1. Alan Deans, 'Speak Softly, Carry an Iron Bar', *The Bulletin*, 25 April 2001.
2. Ibid.
3. Authors' interview with Brad Mills, June 2008.
4. Ibid.
5. Authors' interview with John Jackson, August 2008.
6. Ibid.
7. Ibid.
8. Ibid.
9. Authors' interview with Brian Gilbertson, February 2008.
10. Authors' interview with Don Argus, July 2008.
11. Authors' interview with Mick Davis, September 2008.
12. Authors' interview with Paul Anderson, August 2008.
13. Authors' interview with Don Argus, July 2008.
14. Professor Garnaut would be appointed in 2007 to report on climate-change measures for the Rudd government.
15. Authors' interview with Keith Faulkner, November 2008.
16. Authors' interview with Chip Goodyear, July 2008.
17. Authors' interview with Don Argus, July 2008.
18. Authors' interview with Sir Robert Wilson, September 2008.
19. Authors' interview with Ian Fraser, November 2008.
20. Ibid.
21. Authors' interview with Brian Gilbertson, February 2008.
22. Authors' interview with Marius Kloppers, July 2008.
23. Authors' interview with Brian Gilbertson, February 2008.
24. Authors' interview with Mick Davis, September 2008.
25. Suzanne Kapner, 'Merger in the Mining Industry Would Create a Global Giant', *New York Times*, 19 March 2001.
26. Authors' interview with Brian Gilbertson, February 2008.
27. Ibid.
28. Authors' interview with Marius Kloppers, July 2008.
29. Authors' interview with Marc Gonsalves, October 2008.
30. Shawn Donnan, 'Profile: Paul Anderson', *Financial Times*, 20 March 2001.
31. Authors' interview with Brad Mills, June 2008.
32. Authors' interview with John Jackson, August 2008.
33. Authors' interview with Lord Renwick, September 2008.

[34] Authors' interview with Brad Mills, June 2008.

[35] Authors' interview with Mike Salamon, May 2008.

[36] Authors' interview with Lance Hockridge, February 2008.

[37] Gary Parkinson, 'Billiton and BHP Agree Merger Plans', *Daily Telegraph*, 2 April 2001.

[38] 'Bigger Digger', *The Economist*, 22 March 2001.

[39] Ibid.

[40] Suzanne Kapner, 'Merger in the Mining Industry Would Create a Global Giant', *New York Times*, 19 March 2001.

[41] Authors' interview with Brad Mills, June 2008.

[42] Jan McCallum, 'Merger Data Still too Murky', *Business Review Weekly*, 11 May 2001.

[43] Authors' interview with Marc Gonsalves, October 2008.

[44] Authors' interview with Brian Gilbertson, February 2008.

[45] Benjamin Wootliff, 'Billiton Flies High on Confirmation of Merger', *Daily Telegraph*, 2 April 2001.

[46] Authors' interview with Brian Gilbertson, February 2008.

[47] Authors' interview with Lance Hockridge, February 2008.

[48] Alan Deans, 'Speak Softly, Carry an Iron Bar', *The Bulletin*, 25 April 2001.

[49] Simon Johanson, 'BHP Merger Approved', *The Age*, www.theage.com.au, 19 May 2001.

[50] Ibid.

[51] Authors' interview with Brian Gilbertson, February 2008.

[52] Authors' interview with Don Argus, July 2008.

[53] Authors' interview with Lord Renwick, September 2008.

[54] Ibid.

Chapter 20: Hunters and Skinners

[1] Authors' interview with David Munro, October 2008.

[2] Ibid.

[3] Authors' interview with Mike Salamon, May 2008.

[4] The Australian Competition and Consumer Commission, established in 1995, is an independent authority of the Federal Government.

[5] Authors' interview with Brad Mills, June 2008.

[6] Alan Deans, 'Speak Softly, Carry an Iron Bar', *The Bulletin*, 25 April 2001.

[7] Gillian O'Connor, 'Conditions are Imposed on BHP-Billiton', *Financial Times*, 5 June 2001.

[8] Authors' interview with Brian Gilbertson, February 2008.

[9] Authors' interview with Mick Davis, September 2008.

[10] Authors' interview with Brian Gilbertson, February 2008.

[11] Billiton's Spence copper deposit in Chile had yet to be developed.

[12] Authors' interview with Derek Keys, May 2008.

[13] Authors' interview with John Jackson, August 2008.

[14] Authors' interview with Derek Keys, May 2008.

[15] Authors' interview with David Munro, October 2008.

[16] Authors' interview with Mike Salamon, May 2008.

[17] Lance Hockridge later became president North America of BlueScope Steel and, later still, chief executive officer of Queensland Rail.

[18] Authors' interview with Lance Hockridge, February 2008.

[19] George Trefgarne, 'BHP Billiton Starts with $1.1bn Bill', *Daily Telegraph*, 21 August 2001.

[20] Authors' interview with Mike Salamon, May 2008.

[21] Authors' interview with Graham Evans, July 2008.

[22] Carolyn Batt, 'Billiton Shuffles Top Names', *Daily Telegraph*, 14 September 2001.

[23] Authors' interview with Brian Gilbertson, February 2008.

[24] Authors' interview with Marc Gonsalves, October 2008.

[25] Authors' interview with Brian Gilbertson, February 2008.

[26] Ibid.

[27] Authors' interview with John Jackson, August 2008.

Part IV: The Power
Chapter 21: Life with Brian

[1] Authors' interview with Don Argus, July 2008.

[2] Authors' interview with Mike Salamon, May 2008.

[3] Authors' interview with Brian Gilbertson, February 2008.

[4] 'BHP Halts Iron Plant Deliveries', Reuters, 27 March 2002. In 2005, the Boodarie HBI plant at Port Hedland was closed down permanently. It was later demolished.

[5] Authors' interview with Mike Salamon, May 2008.

6 Brian Gilbertson, 'A Strategic Framework for an Industry Leader', 8 April 2002, published with Brian Gilbertson's permission.

7 Ibid.

8 Dudley White, 'BHP Billiton Posts 33 per cent Profit Drop', *Business Day*, 2 May 2002.

9 Authors' interview with Mike Salamon, May 2008.

10 Authors' interview with Brian Gilbertson, February 2008.

11 Sophie Barker, 'Gilbertson to Lead Billiton Sooner', *Daily Telegraph*, 2 May 2002.

12 Authors' interview with Lord Renwick, September 2008.

13 Authors' interview with John Jackson, August 2008.

14 Neil Collins, 'City Comment', *Daily Telegraph*, 3 May 2002.

15 Authors' interview with Paul Anderson, August 2008.

16 Authors' interview with Michael Spencer, November 2008.

17 Authors' interview with Chip Goodyear, July 2008.

18 Authors' interview with Paul Anderson, August 2008.

19 Authors' interview with John Jackson, August 2008.

20 Authors' interview with Chip Goodyear, July 2008. He explains, 'The "125" was shorthand for US$100 billion market capitalisation at a 25x price/earnings ratio. This would have meant that if we could convince the market that the company should trade at a 25x multiple (we were probably trading at 15x at the time) and we could generate attributable profit of US$4 billion, we should be valued at US$100 billion (a long way from the US$30 billion we were trading for at the time). Ultimately, we achieved US$240 billion of market capitalisation, and earnings were US$13.7 billion (2007) – all without an acquisition – but the P/E multiple was still in the 15x–17x range.'

21 Authors' interview with John Jackson, August 2008.

22 Authors' interview with Marius Kloppers, July 2008.

23 Authors' interview with Mike Salamon, May 2008.

24 Authors' interview with Chip Goodyear, July 2008.

25 Authors' interview with Brian Gilbertson, February 2008.

26 Authors' interview with John Jackson, August 2008.

Chapter 22: Road to Rio

1 'Not One for Career Mistakes', *Financial Times*, 1 May 2008.

2 Authors' interview with Sir Robert Wilson, September 2008.

3 Ibid.

[4] Authors' interview with Marc Gonsalves, October 2008.

[5] Authors' interview with Brian Gilbertson, February 2008.

[6] Ivor Ries, senior research analyst, E. L. & C. Baillieu, 'For BHP Billiton Shareholders and New Boss Brian Gilbertson, the News is All Good', *The Bulletin*, 14 August 2002.

[7] Ibid.

[8] Authors' interview with Mike Salamon, May 2008.

[9] Authors' interview with Don Argus, July 2008.

[10] Ivor Ries, senior research analyst, E. L. & C. Baillieu, 'For BHP Billiton Shareholders and New Boss Brian Gilbertson, the News is All Good', *The Bulletin*, 14 August 2002.

[11] Authors' interview with Brian Gilbertson, February 2008.

[12] Ibid.

[13] Authors' interview with Mike Salamon, May 2008.

[14] Australian publications routinely report that the BHP Billiton board knew nothing about Brian Gilbertson's plans for a merger with Rio Tinto.

[15] Authors' interview with John Jackson, August 2008.

[16] Authors' interview with Brian Gilbertson, February 2008.

[17] Authors' interview with John Jackson, August 2008.

[18] Authors' interview with Lord Renwick, September 2008.

[19] Authors' interview with Brian Gilbertson, February 2008.

[20] Authors' interview with Lord Renwick, September 2008.

[21] Ibid.

[22] Authors' interview with Brian Gilbertson, February 2008.

[23] Michael Chaney resigned from BHP Billiton's board in November 2005 after serving 11 years. He became chairman of Don Argus's old bank, the NAB, and also of Woodside Petroleum. Argus described him as 'a class act' and added in an interview with Matthew Stevens of *The Australian* in October 2008, 'Chaney should be my successor – make no mistake about it.'

[24] Authors' interview with Don Argus, July 2008.

[25] Ibid.

[26] Authors' interview with Brian Gilbertson, February 2008.

[27] Authors' interview with Mike Salamon, May 2008.

[28] Authors' interview with Brian Gilbertson, February 2008.

[29] Authors' interview with Derek Keys, May 2008.

[30] Authors' interview with Don Argus, July 2008.

Chapter 23: Test of Strength

[1] Now renamed Anglican Grammar School.

[2] England won the match by 225 runs; Australia won the series 4–1.

[3] Richard Northedge, 'Business Profile: The Corporate Wizard of Oz', *Daily Telegraph*, 4 November 2006.

[4] Authors' interview with Brian Gilbertson, February 2008.

[5] Authors' interview with Don Argus, July 2008.

[6] 'The MT Interview: Nigel Boardman (Slaughter & May)', *Management Today*, 2 December 2005.

[7] Authors' interview with Chip Goodyear, July 2008.

[8] Authors' interview with Don Argus, July 2008.

[9] Sherilee Bridge, 'Gilbertson Walks Out of BHP Billiton', *Sunday Times*, South Africa, 7 January 2003.

[10] Authors' interview with Lord Renwick, September 2008.

[11] Authors' interview with Chip Goodyear, July 2008.

[12] Authors' interview with Ian Fraser, November 2008.

[13] Authors' interview with Lord Renwick, September 2008.

[14] *Indaba* is the Zulu word for conference or gathering.

[15] Authors' interview with David Munro, October 2008.

[16] Authors' interview with Chip Goodyear, July 2008.

[17] 'BHP Billiton CEO Quits After 6 Months on the Job', South African Press Association-AFP, *Business Report*, 6 January 2003.

[18] Virginia Marsh, 'BHP Billiton Chief Unexpectedly Resigns', *Financial Times*, 5 January 2003.

[19] Ibid.

[20] Authors' interview with Brad Mills, June 2008.

[21] Zoe Daniel, 'BHP-Billiton Chief's Shock Exit', *The 7.30 Report*, ABC, 6 January 2003.

[22] Sherilee Bridge, 'Gilbertson Walks Out of BHP Billiton', *Sunday Times*, South Africa, 7 January 2003.

[23] *ABC News*, 6 January 2003.

[24] Virginia Marsh, 'BHP Billiton Forced to Explain CEO's Exit', *Financial Times*, 6 January 2003.

[25] 'Dirty Diggers', *The Economist*, 9 January 2003.

[26] Virginia Marsh and Matthew Jones, 'Autocrat Who Dealt Himself Out of a Job', *Financial Times*, 7 January 2003.

[27] Authors' interview with Brian Gilbertson, February 2008.

[28] Mark Bendeich, 'BHP Billiton CEO Quit in Row Over Big Deal – Source', Reuters, London, 14 January 2003. The same story ran over the Australian wire service with a different headline the following day: 'Gilbertson Quit BHP Billiton Over Deal, Says Source'.

[29] Ibid.

[30] Adele Ferguson, 'Argus on the Line', *Business Review Weekly*, 16 January 2003.

[31] Authors' interview with Mike Salamon, May 2008.

[32] Anna Fifield, 'BHP Billiton Moves to Rebalance Board', *Financial Times*, 25 February 2003.

[33] Greg Hoy, 'Mining Industry Looks to Further Mergers', *Inside Business*, ABC, 16 March 2003.

[34] Carolyn Batt, 'BHP Settles £4m on Departed Chief', *Daily Telegraph*, 22 May 2003.

[35] Wayne Arnold, 'After Record Profit, Chief Says He'll Leave', *New York Times*, 8 February 2007.

[36] Alec Hogg, 'BHP Billiton's Annual Report Provides New Insight into the Departure of Former CEO Brian Gilbertson', *Business Report*, 10 October 2003.

[37] Authors' interview with Brad Mills, June 2008.

[38] Ibid.

[39] Virginia Marsh, 'BHP Chief Seeks to Redefine Mining Group', *Financial Times*, 6 May 2002.

[40] 'Brian Gilbertson's Success Comes from Being Nimble', *Business Report*, 22 October 2004.

Chapter 24: Digging Deeper

[1] Authors' interview with Don Argus, July 2008.

[2] 'Chip Goodyear's Working Day', *Financial Times*, 21 December 2003.

[3] Ibid.

[4] Authors' interview with Chip Goodyear, July 2008.

[5] Authors' interview with Don Argus, July 2008.

[6] Authors' interview with Lord Renwick, September 2008.

[7] Authors' interview with Brad Mills, June 2008. In 2008, Mick Davis's Xstrata launched a £5 billion takeover bid for Mills's Lonmin. The bid was withdrawn following the collapse of global financial markets in September/October 2008.

[8] Rebecca Bream and Virginia Marsh, 'Goodyear Shakes Up BHP Structure', *Financial Times*, 17 March 2004.

9 Opposition foreign-affairs spokesman Kevin Rudd rode the scandal to national prominence, dominating Question Time in the House of Representatives. The opposition virtually ignored the 2006 Budget in favour of what Rudd called the 'wheat for weapons' scandal.

10 John Howard, House of Representatives, 31 October 2005.

11 *The 7.30 Report*, ABC, 15 February 2006.

12 Authors' interview, July 2008.

13 Authors' interview with Chip Goodyear, July 2008.

14 Authors' interview with Mike Yeager, October 2008.

15 Ibid.

16 Authors' report on Royal Dutch Shell's 2008 annual general meeting.

17 Authors' interview with Marius Kloppers, July 2008.

18 Authors' confidential source, May 2008.

19 Authors' interview with Tim Offor, September 2008.

20 Ok Tedi 2005 CMCA Review Report: 'A Report for the Mineral Policy Institute (Sydney) on the Level of Consent and/or Awareness of the Community Mine Continuation Agreements Signed by the Impact Communities Along the Ok Tedi and Fly Rivers for Ok Tedi Mining Limited'.

21 Tingay, 'Report on Environmental and Health Issues', CMCA *Review*, September 2006.

22 Authors' interview with Alan Breen, December 2008.

23 Tingay, 'Report on Environmental and Health Issues,' CMCA *Review*, September 2006.

24 Authors' interview with Keith Faulkner, January 2009.

25 Chairman's message, PNGSDP Annual Report, 2008.

26 Authors' interview with Marius Kloppers, July 2008.

Chapter 25: Coal Climate

1 First-hand from Robert Macklin, who was among the journalists.

2 Authors' interview with Chip Goodyear, July 2008.

3 BHP Billiton were unable to supply the names of the specific non-governmental organisations from the environment lobby as they had 'requested anonymity'.

4 Authors' interview with Don Argus, July 2008.

5 IPCC Report, 2007.

6 Authors' interview with Don Argus, July 2008.

7 Authors' interview with Geoff Walsh, March 2008.

[8] BHP Billiton Sustainability Report, 2006.
[9] Pearse, p. 3.
[10] Ibid.
[11] Ibid.
[12] Ibid.
[13] Authors' interview with Guy Pearse, March 2008.
[14] Pearse, p. 16.
[15] Ibid.
[16] Ibid.
[17] Authors' interview with Guy Pearse, March 2008.
[18] Ibid.
[19] Former federal director of the Liberal Party and campaign director in 1996, and later shadow minister for foreign affairs.
[20] Authors' interview with Guy Pearse, March 2008.
[21] Authors' interview with Geoff Walsh, March 2008.
[22] Authors' interview with Marius Kloppers, July 2008.
[23] Authors' interview with Don Argus, July 2008.
[24] Ibid.

Chapter 26: The Cakehole

[1] Pearse, p. 455.
[2] Authors' interview with Mick Davis, September 2008.
[3] Ticky Fullerton, 'The X Factor', *Four Corners*, ABC, 22 February 2005.
[4] 'Nazi gold' was a reference to Xstrata's parent company, Glencore International, founded by Marc Rich, a Belgian Jew who had fled Nazi Europe and settled in the United States. Rich later moved to Switzerland after being indicted on charges of tax fraud and illegal oil trading. He was controversially pardoned by Bill Clinton in the last hours of his presidency.
[5] Authors' interview with Mick Davis, September 2008.
[6] Ibid.
[7] Virginia Marsh, 'WMC Looks to Diversify Portfolio', *Financial Times*, 13 August 2004.
[8] Ken Eastwood, 'A Town Like Roxby', *Australian Geographic*, July/September 2007.
[9] Authors' interview with Mick Davis, September 2008.
[10] Authors' interview with Chip Goodyear, July 2008.

[11] Ibid.

[12] Authors' interview with Marius Kloppers, July 2008.

[13] Lachlan Colquhoun, 'WMC's New Estimate Aids Bid Defence', *Financial Times*, 25 November 2004.

[14] Lachlan Colquhoun, 'Olympic Prize in Bid Battle for WMC', *Financial Times*, 29 November 2004.

[15] Virginia Marsh, 'WMC Work Puts Heat on Xstrata Bid', *Financial Times*, 14 January 2005.

[16] Virginia Marsh, 'WMC Board Seeks White Knight to Better Xstrata Bid', *Financial Times*, 4 February 2005.

[17] Peter Klinger, 'Uncertainty in Russia Gives BHP Cold Feet', *The Times*, 17 February 2005.

[18] 'Warriors in the Big Battle', *Mining Journal*, 16 November 2007.

[19] Rebecca Bream, 'BHP Billiton Set for WMC Bid', *Financial Times*, 7 March 2005.

[20] Authors' interview with Don Argus, July 2008.

[21] Authors' interview with Mick Davis, September 2008.

[22] Authors' interview with Chip Goodyear, July 2008.

[23] Authors' interview with Marius Kloppers, July 2008.

[24] Authors' interview with Mick Davis, September 2008.

[25] *7.30 Report*, ABC, 9 March 2005.

[26] Authors' interview with Mick Davis, September 2008.

[27] Later the husband of Maxine McKew.

[28] The precedent was finally abandoned at the 2007 conference.

[29] BHP Billiton says the correct figure is 32 million litres.

[30] Interview with Jessie Boylan on behalf of the authors, September 2008.

[31] Authors' interview with Richard Yeeles, via email, May 2008.

[32] Authors' interview with Chip Goodyear, July 2008.

[33] Authors' interview with Jim Green, Friends of the Earth website, www.friendsoftheearth.com, November 2008.

[34] Interview with Jessie Boylan on behalf of the authors, September 2008.

[35] Authors' interview with Jim Green, Friends of the Earth website, www.friendsoftheearth.com, November 2008.

[36] Authors' interview with Richard Yeeles, via email, May 2008.

[37] Interview with Jessie Boylan on behalf of the authors, September 2008.

[38] Authors' interview with Richard Yeeles, via email, May 2008.

[39] Interview with Jessie Boylan on behalf of the authors, September 2008.

[40] Authors' interview with Mick Davis, September 2008.

[41] *Business Review Weekly*, 12–19 June 2008, p. 20.

Chapter 27: Dragon Dance

[1] Authors' interview with Thérèse Rein, July 2008.

[2] Macklin, p. 75.

[3] By this time, Rudd was Labor's shadow minister for foreign affairs.

[4] Authors' interview with Brad Mills, June 2008.

[5] Authors' interview with Brian Loton, April 2008.

[6] Authors' interview with Russ Fynmore, June 2008.

[7] Authors' interview with Mike Salamon, May 2008.

[8] Authors' interview with Marius Kloppers, July 2008.

[9] Leora Moldofsky and Rebecca Bream, 'BHP Billiton in $9bn China Contract', *Financial Times*, 2 March 2004.

[10] Wayne Arnold, 'BHP Billiton Remains Upbeat over Bet on China's Growth', *New York Times*, 8 June 2004.

[11] Authors' interview with Brad Mills, June 2008.

[12] Arnold, *New York Times*, 8 June 2004.

[13] Kerry O'Brien, 'BHP Continues Bid for WMC', *7.30 Report*, ABC, 9 March 2005.

[14] 'BHP Billiton Profits Soar on China Demand', *The Times*, 15 February 2006.

[15] The great-grandnephew of Lord Forrest, the first Australian elevated to the British peerage, Andrew was born and bred in the Pilbara. A tenacious entrepreneur, he had quietly amassed the Pilbara's largest single landholding for his company, the Fortescue Metals Group, to challenge BHP Billiton and Rio Tinto.

[16] Authors' interview with Mike Salamon, May 2008.

[17] Peter Klinger, 'BHP Billiton Follows Rio Tinto into Russia', *The Times*, 14 June 2006.

[18] Ibid.

[19] Gazprom, Russia's state-controlled gas monopoly, is the world's largest natural-gas producer.

[20] Guy Faulconbridge, 'BHP Billiton Eyes Russian Uranium Market', Reuters, June 2006.

[21] Wayne Arnold, 'As Demand for Copper Soars, BHP Posts a Record', *New York Times*, 24 August 2006.

[22] 'A Generous Pay Deal for Striking Miners Alarms Chile's Copper Producers', *The Economist*, 7 September 2006.

[23] Victor Mallet and Virginia Marsh, 'Transcript of Interview with Chip Goodyear', *Financial Times*, 22 September 2004.

[24] An ironic description of Australia from social critic Donald Horne in 1964 now universally misapplied to mean fortunate.

[25] Rudd turned 50 on 21 September 2007.

[26] From the Richard Condon novel of a 'brainwashed' pro-Chinese politician.

[27] Wayne Arnold, 'After Record Profit, Chief Says He'll Leave', *New York Times*, 8 February 2007.

[28] Authors' interview with Chip Goodyear, July 2008.

[29] 'Let the Search Begin', Mining Journal, 16 February 2007.

30 Authors' interview with Lord Renwick, September 2008.

[31] Barry Fitzgerald, 'BHP Anoints Whizz-Kid to Top Job', *The Age*, 1 June 2007.

[32] Rebecca Bream, 'Kloppers Set to Keep BHP on Same Path', *Financial Times*, 23 August 2007.

[33] BHP Billiton Annual Report, 2007.

[34] Robert Lindsay, 'Broker Flags Miners as China Fund Targets', *The Times*, 5 October 2007.

Chapter 28: Meltdown

[1] 'The Big Dig', *The Economist*, 8 November 2007.

[2] The core Hamersley deposit was discovered in 1952 when mining magnate Lang Hancock spotted bands of oxidised iron on the walls of a river gorge as he flew his light aircraft along it to escape a tropical storm.

[3] *The Australian*, October 2007.

[4] *South China Morning Post*, 12 May 2008.

[5] 'Kloppers Calms Chinese Merger Fears', *The Australian*, 23 November 2007.

[6] Rebecca Bream, 'The Integration Man at BHP', *Financial Times*, 12 November 2007.

[7] Chinalco and Alcoa actually bought a 12 per cent stake in Rio's London-listed shares, giving them a holding of more than nine per cent in the whole group.

[8] Jo Clarke, 'BHP's Bad Cop Talks Tough as Rio Battle Hots Up', *Financial Review*, 28 April 2008.

[9] *The Australian*, 10 April 2008.

[10] Malcolm Maiden, 'BHP Lights Fuse on Takeover Game', *The Age*, 9 November 2007.

[11] Authors' interview with Marius Kloppers, July 2008.

[12] Jennifer Hewett, 'China Told to Shelve Mine Deals', *The Australian*, 25 April 2008.

[13] Authors' interview with Don Argus, July 2008.

[14] *The Australian*, 10 April 2008.

[15] Peter Smith, 'BHP Attacks Rio's Performance', *Financial Times*, 22 April 2008.

[16] Peter Smith, 'BHP's Head Remains Entrenched in Rio Bid', 23 April 2008.

[17] BHP Billiton has led the industry campaign to develop an indexed method of iron-ore pricing to replace the annual contract negotiations, a move which has been opposed by steelmakers.

[18] Authors' interview with Don Argus, July 2008.

[19] Authors' interview with Marius Kloppers, July 2008.

[20] Authors' interview with Ian Ashby, August 2008.

[21] Emiliya Mychasuk, 'All Fun, No Games with Chinalco', *Financial Times*, 19 August 2008.

[22] Matthew Saltmarsh, 'Record Profit at BHP Billiton Eases Doubts', *New York Times*, 19 August 2008.

[23] Authors' interview with Sir Robert Wilson, September 2008.

[24] ACCC press release, 1 October 2008.

[25] CNN, 23 October 2008.

[26] Johanne Gray, 'Timing . . . It's That Simple Twist of Fate', *Australian Financial Review*, 27 November 2008.

Afterword: The Comeback

[1] Du Plessis replaced Jim Leng, the former chairman-elect to replace Paul Skinner. Leng resigned after just two board meetings following a disagreement over the Chinalco proposal.

[2] Pan Kwan Yuk, 'Conciliatory South African Steps Up to Key Position', *Financial Times*, 18 March 2009.

[3] Richard Wachman, 'New Man Must Build a Bridge Between Rio and Beijing', *The Observer*, 22 March 2009.

[4] William MacNamara, 'Du Plessis to be Rio Chairman', *Financial Times*, 18 March 2009.

[5] Bryce Elder and Neil Hume, 'Hopes of New BHP Approach Lifts Rio', *Financial Times*, 14 May 2009.

[6] Malcolm Maiden, 'If You Can't Beat 'Em, Join 'Em', *The Age*, 5 June 2009.

[7] Jamie Freed and John Garnaut, 'Rio's Colleen Lite Bites Dust', *The Age*, 6 June 2009.

[8] John Durie, 'Sweet Victory for BHP as Rio Yields', *The Australian*, 6 June 2009.

[9] Jan du Plessis, letter to Rio Tinto shareholders, 5 June 2009.

[10] BHP Billiton press release, 5 June 2009.

[11] John Durie, 'Sweet Victory for BHP as Rio Yields', *The Australian*, 6 June 2009.

[12] Chris Zappone, 'Iron Ore Behemoth Bad News for China', *The Age*, 5 June 2009.

[13] Peter Smith, 'Rudd Seeks to Reassure China After Rio Deal Collapses', *Financial Times*, 5 June 2009.

BIBLIOGRAPHY

Adelman, M. A., *The Genie out of the Bottle: World Oil since 1970*, Cambridge, Massachusetts, The MIT Press, 1996

BHP, *Seventy-Five Years of BHP Development in Industry: 1885–1960*, Broken Hill, BHP, 1960

Billiton, *Gedenboek Billiton 1852–1927*, Vol. I, The Hague, Martinus Nijhoff, 1927

Blainey, Geoffrey, *The Rise of Broken Hill*, Melbourne, Macmillan, 1968

Rush That Never Ended, Melbourne, Melbourne University Press, 2003

The Steel Master, Melbourne, Macmillan, 1971

Brady, R. Paul, *Don't Go Down to the Mine, Daddy*, Broken Hill, Quadrangle, 2004

Broersma, K. E., *Billiton: Eene Zaak van Regt en Billijkheid*, Leidschendam, Billiton, 1985

Butler, Anthony, *Democracy and Apartheid*, London, Macmillan, 1998

Camilleri, Jenny, *In the Broken Hill Paddock*, Broken Hill, Camilleri, 2001

Some Outstanding Women of Broken Hill and District, Broken Hill, Camilleri, 2002

Carew, Edna, *Paul Keating*, Sydney, Allen & Unwin, 1992

Cockburn, Stewart, *Notable Lives: A Profile of 21 Eminent South Australians*, Adelaide, Ferguson, 1997

Cummings, Ian and John Beasant, *Shell Shock: The Secrets and Spin of an Oil Giant*, Edinburgh, Mainstream, 2005

Dale, George, *The Industrial History of Broken Hill*, Melbourne, Fraser and Jenkinson, 1918

Edwards, John, *Keating: The Inside Story*, Melbourne, Viking, 1996

Farwell, George, *Down Argent Street*, Sydney, F. H. Johnston, 1948

Filer, Colin, John Burton and Glenn Banks, *The Fragmentation of Responsibilities in the Melanesian Mining Sector*, Canberra, Greenleaf Publishing, 2007

Greenhalgh, Stewart A., 'Rudd and Economic Geology', *Records and Reminiscences: Geosciences at the University of Adelaide 1875–2000*, John Coope (ed.), Adelaide, Gillingham Printers, 2001

Haigh, Gideon, *The Battle for BHP*, Sydney, Information Australia with Allen & Unwin, 1987

Hartmann, Thom, *Unequal Protection: The Rise of Corporate Dominance and the Theft of Human Rights*, USA, Rodale, 2002

Hewat, Tim, *The Elders Explosion*, Sydney, Bay Books, 1998

Howarth, Stephen, *A Century of Oil: The 'Shell' Transport and Trading Company 1897–1997*, London, Weidenfeld & Nicolson, 1997

Jackson, R., *Ok Tedi: The Pot of Gold*, University of Papua New Ginea, 1982

Jones, J. D. F., *Through Fortress and Rock: The Story of Gencor 1895–1995*, Johannesburg, Jonathan Ball, 1995

Jonker, Joost, Stephen Howarth, Keetie Sluyterman and Jan Luiten van Zanden, *A History of Royal Dutch Shell*, 3 vols, Oxford, Oxford University Press, 2007

Kearns, R. H. B., *Broken Hill 1883–1893; 1894–1914; 1915–1939; Silverton*, Broken Hill, Broken Hill Historical Society, 1972–75

Lloyd, John P., *The Weeks Royalty*, Sydney, Fortis, 1993

Macklin, Robert, *Kevin Rudd: The Biography*, Melbourne, Penguin, 2007

Maugeri, Leonardo, *The Age of Oil: The Mythology, History and Future of the World's Most Controversial Resource*, Westport, Connecticut, Praeger, 2006

McIlwraith, John, *The Mt Newman Story*, Perth, BHP-Utah Minerals International, 1988

Menzies, Sir Robert, *Afternoon Light*, London, Cassell, 1967

Overington, Caroline, *Kickback: Inside the Australian Wheat Board Scandal*, Sydney, Allen & Unwin, 2007

Pearse, Guy, *High and Dry*, Melbourne, Penguin, 2007

Robinson, W. S., *If I Remember Rightly*, Geoffrey Blainey (ed.), Melbourne, Cheshire, 1967

Tafoya, Onofre, *Mother Magma: A Memoir of Underground Life in the San Manuel Copper Mine*, Mesa, Arizona, HISI Books, 2001

Trengove, Alan, *What's Good For Australia: The Story of BHP*, Sydney, Cassell Australia, 1975

Turnbull, Clive, *Essington Lewis*, Melbourne, Oxford University Press, 1963

Upfield, Arthur W., *The Bachelors of Broken Hill*, New York, Simon & Schuster, 1978

Weeks, Lewis G., *A Lifelong Love Affair: The Memoirs of Lewis G. Weeks, Geologist*, published posthumously by his wife, Anne Sutton Weeks, copyright assigned to University of Wisconsin, Madison, Wisconsin, 1978

Welch, Jack, *Jack: Straight from the Gut*, London, Headline, 2001

Wilkinson, Rick, *A Thirst for Burning: The Story of Australia's Oil Industry*, Sydney, David Ell Press, 1983

Wiseman, John, *Global Nation? Australia and the Politics of Globalisation*, Melbourne, Cambridge University Press, 1998

Yergin, Daniel, *The Prize: The Epic Quest for Oil, Money and Power*, New York, Free Press, 1991

Unpublished manuscripts

Houser, Carrol D., *The Deal of the Decade: An Inside Account of BHP's Acquisition of Utah International*, 1999

Interviews

Paul Anderson, Glen Andrews, Don Argus, Ian Ashby, Carol Austin, Max Banks, Jess Boylan, Alan Breen (by email), John Burton, Kevin Buzzacott, Harley Carey, Mick Carroll, John Clark, Tony Crook, James Curry, Mick Davis, Gary Dillard, Daniel Edelstein, John Elliott, Jerry Ellis, John Elliston, Graham Evans, Paul Everard, Keith Faulkner, Colin Filer, Matt Foraker, Ian Fraser, Russell Fynmore, Brian Gilbertson, Marc Gonsalves, Chip Goodyear, Stewart Greenhalgh, Geoffrey Heeley, Robert Hickman, Lance Hockridge, Juliana Hooper, Carrol Houser, Craig Hoyer, David Irvine, John Jackson, Paul Keating, Derek Keys, Marius Kloppers, Andy Kugler, Peter Laver, Charles Lineweaver, Brian Loton, Robyn Loughhead, J. David Lowell, Benjamin Macklin, Peter Maund, Dave McGarry, Graeme McGregor, Peter McLennan, Graham Menzies, Brad Mills, Aaron Minchin, David Munro, John O'Connor, Tim Offor, Guy Pearse, Ian Plimer, John Prescott, Pat Quilty, Baron Renwick of Clifton, Gillespie Robertson, Mike Salamon, Stan Salamy, Graeme Samuel, Derek Sawer, Michael Spencer, Fred Stojich, Onofre Tafoya, Alan Tingay, Geoffrey Walsh, Robert Ward, Sir Robert Wilson, Tim Winterer, J. Michael Yeager, Richard Yeeles (email)

Journals and Papers

Adler, Peter S., Janesse Brewer and Caelan McGee, 'The Ok Tedi Negotiations – Rebalancing the Equation in a Chronic Sustainability Dilemma', The Keystone Center, 24 August 2007

Fraser, Maryna, 'Review of *Through Fortress and Rock*', *Journal of Southern African Studies*, Vol. 24, No. 2, June 1998, pp. 463–4

Heidhues, Mary F. Somers, 'Company Island: A Note on the History of Belitung', *Indonesia*, Cornell University, Vol. 51, April 1991

Kirsch, Stuart, 'Indigenous Movements and the Risks of Counterglobalization', *American Ethnologist*, 2007

Shaxson, Nicholas, 'Oil, Corruption and the Resource Curse', *International Affairs*, Vol. 83, No. 6, London, Chatham House, 2007

Tingay, Alan, 'The Ok Tedi Mine Papua New Guinea, Report on Environmental and Health Issues', CMCA *Review*, September 2006

INDEX